Noble  k

The Military Life of
Frederick Duke of York and Albany

LIEUT-COLONEL
ALFRED H. BURNE, D.S.O.

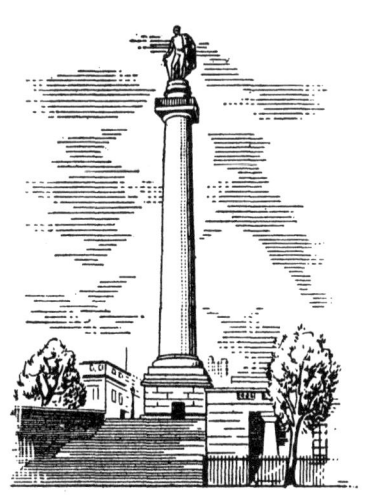

S T A P L E S   P R E S S

STAPLES PRESS LIMITED   STAPLES PRESS INCORPORATED
Mandeville Place, London   70 East 45th Street, New York

FIRST PUBLISHED 1949

SET IN 11 ON 12 MONOTYPE BASKERVILLE SERIES

Made and printed in England by
STAPLES PRESS LIMITED
at their Rochester, Kent, establishment

FREDERICK, DUKE OF YORK

From the statue in possession of the United Service Club

DEDICATED

By Gracious Permission

to

HIS MAJESTY
KING GEORGE VI

ACKNOWLEDGMENTS

In the first place I must express my grateful thanks to His Majesty King George VI for his gracious permission to examine manuscripts relating to the Duke of York in the Royal Archives at Windsor. It is strictly true to say that without this help the book, as conceived and planned by me, would never have been written.

In this connection I would record my indebtedness to the officials at Windsor Castle – especially to Sir Owen Morshead, who not only read the whole of the manuscript, but helped in various other ways; and to Miss Mary Mackenzie, the Registrar of the Royal Archives, for her consideration and courtesy.

I am particularly indebted to Professor C. T. Atkinson, who read and annotated with meticulous care the chapters on the military campaigns and gave me the benefit of his unrivalled knowledge of the military history of the period; to Dr Arthur Bryant, who found time amid his manifold commitments not only to give continued encouragement but also to read the manuscript right through, illuminating it with many an erudite or witty note; and to my brother, the Venerable R. V. H. Burne, who also read the manuscript and amended many slipshod passages.

Among others who have helped in some shape or form I would mention Mr Oliver Millar, of the office of the Surveyor of the King's Pictures, for information and advice; Earl Cathcart, for placing at my disposal the unpublished Cathcart papers; Lord Sherwood, for permission to examine the Lochee bust; Viscount Cowdray, for like permission respecting the Gainsborough portrait of the Duke; Sir Eric de Normann, of the Ministry of Works, for allowing me access to records in connection with the construction of the Duke of York's column; the Secretary of the Historical Manuscripts Commission, and the officials of the Public Record Office; Mr F. G. Rendall, Superintendent of the British Museum Reading Room, and his staff; the librarians and officials of the War Office Library, Royal United Service Institution Library and London Library; the Honourable George W. Bennet for going through the proofs with an eagle eye; finally my publishers, for their endeavours to turn out this book in a manner worthy of its illustrious subject.

CONTENTS

ILLUSTRATIONS

LIST OF SKETCH MAPS

SKETCHES

FOREWORD

By Dr ARTHUR BRYANT

No one who has made any study of the British Army during the Revolutionary and Napoleonic Wars can have failed to be struck by the almost universal respect with which British soldiers of all ranks regarded the Duke of York, its nominal Commander-in-Chief and active administrative head from 1795 to 1809 and from 1811 to 1827. He was the mainspring of almost every important military reform during this period, the friend and patron of John Moore – the greatest trainer of fighting men in our history – a steadfast champion, at a time when there were very few, of the soldier's rights. He deserves a memorial. But though he has a very tall one in the heart of London, a musket's shot from the Horse Guards over which he so long presided, his service to his country has long been forgotten by all but the few and obliterated by the legend of the absurdity and extravagance that surrounds the sons of George III and the brothers of the Prince Regent.

'He is the only one of the Princes who has the feelings of an English gentleman', wrote Greville of him. He might have said, more accurately, the *consistent* feelings of a gentleman, for it was this that distinguished him from his brothers, none of whom were as bad as they were painted by the liberals and moralists of the Victorian age. Had George IV died, as he so nearly did, in the week after his accession, Frederick of York, who would have succeeded him, might have been one of the most popular kings in our history. Had the latter given the slightest encouragement to those who cheered and followed him through the streets during the semi-revolutionary year of Queen Caroline's trial, his brother would almost certainly have been dethroned in his favour. He was an upright and honourable man, the soul of loyalty, and the thing was unthinkable.

Colonel Burne has shown that he was something else, for which neither his contemporaries nor posterity have given him credit. Called by the destiny of his birth and time to the ill-fortune of commanding a British army in the field at the outset of a war – ill-equipped, ill-trained, and ill-supported, as British armies, thanks to the Treasury and public, nearly always are at such moments – the young Duke showed a good judgment and a steadiness of nerve that under happier conditions might have made him as successful a commander as he later proved an administrator. It is Colonel Burne's contention that he was a better soldier in the field than the veterans who stood, so often and unfortunately, at his shoulder, even than the much-lauded Abercromby, to whom he later paid so moving and noble a tribute. Colonel Burne leaves the facts to speak for themselves, and I know he would wish me to do the same. He has written a book based on original research of high military importance and which fills a gap – which has long waited to be filled – in the records of England's worthies.

ARTHUR BRYANT.

Smedmore.

INTRODUCTION

Not only Macaulay's schoolboy but the veriest office-boy of the present day knows this of the Noble Duke of York, that he marched his army up a hill, and then reversed the operation. Frederick, Duke of York, is as indissolubly connected with this imbecile operation as the Duke of Cumberland, his great-uncle, is with the soubriquet 'The Butcher'. Cumberland has of recent years been rehabilitated,[1] but his great-nephew still lacks a champion.

No military biography or even study of the Duke has ever been written. This is curious, when we consider that he spent his whole life in the army from the age of sixteen onwards, that he commanded our army in two important military campaigns, and that he was for thirty years Commander-in-Chief of the British Army – 'the best commander-in-chief the army has ever had', in the judgment of its historian.

The present popular conception of the Duke ranges from the mildly cynical to the openly contemptuous: he is depicted, in descending scale, as an amiable dolt, a dull dunderhead, or an incompetent nincompoop. And small wonder! Whether history repeats itself may be a matter of doubt, but there can be no doubt that the gibe is true that historians repeat one another; there is a suspicious family likeness between the assessments of his military character in the works of modern historians. To take but one example: Hunt, in his *History of England, 1760–1801*, writes: 'The Duke of York was not equal to the command of an army in the field'; while Ward and Gooch, in the *Cambridge History of Foreign Policy*, write: 'The Duke of York was clearly unequal to the ever-increasing difficulties ahead.'

The legend of his incompetence grew, and no one troubled to investigate it until it had become an established 'fact' of history. Even Sir John Fortescue, in his admirable (though far from perfect) *History of the British Army*, 'damned him with faint praise' and asserted that 'The Duke did not shine in the field'. Since no soldier seems to have challenged this assessment, can the historian, still more the man in the street, be blamed

[1] See *William Augustus, Duke of Cumberland*, by Evan Charteris.

if he accepts it unquestioningly? I confess I once so accepted it myself. My eyes were first opened at the end of the Great War, when I found myself close to some of the Duke's battlefields, and began to study them. The suspicion that I then formed that the Duke of York had not had a fair deal has since ripened into a conviction. Any lingering doubts were removed when, by gracious permission of His Majesty, I was allowed to scan the private letters of the Duke to his father, King George III, during his campaigns in the Low Countries. I feel sure that if Fortescue had been able to study these letters before he wrote his great history, he would have reacted to them in the same way that I have. Several years after the appearance of his Volume IV, which deals with the Flanders campaigns, he did go through them and transcribed some in a chapter of his *Historical and Military Essays*. Apart from these transcriptions the letters have never been printed, and thus historians and would-be biographers have been deprived of an essential source of information. It is hardly too much to say that without these letters my book could not have been written.

Thus the name of Frederick Duke of York has only been preserved from oblivion by a cruel and senseless jingle, which is reproduced on the fly-leaf of this book. I have been at some pains to discover the origin of this jingle, and to locate the hill, if such exists. I have failed. The name of the author seems to be 'sunk without a trace'. As for the hill, Mount Cassel in Belgium is sometimes pointed to as the spot, but there can be no substance in this; the nearest the Duke ever got to Mount Cassel was over ten miles away. Nor is there any event in his military career that remotely resembles the operation described in the jingle. Most of the country over which he operated, whether in the Flanders or Helder campaigns, is, as everyone knows, flat; there are no hills worthy of the name. Further south, in the vicinity of Cambrai, the ground is undulating, but cannot be described as hilly. Nor did the Duke take his army forward and then reverse the process, whether up a hill or not. Whence, then, derives this libellous lampoon?

I am driven to the conclusion that, just as the famous song 'Marlbrouck s'en Va-t-en Guerre' was composed long before the birth of John Churchill, so we must look for the origin of this jingle in earlier days. Now, there was in existence at the time an old nursery rhyme, which can be traced at least as far back as 1594, running as follows:

> 'The King of France went up the hill
> With twenty thousand men;
> The King of France came down the hill
> And never went up again.'

The family resemblance between these two squibs is too close to be ignored, and the obvious solution is that some nimble-witted detractor of the Duke unscrupulously adapted the old rhyme to the new subject. And there it has stuck.

Thus the Duke of York is now firmly connected in the public mind with a fatuous military operation, and it is not surprising that the proposal is occasionally mooted to demolish the column erected to his memory on the site of old Carlton House. Meanwhile the column is allowed to remain anonymous, and when Colonial and Dominion soldiers present at the Victory celebrations in 1946 saw this anonymous column most of them departed under the impression that it was to the memory of the Duke of Wellington.

But it was not always so. The very day that the Royal Artillery at Woolwich learnt of his death they decided to open or support a subscription for a memorial to the dead Commander-in-Chief. Another assessment of popularity is the number of inn signs dedicated to a departed worthy. In the county of Staffordshire, for example, there are ten inns under the sign of the Duke of Wellington, and twelve under that of the Duke of York.

Taking it all in all, I hold that Frederick Duke of York and Albany was one of the outstanding figures of an outstanding generation, and that the column that celebrates him, and should bear his name, is no empty symbol.

HOME AND GERMANY

I

On 16 August 1763 a second son was born to King George III. He was given the single name of Frederick.[1] In due course the infant was inoculated by Dr Jenner against the small-pox: we shall see later what influence this had on the Prince. Before he was a year old he was appointed by his father Bishop of Osnabrück. A great deal of heavy humour has been lavished upon this appointment. A modern biographer has written: 'So precocious was the religious growth of the Princes, that the Duke of York was elevated to the wealthy Bishopric of Osnabrück before leaving the nursery.' The fact is, the bishopric was 'a secular dignity with an ecclesiastical designation'. It was one of those numerous tiny principalities that were so common in Germany. It measured forty-five by twenty-five miles, and had already had as its head a member of the Royal Family – Prince Ernest, brother of George II. It may be compared with Mindelheim, a principality that was awarded to the Duke of Marlborough after the battle of Blenheim.

Prince Frederick spent his early years in close companionship with his elder brother, the Prince of Wales. There was only one year and one day's difference in their ages, and during their boyhood they were as inseparable as twins in work and games; indeed, right through life they were the best of friends. As for work, their first tutor was the Earl of Holderness, who put them through a rigorous course of the classics. They studied the Commentaries of Caesar, 'accompanied by a geographical course of explanation', a very sensible idea that might well be more widely adopted. His tutor afterwards observed that 'though the Royal brothers received instruction in Latin and Greek with ease, yet they could never be taught to understand

[1] *The Dictionary of National Biography*, in an article not conspicuous for accuracy, gives him a second name, Augustus, an example that has been followed by several subsequent writers.

the value of money'. It will be well to bear this point in mind.
But their education was thorough in another respect. There
are in the Windsor Archives a series of letters written by
Frederick at the age of ten to Lady Holderness. These are in
elegant copy-book handwriting, which surprises not. What *is*
surprising is that they are all written in excellent French. No
doubt they were closely supervised by his tutor, but even so,
they would be considered something of a *tour de force* nowadays.
Certainly his early mastery of the French language stood him
in good stead twenty years later. All this education the two
brothers shared in common, but Frederick was soon to spe-
cialize in a branch of education not enjoyed by his elder
brother – that of a soldier. He early in life showed proclivities
in that direction, and the King, who discouraged such tenden-
cies in the heir apparent, welcomed these signs of martial bent
in the younger son. The young Prince delighted to accompany
his parent on his numerous military inspections. For his military
education he was placed under the charge of General Smith,
one of the most distinguished engineers of the day. Under this
tuition Prince Frederick studied 'all the most esteemed foreign
works', and we read that 'the gardens of Kew House were
transformed into the terrain of the Seven Years War'. Here the
great Frederick's battles were fought over once more, after the
style of Uncle Toby and Corporal Trim. Frederick was also
attended by a certain Lieutenant-Colonel Lake, whom we
shall meet again.

To broaden their education the two Princes were allotted a
parcel of land at Kew, which they ploughed up themselves,
harrowed, sowed, harvested and threshed. They even took the
grain themselves to the mill to be ground, and finished up by
baking the bread and inviting their proud parents to partake
of it with them. They also had riding and fencing lessons, and
for recreation took part in single-wicket cricket on the green at
Kew, in all probability on the identical ground where cricket
is still played.

On entering his teens Frederick was growing into a great
strapping lad. He was 'particularly distinguished by the
robustness of his frame and the agility of his motions'. As
witness to this, he would get two servants to stretch a garter
between their teeth at his own height and jump it with ease.

We are also assured that he seldom indulged in more than four hours' sleep a night.

Prince Frederick evidently matured rapidly. At the age of 16 he had a youthful *amour* with a dairymaid at Kew, at which his parents must have been much scandalized, if it came to their ears. While only fifteen he wrote a long letter, which has been preserved by the Duke of Buccleuch, in which he discusses gravely the events of the day, debates which party was to blame in a marriage scandal, and attributes the delay in writing the letter to the fact that 'our time is so exactly parcelled out'.

At the age of 17 he was about six feet tall, though of rather slight build—to judge by the oil portrait by Reynolds. He was distinctly handsome in appearance.

Such was the youth who, on 30 December 1780 left his native shore for the first time, accompanied by Colonel Richard Grenville, his military mentor. In the previous month he had been made a colonel by brevet, so it was as a fully fledged soldier that he started out to complete his military education in Germany. He made his headquarters at Hanover, but received most of his military education from his uncle, the Duke of Brunswick (who had married the sister of George III). The Duke was considered the first soldier in Europe – it was before Valmy – and he took kindly to his nephew, and went to great pains to perfect his military education.

But the Duke was not Prince Frederick's hero; the youth had not forgotten those battlefields in the garden at Kew, and he longed to meet in person the great man who had fought them. In due course his wish was gratified; Brunswick accompanied him to Berlin and himself introduced the young Prince to his famous namesake. The King of Prussia also took kindly to the boy and delighted to take him with him on his reviews and field days. On one such the Prince learnt at least how *not* to do it. The Prussian King was quite upset by the bungling of a General Erlach, and after the review he wrote a furious letter to the G.O.C., of which the following is a typical passage: 'Erlach marched his division like cabbages and turnips. . . . I don't intend to lose battles through the laziness of my generals.' Erlach was accordingly placed under arrest. Our Prince was present at the last dinner-party ever given by Frederick the Great, who that evening had a fit and took to his bed. Lord

Cornwallis was also present at that memorable dinner-party. The two Englishmen were destined twenty years later to rule the Army between them.

Meanwhile the young Prince was rapidly rising in rank and honours. On 23 March 1782 he was gazetted Colonel of the 2nd Regiment of Horse Grenadiers (now the Life Guards). On 22 November the same year he was promoted Major-General, and on 27 October 1787 Lieutenant-General, and Colonel of the Coldstream Regiment of Foot Guards. On 27 November 1784 he was created Duke of York and Albany and Earl of Ulster.

The Prussian system of training was looked upon as the best of its day, and it is not surprising that the Duke (as we must now call him) eagerly absorbed its bad qualities as well as its good. Among the bad qualities was the belief in stern corporal punishment, and the Duke was easily converted into a believer in it. His biographer, Huish, sadly relates that 'he imbibed an erroneous opinion of the necessity of corporal punishment, than which nothing is more injurious to the dignity of the service, nor to the high and noble character of the British soldier'. But this attitude was only a passing phase with the young Duke.

But other influences besides military ones worked upon the young Prince. Amongst these was a certain Baron Shetensheim, whom Huish dubs 'one of the most finished gentlemen, and also one of the most finished scoundrels of his age'.[1]

This Baron introduced Prince Frederick, whilst still in his salad days, into the delights and distractions of gambling. It took many forms. Almost every pursuit was made the excuse for a bet. At tennis, for instance, a game of which the Prince was very fond, large sums changed hands, and the Englishman was severely 'plucked', by the simple process of allowing him to win at first at low stakes, and turning the tables as soon as the stakes were raised. He also at the same time acquired a taste for alcohol. It should in justice be remembered that these two vices had then almost attained their apogee in high Society. The worst that can be said for a youth who was obviously endowed to a high degree with strong animal spirits and passions

[1] *Huish*, p. 8.

was that he followed the fashion of the day. The trouble was that he started so young.

From wine to women. The dairymaid showed signs of wishing to join Prince Frederick in Hanover, much to that young man's alarm and embarrassment. The girl was successfully put off, but it would seem that there were not lacking around the Court of Hanover, ladies ready to flaunt their charms before this young Prince Charming. In fact, in women as in wine he seems to have followed gaily and light-heartedly the fashion of his age.

But other activities engaged the interest of the Prince. In a letter to his brother he describes his shooting attainments. 'I have practised five or six times with a rifle-barrelled carabine at a butt, at which I have succeeded better than could have been conceived, as it is very difficult. Grenville and all say that I have the steadiest hand they ever saw.' This was probably no mere Court flattery on the part of his tutor, for he afterwards became an expert shot; only a short time before his final illness he shot ninety-eight pheasants and other game with his own gun in a single day.

He also was in great demand in the ballroom. In short, if his young head was not completely turned by his flattering reception on the part of his father's Hanoverian subjects (who had not seen Royalty for over thirty years), it is much to be wondered at.

One of the most engaging traits of the young Frederick was his devotion to his elder brother George. Thanks to this and to his natural talents as a letter-writer, we are enabled to get an intimate glimpse into the gradual unfolding and development of his character during the half-dozen years that the brothers were separated, since most fortunately the letters on both sides have been preserved. His regular letters to the King help us to complete the picture. These letters have never been published.

As son of the King of Hanover, it was only natural that he should make Hanover his headquarters throughout his stay. Equally naturally the young Prince was fêted and entertained *ad nauseam*. Balls abounded. 'When I return to England I must teach you two different kinds of dances from what we have the least idea of, the quadrilles and the valtzes,' he wrote to his brother.

But quite soon in the correspondence a new and unexpected note is struck. Consider the following as coming from a younger brother aged 17 to his elder brother, who has been ill. 'You know, my dearest brother, that I hate a sermon as well as you, but my affection for you forces me to entreat you for God [sic] sake to take care of your health. You cannot stand this kind of life, and I am afraid it is the Windsor Lodge Duke who leads you into it. [Henry Frederick, Duke of Cumberland, brother of the King.] I have no doubt he means you exceedingly well, but believe me he is not the best adviser you can follow.'[1] This draws an indignant denial that George has even seen the Windsor Duke for ages.

After being ten months in Hanover, Prince Frederick writes triumphantly: 'I have become one of the best shots here, so much so, that I can shoot hare in their full speed with ball at an hundred yards distance. . . . You can have no idea of stag-shooting. I have often run five or six miles as hard as I could on foot with my gun on my shoulder after a stag.'[2]

This, of course, was not to be borne by the heir apparent and hotfoot came the riposte: 'I am become an exceedingly good shot. . . . The first time I ever fired a fowling piece I fired at a sheet of paper at sixty yards distance, and covered it full of shot. . . .' Then he goes on to talk of his fine horses and his hunting feats.[3] This seems to have cured the younger brother of boastfulness – for the time.

The great event of 1783 was the visit to Frederick the Great at Potsdam referred to briefly above. Prince Frederick gives the King a good pen-portrait of his hero. 'He is short and small but wonderfully strong made. Not very well upon his horse, but on horseback Your Majesty would be astonished to see him. One of the days we were with him, he was from three o'clock in the morning till past eleven o'clock without ever getting off his horse. . . . He has exceedingly the air of a gentleman and something exceedingly commanding in his look.'[4]

Next year, while still only 21 years old, we find him gravely advising the King to replace General Walmoden as Envoy at Vienna by Count D'Alvinsleben. He was already in all but name a sort of 'Envoy Extraordinary' of the King in Germany.

And now the interest returns to his elder scapegoat brother,

[1] *Windsor*, 30.3.81.   [2] Ibid., 12.10.81.   [3] Ibid., 2.10.81.   [4] Ibid., 8.6.83.

who writes a rather violent but historically important letter, describing the rift that is growing between him and the King, and adding that he proposes coming over to Hanover to visit his brother whether the King likes it or not. Once again the roles of the two brothers are reversed, and the Prince of Wales receives this truly remarkable reply from young Frederick: 'I never can think of returning without the King's express commands, besides my education and the learning of my profession require my remaining some time in these parts. I am exceedingly sorry to hear of the very unpleasant difference between you and the King. For Heavens sake do everything in your power to put an end to it, for it would be a dreadful calamity not only for us but for the whole country if it was to continue. Let me also entreat you, my dearest brother, to give up the idea of travelling. Indeed, you know not all the inconveniences to which you would be subject; and as for saving money, I can assure you you are very much mistaken if you think you will be able to do that.' (The Prince had given that as one of his reasons!) He ends hastily: 'We arrived here (Vienna) last Tuesday and have been received very graciously by the Emperor. I am obliged this moment to dress for a great dinner. I have therefore no time to add more.'[1]

In a subsequent letter Prince Frederick filled in the details of his Vienna visit: 'During the time I was at Vienna there was a fête every evening, which lasted so long, particularly the balls, that I was hardly ever able to get away before six o'clock in the morning. And as I was occupied the whole morning, seeing everything that is remarkable about the town. I was left hardly a moment for repose. One week particularly, I went to bed on the Monday and I never saw my bed again till the Sunday night following. During the camp, however, we had quite a different life, as we always went out with the troops at 4 o'clock in the morning, I cannot say, however, that I am sorry after so very long and boisterous a journey to be at last returned again to my own fireside. I am afraid you will think me grown very old,' he adds a trifle sheepishly, 'for talking in this manner.'[2]

We begin to see that the early reports as to the physical stamina of the Prince were not mere Court flattery.

Trouble was, that autumn, brewing between Vienna and

[1] Ibid., 28.7.84.   [2] Ibid., 15.10.84.

The Hague, and the Duke of York (as he was now become) begged eagerly from his father leave to serve, if war should supervene. We get repeated instances of this clamouring for service whenever the opportunity seems to arise.

In 1785, the King decided to send his son Edward (later Duke of Kent) to complete his education also on the Continent, and suggested Göttingen. The Duke here exhibits the influence he was attaining in his father's counsels by opposing the suggestion, on the grounds that Edward would have companions of undesirable character at that university, and by suggesting Lüneburg instead. King George acceded to this representation, and young Edward in due course was installed at Lüneburg.

A still more significant letter reached the King next month from the Duke, exposing 'the machinations of the Court of Vienna', who had designs on Bavaria (which they still had eight years later). 'You will see, Sir, that my ideas, which I mentioned to your Majesty at my return from Vienna are verified, that the Emperor had some very great project in view which was not then ripe for execution.'

In April 1785 the Duke refers to his military education, suggesting that he shall go twice a week to some college (which is indecipherable), 'in order that I may be more *au fait* of the manner of treating the affairs than I could possibly be, were I only to *hear* the reports after their conclusion'. He then refers to his brother William (afterwards William IV), who was also now in Germany. He does not expect any real alteration in him 'till he has been kept for some time under severe discipline'. From the context it is clear that he means on board ship. Prince William was, of course, destined for the Navy.

But the chief event described in the letters in 1785 is the great review in Silesia, where Frederick the Great assembled practically his whole army. The Duke got wind of it some months before and promptly wrote to ask if he might attend. He received in reply a delightful letter written in French from the aged King of Prussia, who indeed describes himself as 'un vieillard' who descries in the Duke all the talents that will one day cause him to shine (briller).[1]

A reference to the manœuvres has already been made. In

Windsor, 9.9.85.

the Duke's letters the item that caught his imagination was a mere curtain-raiser to the real business.

'The day before the King arrived the 29 battalions marched in one line, which never was attempted before, and I suppose never will be again. The distance from one wing to the other was 7446 paces [about 4 miles]. It succeeded surprisingly well. . . . The cavalry is infinitely superior to anything I ever saw. . . . One day the King decreed without any previous notice that the 35 squadrons of cuirassiers and dragoons should charge in one line. Never was there seen so finer [*sic*] sight. There was not a single horse out of its place till the word Halt was given, when, as the commander was at the head of the right squadron, it was impossible for the squadron on the left to hear in time enough, so they advanced about twenty paces too forward.'[1]

In the next year, 1786, we find the note of home-sickness constantly occurring. Repeatedly, but respectfully, he asks leave to return home, but the King is obdurate, and it is not till 2 August 1787 that the Duke of York sets foot in England, having been away nearly seven years. His first thought at the end, as it had been at the beginning, of his long journey was for his brother, and the last letter of the series opens with these words: 'My dear Brother, I am this very instant arrived.'[2]

[1] Ibid., 7.10.85.   [2] Ibid., 2.8.87.

THE DUEL

2

In August 1787, after a stay of nearly seven years abroad, the Duke of York returned to England. He was now a grown man, just 24 years of age, tall, still slender in figure and good-looking. Sir Gilbert Elliot described him as 'extremely handsome', a description that is not belied by Sir Joshua Reynolds's portrait, for which he sat immediately on his return home. He was indeed as much a Prince Charming as the second son of Henry VII; indeed, he shared some, though by no means all, of the characteristics of Bluff King Hal. Perhaps if he had lived to be King he would have shared others, too. . . . He was eager to throw himself whole-heartedly into the turmoil of Court society, politics and the Army – and dissipation. To deal with the last item first, General Dyott records the seemingly incredible fact that at a dinner-party given in the year of his return, at which he and the Duke of Clarence were present in a party of twenty, no less than sixty-three bottles of wine were drunk.[1]

In that same year Lord Auckland wrote that Frederick was credited with 'numerous *amours*', and it was supposed that he would soon have '*une habitude*'. It was supposed by some that the King had deliberately kept him abroad for so long in order that the Prince of Wales should not have an evil influence on his younger brother. Whatever the truth of this, the two brothers, who had corresponded regularly throughout the German visit, again became inseparable companions. For some years they maintained a racing establishment at Newmarket: in later years the Duke twice won the Derby.

The Duke's incursion into politics came unexpectedly early, though Grenville had been warned before he left Germany that strenuous efforts would be made by the Opposition to entice him into their ranks. In the autumn of 1788 the King showed

[1] *Dyott's Diary*, p. 65.

signs of insanity, and the Government had to consider the question of a Regency. What followed is well-known history, and the only need to refer to it here is because it had a repercussion on the military life of the Duke. Briefly, then, William Pitt, the Prime Minister, foresaw that if the Prince of Wales were invested with full regal powers as Regent, his own Government would be dismissed, and Fox, the Prince's particular friend, would take his place. In order to counter this Pitt forced through the Commons a Bill limiting the powers of the Prince as Regent, both as regards the control of the person of the King and the right to appoint new Ministers. Fox violently opposed it, and we are tempted, knowing as we do the characters of the two statesmen, to side with Pitt. But there are those who hold that Fox was constitutionally in the right, and that the Prince of Wales was entitled to feel aggrieved at Pitt's action. What turned the public against him and his brothers was the spectacle of them wrangling in public whilst the King lay at Kew apparently desperately ill. Though the Prince did not himself intervene in the House of Lords, he got York to do it for him. The latter spoke two or three times in support of his brother, and rather effectively. However, before the final vote was taken, the King unexpectedly recovered. Burke's verdict on the part played by the Duke was very flattering. 'The Duke of York's whole conduct has been such, with regard to spirit, judgement and correctness of honour, as you and every friend of his could wish.'[1]

A curious aftermath of the affair is preserved in a paper in the Windsor Archives entitled: 'A STATEMENT BY THE DUKE OF YORK'. 'On the 21st day of February 1789 the newspaper called *The Times*, of which one Walter is the editor, contained the following paragraph: "It argues infinite wisdom in certain persons to have prevented the Duke of York from rushing into the King's apartments on Wednesday. The rashness, the Germanic severity, and insensibility of this young man might have proved ruinous to the hopes and joys of a whole nation." '[2] The Duke happened to have had a particularly affectionate meeting with the King about that time (after being kept away as long as possible by the Queen), and he promptly brought a libel action against 'one Walter', who was sentenced to one

[1] *H. M. C. Charlemont*, 98. [2] *Windsor*, 43908.

year's imprisonment and to be placed in the pillory. After the imprisonment the King remitted the remainder of the sentence, so the world was denied the sight of the Editor of *The Times* in the pillory.

This affair of the Regency left a scar, and it was a woman who had been wounded – the Queen. 'Hell has no fury like a woman scorned.' And the results were, if my reconstruction is correct, startling. For it resulted in a duel between a Prince of the Blood and a commoner.

We will give this extraordinary event in the form in which it is usually presented. On 15 May 1789 the Duke of York was exercising his Regiment of Coldstream Guards when a young Lieutenant-Colonel,[1] Charles Lennox (often spelled Lenox), approached him and asked to know if the Duke had said 'that he (Lennox) had put up with language unfit for any gentleman to hear'. The Duke merely ordered the officer back to his post; but, after dismissing the parade, summoned all the officers to the orderly room, where he called upon Lennox to state his complaint. Lennox repeated his question, to which the Duke answered that he had heard the statement referred to. On Lennox asking the name of the person who had made it, the Duke would not give it, but made the reply that 'he desired to receive no protection from his rank as a prince, or his situation as Commanding Officer, but that when not on duty he wore a brown coat, and was ready as a private gentleman to give the Colonel satisfaction whenever or wherever he pleased'.

Lennox then circularized the members of Daubigny's Club, inviting corroborative evidence of the alleged occurrence. Not having received any satisfactory replies, the Colonel, a few days later sent a written message to the Duke, to this purport: 'That not being able to recollect any occasion on which words had been spoken to him, at Daubigny's, to which a gentleman ought not to submit, he had taken the step which appeared to him most likely to gain information of the words to which his Royal Highness had alluded, and of the persons who had used them; that none of the members of the club had given him information of any such insult being in their know-

---

[1] A Company Commander. It was usual for such to carry the rank of Lieutenant-Colonel in the Guards.

ledge, and therefore he expected, in justice to his character, that his Royal Highness should contradict the report as publicly as he had asserted it.'

The Earl of Winchelsea handed this letter to the Duke, who gave a verbal reply which Lennox considered unsatisfactory. He accordingly took York at his word and 'called him out'.

Now, this may seem a trivial pretext for a duel, but the course of events may show that there was a deeper cause.

The first thing to do was to appoint a second. The Duke's choice fell upon Lord Rawdon (son of Lord Moira), who had made a reputation in the war of American Independence. Rawdon was at the time inclined towards Pitt, and only with extreme reluctance did he accept the delicate post. That same evening he and Winchelsea arranged the details of the meeting. It was to take place on Wimbledon Common early next morning, with pistols. The Duke was at the time staying at Carlton House with the Prince, and one would have supposed that he would confide in his brother. But so far from doing this, he took elaborate pains to disguise the affair from the Prince. Next morning, 20 May, he set out in a hired post-chaise, taking care to leave his own hat in the house and wearing one belonging to a servant.[1]

The duel took place as arranged. Its details are given in the words of the two seconds, who drew up the following report for publication.[2]

'In consequence of a dispute already known to the public, his royal highness the Duke of York, attended by Lord Rawdon – and Lieutenant-Colonel Lenox, accompanied by the Earl of Winchelsea – met at Wimbledon Common. The ground was measured at twelve paces, and both parties were to fire at a signal agreed upon. The signal being given, Lieutenant-Colonel Lenox fired, and the ball grazed his royal highness's curl. The Duke of York did not fire. Lieutenant-Colonel Lenox observed that his royal highness had not fired; Lord Rawdon said it was not the Duke's intention to fire; his royal highness

[1] It seems that this did not delude the Prince of Wales, who paced up and down in front of Carlton House in the greatest agitation till his brother's return.

[2] *Watkins*, p. 137.

had come out upon Lieutenant-Colonel Lenox's desire, to give him satisfaction, and had no animosity against him. Lieutenant-Colonel Lenox pressed that the Duke of York should fire, which was declined, upon a repetition of the reason. Lord Winchelsea then went up to the Duke of York, and expressed his hope that his royal highness would have no objection to say he considered Lieutenant-Colonel Lenox as a man of honour and courage? His royal highness replied that he should say nothing; he had come out to give Lieutenant-Colonel Lenox satisfaction, and did not mean to fire at him: if Lieutenant-Colonel Lenox was not satisfied, he might fire again. Lieutenant-Colonel Lenox said, he could not possibly fire again at the Duke, as his royal highness did not mean to fire at him. On this both parties left the ground. The seconds think it proper to add, that both parties behaved with the most perfect coolness and intrepidity.

'RAWDON,
'WINCHELSEA.'

Whatever we may think of this duel, one fact stands out clear; the Duke of York was endowed to no ordinary degree with the military virtue of sheer physical courage. Of the two seconds it may be remarked that Winchelsea afterwards fought a duel with William Pitt, and Rawdon as Lord Moira for a short time commanded a corps under his principal in Flanders. Lennox exchanged to another regiment, and shortly afterwards fought another duel arising out of this affair in which he seriously wounded his antagonist. He later succeeded his uncle as Duke of Richmond, and was the host at the most famous ball of all time – that held at Brussels on 15 June 1815. The quarrel is said to have been patched up during a cricket match at Lord's in the following year.

The duel being over, the first thing was to notify the various branches of the Royal Family. First, naturally, the Prince of Wales. York on his return to Carlton House briefly told his brother, and on his request for more information, coldly replied: 'I have no time to give you particulars now for I must go off to the tennis court.' What a man! The Prince of Wales, with brotherly and filial duty, hastened off to Windsor in order to break the news to his parents before any rumour should

reach them. This was necessary, for, according to Lady Bessborough, 'all London is in an uproar'.[1]

The King received the news with considerable agitation, but
the Queen displayed no particular emotion, nor even interest,
if the circumstantial account that the Prince afterwards wrote
can be believed. And there is some corroborative evidence for
it, which I will give.

One Jack Payne, member of the Prince of Wales's establishment, declared that the Queen had said that the affair was all
the Duke's fault. Relations had for some time been estranged
between the Queen and the Duke. A heated incident had
occurred in the previous January, when the Duke is reported
to have so far forgotten himself as to insinuate that she was as
mad as her Consort. Since then, according to Burke, 'everything is done to disgust the Prince of Wales and Duke of York
with Windsor and Kew and to keep them from visiting there.'[2]

The Duke had himself once complained of not being admitted, and this brings us back to the real origin, in my judgment of the duel – 'a woman scorned'. The Queen had not
forgiven the two brothers for asserting the claims of the elder
when the King was ill. She felt it as a slight to both George and
herself.

Now, the Earl of Winchelsea was a Lord of the Bedchamber,
and very much in her confidence. Some hint of what was in the
air might well have reached her from that source. It seems
almost incredible that she should have secretly abetted the
duel, but it is at least a fact that she afterwards bore no malice
against Lennox, and indeed invited him to a State ball. There
an awkward scene took place between him and the Duke of
York and the party broke up prematurely.

In short, the seeds of the duel can be traced back to the
Regency Bill. This brings us to the spark that set the tinder
alight. I have given the accepted story. But it would seem that
the incident at Daubigny's was only the pretext for the quarrel.
The Duke himself in 1822 related to Greville what led up to it.
In Greville's words: 'At a masked ball three masks insulted the
Prince of Wales, when the Duke of York interfered, desired the
one who was most prominent to address himself to him (the

[1] *Lady Bessborough and Her Family Circle*, p. 46.
[2] *H. M. C. Charlemont*, 95.

Duke), and added that he suspected him to be an officer of his regiment (meaning Colonel Lenox), and if he was, he was a coward and a disgrace to his profession; if he was not the person he took him to be he desired him to unmask, and he would beg his pardon.' Greville adds that 'this did not lead to any immediate consequences, but perhaps indirectly contributed to what followed'. No doubt.

Sir Gilbert Elliot provides the final connecting link. 'Mr Lenox [*sic*] had been amusing himself all this winter with abusing and insulting the Prince of Wales and the Duke of York in the most scurrilous and blackguardly way. . . . Lenox was abusing the princes and talking offensive language about them and their friends in the presence of the Duke of York at Daubigny's Club, when St Leger said that it was very odd that he always chose to say these things to persons who could not resent them. "Why don't you say them to some of us who can answer you?" '[1] This, no doubt, is the origin of the 'some words' to which the Duke alluded.

The whole affair can now be summed up as follows: Colonel Lennox, representing the Court Party, was a bitter opponent on personal grounds of the Royal Princes, and having strong reason to believe that he had the backing of the Court, i.e. the Queen, and being, moreover, a headstrong youth, picked up with alacrity the gage that the Duke threw down.[2]

Colonel Lennox's sister, later Countess Bathurst, begged and obtained the Royal curl that had been shot away, and this led to a lifelong friendship between the two.[3]

A week or two later the Duke of York sickened, and retired to bed with – the mumps.[4]

[1] *Life and Letters of Sir G. Elliot*, Vol. I, p. 313. This work gives much the more detailed account of the whole affair.
[2] Since writing the above, I have discovered that Sir Gilbert Elliot comes to the same conclusion.
[3] It is noteworthy that Lady Sarah Lennox, Charles's aunt, took the side of the Duke, in private. Writing to Lady Susan O'Brien on 4 June, she stated that 'the Prince was cruelly ignored by his Mother in her allowing Mr Pitt to comply with my brother's insulting wish of putting Charles over all the Duke's officers & friends in his *own* regiment without his knowledge. . . . All this enraged the Duke & has tempted him to be, I own I think, a little too ready to punish Charles's impertinence (for impertinent he is, I hear, continually, about the Princes).'
[4] Another possible, or at any rate predisposing, cause of the strange animosity exhibited by a Lennox towards a son of George II has been suggested to me. The first real love of George III was Susan Lennox, daughter of the second Duke of

IN GARTER ROBES, 1787, AGED 24
From the painting by Sir Joshua Reynolds at Buckingham Palace
REPRODUCED BY GRACIOUS PERMISSION OF HIS MAJESTY

COMMANDER IN FLANDERS, 1794, AGED 31
From the painting by Hoppner

The next four years of Frederick's military life need not detain us long. But it must be recorded, in passing, that in May 1791 he set out for Berlin to claim the hand of the Princess Royal of Prussia. She was the niece of Frederick the Great, and the two young people had frequently met during his stay at the Prussian King's Court. It seems to have been more an affair of the heart than most Royal weddings of the period. The Duke wrote from Berlin to his old tutor, General Grenville: 'You knew for many years that the Princess Frederique has been a flame of mine, and you will not forget that when we left Berlin four years ago I then told you that I should be very glad to marry her if it could be brought about. The different events that have happened during the last four years have hindered me till now from declaring myself, but still I can safely say I never lost sight of my object. . . . I have no doubt of being perfectly happy. The Princess is the best girl that ever existed and the more I see of her the more I like her.'[1]

The Princess accepted him and the marriage was solemnized in Berlin, and again on their return to England, where they settled down at the Duke's new acquisition of Oatlands,[2] three miles from Weybridge (now an hotel).

On their journey a significant incident had occurred as they were passing through Lille. The revolutionary mob molested them, and removed the Royal insignia from their carriage. This draws our attention to the revolution that was raging in France, and which was showing signs of spreading to the neighbouring countries.

As the war clouds rose, so did the Duke's hopes and anticipations of active service. The military profession ever held first place in his heart. The Royal Military Calendar asserts, probably correctly, that one reason for his visit to Berlin was to offer his service to the King of Prussia should war break out

Richmond. At one time he had visions of making her his Queen, and the lady's family were aware of the fact. But hopes were cruelly dashed by the King's marriage with Princess Charlotte. This may have engendered a feud – or at least a feeling of animosity on the part of the Lennox family against the Royal House. Edward IV and Henry VIII had set examples which George III had failed to follow. The proud Lennoxes felt slighted.

[1] *Windsor*, 28.8.91.
[2] He had also acquired Dover House in Whitehall (now the Scottish Office), but in 1792 he exchanged it for Lord Melbourne's house in Piccadilly (now known as The Albany, after his second title).

C

on the Continent. Meanwhile he was finding time to command his regiment at home, in the curiously intermittent manner that was usual at the time. It has been asserted that during his apprenticeship in Germany he had been indoctrinated with the harsh Prussian mode of discipline, in short, that he was a disciple of the famous Colonel Martinet. But this influence may have been exaggerated, for in a letter from the Earl of Buckingham to Lord Grenville in December 1792 it is stated that he and the Duke of Gloucester 'have laid down all the little superfluous martinetisms which had discontented the 1st and 2nd Coldstream Regiments last Spring'.[1] Who imposed these 'martinetisms' is not clear. If it was the Duke himself, it speaks well for him that he realized and rectified his mistake thus early in his career.

On 1 February, 1793, Revolutionary France declared war on England and Holland, and the Duke of York was a happy man.

[1] *H. M. C. Dropmore*, Vol. II, p. 349.

THE CAMPAIGN OF 1793

3

The 20th of February 1793 was a proud day for Lieutenant-General the Duke of York and Albany. He had been appointed to the command of an expeditionary force on the Continent – the dream of his life – and that expeditionary force was drawn up on the Horse Guards Parade, and under his own eye and command. For so minute was this force at the outset that it could be contained within the limits of the Horse Guards Parade. The whole of the seven battalions of Foot Guards were present on parade, but only three were detailed for service: the remainder were to furnish drafts to the lucky three, in order to bring them up to strength. This drafting might very well have been arranged regimentally, but the Duke had other ideas. Advancing to the head of the parade, he briefly addressed the four draft-finding battalions, explaining to them what was required. No record of his words has been preserved, unfortunately, but it is evident that they were well chosen, for when, at the end of his address, he called for volunteers for the draft to step to the front, the whole parade stepped forward as one man.

Seldom, if ever, can the Horse Guards Parade have witnessed a more historic and moving scene. It was the first corporate act in the twenty-two year struggle with Revolutionary and Napoleonic France. It was a tiny seed – a grain of mustard seed. . . .

The news of the French declaration of war had reached the Government on 7 February, and nine days later the French invaded Holland from Antwerp. That unfortunate country called on England for help, and, with what was astonishing speed for those times, the expeditionary force set out for Holland only nine days later. The Duke of York was, as we have seen, to be in command. Before ever war was declared, our Ambassador at The Hague, Lord Auckland, had asked for him by name to come over, even without troops if necessary, and take command of the Dutch army. To the King no proposal could have been more acceptable, and he approved of it with alacrity. Thus an inexperienced soldier, only 29 years of age, was suddenly placed in the most responsible military command that the country could offer. Frederick entered upon it with a light heart, and full of self-confidence.

Such an appointment was not so extraordinary in those times as it would now appear. There were big practical advantages in having a Prince of the Blood in supreme command where several nationalities might serve under the same flag and in the same army. (The King had ordered a Corps of Hanoverians also to Holland.) Petty jealousies would be bound to arise between the different components of the army – even with a Marlborough in command. And there was no obvious successor to Marlborough available. The last war had produced few great leaders, and the one soldier who stood high in general estimation, the Marquis Cornwallis, had not yet returned from India, where he was Governor-General. Moreover, on purely technical grounds, York had had a schooling more thorough than that of almost any of his contemporaries. The appointment, then, was probably the best that could be made. The command of the Brigade of Guards was given to Colonel Gerard Lake whom we last met in Germany and who was to earn fame in India. It can hardly be a coincidence that Lake had been a friend of York's boyhood. His staff seems to have been carefully 'handpicked', as indeed was usual in those days.[1]

While this diminutive force of Guards is being hurriedly fitted out for war we must cast a brief glance at the military situation on the continent of Europe. France had already been at war with Austria and Prussia for eight months. After the fiasco of Valmy, the Revolutionaries had taken the offensive, and General Dumouriez had swept the Austrians out of what is now Belgium (at that time the Austrian Netherlands). Yet the French were outnumbered by the Allies, and it seemed a foolhardy act to add to their enemies by deliberately seeking out a war with England and Holland. Dumouriez, however, resolved to maintain the offensive, and on 16 February he advanced from Antwerp into Holland. The Dutch fell back rapidly to the line of the Meuse[2], and the fortress of Breda surrendered to him

---

[1] The staff was normally known as the General's 'family'.
[2] Generally spelt Maas where it passes through Holland.

without striking a blow. It was clear, therefore, that our army must land somewhere to the north of the Meuse estuary, and Helvoetsluys, on the north shore of the Holland Diep, was selected. The choice was a good one, and the Government must be complimented on their prompt action – but not on the orders that they framed.

The Duke's Instructions took the form of a Commission. 'Instructions for our most dearly-beloved son Frederick etc. . . . given at our Court of St James, this 23rd day of February, 1793.'

The gist of these instructions was that he was to act 'for the defence of the United Provinces and for acting against the enemy'. This was rather vague, but 'Separate Instructions' were also issued the same day, in which Hanoverian troops, 13,000 in all, were mentioned, and para. 2 read: 'You will endeavour as far as you can, to avoid dividing our said Troops, or placing them in the Frontier garrisons of the said Provinces. Nevertheless in this respect you are at liberty to act as you shall judge best.' This does not take us much further, but a remarkable paragraph follows: 'You will conform yourself as exactly as possible to the tenor of our instructions given to General Lake.' In other words Lake, who commanded a corps directly under the Duke, received a set of instructions to himself, to which his Commander-in-Chief had to conform.

Lake's instructions open in a similar manner to those of the Duke: 'Instructions for our trusty, well-beloved Gerard Lake, Esquire, Major General of our forces. . . .' These instructions contain the one really explicit order of the whole series, and an amazing one it is. It prohibited operations in any place 'the distance of which would prevent you from retiring hither (Helvoet) in four and twenty hours after receiving an order for that purpose'.[1]

By 25 February all was ready, and again the Horse Guards witnessed a memorable scene. The augmented three battalions were drawn up in line, as the King, accompanied by the Duke and the rest of the Royal Family, rode down from Buckingham House. After an inspection by His Majesty and a march past in slow time, they marched off, across the river, down the Old Kent Road, to Greenwich. Here they embarked amid scenes of

[1] *W.O.*, VI, 11, d. 23.2.93.

enthusiasm and intoxication.[1] One private, cheerfully drunk

'. . . from the centre reeled,
And hiccuping, up to his Majesty wheeled:
"Never mind all these Jacobins, George, rest in quiet,
We'll quell them, my Hearty, as quick as a riot!"

The King was delighted, and laughed out loud, while the
fellow was hailed by three cheers from the crowd!'[2]

The convoy landed at Helvoetsluys. Here the Duke of York
left them for a time, under the command of General Lake. The
Duke quite rightly pushed straight on to The Hague, to concert plans with the Stadholder, the Prince of Orange. And now
his troubles were to begin, for the Stadholder was, in Fortescue's
words, 'a man of almost inhuman dullness, apathy and stupidity'. To make matters worse, his army, if it could be called one,
was utterly inefficient. It is no pleasure to harp thus on the
military failings of one of our traditional allies. The fact is,
while the Burgher party were disaffected towards the Orange
dynasty, the influence of the French Revolution had spread
among the lower ranks in Holland, and their hearts were not in
the war against France. Many of them did not look upon the
oncoming French army as invaders, but rather as liberators
from an unpopular hierarchy. This explains a good deal of
what would otherwise reflect discredit upon the Dutch nation.

The Duke's impressions on his arrival at The Hague are
described in the first letter in that remarkable correspondence
that he kept up with his father, the King, throughout the
campaign.

'I found everybody here in the greatest consternation at the
news which was just arrived of the Surrender of Breda, through
the cowardice of the Governor. . . .'[3]

And a few days later: 'It is hardly to be believed that I have
not as yet been able to find out from any person how many
troops there are really fit for service in this country.

'The Country, from everything that I can see, is perfectly
easy to be defended . . . if proper precautions are taken; the
only danger arises from two causes, first from the irresolution of

---

[1] It should in fairness be noted that the *London Chronicle* reported next day: 'To
their honour they were in general perfectly sober'.
[2] *An accurate and impartial narrative of the war, by an Officer of the Guards*, p. 3.
[3] *Windsor*, 28.2.93.

the Prince, and from an unfortunate jealousy of his authority
. . . and that no one thing can be done without a written
order from him, which from his hurry he very often forgets to
sign . . . and secondly from the astonishing alarm which
prevails. . . .'[1]

Four days later he returned to the same theme. After referring to his efforts 'to spur them on to take some more vigorous
measures', he goes on: 'I at last so far succeeded as to persuade
the Prince [Frederick] of Orange to appoint his son the Hereditary Prince to command from Grave to the sea. . . . It was
likewise agreed that the Hereditary Prince should accompany
me on the tour I was going to make in order to view the posts
for the defence of the country from Berensen to the sea. . . .
We departed on Monday morning and arrived here, Dort [*the
modern Dordrecht*] about three o'clock. As soon as we arrived we
received the unfortunate news of the surrender of Gertruydenberg (12 miles to the south-east). This, besides being a disagreeable piece of intelligence of itself, cast down the Dutch
so much that many of them said everything was over. However,
as it became now of still greater consequence to strengthen
Dort as soon as possible, I set off directly to fetch the Guards
from Helvoet; but luckily I met them half way. From the
awkwardness of our Dutch sailors every boat ran aground
more than once which made us not arrive till noon today.'[2] The
Duke's boat was fired on from the shore as it passed down the
Channel.

Thus early the Duke manifested that prompt and vigorous
action that characterized his conduct throughout the campaign.

In this manner York, fired with youthful zeal, managed to
stir the Prince into some slight signs of animation, and himself
made what Fortescue considers the best possible disposition for
his own troops. Moreover, he proved right in his judgment that
the position could be held, for affairs, following the unpredictable course so common in warfare, took a sudden turn for the
better.

General Dumouriez at this juncture faced a situation not
dissimilar to that which confronted the Allies on the eve of the
Arnhem operation in the autumn of 1944.

[1] Ibid., 2.3.93.   [2] Ibid., 6.3.93.

His enemy was roughly holding the coastline of Holland and thence the line of the Meuse. His original plan was to advance with his principal force northwards on Nimeguen with a subsidiary move from Antwerp on Breda and Rotterdam. But on 1 March the Austrians, under Prince Josias of Coburg, suddenly crossed the Meuse near Maastricht and attacked his eastern flank. Coburg swept all before him, and with ease. Defeating the French at Neerwinden (where William III was so gloriously defeated exactly one hundred years before) on the 18th, he entered Brussels. The French abandoned Antwerp and all Belgium, and Dumouriez came over to the Allies, and indeed tried to bring his army with him.

The situation was completely changed. Coburg had called to the English for co-operation, but the Duke's orders would not allow of it. Fortunately, the Government were for once reasonable, and sanctioned an advance to Bergen and Antwerp. The King had already suggested that such a move should be made by water, in order to co-operate with the Austrians, and his proposal was adopted. Further, three more battalions ill trained, ill equipped, and hastily assembled, were fitted out and sent to join the army at Antwerp, with General Abercromby in command. In short, the rigid instruction which tied the English army to the sea coast was being relaxed, and the Duke thus defines his orders in a letter to the King: 'I perfectly comprehend Your Majesty's intentions concerning my co-operating with the Prince of Coburg and Duke of Brunswick, without forming a junction with either of their corps, or allowing any detachment to be made from the troops under my command.'[1]

The change in the situation required a change in the plans. Accordingly a Congress was held at Antwerp on 8 April, by the heads of the Allies and the civil representatives of their countries.

Three days previous to its assembly Prince Coburg had, on his own initiative, issued a proclamation to the French people, the gist of which was contained in the sentence: 'I enter French territory without any intention of making conquests.' This was distinctly awkward, because the Allies were already

[1] *Windsor*, 31.3.93.

discussing how their conquests should be allotted. Dunkirk was to be the share of England, and the King had already suggested that it should be made our first military objective. On 3 April Grenville, the Foreign Secretary, had written to Auckland: 'His Majesty would be ready if it were desired by Prince Coburg, to act on the side of Dunkirk, the investiture, and still more the capture of which, would so essentially promote the siege of Lisle.'[1]

Hence, the first task of the Congress was to cancel Coburg's *gaffe*. York seems to have taken the lead here, with youthful impetuosity. Chuquet states that 'he cried hotly that Coburg was playing with them'.[2]

The Congress had its way, and, according to Auckland, he, Metternich, and Stahrenberg drafted a new proclamation, retracting the five-day-old original one. Coburg obediently signed this proclamation, the salient passage on which reads: 'It remains for me to revoke my said declaration and to announce that I shall prosecute the said war with the utmost vigour.' This abrupt revocation and recantation made, as may be imagined, a painful impression on the French people.

The Congress, having put that delicate item out of the way, proceeded to draw up a plan of campaign. Writing to Grenville next day, Auckland epitomized it as follows: The British army was to be cantoned in the area Ostend-Menin-Furnes, while Coburg, with 48,000 troops, would capture Condé, Maubeuge, and, if possible, also Lille.

There was nothing very definite about attacking Dunkirk in this, and on the 16th Henry Dundas, the Secretary of State for War,[3] wrote to General Murray, the Duke's Adjutant-General[4] that His Majesty wished Dunkirk attacked. The Secretary of State gave political grounds for this proposal, and thereby has earned the scorn of Fortescue. But political considerations may legitimately be allowed some weight when deciding on major operations. Dundas reckoned, probably rightly, that the cap-ture of Dunkirk (at one time an English possession) would make the war popular in England. In that case recruits would no

---

[1] *Auckland Correspondence*, III, p. 5.   [2] *Guerre de la Révolution*, X, p. 19.
[3] Technically he was Secretary of State for the Home Department till the post of Secretary of State for War was created for him in July 1794, but the War Office was included in the Home Office till that year.
[4] Roughly equivalent to a modern Chief of Staff.

doubt have come forward more freely, and the Army thereby have been strengthened for future operations. Thus do political considerations react upon military ones.

It may be added that on purely military grounds there was much to be said for the project. With Dunkirk in our hands, our line of communications with the seat of war would be shortened, with all the advantages that that would entail; and in English possession it would be as a pistol pointed at Paris; the French would almost certainly react by weakening their centre to a dangerous extent in order to guard against the new menace, and this would allow Coburg with the main army to make big inroads into the heart of France. Dunkirk was weakly fortified, and we had command of the sea. An amphibious operation might lead to its speedy downfall at a light cost. Once firmly in our hands, it would be possible to transfer a portion at least of our field army to another part of the line and co-operate with the main Allied army in a powerful thrust at the heart of France. The port of Dunkirk was a traditional menace to our shipping, so from a purely naval point of view its capture would be also beneficial. I agree with George III that it was an attractive and feasible operation, and if it had been carried out promptly the prospects of success would have been great. I dwell upon this point in some detail for reasons that will in due course appear.

In all this matter one cannot fail to be struck by the total absence of military advice and counsel at the seat of government. No soldier – not even the Commander-in-Chief, Lord Amherst – was taken into the confidence of the Government. All decisions regarding military operations were made by an unofficial triumvirate, consisting of Pitt, the Prime Minister; Lord Grenville, the Foreign Secretary; and Henry Dundas, the Secretary of State, or Home Secretary. This astounding state of affairs was due to various causes. In the first place, at that time, there was not the clear distinction between civil and military officers that now obtains. Every gentleman owned a sword, the insignia of a soldier; whereas every soldier was, when out of uniform, frequently addressed or referred to as a civilian – 'Mister'. Next, it was traditional that the King's confidential advisers, i.e. his Cabinet, should decide these matters. Thirdly, there was no General Staff, or anything approaching one, to which ministers could refer. Fourthly, till the outbreak of war there was not even a commander-in-chief, and had not been since Conway vacated that office in 1783. Fifthly, Amherst, apart from being an overrated soldier, was in his 77th year, and was worn out and incapable. Lastly, the King himself took a prominent part in the deliberations.

The position of the Monarch in this matter was a curiously vague one. Theoretically his ministers acted in his name and took the blame, if not the responsibility for all decisions and actions; but the Sovereign was in fact as well as in name the head of the armed forces, and had a hand in the selection of commanders, and in all matters concerning the troops. Moreover, he was King of Hanover, and thus controlled the Hanoverian portion of his army on the Continent independently of his Home Ministers. He was, indeed, better qualified for this task than the Triumvirate; after all, he had been on the throne during two major wars, immersed in military affairs,[1] which is more than any of them had. Not only was he better qualified, but they knew it. Grenville was a high-minded and gifted Foreign Secretary: no one who reads his correspondence can doubt that. But he was only 34 years of age, and his only connection with the army had been when he was Paymaster, a little more than nominal appointment. Henry Dundas was a shrewd, good-natured, well-intentioned Scotch barrister with no military experience whatever. He has been mercilessly and for all time castigated in the pages of Fortescue for his inept conduct of military affairs. There is no need to describe William Pitt in these pages; even his best friend would not call him a Heaven-born War Minister.

Such was the little group of men who were to direct our armed forces during the first days of our greatest struggle with France. But we are not to assume that mere civilians are necessarily incapable of forming correct military decisions; war is a lottery, and a correct decision is a matter of opinion; there is no acid test. If the Triumvirate were frequently guilty of egregious errors, they sometimes hit – or stumbled – upon the right decision (Dunkirk was an example), so it would be a mistake to assume that everything that Dundas did was wrong, and ungracious not to recognize that he profited by his mis-

[1] On one occasion he wrote to Pitt that the state of affairs 'fills up every crevice of my mind' (*Windsor*, 12.10.94).

takes and eventually became a passable War Minister.

After this digression we must return to the Antwerp Congress. Coburg was averse to the Dunkirk project, and very anxious for the support of the English army in his operations further south. At length he undertook (though Auckland missed the point in his report of the proceedings) that if the Duke would co-operate in the siege of Valenciennes he would, after its fall, come with his whole army, to the support of York at Dunkirk.

This project was submitted to the King, who agreed to it, and the British troops were set in motion towards Tournai.

Meanwhile Abercromby's brigade, consisting of the 14th, 37th, and 53rd Foot, had arrived at Antwerp, and the Duke, who was now promoted full General, set out to inspect them. He had a shock. He found them so lacking in physique and training, due to the large proportion of recruits that they contained, that he considered it positively unsafe to allow them in the field, and left two of the battalions at Antwerp for further training. This was drastic action to take at the outset of a campaign, and showed that at least he had the power of making bold decisions and taking an unpopular course. That it *was* his own decision and not that of Sir James Murray seems clear from the letter in which he recounted to his father the precise reasons for it.

It might seem a bold proceeding for the English army to leave its communications with the sea in Dutch hands, and to plunge south to join the Austrians some 60 miles inland. The Duke was well aware of this, and in spite of his youthful eagerness he did not neglect this vital point.

'His Royal Highness is determined not to advance to Tournai until he shall be assured that it can be done with safety,' wrote Murray to Dundas on 19 April.[1]

But Coburg sent some troops for the purpose, and on 23 April the Duke set up his headquarters at Tournai, that 'unsullied Virgin' that had, despite its proud title, fallen to Henry VIII (whose tower still stands to mark his conquest). Two days later the Duke awoke to encounter another shock – mutiny. He told the story in a letter to the King.

---

[1] *W.O.*, I, 166, f. 125.

'Tournai, 26 April, 1793.

'I was awaked yesterday morning by a Hanoverian Officer who was sent express by Lieutenant General Bussche to acquaint me that the Grenadiers and tenth Regiment of Foot had mutinied on Wednesday (24th) and had refused to march, saying that they had been promised English pay, and that they would not march a step further till they had received it. Though totally unacquainted with the Articles of the Treaty, I thought it my duty to do everything in my power to stop this spirit, and therefore I set off immediately for Vilvorde which was the cantonments of the [Hanoverian] Grenadiers. Upon my road, however, I was informed that the Battalion had marched that morning, and was quartered about a league and a half on this side of Brussels. I immediately went there, and desired the Major to assemble the Battalion directly. Before, however, the Battalion could assemble, I had a good deal of conversation with General Bussche and all the Officers of the Battalion, who seemed more vexed and affected than can be described. . . .

'As soon as the Battalion was assembled, I went out to them and desired General de Bussche to acquaint them from me that I understood that they thought themselves injured, but I would give them my word of honour that though I was not acquainted with the Treaty, I would take care that whatever was their right should be given them, but that I was ashamed of their conduct as Soldiers, and that the first Man who ventured after this promise to grumble again should be punished in the severest manner. I then told them myself that it was the first time I had ever seen a Hanoverian Regiment with disgust, and that the disgrace they had brought upon themselves could only be washed away the first time they met the Enemy. I cannot express to Your Majesty how ashamed and affected the Men appeared, and I have no doubt from what I saw and have heard that this very disagreeable occurrence is totally over. I thought it, however, right to desire General Bussche to acquaint all the Regiments of the Division from me, that whatever is their right should certainly be given them.'[1]

In this affair we cannot fail to note the good sense, tact, and firmness with which the young Duke handled a rather tricky

[1] *Windsor*, 26.4.93.

situation. Note also the decision and speed with which he acted – 'I set off immediately' – and his moral courage in acting in spite of his ignorance of whether he had the technical power to do so. We shall see further examples of these qualities before long. His intervention proved effectual, and the trouble fizzled out.

Murray wrote enthusiastically to Dundas: 'By talking to them with firmness, declaring at the same time his intention to do them justice, His Royal Highness succeeded in re-establishing discipline and order. . . . The Duke seemed to me to act with great judgement in this critical circumstance.'[1]

Round Tournai the British army gradually concentrated, whilst Coburg slowly and methodically perfected his plans for the campaign, blissfully unconscious of the fact that throughout the month of April he had France at his feet, had he risked a blow. The number of troops under the Duke's orders had now reached the respectable total of 35,000, made up as follows: British infantry, 4,200; British cavalry, 2,300; Hanoverians, 13,000; Dutch, 15,000. In addition, 8,000 Hessians in British pay were approaching. It was a heterogeneous collection of troops, and York's Adjutant-General, Sir James Murray, was hardly the man for the job. Though experienced and knowledgeable, and intelligent, he was indecisive, slothful, rather tactless, and consequently unpopular. Someone with the virtue of a Cadogan was required for the post. The Duke had now placed himself completely under Coburg's orders.

Prince Josias of Coburg-Saalfeld was an honourable, kindly, but lethargic old man. Count Langeron,[2] described him as 'an absolute nonentity; he never gives an order, directs a single operation, and never takes a step without his director. But his birth, probity, virtue and equanamity (*docilite*) were sufficient reason for his selection for this command where one required a Prince of a Royal House and a level-headed man.'[3]

[1] *W.O.*, I, 166, f. 173.
[2] This remarkable but little-known Frenchman was one of the last of the Soldiers of Fortune. Born in Paris in 1763, he died in St Petersburg in 1831, having spent more than fifty years almost constantly under arms. He fought for France in the American War, and emigrated to Russia in 1789, where he joined the Czar's staff. From here he was sent to Flanders in 1793, attached to the Austrian staff, with a watching brief from the Czar. In this capacity he accompanied the Duke of York in some of his operations, and his keen eye and sound judgment make his *Mémoirs* an invaluable commentary on the campaign.
[3] *Mémoires sur les Guerres*, by Comte de Langeron, p. 16.

Lieutenant-Colonel Karl von Mack, his Chief of Staff, was a very remarkable man. Backed by twenty-three years' service, he was looked upon as one of the most brilliant officers in the Austrian army, though unpopular with the staff. He has hardly had a fair deal from our historians, who, being wise after the event, can see nothing good in a man who twelve years later had the misfortune to be captured at Ulm. For example, the Cambridge Modern History asserts that 'Mack's ideas of strategy were not sound, as Ulm was to prove later'. All we will say of him here is that he was 'a live wire' – a thing sadly needed in the Austrian army – and that he was the brains and directing genius of that army.

It is, however, true that he was inclined to be a 'defeatist'. In a conversation with Captain Bentinck, R.N., he opined that the only thing to be hoped for in the ensuing campaign was the capture of a few fortresses – and then peace.

*   *   *   *   *

The campaign proper opened on May Day. The Austrian army lay stretched along the approximate frontier of France from Nieuport to Maubeuge. (See sketch map 1.) The barrier fortresses between these places (largely built by Vauban for Louis XIV) were all in French occupation except Ypres, Menin, Tournai, and Mons. The French revolutionary troops were badly trained, and they served under a succession of second-rate commanders. The numbers of the opposing armies were approximately equal.

It was the French, after all, who took the initiative. On May Day they attacked the Austrians near St Amand, fifteen miles south of Tournai. The British troops stood to, in case their help were required, and the Duke sped south to see for himself how things were going. The attacks were driven off without much difficulty; the only point of interest for us is that the Duke must have 'smelt powder' for the first time that day. For, according to Major Jesse Wright (who was in command of the British artillery till Major Congreve came out), the Austrians captured a gun and presented it to the Duke, 'who was near when they took it'.[1] Of course, he had no business to be near; he should have been at his own headquarters, waiting for any call for

[1] *Wright Letters*, p. 7.

help. But one must not be too hard on this young man still in his twenties, who was itching for a fight.[1]

On 8 May the French attacked again, with the intention of relieving Condé, which was then being besieged. The action that followed took place in the Forest of Raismes, midway between St Amand and Valenciennes. At first the Austrians were in a bad way, and the Duke, who had moved some troops down almost to St Amand in case they might be needed, sent up the Coldstream Regiment, followed by the rest of the Brigade, directly the request for aid reached him. The fire-eating Commander could not resist the temptation to follow him in person to see the fun. What ensued let him tell in his own words in a letter to the King:

'I cannot help mentioning to You, Sir, the very remarkable Courage and Intrepidity of the Officers and Men of the three Batallions which went into fire, but most particularly the Coldstream, who bore the brunt of the attack. At the moment I arrived with the Troops, General Knobelsdorf came up to me and said to me "Les Autrichiens plient, Nos Bataillons sont tous repoussés, Au nom de Dieu faites avancer un Bataillon ou nous sommes perdus.' I immediately ordered the Coldstream which was nearest the Batallion to advance: as they were moving along, I went up to them and said to them, My Lads, I have no doubt of Your Courage, but be likewise prudent and cool. The whole Batallion answered me Never fear, we will do You Honor, God save the King. They immediately advanced, formed line, and moved into line, keeping their step and their distance as well as if they had been at exercise. The French as soon as they saw them coming near the wood, ran off and retired behind some entrenchments they had thrown up in the night.[2] Colonel Pennington without any order whatever chose to attack the Battery, and when he came close to it, He received the discharge of three nine Pounders loaded with grape, which mowed down my poor brave fellows most shockingly. This

---

[1] His young brother, Prince Ernest (later Duke of Cumberland and King of Hanover), who commanded the 9th Hanoverian Light Dragoons in this affair, asserts that the Duke 'was the whole time present at this affair.' The Duke did not tell his father.

[2] The ground is dead flat and still covered with wood; it is thus hopeless to attempt to identify the entrenchments.

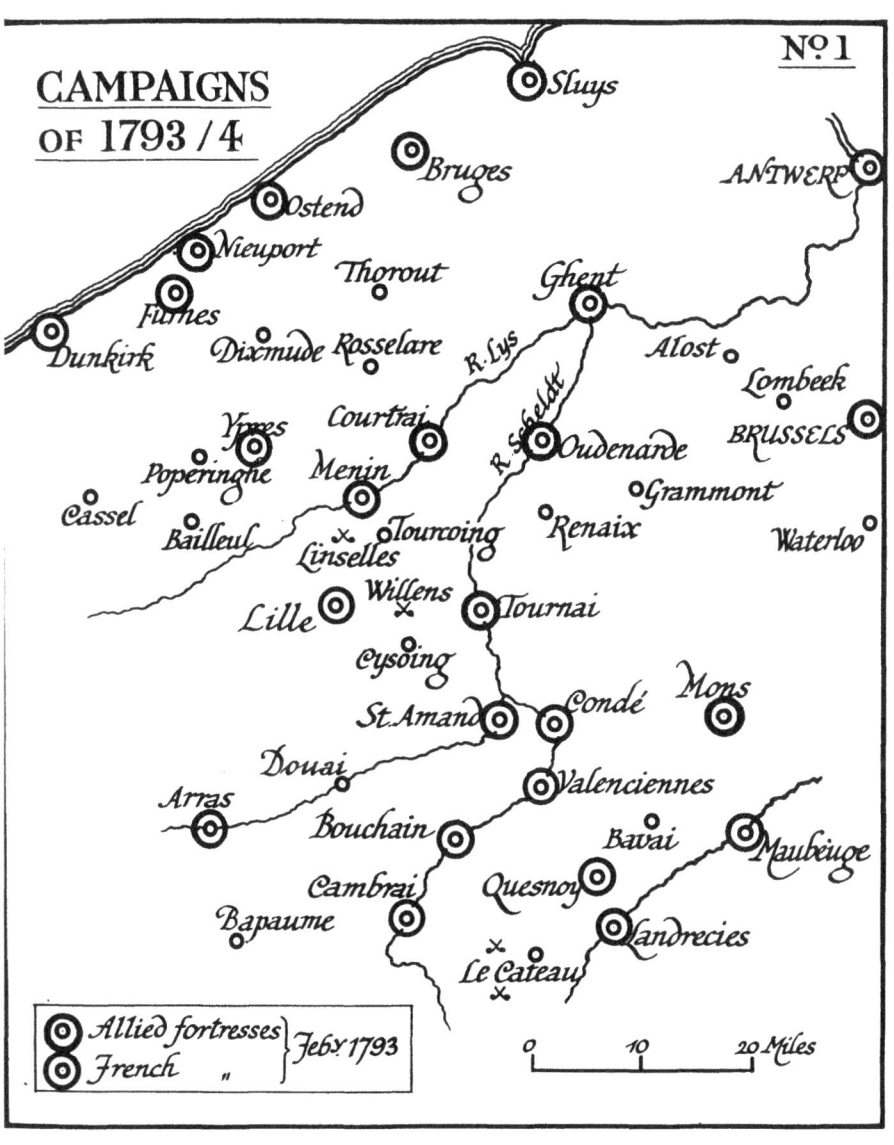

CAMPAIGNS
OF **1793 / 4**

N⁰ 1

Sluys

Bruges

ANTWERP

Ostend

Nieuport

Thorout

Ghent

Alost

Lombeek

Furnes

Dunkirk

Dixmude

Rosselare

R. Lys

BRUSSELS

Ypres

Courtrai

R. Scheldt

Oudenarde

Grammont

Poperinghe

Menin

Cassel

Bailleul

Tourcoing

Renaix

Waterloo

Linselles

Lille

Willems

Tournai

Cysoing

St. Amand

Condé

Mons

Douai

Valenciennes

Arras

Bouchain

Bavai

Maubeuge

Cambrai

Quesnoy

Bapaume

Le Cateau

Landrecies

Allied fortresses
French ,,
Feb.ʸ 1793

0   10   20 Miles

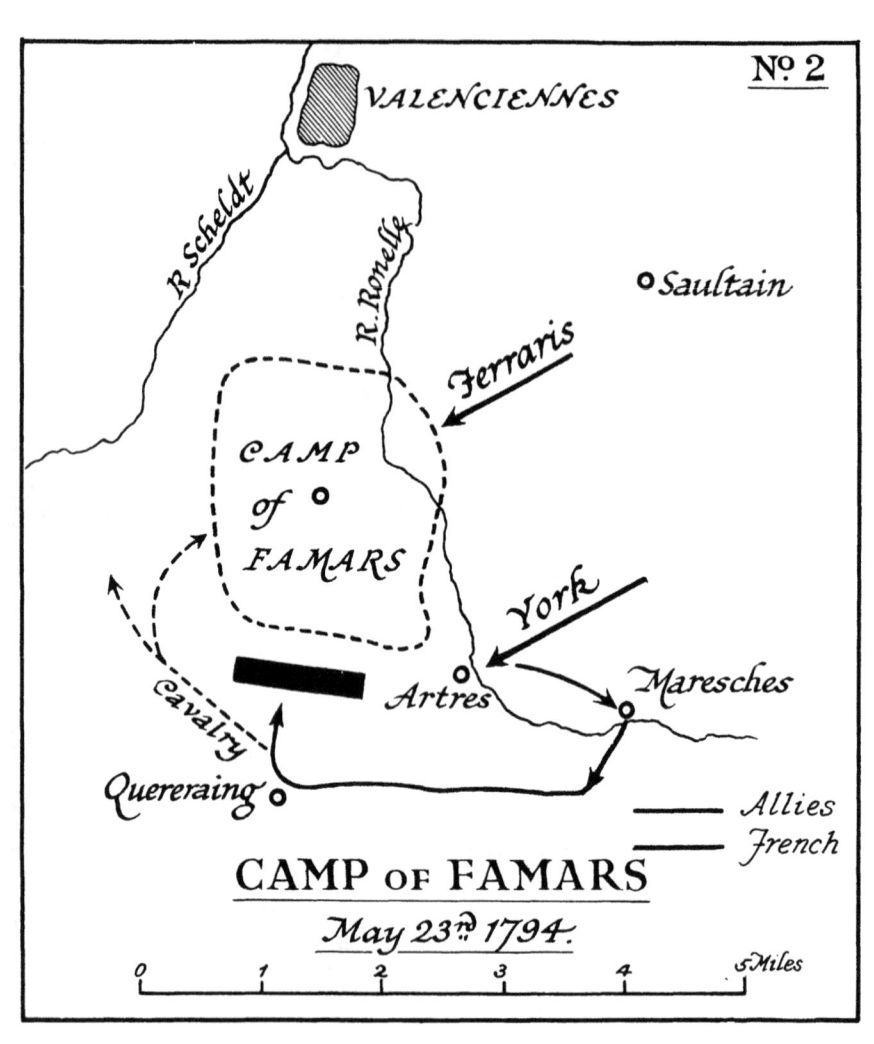

No. 2

VALENCIENNES

R. Scheldt

R. Ronelle

Saultain

Ferraris

CAMP of FAMARS

York

Artres

Maresches

Cavalry

Quereraing

Allies

French

CAMP OF FAMARS

May 23rd 1794.

0   1   2   3   4   5 Miles

however did not make them move till they were ordered to throw back the right wing which they did and then stood a very heavy Canonade without even moving until they were released by the Grenadiers, and third Regiment.'[1]

Major Wright, who sent up four guns and was not far off himself, said that he was not surprised at the casualties the Coldstream suffered; they marched through the wood in line and in step! A certain Colonel Blucher of the Prussian service, later to become famous, probably witnessed the same sublime spectacle, for he declared: 'I have never seen finer soldiers. They marched with such resolution and did everything possible to attain victory.' But we are more concerned with the actions of the Commander than of his troops, and a modern French historian does not find much to praise. 'The Duke of York, young and presumptuous, thought the sight of redcoats would suffice',[2] – which it nearly did: the French gave up their attempt and fell back shortly afterwards.

The Austrians were impressed. 'M. de Clerfait and the Austrians in general speak with the highest praises of His Royal Highness and the English troops. They ascribe in a great measure the complete success on the 8th to their bravery and to a very quick and able manoeuvre of His Royal Highness.'[3]

The heavy casualties suffered by the Coldstream in this gallant action came as a shock to the Guards Brigade, and some officers began the reprehensible habit of writing criticising letters, on inadequate information, to members of the Government. The Duke of the York was attacked, but he refused to defend himself in the only way possible, namely by passing the blame on to his Allies. Sir John Fortescue makes an admirable observation on this. 'The Duke of York, who had never contemplated so foolhardy an attack, wisely thought it best to make no complaint. The Battalion itself, to judge by a letter that one of its officers wrote to Lord Buckingham, was very indignant with the Duke; and there is every probability that its complaints reached the ear of Pitt. I mention this because, though the matter is in itself a small one, it gives conclusive evidence of the incessant friction which arose from the indiscipline of British officers, and from the mistrust which the Allies felt for each

[1] *Windsor*, 10.5.93.   [2] *Chuquet-Guerre de la Révolution*, X, p. 67.
[3] *Auckland Correspondence*, III, p. 58.

D

other. It is safe to conjecture that this uninformed criticism of generals by their subordinate officers continued throughout the campaign; and the preservation of the above-mentioned letter among Lord Grenville's papers is proof that such criticism is not disregarded by their powerful patrons at home.'[1]

This procedure seems to have been as effective as that of soldiers writing home to their Member of Parliament in more recent times.

Meanwhile reinforcements both of British cavalry and Hessian infantry were reaching the army, and by 21 May Coburg felt himself strong enough to launch his long-delayed attack. The French had now fallen back into their entrenched camp of Famars, which took its name from a little village on a ridge three miles south of Valenciennes. This ridge was bounded on the east by the River Rhonelle, the bridges and fords over which had been put out of action. The French army totalled 25,000 men, under General Lamarche. (See sketch map 2.)

The plan of attack had been drawn up by Mack. It was his 'swan song', for he was out of favour at the Austrian Court and among the Austrian generals and was about to be replaced.

The gist of the plan was that a series of holding attacks should be made on the French line to the right and left of the real attack. This attack was to be made frontally against the eastern face of the camp by two columns; the northern, which contained Abercromby's brigade, was under General Ferraris; the southern one, consisting of sixteen battalions, including the Brigade of Guards, was under the Duke of York. It is curious that the British troops were thus split up into two columns, one of them commanded by a foreigner. Nor is it clear what was Coburg's real motive in putting the British contingent into the spearhead of the attack. Was it a compliment to their fighting ability as a result of their action at Raismes, or were they being looked upon as merely convenient cannon fodder?

Mack's order for the attack contained the following paragraphs:

'The destination of the first attack (York's) is to advance on the line (*'rideau'*) between Presceau and Maresches as far as the River Rhonelle; then under cover of its artillery, to throw

[1] *Fortescue*, IV, p. 109.

several trestle bridges in the neighbourhood of Artres, and to pass as many columns as possible over the river; thence to attack the camp of Famars by its right flank.'

Reveille was to be at midnight; staff officers were to give the order to advance and lead each column to its assembly point.[1]

Scorn has been directed against these orders of Mack's as being too meticulously detailed; but judged by modern standards the verdict would be that, if anything, they were not detailed enough. It is, however, a fair criticism that Mack, here as elsewhere, did not sufficiently allow for what Clausewitz called 'the friction of war' – the many little unpredictable incidents and mishaps that between them may mar the best-laid plan. The friction in this case took the form of fog. The assembly-point for York's column was only two miles to the east of Artres, and the advance began soon after 2 a.m. As they were silently filing off, Corporal Robert Brown of the Coldstream caught a glimpse of the Duke riding past, making a rapid inspection of troops on the march. With what suppressed excitement must the 29-year-old Duke have taken that ride. He was going to his first battlefield, and he was the General in command. It was the moment he had dreamed of ever since, just twelve years before, he had his first lesson in soldiering at the Court of Hanover.

Owing to the fog progress was necessarily slow, and it was not till 7 a.m., when it had cleared, that the column found itself close to the eastern bank of the Rhonelle.[2] It was broad daylight, and the surprise that darkness would have provided was lost. To make matters worse, the river bank was actively guarded by both infantry and guns, which promptly opened fire. This was a totally unlooked for situation, for it was implied in the orders that there would be no opposition worth mentioning at the river; bridges could be methodically constructed, and the real battle would only commence when the column resumed their advance up the ridge on which the camp rested.

[1] *Jomini*, III, p. 439.

[2] The spectacle as the fog lifted and the columns advanced silently down the hill to the river was such as to strike the imagination of at least two persons in that host. One was Corporal Brown, who rhapsodizes about it in his book. The other was – the Duke of York, who wrote to his brother: 'The sight in the morning when the fog cleared up was the most beautiful that ever was seen' (*Windsor*, 26.5.93). See Note A at end of chapter.

It was a situation which called for an important decision. If
Mack, the author of the plan, had been at hand, the Duke
might very well have taken counsel with him, and have asked
what – under the new situation that had arisen – he should do.
But unfortunately Mack, who had accompanied the Duke's
column as a 'volunteer', had already been wounded and carried
off to the rear. York had thus to decide for himself, and the
decision he came to was under the circumstances, a striking
one. Leaving some Austrian heavy guns and the troops already
engaged to 'amuse' the enemy in front, he counter-marched
with the remainder of his column, making for Maresches. The
French must have viewed with surprise the column thus
abruptly turning on its heels; they could not be aware in what
respect the plan had gone wrong thus early in the day, nor
could they divine, as their enemy disappeared into the village
of Maresches, two miles away, whether it was going to swing
right or left. But presently the Allies' cavalry, fording the
stream, ascended the low ridge to the south of the village, and
doubts could be set at rest: a turning movement directed at
their right flank was indicated. Forewarned is forearmed, and
the French set about preparing for the new attack. Most unfortunately for York, there was a big delay and great congestion
at Maresches while the bridges were being constructed, and
the column was not across the river till 3 p.m.

The column now turned west, and by a somewhat circuitous
route reached Querenaing an hour or two later. Here the
Duke marshalled his army in line for the assault, at the same
time sending out his light Dragoons to locate the flank redoubts. The patrol on the left almost reached the banks of the
River Scheldt at the Abbey of Fontenelle, according to Arnaudin,[1] completely in the rear of the French position. This fact
(which is not mentioned by any other source) seems to show
that up to that hour the French had made no preparation for
retreat. Other cavalry captured some French guns. The chief
redoubt on the southern face was situated on the ridge about
one mile north of Querenaing. The Duke rode forward to what
Arnaudin describes as a *chemin creusé* between Querenaing
and Maing. This was probably on the ridge of the north-west
of Querenaing, whence he could get a good view of the French

[1] *Arnaudin*, I, p. 85.

position nearly a mile away across the valley.[1] But here the Duke, his brain buzzing with plans and orders of attack, encountered an unexpected obstacle. Not only had Mack accompanied this tyro to his first battle, but Coburg had also sent his new Chief of Staff to shadow the English General, and prevent him doing anything rash or imprudent. Now, General Hohenlohe was 71 years of age. Chuquet describes him as '*toujours circonspect et difficultueux*',[2] prone to raise difficulties. Hohenlohe objected to the proposed attack, pointing out the fatigue of the troops. A wink was as good as a nod, coming from such a quarter – the mouthpiece of the Commander-in-Chief. York therefore regretfully postponed the attack till dawn next day. Morning came – and the enemy was gone. Warned by the double threat to front and flank – for Ferraris had broken into the position without much difficulty, Lamarche had slipped away with his whole army during the night. The Allies had captured the camp, but it was little more than an empty shell.

Whose was the blame? The Austrians tried to attach it to the Duke, so we must examine his conduct in this his first battle rather narrowly. In the first place there can be no doubt that his decision to call off the first attack was sound. The situation was not such as the superior who had given him his orders had envisaged it. The enemy held the river bank, and surprise was no longer possible. A weak commander, fearful of responsibility, will in such a case delay operations by sending to solicit further orders from his senior. But a commander worthy of the name is prepared to shoulder responsibility himself and to take instant decisions on the spot. A commander who, though not necessarily lacking in self-confidence, is plagued with a rigid mind will plunge straight ahead into a sea of difficulties merely because this course has been preordained for him. But flexibility is one of the valid principles of war, and one of the cardinal virtues of the general. A Wellington will turn his own plan upside down at Toulouse; a Montgomery will utterly transform his plan at Mareth Line; even a Buller at Ladysmith showed flexibility eventually and achieved success thereby. The Duke of York is thus to be applauded rather than condemned for scrapping the first plan he was given and substituting another

[1] Since writing this I have identified the actual spot. See Note A at end of chapter.
[2] *Chuquet*, X, p. 93.

and for coming to his decision promptly. As to the delay in carrying it out, we are in the realm of logistics – the affair of the staff. His own staff was at that early stage of the war raw and inexperienced, as also were his troops, and administrative shortcomings must have been considerable. We have not sufficient evidence on which to judge in this matter, nor is it relevant, unless it be maintained that the Duke should somehow or other have given his staff previous training. Before the war he was not in a position to do so, and when the army reached the front it was too late.

The third question is: Would an evening attack from Querenaing have been justified? There is no question that the troops were fatigued. Hamilton states in his excellent history of the Guards that they had been under arms for thirty hours with only two hours' rest and nothing to eat. I should be disposed to consider this a slight exaggeration, but in any case history has shown that time and again when troops have seemed at the last gasp a supreme call has met with a response. Troops often appear at the end of their tether, yet still retain unexpected reserves of strength. Morale is one of the most difficult things to assess in the case of the living; how much harder must it be in the case of troops who have been dead 150 years, and of whom the precise details are scanty? I cannot therefore go further than to suggest that the Guards, at least, would have responded to the call, and that the French, who were then of poor quality and already shaken by the attack on their front, would have melted away on seeing their line of retreat threatened. To sum up, I can find nothing definite with which to find fault in the Duke of York's conduct of his first battle, and a good deal to admire. He had made a promising start.

There are two points to note in his letter to the King announcing the victory (for victory it was, as the capture of Famars Camp was the objective); the first is the note of jubilant enthusiasm that pervades it; the second is his restraint in not throwing any blame on his Allies for putting the brake on his victory. The letter opens by recording 'the glorious success of yesterday's battle which has been more complete than could ever have been expected. The whole plan of this general attack is certainly a masterpiece of military skill. . . . The general officers assembled at the Austrian camp, at 11 o'clock on Wednesday night, and after the last arrangements were taken we returned to our respective columns at 12, and immediately marched. A very heavy fog having come on, I was obliged to delay my attack till about 5 o'clock in the morning. As my attack was the first which was to begin the enemy brought down the largest part of his artillery and we were exposed for near three hours to a very severe cannonade. . . . Luckily it did us little harm. . . . Finding however that I should with difficulty throw a bridge of boats over the Rhonelle at Artres (which was the place intended for me to pass) under so heavy a fire I took the second line, composed of the Brigade of Guards and the Austrian Regiment of Steray, and of Hohenlohe and the six English and four Hanoverian squadrons of Light Dragoons, and passed over the Rhonelle at Maresches, and immediately advanced on the enemy, who directly fled before us, and took refuge in three large redoubts, which were just in front of the village of Famars. As it was impossible to bring my artillery as fast as the infantry marched I was obliged to halt till it came up. . . .'[1]

THE SIEGE OF VALENCIENNES

In the eighteenth century sieges played a prominent and sometimes a dominant part in war. It seems never to have occurred to Coburg that he could leave the frontier fortresses behind him, like so many 'hedgehogs' (to use a modern term) and march boldly on to Paris, living on the country. In his view it was a prerequisite that the fortresses must be taken. In this he was merely echoing the military opinion of his age. That being so, it is easy to understand that he should now turn to the siege of Valenciennes, into which town many of the troops from Famars had taken refuge. Like Marlborough at the siege of Lille, who deputed the actual siege to his colleague and himself commanded the covering army, Coburg placed the Duke of York in command of the siege, attaching to him General Ferraris, to supervise the technical siege operations. The English were averse to a 'sealed pattern' siege, believing that the place could be captured by a *coup de main*. But the Austrians insisted on going through the stereotyped procedure of parallels, covered ways, saps, mines, etc. In this matter the

[1] *Windsor*, 24.5.93.

Duke and his staff were unversed, for there had been little of
the sort in the recent war in America. But the Duke was far
from being the mere figurehead that is widely imagined. Here
is the description of the siege that he sent to his father:

'I am exceedingly happy to be able to acquaint Your Majesty
that we opened the first Parallel last night and that We were
so fortunate as totally to escape the notice of the Enemy during
the whole night, so that the Men were enabled to sink the
trenches so very deep that they were compleatly under cover
by daybreak. We have four thousand five hundred Soldiers at
Work in the Trenches who are relieved every twelve hours, and
three thousand to cover them, who are relieved every evening.
During the whole time I was in the Trenches which was till
between three and four o'clock this morning, the Enemy fired
only five random shots; they have however (fired) a good deal
since six o'clock.'[1]

This reference to the trenches disturbed his father, who
wrote enjoining him to take no undue risks.

The Duke replied soothingly:

'I feel in the strongest manner Your Majesty's gracious and
affectionate hints concerning the risks I may run in action,
though I trust that though I have never improperly shrunk
from any danger, yet I can assure Your Majesty I never have
wantonly exposed myself wherever I thought that the service
could be carried on equally well without it.'[2]

The Austrians pursued their course with methodical and
maddening slowness. This dilatoriness aroused the impetuous
Duke, and we are told that 'he sharply remonstrated with them,
and in return was reproved for his excessive zeal'.[3]

That close observer, Count Langeron, notes that 'the siege
proceeded very slowly'.[4]

Two welcome successes attended the Allies' arms during the
siege. On July 10 Condé fell, followed on the 22nd by Maintz.
Four days later the main hornworks of Valenciennes on the
eastern side were stormed by three columns, in one of which
British troops played a prominent part.

The Duke and Murray between them were responsible for
this success being made possible, as this letter from Murray to
Dundas will show: 'The keeping the hornwork was entirely

[1] *Windsor*, 14.6.93.   [2] Ibid., 21.6.93.   [3] *Fizgerald*, II, 111.   [4] *Langeron*, p. 16.

owing to us putting the Duke of York at the head. Repeated orders were sent by General Ferraris to evacuate it. Knowing the Duke's wishes on that head, convinced of the folly of such a measure, and strongly supported by Colonel Moncrieff, I gave positive orders to the contrary, which was approved in the fullest manner by His Royal Highness who was at that time at a redoubt a little in the rear. . . . The Duke had been fighting the point the whole morning.'

The direct result of this vigour was that on the 28th the fortress surrendered, and the Duke of York was acclaimed by the fickle inhabitants as King of France. The obsequious Director of the Opera inquired what play the Duke would like put on that evening, and suggested *Richard Coeur de Lion.* Throughout the siege Coburg had kept tactfully and discreetly in the background, and the Duke of York was given sole charge of the protracted surrender negotiations. There is a circumstantial account of his interview with a deputation from the garrison, who pleaded for better terms than he was demanding. 'After a moment of reflection, the Duke replied that the garrison could leave with the honours of war, but that they must be regarded as prisoners, must hand over their arms, cannons, munitions, etc.'[1]

When he entered the town, though accompanied by Coburg, it was to himself that the keys of the town were ceremoniously handed. No doubt Coburg had good reason to leave all this to the English Prince, for the French would be more likely to come to terms with him than with the hated Austrians. Indeed, the Duke became quite popular among the French, and it is related that the French garrison, on their way home, told the inhabitants of Soissons that they loved the Duke of York, who seemed to them worthy of the throne of France.[2]

The siege of Valenciennes attained world-wide fame, and was certainly the most considerable operation carried out in the first campaign. Novel methods were employed by both sides. The French sent out balloons in order to keep touch with the outside world. The Duke made use of what is usually considered the modern device of firing propaganda material into the town

[1] *Chuquet*, p. 319.   [2] Ibid., p. 332.

in hollow shells.[1] He also made use of incendiary shells, fired
at night. But though success enhanced his reputation, it throws
no light on his ability as a general in the field. Nevertheless his
powers of leadership were put to the proof in two disagreeable
incidents, which are best described in his own words:

'About a week ago, it was reported to Me that the Privates
of the Hanoverian Footguards had twice without leave left the
Trenches, and returned to their camp without their Officers or
Non-Commissioned Officers, making use of very improper
expressions, and calling to the other Regiments to follow them;
the first time this happened the other Regiments continued
their work, but the second time, they followed them. At the
same time that Count Walmoden, under whose command they
then were, reported this to the Field Marshal, and to Me, he
said that He was very sorry to add that he had every reason to
believe that the Soldiers were set on and encouraged by some
of their Officers, who, though he could not then prove it, he
had been informed, held forth continually before them in
praise of French Principles.

'Yesterday morning Count Walmoden wrote to Me to inform
Me that things were got to such a pitch that unless strong
measures were taken very speedily, it was impossible to know
what might be the consequences. He at the same time mentioned Captains Bulow and Mecklenburg of the Footguards as
two of the Officers who encouraged the Men and who made use
continually of expressions little short of mutiny and treason.

'I immediately went to the Feldt Marschal and after consulting with Him, it was determined that as it was absolutely
necessary to remove these Officers immediately from their
Regiments, I should write to Him and desire Him to order them
to quit the Camp directly which was done this morning.

'I hope Your Majesty will not disapprove of the measure,
which was dictated by necessity, as the Hannoverian Courts
Martial are so exceedingly slow, and though it is not my business to interfere in the internal arrangements of Your Majesty's
Electoral Troops, yet it is My duty not to allow any Officer to

[1] Described genially by Foucart et Finot in *Le Defence Nationale* as 'cette plaisan-
terie du général Anglais'.

serve in the Troops under My command who cannot be trusted.'[1]

The King's approval led to the following letter:

'Before Valenciennes, 16 July 1793,

'I am extremely happy that Your Majesty approves of My conduct with regard to the two Officers of the Hannoverian Footguards. It was absolutely necessary that some vigourous step should be taken at the moment, or it would be impossible to say what might have been the consequences, at the same time that I certainly had not the least right to interfere in the interior discipline of the Hannoverian Troops. It gives Me however the greatest satisfaction to inform Your Majesty that I have every reason to believe that the step has had the desired effect, and that there is nothing more to be feared from any spirit of mutiny or disaffection among the Hannoverian Footguards; on the contrary, from everything which I can learn it appears as if the Men themselves seemed pleased at these Officers being sent away and called them "Patriots".

'On Saturday I went to Condé to see the French Garrison march out. I found the Troupes de Ligne, of whom there were three Batallions, better in point of Men than I had imagined, but the Gardes Nationales were worse than I could have had an idea of; they behaved on the whole in a more orderly manner than could have been supposed, except one man who was drunk, and was repeatedly desired to hold his tongue without effect, upon which the Prince of Wurtemberg had Him heartily thrashed.'[2]

Three days later more trouble occurred.

'I think I ought to mention to Your Majesty a disagreeable circumstance which has happened in the Coldstream, and which I am sorry to say is totally owing to Colonel Pennington's unhappy temper which has grown so much worse that it is now little short of insanity.

'I believe no Corps of Officers ever left England to go upon Service better disposed, or more cordial among themselves than that of the Coldstream. We had been however but a very short time from England when I was informed that Colonel Pennington's behaviour was so very unpleasant to the rest of the

[1] *Windsor*, 3.7.93.   [2] Ibid., 16.7.93.

Officers that they could hardly bear it. As it has always however been my rule to support the Commanding Officer in
every instance in which it is in My power, I sent the Officers
privately a word to be very careful of their behaviour, as I
thought myself in duty bound to support Colonel Pennington.
I must do the Officers justice that they uniformly did everything
in their power to please him; but in vain, and he in many
instances made use of his authority over them to gratify his
ill-nature; at last, however, on Sunday morning, he put Captain
Wynyard the Adjutant in arrest and reported Him to me for
a Court Martial for not handing in his Report to Him of the
Parade mentioned Lieutenant-Colonel Finch being absent.
This accusation, had it been true, was so very frivolous that in
any other case I should have quashed it, but as Wynyard is one
of my own family, Pennington was likely to have said that I had
done it to serve him. I therefore allowed him the Court Martial
he had applied for, when He was not only not able to prove the
charge He had brought, but on the contrary the very opposite
was proved, upon which the Court honourably acquitted
Wynyard. It is to be hoped that after this and after the Conversation I had with Colonel Pennington before all the Officers
in which I told Him very plainly my opinion of His conduct, he
will think of retiring, as really he is perfectly Mad, which is the
only excuse for his conduct.'[1]

The English Government now ordered the Duke to march
his army against Dunkirk. But before the armies parted
company a combined attack on the French position in Caesar's
Camp was undertaken.

CAESAR'S CAMP (Sketch map 3)

The centre of this camp lay two miles to the south of Bouchain, but its left flank lay far to the west, on the Sensee near
Arleux, a place made memorable by Marlborough in 1711.
Indeed, the position on this flank followed the famous lines of
Ne Plus Ultra. The right flank bent back in a southerly direction, almost to Cambrai, and the extreme flank was protected
by entrenchments at Bourlon Wood, with a cavalry screen still
further to the south and east. The garrison of the camp consisted

[1] *Windsor*, 19.7.93. It is only fair to add that subsequently Pennington earned the
Duke's praise.

of 35,000 men under a general of Irish extraction, Kilmaine by name. Coburg's plan for the attack has been generally misunderstood. The Duke of York was given the largest column, 25,000 strong, but his attack, which was to be made against the southern face of the camp, was really intended only as a diversion; the real attack was to be delivered by 15,000 Austrians against the eastern face, after the Duke's column had started off on its long flanking march to the south. This is made clear in Murray's private letter to Dundas of 8 August, wherein he writes: 'In the original plan of the attack . . . there is no mention of the Duke's column, which was, however, what determined the affair. We made it (the new plan) out at the conference when the first plan was regularly proposed. I begged 20 times, and more earnestly every time, as the event drew nearer, to have the cavalry of General Coleredo's column, if not that of the other, and to regulate our measures beforehand, upon the certainty of their running away.'[1]

This plan appears nonsensical, for the diversion would probably warn the defenders of the camp, and give them time to evade the blow that was being prepared against the front face. The roles should have been reversed. Another error was that the Duke was only allotted a few squadrons of cavalry, though he was operating in ideal cavalry country, whereas the main attack would be over ground unsuitable for that arm. In fact, everything goes to show that the Duke's role was a mere afterthought, and that Coburg pinned his faith in the frontal attack by his Austrians.

At 3 a.m. on August 7 York's column set off from Villers en Cauchie. The force marched in a single column via St Hilaire towards Crevecoeur and Masnieres, ultimately splitting into two columns. But even these must have widened out, for Corporal Brown states: 'We made our own roads.' This seems likely to be true, for the country thereabouts is very open – as those who fought at the battle of Cambrai in 1917 can testify.

The day became extremely hot, and skirmishes with French cavalry on the right flank near Cambrai further delayed the column. It was therefore not till evening that the Scheldt was reached at Crevecoeur and Masnieres, and only part of the column crossed the river that night.

[1] *W.O.*, I, 167, f. 731.

Meanwhile the French cavalry gave Kilmaine due warning, as was only to be expected. He thereupon held a council of war. This was attended by a civilian deputy, Delbrel by name. Delbrel played the part to Kilmaine that the Dutch deputy Goslinga had played to Marlborough; that is, he advocated a quite impracticable but interesting plan. This was that the French should sally forth from the camp, ignoring the threat from the east, and hurl themselves on York's column while it was still on the march. It was just such a blow that Wellington delivered at Salamanca, but Wellington's troops were highly trained, whereas Kilmaine's men were little better than a rabble. Kilmaine wisely declined to make the attempt, but decided instead to decamp during the night. To do this it was necessary to fall back due west to Arras, instead of south-west, as that way would be barred by the Duke's column. To cover the movement he left a rearguard on the line Bourlon-Marquion.

Soon after daybreak on August 8 the Duke's column moved off. York wished to move off punctually at daybreak, but Hohenlohe, who accompanied the force, demurred. Exactly how much postponement there was, I cannot discover, but Taylor, who related it, is a reliable witness.[1] But it may have been Coburg himself, who also accompanied the column, who was the real opponent of an early start.

The army advanced in line of three columns. The right column, consisting of Austrians under Hohenlohe, heading for Bourlon, halted at Cantaing and remained there the rest of the day. The centre and left columns, under York, advanced respectively through Anneux and Graincourt and pushed on to the Cambrai-Bapaume *chaussée*. By this time the French rearguard had evacuated the Bourlon-Marquion line, for Kilmaine had slipped away before dawn. But from the ridge to the west of Bourlon Wood there is a clear view of practically all the ground down to the little village of Marquion, two and a half miles to the north.[2] Over this open stretch of country the Duke of York could descry the rearguard of the French army

---

[1] *Taylor*, p. 42.

[2] The Duke probably spotted the enemy from the spot where the Bourlon water tower now stands.

trickling away. His ardent spirit was aroused. He had only a
tiny force of cavalry under his direct command, so he applied to
Prince Hohenlohe for help. Captain Taylor, who was present
as A.D.C. to the Duke, states that 'The Duke of York urged
Prince Hohenlohe early to press them, but he declined, and
told His Royal Highness later in the day that he might follow
them with his own cavalry. H.R.H. did so, and I was one of the
party.'[1]

Unfortunately Taylor does not, for some reason, give the
details of what followed, and we are obliged to have recourse
to French sources. As this was one of the most memorable days
in the military life of the Duke, it is worth recounting it in
detail. Dupuis writes: 'As his troops crossed the Cambrai-
Bapaume road, he learnt that a strong French cavalry force
was advancing towards him. Immediately he faced this menace.'
The French then retired and, 'realizing that the enemy were
trying to make off and that he ought to harass them as much as
possible during their retreat York quickly collected a mixed
corps composed of all the cavalry, of his two columns, less four
squadrons, total just over 2,000 men – a detachment of infantry
and some guns and dashed forward at their head in the direction
of Marquion'.[2]

At this moment his opponent Kilmaine was also approaching
Marquion as rapidly as possible, leading up a reinforcement of
cavalry to the threatened rearguard. Thus the rival commanders were galloping straight towards one another, just as forty-
six years before York's great-uncle, the Duke of Cumberland,
and Marshal Saxe almost came to blows at the bloody battle of
Laffelt. Count Langeron, who was present, tells the story.

'This day I had the happiness to save the life of the Duke of
York. On arrival at the Agache he ordered the Austrian cavalry
on the left to make for the bridge of Saing-les-Marquion [one
and a half miles south of Marquion, also on the Agache] and
intended himself with the English cavalry to cross at Marquion,
where we had captured the bridge. The village was on fire, and
we were so roasted by the fumes that it was impossible to cross.
The cavalry halted. The Duke of York who was leading with a
single orderly and myself, dashed through the burning village,
however, at a gallop, and a hundred yards beyond it reached

[1] *Taylor*, p. 41.   [2] *Dupuis*, p. 159.

a small height[1] from which we saw, only 20 yards away, two lines of French cavalry. As they wore practically the same uniform as the Hanoverian cavalry, the Duke, who had more personal bravery than experience of war, cried "There are my Hanoverians!" He continued to advance and almost reached the line of enemy officers, when I cried out to him "Monseigneur, those are the French!" and seizing his horse's bridle turned him and led him back to Marquion. But for me he would have been killed or taken – which would have been the same thing for him, for the Convention spared no Englishman.'[2]

Doubtless Langeron made use of the old soldier's prerogative as described by Shakespeare, of telling his story 'with advantages' – to himself. Nevertheless, there is no reason to doubt the essential truth of his account.

Dupuis throws further light on the action. The bridge at Marquion was partially broken, and the cavalry could only cross it in single file. Meanwhile York supposed that the Austrian cavalry had succeeded in crossing at Saing, but the ground was, in fact, marshy and the approach narrow, and only a few of the horsemen managed to get across. The cavalry that the Duke nearly crashed into had been rallied by Kilmaine, so that the Englishman and Irishman may have come within pistol shot of one another. Not since his duel had the Duke been under such close-range fire.

Eventually some Hanoverian cavalry, commanded by Prince Ernest, succeeded in getting across the river, and then engaged the French cavalry on the ridge beyond. The Prince wrote enthusiastically to his father: 'I have had the good luck to fight hand in hand with the French cavalry. . . . We killed about 20 of the enemy. Though I was in the midst of them I cut my way through. I received one cut on my head, but it fell flat and only made a small impression on my hat without doing me the least harm. About 200 shot fell about me.'[3] Thus in this exhilarating action two of the sons of King George played a prominent and contiguous part. But Kilmaine's prompt action checked the pursuit, and York went back in high dudgeon, to vent his feelings on Hohenlohe. Hot words passed between

[1] The gallant Langeron has somewhat foreshortened the distance. It is a good 1,000 yards from the river to the crest of the hill.
[2] *Langeron*, p. 20.   [3] *Windsor*, 9.8.93.

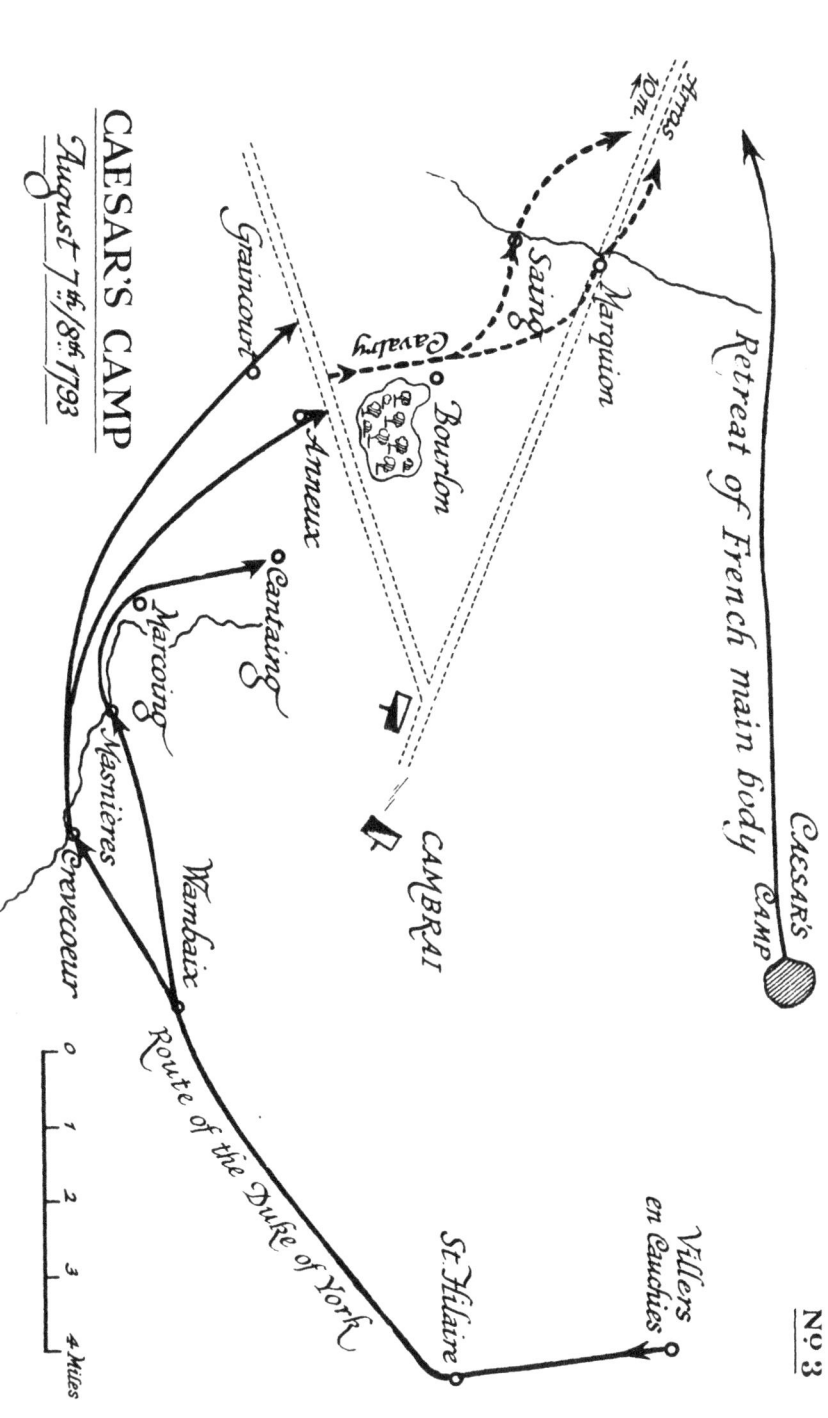

CAESAR'S CAMP

August 7th/8th 1793

Nº 3

Retreat of French main body

Caesar's Camp

Arras 10m.

Marquion

Saing

Cavalry

Bourlon

Graincourt

Anneux

Cantaing

Marcoing

Mosnières

Crèvecœur

Wambaix

CAMBRAI

St. Hilaire

Villers en Cauchies

Route of the Duke of York

0 1 2 3 4 Miles

them. Langeron states that 'the Duke returned to Bourlon and had a sharp altercation with Hohenlohe, whom he accused, with reason, of the small success of the day.'[1]

Dupuis, a most fairminded historian, agrees with this judgment. 'Kilmaine's success must be mainly attributed to the very provoking hindrances that York encountered.'[2]

A certain Colonel Scharnhorst of the Prussian service (afterwards to become famous) who was present also supported the Duke against the Austrians. He probably pointed to the heart of the trouble when he said that Coburg's orders (to Hohenlohe) were 'only to trouble the enemy for a while'.[3]

If this be as Scharnhorst asserted, it vitiates the criticism of Jomini, which was that the English should have made a night march, since in daylight they were visible from the heights of Cambrai; for if Coburg did not really aim at crushing Kilmaine, but merely at ejecting him from Caesar's Camp, there would be no harm done – rather the reverse, if York's column was seen and a bloodless victory thus obtained.

Yet even so, and in spite of delays on the march, due to the extreme heat and to the passive resistance of the Austrians, there was a chance of a smashing victory as late as noon on the 8th. Quite unknown to the Allies, who could not penetrate what was passing 'the other side of the hill', the mere presence at Marquion of the Duke of York's small force had induced a panic in the ranks of the retreating French army which was not quelled till it had reached Arras and beyond. It was an opportunity for a cavalry pursuit such as occurs only about once in a campaign. But the bulk of Coburg's excellent cavalry were lying inactive far away to the east.

Now, what had the Duke to say to his father about this, one of the most exciting and creditable days of his life? One might perhaps expect a detailed account of his experiences, such as he had given freely in previous letters. But no: his account is extremely bald. Here are the salient passages:

'At the village of Bourlon.

'By the time we arrived near their camp we received information that the enemy had retired from all his posts and was retreating towards Arras. I immediately resolved to pursue as

[1] *Languon*, p. 20.　　[2] *Dupuis*, p. 162.　　[3] *Chuquet*, X, p. 89.

E

far as I could with the cavalry and having assembled all the cavalry of my column except the Régiment de la Tour, I followed them for about two leagues, when I came up with them at the village of Marquion, to which they set fire to cover their retreat. We however managed to get round, and after taking three pieces of cannon we obliged them to pass a large ravine, behind which they formed themselves again, and which it was not thought prudent to pass.'[1]

The explanation of his marked reticence is no doubt twofold: the fear of reproof from his father for needlessly exposing himself at Marquion as he had done at Valenciennes, and a natural desire to keep on good terms with the Austrians. He worked on the sound principle: 'least said, soonest mended.'

*   *   *   *   *

In spite of all disappointments, the French army had been severely shaken, and a sound strategy pointed to taking advantage of this situation by concentrating all available forces against the weak spot that had developed in the hostile defensive system, and to do it promptly before the enemy had time to 'recover his wind'. Coburg, to do him justice, seems to have genuinely wished for this. Unfortunately, the English Government still clung blindly to their Dunkirk project. Now, this project would have been perfectly sound in April, when the Allies were dispersed, but the situation in August was changed; the Allies were fairly well concentrated in the centre of the line, where a breach had just been made, and to disperse the striking force just when an outstanding victory was within their grasp was fatuous.[2]

[1] *Windsor*, 9.8.93.
[2] The explanation for Pitt's mania for dispersion, that vitiated our efforts throughout his war administration, has not, I think been given by Fortescue, and it is only fair that it should be placed on record. It is contained in a letter from Pitt to Murray on July 19: 'If we can distress the enemy on more sides than one when their internal distractions continue it seems hardly possible that they can long oppose any effective resistance.' (*Chatham Papers*, Vol. 102.)
This is a good example of political considerations dominating military ones. Assuming that the politicians were correctly informed as to the internal state of the enemy country (which they in this case were not), they would be justified in overriding purely military considerations. Thus the Dunkirk project must not be condemned out of hand merely because it transgressed the military principle of concentration.

The Duke was strongly opposed to the Dunkirk venture, but the English Government was obdurate, and York – always a pattern of loyalty to his seniors – regretfully parted company with Coburg, and marched north for Dunkirk, taking with him a force of 10,000 Austrians, while Coburg turned placidly to besiege the minor fortress of Quesnoy (midway between Maubeuge and Cambrai).

LINSELLES[1]

On 16 August the British army was back at Tournai, and next day reached Tourcoing. This sector of the line was held by the Dutch, who, taking advantage of the presence of British troops in the vicinity, sallied forth to attack the French posts at Baton and Linselles (seven miles north of Lille). The French, however, reacted vigorously, and as the Duke's army was passing from Tourcoing to Menin on the 18th, the Dutch were ejected from Linselles, and fell back hastily, calling out to York for assistance. The latter, with some perspicacity, had envisaged such an eventuality, and had prepared against it by prescribing a short march of only six miles for that day. Just as the Guards were pitching their tents at Menin after what Fortescue calls (for some reason) a 'severe' march, the Dutch cry for help arrived. The Guards happened to be the nearest unit to the scene of action, so the Duke sent them straight off at once to the support of the Dutch. Gerard Lake marched his men, a mere 1,100, supported by a few guns, straight at the French position, and in one of the most brilliant actions of the war retook the hill. The French fled precipitately; in fact their General, Jourdan, who tried in vain to stop the rot and even to mount a counterattack, declared: 'It was not a retreat, but a rout'.[2]

The Duke wrote a very clear account of it to the King next day:

'Menin, 19 August 1793.

'The Hereditary Prince of Orange very unadvisedly and as it turned out very unfortunately for Himself thought to take advantage of My March to attack the French Advanced Posts

[1] On the Duke's campaign map (which I have examined) the first 'S' in Linselles is obscured. The Duke read it as a 'C', and thus spelt the name in his dispatch. This spelling has persisted.
[2] *Phipps*, I, p. 216.

of Lincelles, Pletten and Mouveaux.

'In this attack upon the two first of these posts he succeeded with very little loss in the morning, the enemy having evacuated them after very little resistance.

'The attack upon Mouveaux, however, did not turn out so advantageous as the Dutch were repulsed with some loss, and pursued into the very village of Turcoing.

'About three o'clock a report was brought from the Dutch General, who was left with three Batallions and two Squadrons to defend Lincelles, that he was attacked and begged for succour. The Prince of Orange told me he had not a batallion to spare, and desired Me to assist Him, which I did not hesitate to do, as I thought my own Honor and that of the Corps I commanded concerned in not allowing an Ally's post so near to us to be attacked without affording Him every assistance in my power. I therefore immediately ordered the three nearest Batallions to march, which were the 1st, Coldstream, and 3rd Regiment of Guards under the command of Major General Lake. When they arrived at Lincelles, they found that the Enemy had got Compleat possession of the Village, and that the Dutch Troops had run away in the most cowardly manner possible. General Lake immediately took His resolution in the handsomest manner possible, and thinking that if He retreated the enemy might imagine that they had gained some advantage over us, He resolved to attack the Village, which was covered by very strong entrenchments, most part of which were palisaded. He immediately formed the Batallions under a very heavy fire of Grape shot, and led them on to the Storm; nothing could exceed the coolness and courage of the Troops; not a piece was fired till the word was given, and they then rushed forward with the Bayonet; the entrenchments were directly taken, the Enemy fled on all sides, and were soon compleatly driven out of the Village, with the loss of all their Cannon. Having received some reinforcements, however, they attempted to attack the Village again, but were repulsed with great loss. Upon the first intelligence of what had happened, I sent six Batallions to General Lake's support, and went there myself, but before We arrived everything was over and the enemy was compleatly gone.'[1]

[1] *Windsor*, 19.8.93.

The final sentence in this letter is corroborated from other sources. The Duke sent not only some Hessian battalions, but two English battalions, the 14th and 53rd. It is therefore difficult to see the grounds for Fortescue's criticism: 'It is a grave reflection upon the Duke of York that he should so thoughtlessly have exposed some of his best troops to needless danger, leaving them isolated and unsupported for several hours.'[1]

Lake did indeed call for help, but on what seems inadequate grounds: he was in no real danger. To have diverted a bigger proportion of the British army from the march to Dunkirk merely to engage in a transient fight in order to oblige the Dutch would have been to infringe the principle of economy of force.

The Duke was naturally delighted with the performance of the close friend of his boyhood, Gerard Lake, and wrote exultingly to his brother: 'You will have been pleased with the bravery and spirit of our friend Lake and the Brigade of Guards.'[2]

* * * * *

DUNKIRK

York was now urged to follow up his success and attack Lille, but regretfully declined, saying: 'My orders are imperative.' To use modern jargon, this would be described as observance of the principle of maintenance of the objective. Resuming his march, therefore, and realizing the value of speed, York urged his men forward, and covered thirty-five miles in two days – good going for those days.

The Duke had divided his army into two columns, allotting Field-Marshal Freytag (an acquaintance of Hanover days) the left-hand column, consisting of Austrians and Hanoverians with ten British squadrons, with mission to cover the actual siege operations whilst he himself pushed on from Furnes to undertake the siege. Driving forward with some vigour, he unceremoniously bundled the French back within the walls of Dunkirk on the 24th. (Sketch map 4.) Next day the French counterattacked, and the result is given in the following letter from the Duke:

[1] *Fortescue*, IV, p. 122.   [2] *Windsor*, 21.8.93.

'The enemy attacked. They were however repulsed with great loss and we took one piece of cannon. Unfortunately the ardour and gallantry of the troops carried them too far and in spite of a peremptory order from me, three times repeated, they pursued the enemy upon the glacis of the Place, when we had the misfortune to lose many very brave and reliable men by the grapeshot from the town.'[1]

Meanwhile Murray was openly confident of success. He wrote rashly to Dundas.

'I rather hope that Dunkirk will surrender immediately, certainly soon after we get up our cannon. Bergues may be more tedious, but will come of course. I shall keep up my hopes of St Venant, for which I have a great fancy, and which is very material for Lisle.'[2]

But York had now to face a series of disappointments and setbacks. An English fleet, with a convoy of siege guns, which had been promised, was due at Nieuport on the 22nd, but had not appeared; instead, French gunboats appeared off the coast and harassed his seaward flank. But this was not all, as the following letter from the Duke will show:

'Before Dunkirk, 31 August 1793.

'Our good friends the Dutch have again behaved with their usual cowardice. On the 28th the Enemy attacked their posts at Tourcoing, Waterlos and Lannoi, all of which they abandoned without firing a shot, and retreated with the utmost precipitation to Roncq, (near Linselles), where the Prince of Waldeck got them at least to make a stand, and they drove the Enemy who had pursued them thus far, back to Moucron and took as they say four pieces of Cannon, but they do not add what is however very true that they had lost two Cannon themselves before. The allarm was so great among the Dutch, in spite of this soi-disant advantage that they had gained, that the Hereditary Prince of Orange wrote to me to acquaint me, that he did not intend to keep His position at Menin and along the Lys any longer, but meant first of all to retire to Courtrai and probably afterwards to the frontiers of Holland.

'This shameful resolution which nothing but fear or ill-will could have occasioned, put Me to the greatest perplexity as had

[1] *Windsor*, 26.8.93.   [2] *W.O.*, I, 166, f. 799.

the Prince of Orange executed it, the whole of Austrian Flanders was left uncovered, and the Enemy could have without the least opposition laid siege to Ipres, which covers the left wing of Field Marshal Freytag's Corps.

'At the same time that the Hereditary Prince of Orange wrote to Me, the Prince of Waldeck sent his Aide de Camp to Field Marshal Freytag to acquaint him with the resolution which had been taken, to retire, but added at the same time, that if He could send Him some squadrons of Cavalry, he would persuade the Hereditary Prince to delay His retreat for some days.

'In this situation there was no time to hesitate, and therefore, thinking it absolutely necessary not to give the Hereditary Prince the least excuse to retreat, though but ill able to spare any Troops from my Corps, I detached the Six Squadrons of Hessian Cavalry to his assistance. . . .'[1]

The delay in the arrival of the siege guns was most unfortunate, for the fortress was in a state of dilapidation. The rapid flank march of the British army had surprised and mystified the French, each sector that it passed in turn believing itself to be the target. No one correctly defined the Duke's objective. Observers judged that Dunkirk could only hold out for five or six days if bombarded, and a contemporary French historian even says: 'It would doubtless have been taken if the fleet had arrived before the town at the same time as the army.'[2]

An English gentleman who escaped out of Dunkirk wrote to the *Public Advertiser* that the town would have surrendered outright had not Commissioners from Paris arrived and prevented it.

This estimate is partly corroborated from the English side by a civilian, Crawford by name, writing to Lord Auckland from Brussels on 18 September. 'Professional men still persist in blaming the attack . . . and say that nothing could justify it but the Duke of York's finding everything in readiness on his arrival before Dunkirk for immediately besieging the place: that in that case, and with a powerful co-operation from the sea it might perhaps have been carried immediately . . . but

[1] *Windsor*, 31.8.93.   [2] *Victoires*, pp. 11, 12.

they observe that, instead of this, after the most rapid successes in carrying all the enemy's advanced posts, His Royal Highness was under the necessity of waiting above a fortnight without being able to do anything, during which time the enemy were masters of the shore and entirely commanded it by their gun-boats.' He ends with the curious observation: 'They say that the lateness of the season and the probability of big rains, as well as in order to give as little time as possible to the enemy to render the approach to the place still more difficult, justified after occasion some awkwardness.'[1]

This semi-apology for the speed of the Duke's march seems rather amusing to us nowadays. But the 'professional men' were Austrians, it must be remembered.

During the course of the siege the Duke was informed that the Emperor wished to mark his appreciation of his conduct in the campaign by bestowing on him the order of St Theresa. York referred the matter to the King, observing: 'I do not know how far Your Majesty may approve of Your Majesty's family or any Knight of the Garter accepting any foreign order whatsoever. Besides as it is impossible to know how long con-nections between different countries may last, it might here-after occasion some awkwardness.'[2]

The delay resulting from the non-arrival of the siege guns allowed the French, under the vigorous direction of Carnot, to concentrate troops for the relief of the place. This force attacked Freytag on 6 September and penetrated his lines; whereupon the Austrians fell back to Hondeschoote, and were again success-fully attacked there on the 8th. A glance at the sketch map will show the dangerous situation in which the investing force now found itself, and the Duke rightly decided to extricate himself from it with the greatest promptitude. The move was made at short notice and in some confusion – natural under the circum-stances – and the heavy siege guns had to be left behind. From midnight to dawn on 9 September the army, however, managed to cover eleven miles to Furnes and safety, being entirely un-molested by the enemy the while. Fortescue speaks of bad

[1] *Auckland*, Correspondence III, p. 115.

[2] *Windsor*, 31.8.93. Some awkwardness of this nature was, in fact, occasioned in 1914 – and again in 1941.

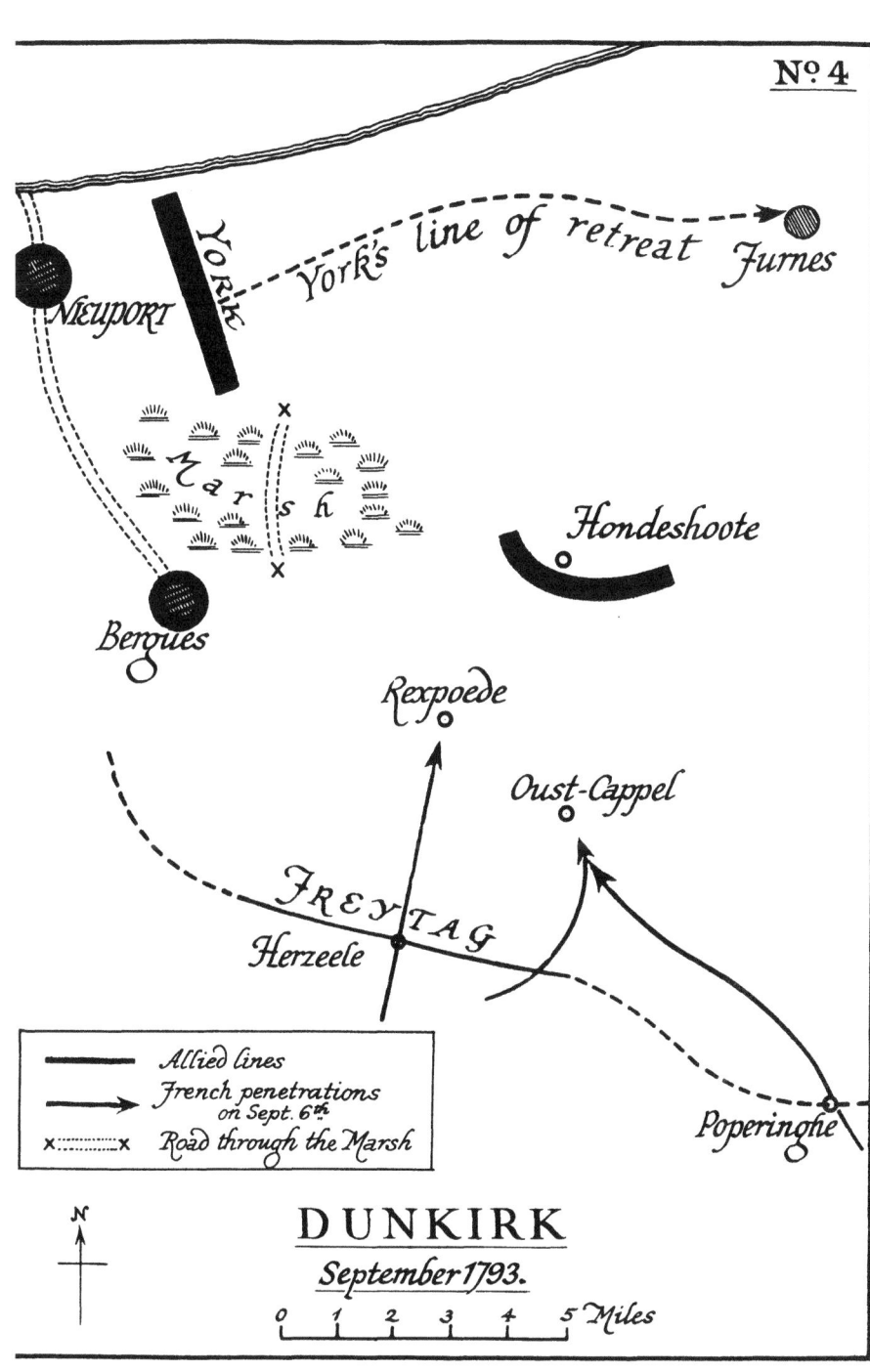

NIEUPORT

YORK

York's line of retreat — Furnes

Marsh

Hondeshoote

Bergues

Rexpoede

Oust-Cappel

FREYTAG

Herzeele

Poperinghe

Allied lines
French penetrations
on Sept. 6th
Road through the Marsh

N

DUNKIRK
September 1793.

0 1 2 3 4 5 Miles

work on the part of the Duke's staff, but I think that considering the abnormal difficulties it must have been surprisingly good. Be that as it may, the army did get away and form a new front, covering Furnes.

Next day the fleet arrived. . . .

Such, in brief outline, is the history of this sad chapter in our military history. Disaster had been narrowly averted – as it was also on the same spot 147 years later – but England, instead of being thankful for this escape, gave voice to a howl of disappointment and criticism. Indeed, the Duke's military reputation is more nearly identified with his conduct at Dunkirk than with anything else. We must therefore examine closely what he has to say in his own defence. Fortunately, that is not difficult, thanks to his letters written at the time and in confidence to his father.

In public he said nothing. He wrote rather pathetically, but with dignity, to his brother: 'I confess I have been exceedingly hurt at having been obliged to retire from before Dunkirk; however, being convinced that it was not owing to my own fault, and that I was only (illegible) in that business I bear it with all the philosophy and resignation I am master of.'[1]

But to his father, the King, he wrote in confidence a full account. Fortescue (who had not seen this very important letter when he wrote his history) printed it in his *Historical and Military Essays* in 1928; but as probably ten persons will read his *History of the Army* to one who reads the relevant chapter in the later book it merits transcription almost in full.

'Menin, 18 September 1793.

'. . . At the moment these plans [to besiege Dunkirk] were fixed, Sir James Murray applied in My name to Your Majesty's Ministers for the artillery necessary for the siege of Dunkirk, as well as for a sufficient Naval force to co-operate with Me, and to protect Me against the Enemy's Vessels. All of which was immediately promised and with regard to the Naval part Mr Pitt in a letter to Sir James Murray said that Your Majesty's Ministers undertook to furnish a compleat Naval force, and desired me to leave it totally to them.

[1] *Windsor: to P. of W.*, 21.9.93.

'I received repeated hints to hurry my March to Dunkirk and repeated assurances that everything should be ready at Nieuport by the twentieth of August. I therefore engaged to be at Furnes on the twenty-second, and was so exact to My time as to arrive there on the twenty-first, but to my great astonishment and disappointment I found no one ship arrived.

'Still however after the repeated assurances I had received I did not hesitate to move forwards and after obliging the Enemy to quit the Camp of Gyvelde, I took up a position before Dunkirk.

'As it was absolutely necessary for the carrying on of the Siege, that a part of my Army should be detached in order to cover it, I proposed to Field Marshal Freytag to take the Command of His Corps of Observation, and allotted Him the largest part of the Troops. In order likewise that He might fully understand My intentions, I gave Him the enclosed Instruction with which he appeared fully satisfied.

'Encouraged however by the success which He had at first, He moved forward, and in a manner blockaded Bergues, which He summoned.

'As soon as I received intelligence of this, I went immediately over to Him, and begged Him for God's sake to give up all thoughts for the present of Bergues and confine Himself wholly to keeping up with the greatest care His communication with Ipres and with My Corps, and therefore desired Him to draw into His line as many of the Troops which were round Bergues under the Command of General Count Walmoden as possible. I likewise added that, should He receive Intelligence that the enemy's force at Cassel ever increased to any considerable amount, for at that time it was little more than three thousand men, and would let Me know, I would immediately join him with all the Force I could collect, leaving only a sufficient number of Troops to defend the Works of Countervallation, and we would jointly make an attack upon Cassel. This He promised to do and repeatedly assured Me that the left of His position was perfectly secure, but that He did not think His right flank by any means so safe, to which I answered that I had left it totally to Him to take up the position which He judged the best; that I had but two objects which I wished Him particularly to look to; the one was to keep up His communication with Ipres and the other with Me.

'I again repeated my offer of joining Him should the Enemy ever be in force at Cassel, but he regularly refused it, and even the night before he was attacked, when upon receiving certain intelligence that the Enemy were assembling in great force, I again made him the same offer through His Aide de Camp, Captain Murray. I received for answer that if it was necessary, He would certainly send to Me, but that He did not believe in the Enemy being so strong and that He thought himself fully strong enough alone to attack Cassel, if necessary.

'During the first four days (that) I was encamped before Dunkirk, nothing arrived from England though the wind was perfectly fair. At last One Convoy arrived containing only half the Artillery and Stores, but not being arrived in time for the Spring tides only four of the lightest transports were able to come into the Harbour of Nieuport, and the rest were obliged to go into Ostend, which made such a prodigious difference in the bringing up of the Stores to the Artillery Park near Dunkirk on account of the numerous changes of Boats which it required in the different Canals through which these stores were obliged to be brought by Water, as we had no horses to draw them (that) the very last morning that I had a conference with poor Colonel Moncrief[1] and Lieutenant Colonel Congreve in order to settle when the Trenches should be opened Lieutenant Colonel Congreve declared that it would be impossible for the Artillery to be in readiness under a week.

'As for the Naval force, none appeared till the very night that I was obliged to retire, so that whenever the Enemy chose to make sorties, their Gun Boats advanced and fired in the rear of our Works, which though they did not do much execution, very much incommoded the Troops.

'About a week after My arrival before Dunkirk, I received intelligence that the Enemy were assembling a considerable force with the resolution to try and oblige Me to retreat from before the Town. I immediately sent Major Calvert to the Prince of Cobourg, with the intelligence, who sent Prince Reus back to Me, in order to talk the matter over, and to propose that as soon as Le Quesnoi surrendered He should march with

---

[1] The commanding Royal Engineer.

his whole force to my relief, but before Prince Reus returned, the whole mischief was done.

'I sent the Field Marshal the same intelligence, but he disregarded it.

'On the 6th of September, the day of the first attack upon the Field Marshal's Corps, He never would believe that the Enemy had forced the post on His left and turned His left flank in spite of repeated reports which were sent to Him, nor was it till six in the evening, that he consented to retreat, which he did in two Columns. Instead however of sending the Artillery and baggage with General Count Walmoden's Column which was the furthest from the Enemy, He chose to take them in the rear of His own Column. I shall not touch upon the subject of His and My Brother Adolphus's[1] being taken Prisoners. I do not imagine that there can be two opinions on that subject. I will only say that in consequence of this misfortune, everything would have been lost if it had not been for the presence of mind and coolness of Count Walmoden,[2] who upon the first intelligence of what had befallen the Field Marshall and His Column, resolved immediately to disengage them by turning and attacking the Village of Rexpoede, which thoroughly succeeded, and enabled the Column to proceed upon its march to Hundschoote without the loss of any of its Cannon or its Baggage.

'During four and twenty hours I was totally without any account of the Field Marshal's Corps except what I could learn from one of His Advanced Posts, which was attacked and which I supported and which in the evening received an order from the Field Marshal to retire and join Him, and it was not till the middle of the next day that I received a letter from Count Walmoden to inform Me of what had passed, and that He had made good his retreat to Hundschoote, that His position was by no means good, but that He would attempt to defend it as long as possible, as otherwise I might be compleatly cut off with the whole of my Corps.

'Upon the first allarm I had detached three Hessian Batallions to Furnes in order to secure if possible that place, two of

---

[1] Afterwards Duke of Cambridge. The only Royal Duke to be taken prisoner in battle since the Wars of the Roses.

[2] Whom the Duke, it will be remembered, had recommended to be removed from the Embassy at Vienna just ten years before.

whom afterwards I sent to reinforce Count Walmoden. I like-wise sent the 53rd Regiment to cover the Depot of Artillery which was about a League in my rear towards Furnes, and to occupy a large Dyke over which the Enemy might pass and get behind Me, should Count Walmoden be obliged to retire.

'In this situation it was impossible for Me to think any more for the present of beginning the Siege of Dunkirk and I therefore began to move the Artillery and Stores as quick as possible back to the Depot near which I intended, if Count Walmoden could have kept His post at Hundschoote, to have taken up a position and to have waited there till some succour arrived.

'The Enemy had during those two last days made every afternoon a violent Sortie upon our Lines, but had been each time repulsed with considerable loss, and driven back into the Covered Way. However this naturally harassed My troops very much, as they were almost continually under arms.

'On the 8th the Enemy made two Sorties, the one in the morning, the other in the afternoon, in both of which they were repulsed with considerable loss.

'In the middle of the last Sortie I received the unfortunate intelligence that after doing everything that Troops could do, Count Walmoden had been overpowered through numbers, and that he had been obliged to retreat close to Furnes, by which means the Enemy had got possession of the roads which led down from Hundschoote upon my rear, and had it in their power to bring down any force they chose, and after over-powering the 53rd Regiment, to cut Me compleatly off.

'Under these circumstances there was not a moment to hesitate, nor could I any more take up the position I had inten-ded in order to save the Depot of Artillery. I immediately therefore ordered the Tents to be struck and all the Baggage to be sent off, and as soon as it was dark, after putting out my outposts as usual in order to hide my march from the Enemy, I began my retreat in two Columns, after having sent away as many stores as it was possible in that short space of time, and having destroyed the rest.

'I have now given Your Majesty as exact an account as I can of everything that passed; I think it right to add that upon examining the different Prisoners who were taken, of whom there were a considerable number, they all agreed in saying that this very great force which was assembled and brought to act upon Field Marshal Freytag's Corps, was composed of the Garrisons of Valenciennes and Mayence, who in defiance of their oaths had been sent by the National Convention, and the whole Army of the Moselle, who had been most unfortunately left unoccupied by the King of Prussia and General Wurmser having altered the place proposed for the Campagne, and having both moved to their left towards Strasbourg.

'I think therefore that I am justified in saying that there were three grand causes which made this expedition miscarry: the first owing to the promises and assurances I so repeatedly received from Your Majesty's Ministers not being in any way fulfilled; the second owing to the alteration made in the plan of campaign by the Armies of the King of Prussia and of General Wurmser, by which means the Enemy was enabled to bring the whole Army of the Moselle against the Field Marshal and Me; and the third owing to the Field Marshal's own conduct.

'As this paper is merely drawn up for Your Majesty's own inspection, in order to clear up my Conduct to You, and never intended to be produced to any other Person whatsoever, by Me, I have stated every fact as fully as possible. Your Majesty however may be assured upon My honor, that However I feel myself hurt and grieved at what is passed, I never will make my complaint publick, nor shall any thing which has befallen me be brought forward to weaken the Heads of Your Government and Administration.'[1]

After this masterly exposé little remains to be said – unless, that is, anyone should doubt the strict veracity of the Duke when writing his own defence. To any such I would say that, in all his correspondence that I have been privileged to examine I have not in a single instance discovered any misstatement, where it can be checked from other sources.

We cannot, however, ignore Fortescue's strictures, for the opinions of most people are founded upon them.

He suggests that York should have prevented Freytag holding the advanced line that he did, from south of Bergues to Poperinghe, but that Hondeschoote should have been held in the first instance. But there are many weighty objections to the Hondeschoote position.

[1] *Windsor*, 18.9.93.

(1) It was too narrow, only three miles wide, consequently the enemy would have been able to slip past this, his strategic flank, and involve the investing army in disaster.

(2) The position was nearer to Furnes, on the Duke's lines of communication, than was the British army. It would give the enemy the big strategic advantage of covering their own communications whilst threatening the enemy's.

(3) If Freytag were defeated at Hondeschoote, he would have to fall right back to Furnes (as ultimately he did), as there was no intermediate position. In short, the position lacked depth: the smallest penetration would jeopardize the whole besieging army.

(4) Freytag would be cut off from effective direct communication with the Duke, by the road across the marsh to the east of Bergues (see sketch map 4), whereas the position that he actually occupied adequately covered the vital link.

(5) The terrain round Hondeschoote was unsuitable for cavalry, the arm in which the Allies were markedly superior to the French both in number and efficiency.

In view of the above it is difficult to see on what grounds Fortescue asserts that 'the position at Hondeschoote would have covered the besiegers quite as efficiently and with less risk'.[1] In my opinion Freytag occupied the best possible position; his mistake was that he was forgetful of the principle of maintenance of the objective – namely, to cover the besieging army – till pulled up sharply and rightly by the Duke. Indeed, no impartial reader could study the Duke's long letter to his father closely without being impressed by many things in it – the sound military judgment in the case mentioned, and in proposing to concentrate against the French should they attack. The fact that even without the Duke's aid Freytag very nearly held up the French is a clear indication that with it the victory would almost certainly have gone to the Allies. The lucid and concise manner in which York marshals his facts in this paper shows that his experience in letter-writing while a boy in Germany had stood him in good stead.

The importance of the assertion that the prisoners taken at Valenciennes had been used at Hondeschoote should not be overlooked. It was a factor that could hardly be taken into

[1] *Fortescue*, IV, p. 30.

account, yet it upset the Duke's calculations, and led directly
to the French victory. Yet this important – indeed vital – fact
has been ignored by all historians of the campaign.

The cumulative effect of all the facts that he sets out is irresistible, and in my opinion places the whole affair outside the
range of controversy. What a pity Sir John Fortescue had not
this letter before him when he wrote his *History*. Finally, and
perhaps strongest of all, is the impression made by the Commander-in-Chief's self-abnegation and silence under obloquy,
self-imposed for fear of creating discord between the Allies.
Even Marlborough could not have shown greater restraint.
But from the King he hid nothing. He could not bear the
thought that his own father should lose faith in him. 'I never
will make my complaint publick,' he declared, and he was as
good as his word.

But if the British commander would not make his complaint
public, there were not lacking in his army officers prepared to
make good the omission. Only two days after the battle one
such officer wrote to the *Morning Chronicle* a letter in which he
roundly declared: 'There is but one sentiment through the
whole camp. If the gun-boats and floating batteries had been
ready, according to the express promise to co-operate with the
Duke of York, and if his alacrity had been at all seconded on
the part of the officers in England there is no doubt that Dunkirk would have fallen at the first attack. Every man that has
since perished . . . is to be set down to the score of the
ministers, who have sacrificed their duty to the holiday mum-
mery of camps or to the amusements of partridge shooting.'

The Duke outwardly remained cheerful. 'I do assure you,'
wrote one of his staff the day after the retreat, 'the Duke's
character rises very much by this reverse of fortune. His good
humour and spirits never forsake him and he meets the unfortunate events which have happened with a degree of constancy
and resolution that do him infinite honour. He has had many
mortifications and disappointments, but I have a presentiment
that though the situation at present is but so-so he will rise
superior to them all.'[1]

But secretly he was terribly distressed. Indeed, he openly
admitted it himself in a letter to his brother. But it was not for

[1] *Calvert*, p. 127.

long: his natural resilience of spirit soon asserted itself, and only thirty-six hours after taking up a new position covering Furnes we find him writing to the King that he intends to attack the French at Ypres.

'Furnes, 10 September 1793.

'I have this day received the Intelligence that the French have made an attack upon Ipres and were bombarding the town; at the same time I have been informed that the Hereditary Prince of Orange has as usual taken fright and means to retire from his present position at Menin, by which movement I find myself compleatly abandoned by every body. I have therefore resolved to try if possible to save the Troops under my command towards Ipres; should I find it possible, I mean to attack the French Army; if that is impracticable, I shall fall back and take up a position between Nieuport and Dixmude. Whatever may be the event, I can only say that I will do my best, and with such brave troops as I command, everything may be expected what men can do.

'This morning Colonel Sporken came to Me from the Field Marshal Freytag to acquaint Me that the Marshal intended to send him to England in order to relate to Your Majesty the unfortunate events of the last four days. As I have not received a single report from the Marshal ever since the attack of the sixth, I cannot say anything concerning Him. Should however any thing be laid to my charge, I trust Your Majesty will delay Your judgement till I lay before you the exact account of every thing which has passed.'[1]

This he did in the long letter of 18 September which we have already printed.

However, just after this move had been got under way, fresh information arrived that the enemy had relinquished the attack. Major Wright of the Artillery wrote at this time: 'I pity from my heart the poor Duke, it is entirely over with his prospects, I fear.'[2]

Major Wright no doubt reflected the general view in the army. A scapegoat was called for, and the Commander or his Adjutant-General was the obvious choice. To make the shock

[1] *Windsor*, 10.9.93.   [2] *Wright Letters*, p. 24.

F

all the greater to the Government at home, York had during the siege been quite cheerful in his letters, in spite of the non-appearance of the fleet, whilst Murray had been positively exuberant; he wrote Dundas a letter only three days before the French struck their blow in which he expressed the opinion that 'everything is going on extremely well', and invited Dundas to come over and see the fun. It was not likely that ministers would in the first shock of disappointment realize the fact that York had done exceedingly well to extricate his army at all. Yet such was the case: he had not lost his head, and I have read no criticism, either contemporary or subsequent, that he should have done other than he did from the moment that the Hanoverians gave way. An indirect indication of this is that the Committee of Public Safety were so disappointed at the escape of the British army that they sent Houchard to the guillotine, and appointed General Jourdan in his place.

Historians of all nations have united in condemning the strategy which directed the army of the Duke of York against Dunkirk. Sybel, Jomini, and Fortescue combine to criticize it, and the French military historians Fouchard et Finot go so far as to describe it as 'une des sottises stratégiques les plus énormes dont fasse mention l'histoire militaire de tous les peuples'.[1]

Undoubtedly it transgresses the principle of concentration; and assuming that the Austrians were prepared to hazard a direct advance towards Paris, an eccentric move on Dunkirk was a mistake. But strategy is not an abstract science that can be treated in a vacuum: it is only one of the many factors or strands of war that affect the issue. In this case it is extremely doubtful whether the Austrians would have consented to advance boldly into France before reducing the fortresses of Quesnoy and Mauberge; and if that were so the British army was better employed taking Dunkirk than in helping the Austrians to take Quesnoy.

Moreover, it is easy to be 'wise after the event'. Dunkirk did, in fact, hold out, but in the first few days of the siege the issue was in doubt, in spite of the mishandling of the operation by the British Government. Had the French not broken the terms of the capitulation of Valenciennes and used its garrison for the relief of Dunkirk, that town would probably have fallen. It

[1] *Foucart et Finot*, II, p. 15.

was perhaps a gamble, but war is one big gamble.

The situation had now become fluid and obscure. The French had sent the Dutch reeling back from Menin and Courtrai, and had made a nasty salient in the Allied line, threatening to cut the communications of the British with the main army which was still besieging Quesnoy. Evidently the Duke had two main tasks:

(1) To safeguard his own communications with England.

(2) To afford relief to the Dutch.

To achieve both these objects he therefore marched on 14 September to Thorout, a good central position from which he could reach Ostend, Bruges or Ghent equally easily. (Sketch map 1.) Here he held an important council of war, of which the amusing rhymester, 'An Officer of the Guards', who must have been present, has given some illuminating particulars.

First Sir William Erskine proposed an attack on Menin, to which Sir James Murray made a shilly-shallying reply.

'But Sir Wullie arose, with a steady grave face,
And said "Do ye ken this same Menin's a place
Of the utmost importance, and troth I advise
That we march, and those d—nd Sons of Licence chastise.
All our laurels by this we at once shall regain.
Having told ye my mind, I'll sit down again."
The Duke smiled applause: and Sir Jamie demanded
Permission to speak, which was not countermanded.
'Twas a pity, he said, it appeared to him plain,
Our Allies were unable their post to maintain;
But we sure might retake it, *or let it alone.*
He was much at a loss which was best to be done.
In short, what the Duke might think proper to do
Was surely the properest plan to pursue.
And Johnstone,[1] Prince John, nay, *we all* to a man,
Declared he had struck out a wonderful plan.
The Duke then triumphantly rose to his feet
And said: "'Tis resolved: – we'll the enemy meet." '[2]

Here we get an invaluable and rare glimpse into the proceedings of one of the Duke's councils of war. It brings out two

[1] A Staff Officer.   [2] *Officer of the Guards*, I, p. 95.

points: one, the feeble attitude of his Adjutant-General; and
the other the clear indication that the Duke was, in fact as
well as in name, the real commander of the British army.[1] One
can almost see him nodding approval when offensive action is
urged, and then rising 'triumphantly' to clinch the point.

Pursuant to the decision taken at the council of war, the army
marched south next day *en route* for Menin. They reached
Rousselare (Roulers) that evening, and found that simultaneously a force of Austrians under General Beaulieu, who had
occupied Courtrai overnight, had driven the French back to
Menin and had entered the town. In this operation Beaulieu
was assisted by some Hanoverian infantry and British cavalry
whom the Duke had sent forward to his assistance. The Duke
sent the King the following particulars:

'Upon my arrival at Rousselare I received intelligence that
the enemy had made an attack on General Beaulieu who was
covering Courtrai with 6 battalions and 6 squadrons. I immediately ordered Lieutenant-General Erbach with my advanced
guard, to march to his assistance, and afterwards detached 4
battalions more . . . to support them. But the enemy, upon
the arrival of General Erbach immediately retreated and
evacuated the town of Menin, of which General Erbach took
possession the same evening; and the next day I proceeded
with the whole army and am now encamped under the walls of
this place.'[2]

It seems from Jomini's account of this action that the success
was largely due to the incursion of the British cavalry on the
French left flank, though the actual fighting was only slight.

This sudden retreat of the French deprives the student of
war of an interesting strategical study. For, Quesnoy having
fallen, Coburg was on his way with the bulk of his army to the
help of the Duke. He sent word to York that he would reach
Cysoing, ten miles south-east of Lille, on the 15th, the day that
the Duke reached Rousselare, and that he was ready to co-
operate. This news delighted the British commander. A situation full of possibilities had suddenly arisen, and it was not lost

---

[1] Fortesque dismisses this verse as 'miserable doggerel' and confines his attention
to its footnotes. But it is thanks to its being doggerel that the author can give a
more exact description of the scene than if he had tried to put it into polished verse.
It is, in fact, one of our most valuable sources for the campaign.
[2] *Windsor*, 17.9.93.

upon the English Commander. To explain it, a few distances must be given. The French were holding Menin; three hostile columns were now pointing towards them; eleven miles to the North, at Rousselare, was York; six miles to the east, at Court-rai, was Beaulieu; seventeen miles to the south, at Cysoing, was Coburg. A grand operation on exterior lines was indicated. Two things were requisite, first, that the French should hold on to their present position, second that the three columns should attack simultaneously. There seemed good prospects of these conditions obtaining, and York wrote off jubilantly to his father:

'On my arrival here (Rousselare) today I received the agree-able intelligence that the Prince of Coburg was to arrive with a considerable part of his army at Cysoing today, in order to co-operate with us, and to make a general attack. I have immediately written to him, acquainting him with my motions and intentions and begging him to fix the day (either tomorrow or next day) in order to make a general attack, which I trust from the courage of the troops and the thirst they appear to have to avenge their comrades, I cannot but think will turn out most glorious.'[1]

Unfortunately, as we have seen, the French incontinently retreated, the salient was flattened out and the opportunity for a smashing blow was gone.

General Houchard's plan had been merely to hold the Duke of York with a force of 20,000, whilst he marched south with the remainder to relieve Quesnoy.

The Duke of York seems here open to the criticism that if he schemed a converging attack on exterior lines he should not have engaged the French left flank on the previous day as he did. If he had held his force in hand that day, the enemy might have held on to their position in front of Menin that day and fallen into the trap on the following day. In order to pronounce judgment on this point it would be necessary to know whether the Duke received Coburg's letter before or after he sent off his advanced guard. If before, it looks as if he should have held his hand. We have no information on this point. But the prob-ability is that Coburg's letter arrived after the troops had been put in motion, though before York knew what the upshot of the

[1] Ibid., 15.9.93.

day's fighting would be. Thus he would be justified in making plans for all eventualities, and concerting with Coburg for a combined attack, if the French stood their ground. Moreover, Beaulieu had only a weak force, and it would have gone hard with the Duke's reputation if he had stood aside while his ally was grappling with a superior enemy and had thereby been beaten. 'March to the sound of the guns' is a good maxim, and York had showed on more than one occasion that it was part of his military creed: if an ally seemed in difficulties the Duke instantly marched to his assistance. We shall see a further example of this in a very short time. Moreover, the abrupt retreat of the French could hardly have been foreseen. It still remains rather inexplicable to French historians.

On the balance of the evidence I think the English commander showed a sound grasp of strategy. In point of fact – though it does not affect our assessment of the General, for he could not possibly be aware of it – the French at Menin were about to receive orders to march away south with the bulk of their force. So an attack on the 16th would have been too late, even if Coburg had consented to join in it.

The French having retreated, fresh plans had now to be made, and as may be imagined, Coburg's glance was at once directed on another fortress, this time Maubeuge. To assist in the siege of this place, he asked the Duke to hold the line from Nieuport to Cysoing (ten miles south-east of Lille). This the Duke consented to do, although his army had been depleted by the Government in order to find troops for the West Indies. Soon there were only 4,000 fit English troops left in Flanders.

After a short stay at Menin the army was on the move again. This letter to the King explains the reason.

'Just after I had sent my last letter to Your Majesty I received intelligence that the enemy had suddenly withdrawn part of their troops from this position and were assembling them near Cambrai. I likewise received a letter from the Prince of Coburg pressing me very hard to move with as many troops as I could to Cysoing, and this morning I have received a second letter from him to the same purpose, only much more pressing. Under these circumstances I trust I shall meet with Your Majesty's approbation in fulfilling the Prince of Coburg's wishes, I mean therefore to leave General Erbach with 6,000 men here and shall move tomorrow morning with the rest of the troops to Cysoing. . . .'[1]

This march was carried out as planned, and the army halted on 11 October at Cysoing. But not for long.

On 7 October the Committee of Public Safety had sent General Jourdan to relieve Maubeuge, whereupon Coburg called on York for still closer support. Again let the Duke tell his own story.

'The night before last the Prince of Cobourg sent an Aide-de-Campe to me to acquaint me that the Enemy were assembling the whole of their forces at Guise, which by some reports are said to be near ninety thousand men; that in spite of all his entreaties the Hereditary Prince of Orange had peremptorily refused to pass the Sambre or to give them the least assistance, saying that the Dutch had engaged themselves for the Siege of Maubeuge, and not for the attack of the fortified Camps, and that till that was forced, they would not move; under the circumstances He begged Me for God's sake, I would march as soon as possible and join him, with all the Troops which could be spared. . . .

'As the whole Event not only of this Campaign but of the whole War appears to depend upon forcing the Enemy to an action and takingMaubeuge, I did not think it right to hesitate, but immediately agreed, and in consequence I marched yesterday, with the Brigade of Foot Guards, the 37th Regiment, the 6th and 11th Regiments of Hannoverians and twelve British Squadrons, and hope tomorrow to arrive at Engelfontaine, where I am to command, and where I am to meet Lieutenant-General Winkheim with ten thousand Austrians. Engelfontaine is at the Edge of the Forest de Mormal and covers the right Flank of the Prince of Coburg's army.

'I trust that I shall meet with Your Majesty's approbation for this step, which the exigency of the Moment seems to require, as in reality the fate of the whole War depends upon this action.'[2]

An important point should be noticed here. Though the Duke uses the words 'join him', it is clear from a later sentence

[1] *Windsor*, 9.10.93.   [2] Ibid., 15.10.93.

that he meant for the time being to take his station at Engelfontaine, about ten miles from the Austrian main army. This
he proceeds to do, starting off next morning, i.e. 14 October.
That day he marched about fifteen miles to near St Amand,
and on the 15th fourteen miles to near Valenciennes. During
that night he received an urgent message from Coburg, to the
effect that Jourdan had attacked him that day, and though he
was holding his own he would like the Duke to hurry forward
as quickly as possible. The Duke responded with alacrity,
marching at dawn. So speedy was the march that he reached
his prescribed destination, Engelfontaine, at 11 a.m., having
covered thirteen miles in about four and a half hours. Here
he met the Austrian General as arranged, and took over the
command of the sector held by him. It was a wide one, stretching
from Solesmes, eight miles to the west, to Berlaimont,[1] nine
miles to the east.

He sent a staff officer, Calvert, over to Coburg to report his
arrival and to observe how the battle was going, and meanwhile
he discussed plans with General Winkheim for an attack on the
following day.

But it was not to be. After fighting a drawn battle – the
battle of Wattignies – during the day, Coburg seems to have
lost his nerve in the evening, and threw up the sponge: that is
to say, he abandoned the siege of Maubeuge and fell back to
the north side of the River Sambre.

York's letter of 18 October to the King comes in here:

'During the night of the 15/16th October, while I was at
Valenciennes I received intelligence that the enemy had attacked the Prince's army on the morning of the 15th, but had been
repulsed with considerable loss . . . but however, as he
expected the attack to be renewed in the morning he wished
that I would hurry on with the troops as soon as possible. I
therefore determined to march at daybreak, and arrived at this
place [sixteen miles west of Maubeuge] about eleven o'clock. I
found that the attack had been renewed upon the Prince's army
with redoubled vigour. . . .'

After relating how in consequence the siege of Maubeuge
had been abandoned, he proceeded:

'The enemy's spirits are raised, and there is no probability of

[1] Where part of the B.E.F. detrained 120 years later.

the siege of Maubeuge being begun again this campaign. . . . [This prognostication proved correct.]

'In consequence of this check I thought it right to go over myself to Bavai where the Prince of Coburg had taken up his headquarters to enquire what his intentions were. He has desired me to keep for the present the position I now have, which is from Solesmes to Berlaimont and declared at the same time that if it was possible he intended to attack the enemy.'[1]

This was a hollow intention on the part of Coburg; his army had fallen back behind the stretched-out line held by York's tiny army, which now found itself in a salient which was rendered more pronounced by deep incursions by the Duke's cavalry into enemy territory past Le Cateau.

The question now to be examined is: Could the British contingent, by marching more rapidly, have been in time to intervene in the battle? The Austrian historian, Witzleben, thinks it could. Dupuis quotes him as reproaching the Duke with excessive slowness: Witzleben considers that he might have reached Maubeuge on the evening of the 15th, or at least in the morning of the 16th, adding that the distance from Cysoing to Maubeuge was eight and a half miles.[2]

This is a manifest mistranslation by Dupuis of miles for leagues. But even so, it will not hold water. The distance from Cysoing to the Austrian army south of Maubeuge was fifty-four miles, as near as I can estimate it. Now eight and a half leagues is only twenty-five miles. Witzleben has misread his map. But let us work out the speed and mileage of the British army.

14 October	. .	15 miles
15 ,,	. .	14 ,,
16 ,,	. .	13 ,,
TOTAL .	. .	42 miles

To have covered fifty-four miles in two days would be at the rate of twenty-seven miles per day, or if they took two and a half days it would still come to over 20 miles per day. On the bad Flanders roads of mid-October for the infantry to have

[1] *Windsor*, 19.10.93.   [2] *Witzleben*, II, p. 238.

achieved this would have been phenomenal; for the artillery of that day it would have been utterly impossible. To add to the achievement, détours had to be made round St Amand and Valenciennes, for the Austrians would not allow English troops to march through towns garrisoned by themselves.

There remains the consideration, should the Duke, then, have sent his cavalry on ahead to join Coburg? This would have been to split up his army and place a part of it under the Austrians, a course which the Duke was not competent to take upon himself; permission would be required from the King. In any case, there is no sign that Coburg expected or even wanted the cavalry by itself. Major Calvert was with him during the 16th and received no complaints of non-arrival, and everything points to the fact that Coburg himself assigned Engelfontaine as the meeting-point with Winkheim. Nor was there any necessity for Coburg to retreat at the end of the battle. If he had remained *in situ* the English army was well placed to threaten the hostile flank next day. Our conclusion is that, so far from marching with excessive slowness, the Duke of York pushed forward with an alacrity and speed unusual in those days and in that season of the year, to the help of his ally. A modern French historian says he responded to Coburg's appeal *'avec empressement'*.[1]

A possible line of criticism is that, instead of halting at Engelfontaine for the rest of the day, the English army should have pushed on towards the battle. Unfortunately, the dispatch and Murray's accompanying letter to Dundas are both missing from the Public Record Office, and the Duke is silent on the point, and so it is not clear what dispositions the British troops took up that day. But it must be remembered that they were bound to be fatigued after their rapid three days' march; and reliefs had to be arranged and made with the Austrian troops, who were holding an extensive defensive position there. And no doubt the Duke presumed that if Coburg wanted him on the field at once he would have sent back Calvert with the necessary message. Calvert, though he does not explicitly say so, must have informed Coburg of the position of the Duke's force.

For the next few days the Duke maintained his position by arrangement with Coburg, though it was far advanced, in a

[1] *Dupuis*, II, p. 106.

pronounced salient, as we have seen, and with the Forest of Mormal between it and the Austrian main army (just as this same forest separated the British 1st and 2nd Corps on the eve of the battle of Le Cateau).

But the halt was not destined to be for long. On the morning of 23 October, Coburg sent York word that an irruption by the French towards Menin was expected, and asked him to return to Tournai. The Duke then made another of his rapid marches. Setting off that very day, his army reached Saultain by nightfall, a thirteen-mile march.

The Duke himself dashed off to see Coburg, and after conferring with him, rode on to Valenciennes for the night. That night he received very bad news: the enemy had retaken Menin, and the Austrians whom he had left at Cysoing had fallen back almost to Tournai under pressure. He therefore called for a supreme effort from his men: marching at daybreak on the 24th, they went straight through to Maulde, a distance of seventeen miles. Halting there for a while for refreshment, they were then to continue to Tournai, another ten miles, making twenty-seven miles in all – a forced march indeed! The cavalry completed this march without making the Maulde halt, and the Duke pushed on rapidly ahead to see for himself, according to his wont, what the situation was at Tournai. Arriving there, and finding things were not so bad as reported – but that the Austrian general had lost his head and retreated unnecessarily – he sent back word to the infantry to remain at Maulde for the night, and to continue their march to Tournai at 2 a.m.

York was highly incensed with the Austrian General and wrote to his father that night:

'. . . This [the retreat from Cysoing] is a most unlucky step and done contrary to the opinion of all the officers who were consulted. . . . It will be necessary to retake the position of Cysoing as soon as possible.'[1]

The military significance of Cysoing was that it stood on comparatively high firm ground suitable for cavalry – the arm in which the Duke excelled – and, being midway between Tournai and Lille, formed a suitable defence line against that perpetual danger spot.

[1] *Windsor*, 24.10.93.

Next day the Duke wrote again on the same subject to the King:

'As I have had every reason to be dissatisfied with the conduct of the Austrian generals who have commanded the detached corps of this army during my absence, I have ordered Count Walmoden, in whose talents, courage and prudence I have the fullest reliance to take command of the corps which was at Menin. . . .' And he detailed other replacements.[1]

Was this a case of making a scapegoat? There is insufficient evidence to be positive on the point, but it would only be 'running to form' if the Austrian Generals were at fault. The Duke certainly took prompt and drastic steps to show his displeasure, and his action probably had good moral effect on the remaining Generals.

The news was better all round on the night of 25 October, but before continuing to the relief of Menin it was essential, as he had told his father, to push the enemy back from their dangerous proximity to Tournai, and to recapture the Cysoing position. This he carried out brilliantly on the 27th at the action of Sainghin, the enemy falling back helter-skelter through Lezennes, and being pursued by the Royals[2] and Bays almost to the ramparts of Lille.

The road was now clear for a resumption of the northern march of the army. News had by this time come in that Ypres had been unsuccessfully attacked, but that the enemy had taken Furnes and were threatening Nieuport. Even Ostend seemed in danger. It was indeed a general concerted attack all along the line from Nieuport in the north to Marchienne (five miles west of St Amand) in the south.

On the day following the Sainghin success the flank march was resumed. The Duke had formed a plan, by which Walmoden would attack Menin with the Hanoverian troops in that vicinity, while the British army pushed forward in that direction from Tournai with the intention of attracting the enemy's attention in their direction by a brisk demonstration. With this object, the Duke pushed a corps forward under Abercromby

[1] *Windsor*, 25.10.93.
[2] Commanded by Prince Ernest. 'Never did I see such havoc and chopping,' he wrote with relish to his father. The ground is a gentle descent, admirable for a cavalry charge.

to attack the French position at Lannoy (midway between Tournai and Menin). The attack was brilliantly successful and 100 French prisoners were captured. The French fell back from Menin, which Walmoden entered the same day. Likewise the French fell back from before Nieuport and the position was restored all along the line.

The Duke was naturally jubilant at the result of his swift and decided motions, and wrote in that strain to the King: 'My attempts to save West Flanders have been crowned with success.'

This claim, though no doubt genuinely entertained, was only partially justified. The Duke had taken prompt and vigorous steps to counter-attack the French irruption, but it was in truth a feeble affair at best, ordered by Paris and reluctantly complied with by the Generals all along the line. The mere threat of a counter-attack by the English was enough to put them all into reverse. But it certainly does seem that the mere name of the Duke of York was at least held in respect by his French opponents. Indeed, the thrust from Tournai almost to Lille on the 27th probably decided the French evacuation of Menin.

The strategical situation at Menin had, for a brief time, been not unlike the situation at the same place on 15 September. The French held a salient at Menin, and on each occasion York schemed to mount an operation on exterior lines against it. On this latter occasion Walmoden was to attack from the east, a Hessian General Wurmb from the north, while his own army applied pressure from the south. But, apart from the fact that the French, as before, took fright and slipped away before the blow could be properly developed, a serious hitch in the plan was caused by Wurmb, who, ignoring the instructions, marched north towards Ostend instead of marching south. In the upshot this did not matter, but it is mentioned here as throwing a light on York's conception of utilizing the strategy of exterior lines, and the difficulty he encountered in obtaining intelligent co-operation on the part of the Austrians. The Queen's Bays had captured 100 French prisoners at Lannoy, which afforded a good example of the Duke's natural humanity and chivalry. 'Every possible assistance was given to the suffering Frenchmen. All the surgeons in the camp were sent to dress their wounds, and His Royal Highness the Commander-in-Chief, humanely ordered wine and food to be distributed among them.'[1] The French soldiers, it may be observed, had orders to give no quarter to English troops.

In the midst of these invigorating and successful operations, while the Duke was feeling on the top of his form, suddenly there came a 'bolt from the blue' in the form of a sharp private letter, together with an official one in more guarded terms, of complaint and criticism from Dundas. When we peruse these faded lines of Dundas's letters it is easy to conjure up rather a pathetic picture of this Scottish barrister grappling single-handed in his Whitehall office with complicated problems of strategy. Singlehanded, for he had not had time to consult the King, whose knowledge and good sense were profound; single-handed for it simply did not occur to him to seek expert military advice before issuing a *mélange* of advice and directives. But the official letter opens modestly enough:

'If, not [being] versant in military operations and probably unqualified to reason with accuracy on the subject, I was to form an opinion founded solely upon a retrospect of the last transactions of the campaign, I should be disposed to draw two conclusions.'[2]

The two conclusions he drew were:

(1) That the enemy will profit by taking the offensive.
(2) That we ought to concentrate our forces, rather than disperse them.

From this we gather that, however egregious and fatuous some of the Home Secretary's military judgments and measures may have been in the early part of the campaign, at least he was learning by dear experience; for he had stumbled upon the two most fundamental principles of war – offensive action and concentration. It is to be presumed that the Commander-in-Chief and his Adjutant-General were not unaware of the soundness of these two principles; in point of fact, the Duke had been advocating them incessantly since the beginning of the campaign.

Hence neither paid much attention to these opening remarks: but when the Secretary proceeded to badger them for a plan of campaign their choler began to rise, for, as any soldier

[1] *An Officer of the Guards*, p. 110.   [2] *W.O.*, VI, 11, f. 81.

knows, at the moment when the enemy is delivering a powerful attack it is he that makes the plan. When Wellington was asked on the eve of the battle of Waterloo what his plan was he replied by merely asking: 'Who is attacking – Boney or me?' After giving some further advice on the right strategy to be pursued Dundas ended this letter with some rather confusing instructions as to the role of the reinforcements, under Sir Charles Grey, that he was sending to Ostend 'on loan'.

The private letter, as I have said, was more outspoken, and contained some severe strictures on the Duke's conduct of operations. (This letter is not in the file of Dundas's correspondence.)

Murray received this letter on the 29th and replied to it next day, while York wrote to the King. Both letters deserve long extracts. That of Murray said:

'It would be in vain to disguise from you that the Duke of York is much hurt at the dispatch that has been received this day. . . . Such reflections are not likely to be more patiently received that they come at a moment for him perhaps the most glorious of the campaign, when by his (?), with a very small additional force he has entirely changed the face of the war in this part of the country, where by the vigorous and just measures which he has embraced, universal defeat and despondency have given way to confidence and success. . . . The paper [written by a friend of Dundas and enclosed in his letter] in question seems to me to be like some others written at a distance from the scene of action, specious in the general principles and inapplicable to the use in question. . . . I rather imagine, but this is in confidence, that something has come to your ears from Marshal Freytag or General Ainslie; if it were possible that anything said by them should make impression, a very few minutes conversation, or a knowledge of the facts would enable me to set it to rights.'[1]

This was a pretty shrewd guess on the part of Murray, for the chain of events is clearly indicated by some letters in the Public Record Office. Ainslie was the General in command at Ostend, and on 23 October he wrote a panicky letter to Dundas, on the strength of reports – equally panicky – that he had received from Nieuport, stating that the town was being attacked and

[1] *W.O.*, I, 167, f. 493.

was not likely to hold out long, and adding: 'If the garrison (of Nieuport) gets safe hither, Ostend may hold out a short time, as I have landed 400 men. . . . I wish there may not be reason to regret that my repeated representations[1] on this head had been a little attended to. . . .'

Dundas had received the above letter on the 25th, and two days later wrote the reprimand referred to above.

And now for the Duke's own letter:

'It is with very great concern that I find by a dispatch which Sir James Murray received last night that my conduct is disapproved of for not having taken more care of Ostend. . . .'

He then points out that he had received the King's 'approbation' for his march towards Maubeuge, and proceeds to argue in great detail and with soundness why Ostend was of less value to the Allies than places such as Ypres and Tournai, and ending with a remark which reminds one of the Flanders campaign of 1944: 'Should Ostend, on the other hand, be taken . . . the only unpleasantness would be the temporary inconvenience of want of communication with England, which could be restored in a very few hours through Sluys or by the mouth of the Scheldt.'

The letter ends: 'Before I marched to join the Prince of Coburg I gave written orders to the general commanding the different corps, in what manner they were to act, and particularly ordered them to support one another if attacked, and pointed out in what manner that assistance was to be given. I am very sorry to say my orders were not obeyed and that in particular at Menin some very egregious faults were committed, by whom I cannot as yet make out, but it must be found out. . . .'[2]

The King replied to this in a letter which is not extant, but which evidently assured the Duke that he was *not* displeased with him.

The Commander-in-Chief had a perfectly good case against the Home Secretary, had he cared to avail himself of it, for on 13 October Dundas had written: 'Every measure essential for the success of the attack on Maubeuge merits approbation, and

[1] These 'representations' evidently refer to a letter he had written to Dundas on the 12th, stating that 600 Frenchmen could take the town in its present state.
[2] *Windsor*, 30.10.93.

as you represent the chief body of the French forces to have moved towards that quarter, I flatter myself the troops left in the different places of Nieuport and Furnes, and under the command of General Wurmb, will be sufficient for the protection of that part of Flanders.'[1] As, in fact, they were.

This letter was in reply to one in which Murray specifically warned Dundas that 'it may be impossible not to expose Ostend in some degree', adding: 'The public stores there are inconsiderable, the communication with England for the moment of little consequence.'

The gallant Murray, a day or two later, fired another shot in defence of his revered Chief, whom he rightly felt was getting into ill odour at home. He assured Dundas that: 'It is not in letters only, but in private conversation, when neither the Duke, nor anyone connected with him are present, that he is spoken of in the highest terms by the Austrian Generals.' The Emperor, indeed, asked that the Duke might be raised in rank.

But if the Duke was not in favour with Dundas, neither was Murray himself. The army had suffered much owing to the War Secretary's amateurish bungling, all of which is well and adequately dealt with by Fortescue. Murray had that dangerous gift, a sarcastic pen. Stung to anger by Dundas's latest imbecility, the Chief of Staff unburdened himself of this cutting passage: 'Let me point out to you that the same messenger brought to me from you, advice to besiege St Quentin: secondly an order to keep some troops at Ostend; and thirdly strong exhortations against division or detachment of our forces. . . . I think it right to show that perhaps people in England are not more infallible in their judgment than those upon the Continent.' Dundas never forgave this audacious soldier; Murray did not survive the campaign.[2]

*   *   *   *   *

Both armies now relapsed into the dreary routine of forming a 'cordon', to be followed in late November by winter quarters. On the conclusion of this the Duke of York's first campaign, it is important to examine the position and estimation in which he was held both *vis-à-vis* the army and the Government. Unlike

[1] *W.O.*, VI, 11, f. 37.
[2] But we shall come across him later as General Pulteney.

G

Coburg, his position seems to have been unimpaired in the army. At Brussels 'the cry against Coburg is great indeed. They say he has done nothing since Colonel Mack left him and that he is not equal to the command he holds.'[1]

No such feeling existed about the Duke. His tongue, it would appear, was his worst enemy. The nearest approach to contemporary criticism that I can find comes from the same source. 'Some of the things reported in England may be true, but I am persuaded he is both good natured and humane, although by sometimes talking absurdly he gets a contrary character.'[2] We shall see somewhat similar criticism later in the story. The fact no doubt was that in the privacy of his own headquarters he was indiscreet, assuming that his confidences would not be divulged. Other great men of more recent date have shared this weakness – if weakness it be. He was congenitally careless; as early as 1789 General Grenville told Lord Cornwallis that he was 'beyond measure careless', leaving private letters lying about opened, and so on. This trait of carelessness was to be his undoing in years to come.

But if the Duke still retained the confidence of his troops at the front, his stock was undeniably low at home. A scapegoat was required, and Ministers could hardly be expected to drive themselves out into the wilderness. York fully realized this, yet he refused to speak out in his own defence, for he could only defend himself by exposing the shortcomings of his Allies and the futilities of the Government. Nor were his staff under any misapprehensions. When he went home that winter for a conference:

'it was with confidence stated our Chief would remain
On this side the water the ensuing campaign,
And Pitt (*entre nous*) it was pointedly hinted
Towards the Marquis from India had frequently squinted.
All things put together, bets ran five to four,
The Duke would return to the army no more.'[3]

Lord Malmesbury, on his way to Vienna, in December, visited the army, and records in his diary some notable tributes

---

[1] *Harcourt*, p. 395.   [2] Ibid.
[3] *An Officer of the Guards*, II, p. 7. The Marquis was Lord Cornwallis, who had just returned from being Governor-General in India.

paid to the Duke (and the reverse to Murray). Colonel Fox 'spoke most highly of him as a man and an able general', while Colonels Fox and St Leger 'both think Sir James an unfit man for his station'.[1] Count Mercy, the Austrian Minister at Brussels, 'praised the Duke and his army and said "La grande cause lui devait les plus grandes obligations." ' Bentinck, the Dutchman, 'blames the Prince of Orange, praises the Duke'. Lord Elgin 'states Sir James Murray is unpopular, and thus makes the Duke so'.

And then comes his important interview with the Duke himself on 6 December, which must be transcribed in full.

'[The] Duke brought Sir J. Murray with him, but he left us often alone. He said the army was ill provided. Condemned the whole measure of Dunkirk and separation of the armies; spoke slightingly of the Dutch, and still more of the hereditary Prince of Orange, whom he called "Young Hopeful".

'On my hinting a possibility or rather a certainty that Grey would make *Dunkirk* the first object on the opening of the Session, the Duke said he trusted none of *his* friends would be so over zealous as to think it necessary to defend him at the expense of others. That whatsoever he might feel or think as to himself, and the *usage* he had met with, yet, that this consideration was a very secondary one indeed, if the obtaining it stood in the way of the great cause for which we were contending, and he should be very sorry indeed that any blame should be thrown on any particular measure, or any particular Minister, as it certainly would go to censure the principle of the War and produce the worst consequences. The Duke of York (Sir J. Murray being absent) went into a detail of his own situation, which he said was unpleasant; he had *nobody* about him, no Secretary to write for him as the old Duke of Cumberland had; no *really experienced* officer. He had written to the King; had been forced to say, Sir James was unpopular. The Duke read me the King's Answer, which was that of a most affectionate Father to a favourite Son. His Majesty entered into all he said, proposed giving Murray rank and a Scotch brigade, to appoint Craggs[2] in his stead, and in answer to a request of the Duke's to return home, advises him not to ask it, in order to keep his officers abroad, but that he will send for him to England soon.

[1] Fox and St Leger were both on the Duke's Staff.   [2] A mistake for *Craig*.

This was an excellent and most affectionate letter, and the Duke's answer, which he read me, was equally so – all respect and proper attention.

'The conversation confirmed me in the opinion, that the Duke of York has a very good understanding; but he *talks* too much, and is careless to whom. I ventured to tell him so, and took an opportunity of recommending him to ask the superior officers to dinner; and, as he could not prevent their writing home, to try at least to furnish them by *his* conversation there, with *materials* which would do *no harm*. Now they, and particularly the Guards, write nonsense, almost equal to mutiny. To this he attended with great good humour. I staid till one in the morning, and then returned to Tournai. I remained at Ath all night – on the morning of Saturday, December 7th, Lord Herbert came to me, and we returned together to Brussels. He was very glad to see me – complained very much of the insubordination of the army, that it was greater than could be believed, that the Guards were so beyond measure; that the Duke of York was most unjustly unpopular, and he believed the worst used man in the world, as all his foibles were cried out against, and none of his good qualities, which were many, noticed.'[1]

The Duke's letter to the King referred to in the interview is in the Windsor archives and will be quoted on a later page.

Malmesbury's assessment is corroborated by a letter written on 11 January, 1794, by John St Leger, a member of the Duke's staff, to Thomas Pelham:

'I should hardly conceive that any attack would be made on the Duke, but even supposing there was, I believe he would suffer it rather than be defended in any way that might injure what he conceives to be the general cause.'[2]

To Thomas Pelham Malmesbury wrote, a few days later, saying that the interview 'went to confirm me in the good opinion I always was disposed to have of him, and in general not to alter that I had of many mistakes which had defeated the effects of his exertions and abilities, and rendered the end of the campaign less brilliant than its beginning.'

William Windham (Samuel Johnson's young friend) also paid him a visit in December – and a tribute. 'These clamours

[1] *Malmesbury*, III, p. 17.   [2] *Add. MSS.*, 33/133, f. 6.

against the Duke are for the most part utterly without founda-
tion; and in *all* very nearly so. They originate in the mere
licentiousness of the officer part of the army. . . . Nothing
material in the campaign has suffered from him, if anything at
all has; and all the latter part has been of a sort to do him the
highest honour. Both the Court at Vienna and the Austrian
army are full of his praises.'[1]

Praise also came from an unexpected direction – from
Frederick's old military mentor, the Duke of Brunswick, who
wrote him a flattering letter referring to 'the talents which
place you in the ranks of the great men of the century'.[2]

It was only in his own country that the Duke's stock had
fallen.

That the origin of the campaign of slander was a disgruntled
set of officers is corroborated from another source. Lord Portland, writing to Malmesbury from England, speaks of 'the
licentious, not to say mutinous spirit against the Duke of York
which prevails among the troops and which originated in and
is even cultivated in the Guards'.[3] He also throws out hints as
to its origin, but that is as far as I have been able to trace this
wretched matter.

Many of these officers were persons prominent in Society
and politics, who had joined the army at the outbreak of the
war, 'just to see the fun'. An example of the sort of difficulty the
Duke had with them, and his method of dealing with it, is
afforded by the following letter:

'I had the Honor to mention to Your Majesty in my last
letter the very improper behaviour of Captain Gage of the 1st
Regiment of Guards. On Saturday morning, he sent Me a
written request to sell, and at the same time, in a manner
insisted upon setting off directly for England. Had he been any
other Person, I never should have allowed him to go, but out of
respect to the Duke of Gloucester, in whose family he is, I sent
him word that He might leave the Army directly, and I at the
same time gave him notice, that I disapproved so much of his
conduct that I should certainly write to the Duke of Gloucester
about Him, and that I hope Your Majesty would not consent
to His selling His Commission. Indeed, if Officers are allowed

[1] *Malmesbury*, III, p. 23.   [2] *Diaries and Correspondence of George Rose*, II. p. 15.
[3] Ibid., III, p. 69.

to behave as He has done with impunity, it will be difficult to keep up any discipline.'[1]

Amid such vexations as these, the army settled down into winter quarters between Ghent and Courtrai, where it seems to have made itself tolerably comfortable.

[1] *Windsor*, 19.11.93.

NOTE A. FAMARS CAMP

The camp was situated on a well-defined ridge. Preseau is one and a half miles east of the River Rhonelle by Artres, and is in a slight dip. The advance from the village was thus under cover from Artres till the crest was reached, only 600 yards from the river. It is easy to locate approximately what must have been the Duke's command post on the roadside descending into the valley. The French guns were probably on the opposing heights, the two artilleries being about 1,200 yards apart. The Rhonelle is here 18 feet wide, shallow, with a firm bottom.

In order to gain Maresches the army must have countermarched over the crest, and then turned to their right. There are still two bridges at Maresches; in the summer the foliage would hide the crossing from the Artres ridge. But the movement would become visible after crossing the river, even if French cavalry had not discovered the march, as they did.

Querenaing is situated on the flat top of a ridge, and the French redoubts were not visible from it. Consequently the Duke had to move to his left in order to view the position. The exact spot whence he viewed the position can be located, for the *chemin creusé* still exists. It affords a splendid view of the French position and the remains of the principal redoubt are still in existence on the opposite side of the valley, 250 yards beyond the railway and distant 1,200 yards from the Duke's command post. The British troops would undoubtedly have been very exposed in their approach to this position.

THE REVIEW OF THE CAMPAIGN

4

The best-known portraits of the Duke of York depict him as a portly, if not corpulent, elderly gentleman. This is a relevant factor in our estimation of his military qualities, for we absorb through the eye, and are thus apt to regard the Duke's military motions as slow, ponderous, and unimaginative. It is therefore with something of an effort that we realize, from an unbiased study of his operations, that this portrait simply does not fit this his first campaign.

Right from the outset we find him, young and inexperienced though he was, acting with self-confidence, initiative, and drive. Fortescue somewhat grudgingly writes of him at this early age that 'Youth can be at any rate energetic'. There is no doubt that his enthusiasm and energy did pump some symptoms of animation into the somnolent Stadholder. It is equally clear that his presence and actions with a mere handful of British soldiers did save Holland from being overrun in the first few days of the campaign.[1]

Yet if ever a commander in the field was 'cribbed, cabined, and confined' by the instructions of his Government, surely York was at this time. To be tied down to an area within a day's march of a given spot is to be as effective in defence of a country as a dog chained to its kennel is for the defence of its master's property. Yet by his skill, tact, and patience the Duke gradually obtained relaxation of these deadening restrictions, and for all practical purposes they did not impede his motions during the first part of the campaign.

A further charge against the Government is that they stinted the army of supplies in all its branches, even sending out recruits to the front unarmed. Dundas must not receive the sole blame for this. It must be shared by the Ordnance Department

[1] Winston Churchill's sudden appearance at Antwerp in October 1914 had a very similar effect.

which was at the outbreak of the war in a shocking state of inefficiency. Dundas and the Government could not 'make bricks without straw'. The trouble was that they tried to make too many: that is to say, they had 'too many irons in the fire' at the same time. The West Indies, La Vendée, and Toulon in turn attracted them, with the natural result that the army in Flanders was starved for men and stores. When, in an emergency, reinforcements were rushed out, they were usually 'lent' as a temporary measure, 'to be returned' in a stated time for some other operation – much as one might lend a neighbour one's garden roller, expecting it back intact on a stated date. It does not seem to have occurred to Pitt and Dundas that troops in action are an 'expendable store'.

All things considered, it is surprising that the Duke of York accomplished as much as he did with such inadequate resources.

But the Duke had other difficulties besides those imposed by his own Government. Ever since the Hundred Years War our operations upon the Continent have been in conjunction with allies; and in practically every case these allies have provided difficulties that have taxed the qualities and patience of our commanders in the highest degree. Especially, it must be admitted, has this been so in the case of the Austrians and the Dutch. In particular, Francis Vere, Stair, Marlborough, and Cumberland experienced them to the full. But none of the above had the same degree of difficulty as the Duke of York in his two campaigns of 1793 and 1794. Yet on the whole he surmounted them at least as well as could be expected. The patience of a Job – or rather of a Marlborough – was required; and York was undeniably well endowed with this virtue. He might write scathingly of the shortcomings and misbehaviour of his allies privately to his King – as Marlborough did to his Queen – but his outward and personal relations with them remained surprisingly good. I am not sure, indeed, that this is not the most notable quality of all displayed by the Duke. It is true that he possessed an advantage not enjoyed by Marlborough, that of being a Prince of the Blood. In the eighteenth century this meant much in Europe, not only among the higher officers, but among the common soldiers, too. The Duke was a fine figure of a man, and he kept a princely board during the quiet moments of the campaign. All these things helped in an intangible, but very real way. If an Allied General felt aggrieved and wished to let off steam, he found his style cramped, in writing to the Duke, by having to use the words 'Your Royal Highness' in almost every line of the letter. In this respect York had the advantage over Marlborough: consequently his achievement in this matter does not quite come up to that of his great predecessor in Flanders.

Part, and a large part, of his success in maintaining good relations with his allies can be attributed to his integrity in keeping his word, and promptness in responding to any calls for help. We saw it at Raismes, at Linselles, at Ypres, at Menin, at Maubeuge, at Cysoing, and finally again at Menin – surely a notable record for one short campaign. Of the difficulties imposed upon him by the home Government there is no need to say more, for it is common ground with all historians, and Fortescue has dealt with the egregious Dundas with such shattering castigation and irony that my pen could not add to it. If anything, he piles on the agony overmuch: the unfortunate War Secretary did at least learn something from his mistakes, as we shall see when we come to the Helder Campaign.

A close study of this campaign clears away another misconception that is common – namely, that the Duke was a mere Royal figurehead, and that Sir James Murray was the real director of operations. Nothing could be farther from the truth. From the very moment of his setting foot on the Continent we see him thinking and acting for himself. The first thing he does is to write a hurried letter to the King saying he is going to The Hague and hopes to get there in seven hours. There is not a word about his Adjutant-General. From that moment the Duke is in the centre of the picture and Murray takes second place. Thus we find Lord Bonington writing from the camp at Valenciennes; that he was impressed by 'the very great clearness, precision and quickness with which he gave his orders.'[1] We begin to suspect already that the Duke of York was a great man in his own natural rights.

Whether his training in Germany had taught him resolute and prompt action we cannot be sure: certain it is that he exhibited this essential military virtue in the field. Notice, for

[1] *Private Correspondence of Lord Granville, Leveson Gower*, I, p. 67.

example, the prompt and resolute way in which he tackled the Hanoverian trouble. We shall see a still more striking example of this quality in the next campaign. Nor can we fail to be impressed by his sheer magnanimity in scorning to defend himself against the clamour resulting from Dunkirk, simply because to do so would damage the Allied cause. Yet another quality to admire is his natural resilience – due perhaps to his youth – a strain of robustness in adversity that Lord Wavell has taught us to admire above nearly all virtues in a general. On 9 September his army was reeling under its first defeat, having narrowly escaped a 'Dunkirk': yet twenty-four hours later we find him issuing orders to advance to the help of his allies in Ypres, and to attack the French wherever found – a truly Fochian attitude.

So much for the general military qualities displayed by the Duke of York in the campaign of 1793. A word now regarding the actual operations in the field.

There are certain well-established principles or factors of war, prominent among them being mobility, offensive action, co-operation, and concentration. It is unlikely that the Duke of York had ever tabulated them in this precise enumeration, but they contain nothing new: they have been recognized or at least adopted by the great captains, and not least by Frederick the Great, who had a big influence on the young soldier at an impressionable age. It is reasonable therefore to suppose that his military training in Germany had stood him in good stead in this respect. Frederick's own writings on strategy do not carry us far: they are rather contradictory and equivocal. But his disciple Guibert wrote in 1772 a book which was all the rage while Prince Frederick was in Germany, and with which he probably was acquainted. In his first book, *Essai Générale de Tactique*, Guibert calls for a war of movement, in contrast to the Austrian school of thought whose chief aim was the reduction of fortresses. His other views he afterwards modified, but not this essential principle. Now, it is clear that York believed heartily in a war of movement – and speedy movement, too. Speed is a relative term. We must consider every campaign in its own setting. Judged by this criterion, York's marches were characterized by speed to a notable degree. With *speed* was bracketed *surprise*: to achieve this he frequently marched by night or early morning, a course that was not popular in that epoch. In fact, if we compare the motions of his army with the Prince of Coburg's army, we find a remarkable contrast. From first to last Coburg never had his headquarters more than twenty miles from Condé; whereas the Duke of York's movements may be summarized thus:

Tournai – Valenciennes	.	.	. 20 miles
Valenciennes – Cambrai	.	.	. 25 miles
Cambrai – Dunkirk via Linselles		.	110 miles
Dunkirk – Menin via Thorout	.	.	50 miles
Menin – Engelfontaine	.	.	. 66 miles
Engelfontaine – Lannoy	.	.	. 60 miles

331 m.

All these marches, be it noted, were flank marches across the front of the enemy's line; consequently, as his army progressed each sector in the line in turn fancied itself threatened: this was notably so in the march to Dunkirk. By constant movement the British army kept its opponents guessing. As regards the principle of offensive action, we have seen that it was strongly developed in the young Duke right from the start. Like Robert E. Lee, he was for ever asking himself: 'How can I get at him?' Well did he realize that it is only by offensive action that decisive results can be achieved in war. In this respect he parted company with the King of Prussia – in his latter days, at any rate.

As for co-operation, in his very first letter to Coburg, written from Antwerp, he impressed on him the desirability of close association between the two armies, even though at that moment he had hopelessly restrictive instructions from his own Government. And he was as good as his word; as we have seen, whenever an ally asked for help or co-operation it was forthcoming and prompt.

Finally, the principle of concentration was firmly imbued in his military philosophy. To a certain extent this principle merges into that of co-operation. At Famars and Caesar's Camp he was a mere column commander, with no scope to initiate anything on his own. At Dunkirk he had every intention of concentrating all available forces to meet the French attack, but Freytag spoilt his plan by keeping essential information from him. At Menin he eagerly embraced the possibility of a grand concentration against the French, but his design was nipped in the bud by the premature retreat of the French; at Maubeuge he was planning to take part in a concentrated attack when Coburg incontinently retreated across the Sambre. Finally, his second attempt to envelop the French at Menin was frustrated for the same reason as previously – the enemy took fright before the plan could be put into force.

It is a speculation, but a natural one, that York had when in Germany read *The Seven Years War in Germany,* by that remarkable renegade Englishman, General Henry Lloyd. In this work the author advocated an enveloping concentration on the battlefield, such as York repeatedly attempted to bring about. 'No enemy,' declared Lloyd, 'can keep his ground if you advance against him in front and at the same time send a powerful corps to act on his flank and rear.'

To sum up, the young Duke of York seems from his actions to have been unusually well grounded in what we now know as the principles of war, and if he was not uniformly successful in applying them, we must look for the explanation to the shortcomings of his Allies rather than to those of himself or of the British army.

If I appear to be unduly eulogistic about the qualities of the Duke of York in his first campaign, and indiscriminate in his praise, it is simply because I have not succeeded in the course of my search in discovering any obvious blemish in his operations. Critics almost invariably confine themselves to stating that he was a mediocre General, without indicating in what specific respect he erred. In two cases Fortescue criticizes; in each of these I have tried to show that his criticism is unsound. There is no one else to answer!

WINTER QUARTERS

5

Early in December both sides went into winter quarters. Such a course was customary and almost inevitable in those days. Even Marlborough was obliged to observe the custom. But this meant nothing to Dundas, the civilian; he induced the King to write a letter to Coburg, urging him to remain active during the winter season. Dundas sent it to the Duke, suggesting that some senior officer, preferably Abercromby, should take it to Coburg. The Duke replied that he would take the letter himself, and urge it on the Prince, adding that he would support with his cavalry any inroads made by the Austrians. It is to be noted that he did not undertake to use his infantry and artillery; the reason for this he gave in a subsequent letter – it was an obvious one – that artillery could only move off the *chaussées* for eight months in the year. The Government's motive in urging activity during the winter was that of holding French troops in Flanders, thus preventing reinforcements for the attack on Toulon, where our garrison was hard pressed.

Nothing came of Dundas's well-meant prompting, and, apart from patrol activity, both sides settled down to make themselves as comfortable as they could for the next four months. The British army quartered in the area between Ghent and Courtrai, the Duke's headquarters being near the latter town.

The first problem that arose was naturally the question of leave. For various reasons the Duke was anxious to get home for a spell, but the King would not listen to it. He pointed out with shrewd sense that if the Commander took leave the other officers would expect it, too. England was so temptingly close. But, said the King in effect: 'In due course I will *order* you home for consultation; that will avoid trouble.' Wise old Monarch!

During those winter months there was a good deal to keep the Commander employed. Relations with foreign contingents engaged his attention throughout; the Hessians, being mere mercenaries, gave most trouble. But it is a dull subject, and we need not go into it.

In the course of the winter the Duke sent one of his staff, Captain Crauford, on a mission to the Emperor at Vienna. Crauford had a most enlightening interview with Baron Thugut, the new Austrian minister, at which Thugut gave him an appreciation on the causes of the lack of success in the past campaign. One would not be disposed to expect much of value to originate from such a source, but in fact the paper is most illuminating, and full of sound sense. I will summarize the five reasons given by him for the failures.

1. Slowness in bringing up the Austrian siege train to Valenciennes.
2. Missing the opportunity afforded of delivering a knock-out blow to the French army at Famars.
3. Failure to besiege Maubeuge immediately after the capture of Valenciennes.
4. The abandonment of the siege of Maubeuge after the battle of Wattignies.
5. Engaging in field operations in terrain unsuitable to cavalry, the arm in which the Allies chiefly excelled.

The modern historian, with all the advantages of fuller knowledge of both sides, could hardly improve on this appreciation. It goes to show that there were at Vienna some people, surprisingly enough, who had a flair for war.

It will be noted that over none of these causes had the Duke any control, or the British army any responsibility.

Such were some of the lessons from the past. The Duke of York was already casting his mind forward to the approaching campaign, and considering how to profit by these lessons. His first problem was a delicate one – how to bring about tactfully a change of Chiefs of Staff, both British and Austrian. The relations between himself and Murray were excellent. I find it hard to assess the military capacity of the Adjutant-General. Fortescue gives a vivid pen-portrait of him, but I can discover little positive data on which to judge of his actions and advice during the previous campaign. He was evidently modest, self-effacing and intensely loyal to his master, and it is difficult in most cases to say to what extent he influenced the decisions taken in the field by the Duke, and how far he merely endorsed them. But he seems to have been unpopular in the army, as well as with the Government, and that solid fact may have in itself justified a change. At all events, the Duke of York approached the problem, as was his custom, through the King.

'I trust Your Majesty is thoroughly sensible of the extreme delicacy I felt concerning Sir James Murray, who is without doubt a perfectly good Man, and has very good Military talents, but unfortunately is not endowed with that spirit of exactness and order which are absolutely necessary in an Adjutant-General, besides that he actually does not possess that manner of writing which is requisite for His Publick Correspondence. I feel exceedingly happy in knowing Your Majesty's intention of placing him at the Head of the Scotch Brigade, by which he will be equally of use to the Service, though removed from an Office to which certainly His genius does not fit him. I really know no one Officer whom I could wish to propose to Your Majesty as Adjutant-General, but from everything which I have heard, for I am very little acquainted with him, Colonel Craig is a very exact Officer, and one who is thoroughly fit for that Office'.[1]

Ten days later we find him writing again to suggest that, as Murray was at present in England, the appointment of Craig as Adjutant-General in his place should be made at once, before Murray returned to the army. This resulted in an interview between Dundas and Murray on 21 December, at which the War Secretary suggested that he might like the command of the Scotch Brigade (the spelling is that of Dundas, himself a Scotsman). In reporting the matter to the King, Dundas wrote: 'He did not say much, but seemed much hurt and pressed much that Mr Dundas would give the reasons which had induced Your Majesty to take this determination.'

However, the affair was thus settled, and Craig appointed in his place, for which the Duke in his letter of New Year greetings to the King dutifully renders thanks.

That matter being disposed of, the next thing was the still more delicate problem of getting rid of the Austrian Chief of Staff, Prince Hohenlohe. On 4 January 1794 the Duke fired

[1] *Windsor*, 3.12.93.

the first shot. As may be imagined, it took the form of a letter to the King.

'As long as Prince Hohenlo [*sic*] remains in his present situation as Quartermaster general and has the direction of all operations, nothing of any consequence can be expected. Indeed, his conduct has alienated the minds of all the troops upon this frontier, and if he is not removed before the beginning of the next campaign I am afraid everything will fall very short of what is expected or necessary to be done. It would therefore be very much to be wished that by some means or other the Emperor could be persuaded to let Colonel Mack return to the army. His presence alone would restore confidence to the troops, and instil a degree of spirit, etc. . . .'[1]

This letter worked the oracle; Mack – now promoted Major-General – was appointed to succeed Hohenlohe.

The next step was to get in touch with Mack and concert plans with him for the next campaign. Mack soon informed York that he had a plan prepared and would presently submit it to him. Thereupon York suggested to the King that he should procure a copy of this plan and bring it over to England himself, adding: 'I have no doubt that I shall easily persuade General Mack to follow me over likewise in order that the whole may be fully discussed and arranged.'[2]

Note the words 'I have no doubt . . .' It is clear that the Duke had acquired a certain ascendancy over the brilliant Austrian Staff Officer during their brief co-operation, and that he could secure what seems so sensible and obvious to us nowadays, but which was unprecedented then, namely a visit to this country by a Staff Officer of one of our Allies. The Duke of York must be given the credit for having established a useful precedent.

The British commander purposed to go over to Coburg's headquarters at Mons directly he heard of the arrival there of Mack. But Mack took the significant course of coming to Brussels to meet York and to show him his plan before ever reporting to his own Chief! Evidently he felt it advisable to win over the English Commander-in-Chief first and then present the plan as a sort of joint affair, agreed upon between himself and the Duke. This was to treat the Prince of Coburg

[1] *Windsor*, 4.1.94.   [2] Ibid., 22.1.94.

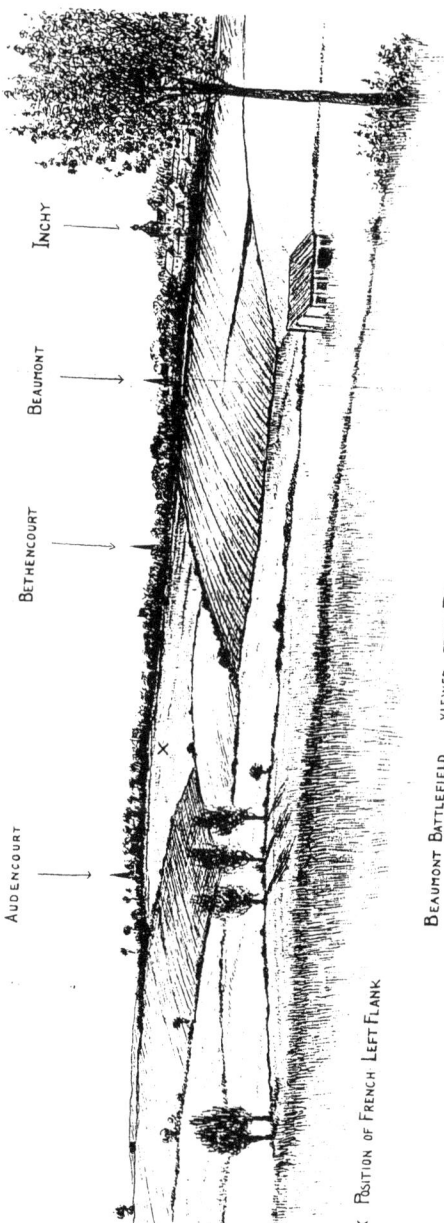

AUDENCOURT   BETHENCOURT   BEAUMONT   INCHY

×   POSITION OF FRENCH LEFT FLANK

BEAUMONT BATTLEFIELD   VIEWED FROM TROISVILLES WINDMILL

with scant respect – but it was successful.

The meeting between the two friends took place in Brussels, on 1 February. Mack showed York his plan – a lengthy document – but did not at this stage give him a copy. The Duke, however, absorbed it pretty thoroughly, for he sat down that night to send the King a précis of it from memory. The full plan, signed by Coburg some days later does not differ in material points from this précis. He sent this off to the King, adding the welcome news that he had obeyed His Majesty's commands to invite Mack over to England. Evidently the King had, as usual, fallen in with his son's advice.[1]

All was now going swimmingly. Mack set off for Mons, there he soon obtained Coburg's signature to his plan and he then followed the Duke, who had already departed for England.

But all was not going as swimmingly for the Duke of York as he himself believed. His visit almost coincided with the return from India of Earl Cornwallis. Pitt and Dundas had for some time been wanting to get rid of the Duke, but they had no illusions as to the delicacy of the task and of the difficulty they would experience in persuading the Monarch, who possessed, and jealously preserved, the constitutional right of nominating the commander of his forces in the field.

The timely arrival of Cornwallis therefore was hailed by the Ministers as a God-given opportunity to achieve their purpose. Cornwallis had come home with his Indian military honours thick upon him; he was universally recognised as the leading soldier of the day; the only question was, whether he would accept the command. Dundas soon made himself sure upon this point. He summoned the Earl on 9 February to an interview, which seems to have satisfied him. Meanwhile Mack arrived, and a conference was held. At it were present Pitt, Grenville (the Foreign Secretary), Dundas, and Mack; but not York, for sinister reasons. Mack was to be informed of the projected change in the British command.

But the British Government had reckoned without the Austrian staff officer. He reacted so strongly to this suggestion of the supersession of York and spoke up so vigorously on behalf of the Duke that, surprising as it may seem, he carried the day. He praised the Duke's character, 'decrying his critics

[1] It is unfortunate that none of the King's letters to the Duke has been preserved.

H

as a set of influential but inexperienced youths.'[1]

Mack also made the startling announcement that he declined to serve further under the Prince of Coburg. This was going a bit too far. But, to anticipate, the matter was smoothed over by inducing the Emperor to take the supreme command himself.

Mack then produced his famous plan. There is no need to describe it here in detail; the gist of it was that the main attack would be delivered by the Austrians in the centre, directed upon Paris while the British army (which was to be raised to 40,000) was to protect the Austrian right flank, directing their march upon Amiens. A second meeting was held next day, which York was invited to attend.

So the die was cast; the Duke of York returned, after all, to his army.

At this point it would be interesting, though perhaps profitless, to speculate as to the effect that the proposed change of command would have had on the fortunes of the coming campaign. In spite of Yorktown, Cornwallis had achieved a considerable military reputation in America, and he enhanced it by his victories over Tippoo Sahib in India. But conditions would have been very different in Europe, where he would have had to deal with foreigners as allies. Judging by his conduct when on a military mission to the court of Prussia in the summer of 1794, he would not have shone in his relations with these people – certainly not in the same degree as Marlborough and York did.

It is always difficult to compare one General in the field with another. In popular estimation the Marquis would be placed much higher than the Duke; but I do not feel that the evidence is conclusive on the point. Cornwallis did not show real brilliance either as a strategist or as a tactician; indeed, his biographer Kaye admits that 'he was not inspired by any lofty genius'. Nor, it may be asserted, was the Duke. That may be so, but we are merely concerned with the question as to which of them would have conducted the better the 1794 campaign; and here, as will be presently seen, genius in the British commander would have availed nothing. So the question of genius cancels out, and we are left with the personal factor. As regards

[1] *Holland Rose*, p. 205.

relations with the British officers, Cornwallis would have the advantage, but York did, in fact, receive loyal service from them in '94. As regards relations with the Austrians, I have no doubt whatever that Cornwallis would have failed even more dismally than York. And as for the Hanoverians, the Duke was almost one of themselves – 'My Hanoverians', he called them. Thus, on balance I am inclined to the opinion that the Duke of York was the best man for the task, and that the British Government showed good judgment in acceding to Mack's wishes.

*   *   *   *   *

Meanwhile Sir James Murray had passed on to his Scotch Brigade and Colonel John Craig reigned in his stead. Craig was a little stocky man, who was said to have started his military career as a private in the Household Cavalry. He had had considerable experience in the American War, notably at Wilmington.

Arriving at the Front early in January, he did not write his first letter to Henry Dundas till the 21st of the month (though he had written to tell Nepean, the Assistant Secretary, on the 14th, that the Duke had received him cordially). This letter to Dundas is so illuminating as to the characters and methods of life of both himself and his chief that in spite of its length it merits very full quotation. Craig starts by explaining why he has not written earlier. Dundas had instructed him to write to him freely and fully (as he had also instructed Murray); but after his arrival at headquarters one of the first things that his new Chief told him was that 'he had the King's direction to take all the official correspondence into his own hands'. (After the unfortunate experience of Murray, this was not to be wondered at.) Craig proceeds:

'It is impossible to be too grateful for the reception which His Royal Highness received me with, nor have I the smallest reason to believe from his conduct towards me that His Royal Highness does not intend to honor me with his entire confidence. I think it however indispensably requisite that I should observe to you, Sir, that as it is impossible for me to take the liberty of questioning His Royal Highness, I am obliged to obtain my information on many points by indirect measures. . . . I have had no opportunity yet of seeing General Abercromby, but I

have infinite satisfaction in assuring you that whatever may
have been the case formerly there certainly is not now the
smallest appearance of any distance between His Royal Highness and Sir William Erskine.[1] I have opportunities daily of
witnessing the confidence with which the Duke treats Sir
William, and the zeal with which Sir William returns it. Indeed, it appears to me that His Royal Highness treats everybody with a degree of good nature and politeness which I know
have not had justice done to them in the accounts which have
been given of him in London. I believe the late Promotion has
in a great degree removed the sources of the misrepresentations
which have been made on this subject; at least it is very clear
that a certain corps,[2] amongst the officers of which it has occasioned the principal removals, has been infinitely more quiet
since, and I am led very much to believe that matters will go
on now more smoothly than they did before.

'The only circumstance which I have observed in the Duke's
treatment of the officers which I could wish changed, is with
respect to the invitations to his table; in this it appears to me
that sufficient attention is not paid to the field officers and those
of a higher rank. I am endeavouring as much as lies in my
power, at present to bring about a little alteration in this
respect, which if I can accomplish it I am sure will tend to
increase the Duke's popularity in the army.

'It would not perhaps be unpleasing to you to know that the
Entertainment that His Royal Highness gave on Her Majesty's
birthday – a ball and supper – was perhaps one of the handsomest and best conducted things of the kind that was ever
given. There were about 800 people at it. Prince Ernest was
here but Prince Adolphus did not arrive till next day.'[3]

We are struck in the above letter by two aspects of Craig's
relation to the Commander-in-Chief: first, his marked and
almost excessive reverence and awe for the Royal Prince: it is
an astonishing state of affairs when a Chief of Staff dare not
ask his chief elementary questions concerning the military
situation. (One should however remember that the office of
the Chief of Staff as we know it did not then exist: Craig was,
strictly, only Adjutant-General.

[1] In command whilst the Duke was in England.
[2] Presumably the Guards Brigade.   [3] *W.O.*, I, 168, f. 189.

The second aspect was his quick perception of 'where the shoe pinched' – as to which Murray had been completely blind – and his tactful steps to remedy matters. The fact is, the Duke preferred the company of his 'family' – men of his own age – to that of the generals.

As for the misleading accounts from London, it is the old story. London has always contained a set of malicious gossipers and slanderers, only too ready to blacken the character of the commander in the field. I can think of no important commander, with the exception of Sir Ralph Abercromby, who has not been the target for these gentry, however successful he may have been. Stories circulate by word of mouth – these folks take care not to commit them to paper – hence it is almost impossible to track down and refute them. In the case of the Duke of York it is even difficult to discover what the specific charges were, except that he was too unguarded in his talk, and that he is said to have kept too lavish a table. No doubt the entertainment here described was added to the charge, though his open hospitality must have been instrumental in fostering good relations between the British army and the inhabitants of the occupied country. The reference to the way the Duke treated all alike with bonhomie echoes back to Cornwallis's observation as to his approachability when he met him in Germany many years before.

*   *   *   *   *

On 8 March the Duke of York arrived back at his Flanders headquarters, and duly notified the War Secretary. In signing his name to this and future letters (as opposed to dispatches) he makes a break with the etiquette of the time. In place of the usual circumlocution – 'I am, Sir, Your most obedient servant' – he ends up abruptly:

> 'I am, Sir,
> 'Yours,
> 'Frederick',

an innovation with a very modern flavour.

As soon as the Duke had resumed the threads of office, he sent Craig off to Berlin to try and procure some light troops. He himself then hurried on to Valenciennes, where an important war council was held. Mack had had his way; the Arch-Duke

Charles (brother of the Emperor) had gone back to Vienna on purpose to persuade his brother to assume the supreme command in the field, and in this he had been successful. The British Government, not fully trusting York, had now swung from one extreme to the other: in the previous campaign they had impressed upon him that he must not get committed in any Austrian schemes; now they placed him absolutely under Coburg, with an Austrian detachment in his command in order to tie him the more effectually to the Austrians.

The dispositions settled were as follows. On the right the Austrian General Clerfait[1] (or Clairfait) commanded from the sea to the south of Tournai. York had the next sector, centring on St Amand; Coburg was at Valenciennes, and the Prince of Orange held the left wing, reaching almost to Maubeuge. To 'marry' the two armies the more effectually, an English brigade, was attached to Clerfait's army. All this was verging on an insult to the Duke, but he accepted the position calmly and obediently, though inwardly he must have raged.

After protracted negotiations skilfully conducted by Lord Malmesbury, the Prussian King on 19 April promised an army of 62,400 men, to be paid by England, and in return to operate in whatever theatre we wished.[2] It was to take the field by 24 May, and Dundas requested its presence in Flanders. Thus the Allies were making great efforts to deliver the knock-out blow in the forthcoming campaign. But, as so often happens in war, the enemy were attempting exactly the same thing, under the energetic direction of Carnot.

The first blow struck was a verbal one – a letter from the new French commander, General Pichegru (nearly all the previous ones had gone to the guillotine), addressed to the Prince of Coburg. It was in the following elegant terms:

'General,

'I summon you in the name of the French Republic to render up immediately Quesnoy, Condé, and Valenciennes, or be assured I shall attack and vanquish you.   'Pichegru.'

---

[1] Fortescue always calls him Clerfaye. The origin of his mistake was, I conjecture, as follows. Towards the end of the campaign the Duke had a secretary or copyist who made fair copies of Clerfait's letters. I suspect that Clerfait did not cross a final 't' and that the clerk read it as an 'e': he certainly transcribed it Clerfaye and York consequently adopted that spelling in his later dispatches.

[2] *Malmesbury*, III, p. 92.

Before the two sides came to actual blows, the English commander, apart from trouble with his foreign troops – which was
only to be expected – also had trouble with his own men, which
put his powers of leadership to the test. It is therefore worth
giving the story in detail, and as much as possible in his own
words.

The first extract is from a letter to Thomas Pelham, a M.P.
who had visited the Duke's headquarters during the previous
campaign. Evidently York, judging by bitter experience
guessed that malicious and garbled accounts of his action would
filter to England, and therefore resolved to get his own word.in
first. The letter is also a good example of that clear, well-
arranged exposition which characterized the Duke's letters.

'For some time, I am sorry to say, the British troops under
my command have committed various outrageous acts of
murder, robbery and plunder, against the poor and *well
inclined* people of this country, in spite of every effort of mine
to prevent it. About a week ago one unfortunate peasant was
robbed and murdered by a man of the 14th Regiment of Foot.
I had him tried by general court martial, who found him
guilty but sentenced him only to a corporal punishment.
Though this sentence is not published, because I would not
confirm it and have sent it to be laid before His Majesty, yet
the soldiers immediately suspected that I would (?) and therefore became more daring. On Tuesday after the regiment was
ordered to march the next morning, two men of the same regiment went to a farmhouse, forced the door open, robbed the
poor unfortunate woman of everything she possessed, and since
she had only two crowns in money they shot her and likewise
her child, who was about four years old. They were immediately
taken and confessed their crime. General Abercromby was
directly here and reported the circumstance himself. There was
no time before the Regiment to assemble a court martial, nor
would it have been possible to have brought the necessary witnesses after the Regiment. . . .'[1]

The next extract takes the form of an official letter from the
Adjutant-General to General Abercromby. 'His Royal Highness has received with the deepest impression of concern your
report. . . . His Royal Highness has directed me, Sir, to order

[1] *Add. MSS.*, 33, p. 133.

that you do give immediate directions for assembling such part of your brigade as you can conveniently get together in the time, particularly the 14th Regiment, and that you do cause both the persons to be executed by hanging them till dead, before sunset this evening, if this order arrives in time, for that purpose, if not before your brigade marches tomorrow morning.'[1]

The final extract is from a special order which the Duke issued next day.

'Famars, April 10, 1794.

'His Royal Highness the Commander in Chief earnestly requests that the General and Field Officers, Captains and Officers commanding companies, will take pains to explain to the men of the army under their command the following order, addressed in particular to the *private* men of the army.

'His Royal Highness feels it to be unnecessary that he should seek for any other than the plainest and most direct language, to convey to them the sentiments under the impression of which it was dictated.

'His Royal Highness therefore announces his full determination to exert every effort of severity and rigour to put a stop to the scenes of plunder and outrage of which so many instances have lately occurred, to the dishonour of the British Army.

'Major General Abercrombie reported yesterday to His Royal Highness, that two men of the fourteenth regiment had, during the preceding evening, attempted to rob the house of a country man, that in the course of the attempt they had murdered the woman of the house, and that a child had also been so much wounded that there were little hopes of its living.

'His Royal Highness leaves it to those among the class of his brother soldiers, whom he now addresses, and in whose minds there exist those principles of honour and integrity which can alone render them worthy the appeal, and which he trusts and believes is by far the greater number of them, to judge of the feelings which must have forced themselves upon his mind at receiving a report of an act so atrocious and inhuman in its nature, and so well calculated to cast the most injurious stigma on the national character in general, and that of the army under his immediate command in particular.

[1] *Add. MSS.*, 33, 133, f. 8.

'His Royal Highness is persuaded that there can be but one sentiment of detestation and horror upon the occasion, and he relies so much upon this conviction, that he forbears, as unnecessary, to make further observations upon it.

'His Royal Highness feels himself called upon by every tie of justice, humanity and duty, to punish by a single act of severity, the perpetrators of so horrid a fact. Under this impression he did not hesitate a moment to order the provost to proceed to the spot, and by instant execution of the offenders to make atonement to the violated laws of God and man, and endeavour by that terror, which he is convinced can alone have any effect upon minds lost to every feeling of religion, humanity, and honour, to put a stop to a conduct, of which too many instances have lately occurred, to leave His Royal Highness any doubt of the necessity of an immediate and rigorous interference.

'His Royal Highness trusts the army will do him the justice to believe that it was not without the utmost regret and concern, that he thus gave way to the necessity which urged him to doom two of his fellow creatures to so awful a fate, which they indeed too well merited.

'It was the future advantage of the army, and the hope that such an act of severity would render a repetition of it unnecessary, which alone actuated His Royal Highness to depart from the ordinary proceedings of justice. He most earnestly and ardently prays that it may have the effect which he had in view; at the same time he repeats his full determination, to persist in the exercise of the most rigorous means in the discharge of the duty which he owes to God, to his King, and to his Country, and to the Brave and Good of the Army, which it will be his pride to command, only, while by its conduct, it may merit the general approbation of our country, as much as he is sure it will at all times by its courage.'

This 'disciplinary order', as Corporal Brown calls it, coming on top of the execution, achieved its purpose: the Duke had the satisfaction of reporting to the King that there had been no further trouble, and this is corroborated by Captain Jones, who in his *British Campaign on the Continent* writes: 'This order was of the greatest importance to the army, and the immediate execution of these unfortunate men put a total stop to plundering.'[1]

[1] Op. cit., p. 8.

Comment seems unnecessary. We see here a happy blend of prompt and courageous action (the Duke was technically exceeding his powers), firm determination, combined with a skilful and tactful appeal to the better nature of the troops. It could hardly have been bettered. York undoubtedly penned the order with his own hand.

Meanwhile the French evidently considered the presence of the Duke of York was a hindrance to the success of their cause, for they hatched a plot to remove him. Dundas warned him of it, enclosing a French paper which said: 'Coute que coute, on tentera d'enlever le duc d'York; il y a 150 hommes choisi pour cet effet.' This plot came to nothing.

On 15 April the Emperor of Austria arrived at the head-quarters of the Allied army at Valenciennes, and the scene was set for the opening of the decisive campaign of the war.

THE 1794 CAMPAIGN IN FLANDERS

6

At the opening of the campaign of 1794 the two contestants in Flanders were approximately equal, the French being very very slightly superior in numbers. But their respective plans were strikingly different, and looked like producing an extremely interesting strategical situation. For whereas the Allies were massing in their centre for a blow towards Paris, the French were massing on their two wings – only a small holding force being in the centre – with the object of turning the Allies' two wings. Thus each side was in a sense playing into its adversary's hands: the Allies by making the French envelopment all the easier; the French by denuding their centre, the point where the Allies intended to attack. A quick decision one way or the other might very reasonably be expected.

But it is seldom that affairs in war pan out as they are planned. The first thing that modified the Allies' plan was that, realizing how the enemy was massing on their flanks, they did not dare to attempt a big penetration in the centre, lest they should have their communications cut. They therefore confined themselves to besieging Landrecies. The French, on the other hand, did not time their two attacks to take place simultaneously – an essential step when operating on exterior lines. An attempt was first made by the left wing, but was half-hearted and was easily repulsed by the Austrians.

After a series of conferences had been held at Allied headquarters at Valenciennes the Emperor himself arrived to take supreme command, on 15 April. Next day he held a grand review of his army on the ridge by Montay, a mile north of Le Cateau.[1]

The dumpy, swarthy figure of the Emperor did not impress the British troops, but the review served its purpose: it was in

[1] See sketch map No. 5.   It was on this ridge that the British artillery did such execution on the German infantry at the battle of Le Cateau, just 120 years later.

reality a blind – a means of concentrating the army at the decisive point without creating suspicion. Mack's handiwork can
be detected here, I think.

An Officer of the Guards' 'miserable doggerel' is worth
quoting here:

> 'Of diminutive stature, eyes sunk in his head,
> Resembling a Mercury moulded in lead,
> With swarthy complexion and pitiful mien
> Judge, beside him, to how much advantage was seen
> With the form of a hero and strength of roast beef,
> Great Frederick! our noble Commander-in-Chief!'

The French were holding a thinnish cordon running east to
west about six miles south of Landrecies – the fortress next to
be besieged. Coburg therefore set up his headquarters at Le
Cateau, whence he issued orders for a general attack upon this
line. Five columns were detailed for the actual attack, the three
eastern ones being Austrian; the fourth, under the Duke of
York was directed on Vaux, six miles south of Le Cateau; the
sixth, under Sir William Erskine against Prémont, five miles
still farther west. On the capture of their objectives the columns
were to halt.

Fortescue waxes scornful about this operation, and indeed,
as an attempt to strike the enemy a hard blow it must be held
to be extremely feeble. But, to do him justice, the Emperor was
not at the moment concerned with defeating the enemy in the
field, but merely with sweeping clear an area sufficiently wide
to enable him to proceed to the siege of Landrecies without fear
of interference. In fact, it was a 'limited objective', undertaken
for a specific purpose, of which there are plenty of examples in
later times. We may condemn his strategy, but not, I think, his
tactics in this instance. At any rate, he achieved the object he
had set himself: the enemy was taken by surprise and driven
back everywhere without much trouble.

BATTLE OF VAUX

The battle took place the very day after the review, that is on
17 April. Erskine's column of British troops advanced up the
road from Le Cateau to Reumont (crossing the position where
our Fifth Division earned fame at the battle of Le Cateau, and

ascending the road down which the gun limbers thundered to the rescue of their guns in that notable battle). Prémont fell quickly, and Erskine swung to his left to co-operate with the Duke's column. Meanwhile the latter advanced south, by St Souplet, till it encountered the French in position on the ridge just to the north of the little village of Vaux (now known as Vaux-Andigny).[1] Let the Duke tell the story in his own words:

'Having examined the enemy's position, and finding it very strong, I determined to endeavour to turn it by their right, and for this purpose, ordered the whole of the column to move forward under cover of the high ground, leaving only a sufficient quantity of cavalry upon the heights to occupy the enemy's attention. Strong batteries were likewise formed, which kept up a severe fire and protected the movement very considerably.

'As soon as the troops had gained sufficiently the enemy's flanks the advanced guard, under the command of Major-General Abercromby, was directed to begin the attack.' (These troops stormed the Star Redoubt, above the village of Vaux, and the Austrians took the woods on the right. The enemy was put to flight.) 'I immediately detached a party of the cavalry round the wood to the right, who completely succeeded in cutting them off, took four pieces of cannon and one howitzer.' Other cavalry pursued the enemy into Bohain, four miles beyond Vaux.

The Duke ended his dispatch in the customary way – mentioning the names of his chief generals; but he adds one name to the distinguished list – that of a humble subaltern, Lieutenant Fead (he wrote Fage, but he misheard the name). Thereby hangs a tale.

There are certain unusual features about this interesting action (to which Fortescue devotes a single sentence). Notice first that the Duke starts off in the orthodox fashion: as soon as the advanced guard is held up he goes forward and makes a personal reconnaissance. Here he apparently spots two things: first, the hostile right flank rests 'in the air'; second, the lie of the ground is such that he can initiate an outflanking movement under cover. Such had not been the case at Famars, nor at Caesar's Camp. In the first case the French had benefited

[1] Sketch map No. 5.

by this to strengthen their flank defence; in the second case, to evacuate their position in time. Profiting by his past experience and utilising his 'eye for country', York was able this time to surprise the enemy. But he did it in a peculiar way. The natural and normal method would be to hold the enemy in front with infantry, while the cavalry made the turning movement. But he reversed the process. Such a procedure is very rare in battle. It is true that Sir Ralph Hopton did it successfully at Lansdown in 1643, but I can think of no intermediate example. Finally he rounded off the action by a cavalry pursuit quite 'according to Cocker'; the only unsatisfactory feature being that they did not obtain effective contact with Erskine's column, five miles away on their right.

Notice also the co-operation rendered by the artillery, thus making the action essentially one of all arms.

And mention of the artillery brings us to this matter of 'Lieutenant Fage'. The explanation of the inclusion of this name is that the Duke had himself witnessed the very fine performance of a Gunner subaltern with two heavy guns, and had inquired his name. Mistaking Fead for Fage in the noise of the engagement, he has sent Fead down to posterity under a false name. But he did more than 'mention' him in his dispatch. He did a very imaginative thing; he ordered Fead's section to parade before his whole army next morning, as a token of his admiration of its good work. Thus did the British Commander foster morale in his army.[1]

The battle was over, and the Duke established his headquarters in a house in the village of Vaux for the night. But some unruly Austrian troops looted and set fire to the village, from which the inhabitants had fled, and the Duke had to seek safety out in the open. That night there was a deluge of rain, and for part of the time he took shelter in a windmill.[2] Next day, as the Emperor had ordered that there should be no pursuit, the Duke returned to Le Cateau. The misbehaviour of the

---

[1] See Note B on the Battlefield at the end of this chapter.

[2] The ruined windmill 1,000 yards north-east of the village is the probable one. The detailed description in the spirited poem of the 'Officer of the Guards' is well worth reading. The remainder of the night he spent in a redoubt, no doubt the one near the windmill, for an officer writes to *The Times* a few days later: 'The Duke of York himself, being burnt out of the village, passed one night with General Fox, Colonel Craig and some others in a redoubt taken from the French.' Characteristically, the Duke did not tell the King.

Austrians was widespread. The Emperor himself confessed to the Duke that he had seen 'thirteen villages on fire at once – set on fire by his own troops'.[1]

*   *   *   *   *

The Allies now proceeded to the investment of Landrecies in earnest. The British contingent formed part of the covering force, and held the Le Cateau sector, which ran from a few miles south of that town to Beaumont, six miles north-west, on the Cambrai road. (Thus their position crossed at right angles that of the Fifth Division at the 1914 battle.)

The investment of Landrecies by the Allies had a big effect upon the strategical plan of General Pichegru. Instead of proceeding resolutely to carry it out, massing every available man on the two flanks, he began to reinforce his centre, partly because he was nervous for the safety of Paris and partly in order to relieve the fortress of Landrecies. Thus a good deal of inconsequential fighting took place in that neighbourhood during the latter half of April. Most of it does not affect our story, but on the 24th a cavalry action was fought at Villers en Cauchies (ten miles north-west of Le Cateau) which demanded the Duke's close attention. It was a brilliant affair – especially on the part of that marvellous regiment, the 15th Light Dragoons – but unfortunately it was marred in its closing stages by the failure of General Mansell's cavalry brigade to render support. The matter is still obscure; probably Fortescue's conjectural solution is correct, though it may have been purely due to the miscarriage of an order. At all events, it made an unpleasant impression on General Otto, who was in command, and he duly informed the Duke. Now, it happened that Craig had noticed some inefficiency (we are not given details) on the part of Mansell at the battle of Vaux; the story also spread rapidly through the army that Mansell's cavalry had mis-behaved. It was therefore incumbent on the Duke to investigate the matter, and if necessary to get rid of Mansell. He therefore rode over to see and consult with Otto next day, the 25th. Mrs Harcourt relates that 'the Duke was angry and talked of an inquiry'. No doubt he was angry; there was not only the problem of what to do with the General, but how to restore the

[1] These fires were seen by Mrs Harcourt at Condé, nearly thirty miles away.

morale of his troops, which had been lowered by the affair. We shall see very shortly how he tackled this problem.

*   *   *   *   *

BATTLE OF BEAUMONT

Early next morning, April 26 – the same day of the month as a battle fought on the same ground just 120 years later – a thick fog lay on the ground. All was quiet and peaceful in the British lines, which were strung out along the ridge running south and facing Inchy, Troisvilles, and Bertry.[1] Suddenly there was a splutter of musketry from the front, the outposts began falling back in some confusion into the village of Troisvilles, and out of the fog loomed several immense French columns. Slowly and clumsily they deployed, whilst the alarm spread rapidly through the British post. The infantry took up their battle posts, the guns came into action, and 'boots and saddles' sounded in the cavalry lines.

At the first warning the Duke of York came galloping out of Le Cateau up to the top of the ridge between that place and Troisvilles. Here, as the fog lifted, he took up his position on the ridge-top – according to one account, in Redoubt No. 1, at the highest point on the ridge; according to another account, in a windmill on the same ridge. In all probability both accounts are true of some period in the battle, for it lasted for some hours. Presently he was joined by General Otto, and together they narrowly scanned the hostile movements and dispositions, the Duke lending the Hanoverian his own telescope for the purpose. One or other of them (Otto claims that it was he) spotted that the French left was 'in the air'.[2] As the Duke had made just such a discovery in the action of ten days previously, it is likely that he did so again. All he commits himself to in his dispatch is: 'These movements being now plainly seen, and their left appearing to be unprotected, I determined to detach the cavalry. . . .' But the Duke was always reticent about his own movements and exploits, as we have seen at Caesar's Camp. It is probably right to say that while Otto delivered the blow that was now to be struck, York

[1] Sketch map No. 5.
[2] The panorama, drawn from approximately the Duke's command post, shows the exposed left flank of the French army (See Note C).

planned it; just as at Salamanca 'Ned' Packenham delivered the blow, but it was Wellington who planned it.

Be that as it may, Otto was entrusted with the task of leading a huge force of eighteen British and Austrian squadrons round the hostile left flank, with a view to rolling up their line.

But before they moved off the Duke had a task to perform. The chief British contingent consisted of Mansell's Brigade, that same brigade and that same commander in whom the Duke had momentarily lost confidence. Whilst therefore they were forming up York left his command post and rode up to their head. Here he addressed a few stern but stirring words to their officers. 'Gentlemen, you must repair the disgrace of the 24th!' he exclaimed. 'I am confident you will regain my good opinion of you.' His words evidently sank home, both on the commander and on his subordinates; for the brigade surpassed itself that day.

Meanwhile the Duke was repeating the tactics that had proved so successful at Vaux. Whilst the turning force was marshalling and manœuvring, he ordered the artillery, ably commanded by Colonel Congreve, to keep up a heavy fire to to the front, in order to draw the enemy's attention to that part of the line. To add to the deception, shortly before he judged the cavalry blow would be struck, and in order to add to its effect, he ordered his light troops in front of Troisvilles to fall back through the village. This was successfully carried out, and the French infantry began to follow up triumphantly.

We often hear of feints of this sort in battle – notably at Hastings – but there is reason to believe that they have very seldom been successfully carried out. But this, on the testimony of a French authority,[1] was successful. Moreover, a further demonstration was made by light troops on the opposite (southern) flank for the same purpose of misleading the enemy. The Commander-in-Chief had now done all he could to further his design; he had merely to wait with as much patience as he could summon up for the *dénouement*.

In this calm before the storm we will take a brief glance into the French lines. A general attack had been ordered for that day, for the relief of Landrecies. The portion of it with which we are concerned debouched from Cambrai in three columns.

[1] *Coutancea*, II, p. 426.

I

The northern one, heading east, did nothing of note. The second, nearly 30,000 strong, under General Chappuis, advanced straight down the *chaussée* towards Le Cateau, whilst the third, 4,000 strong, marched parallel and two miles farther south, through Ligny. It then closed in to its left and joined the battle near Troisvilles. For about two hours the French manœuvred feebly in front of the British position, whilst the storm was brewing.

Meanwhile Otto was leading his cavalry round to the north, hidden by convenient folds in the ground, till he reached a hollow about half a mile west of Beaumont and just north of the main Cambrai *chaussée*.[1] At the last moment Chappuis spotted this movement and hurried two battalions and a few guns to his left to ward off the blow.

As well might he have tried to turn back the oncoming sea. The avalanche of mounted men descended upon him and his doomed army. It was swept through and through from left to right and the whole force as one man took to flight. The English cavalry surpassed themselves, and none better than the Mansell's Brigade. That unfortunate man fell, under almost as disputed circumstances as those in which he had fought two days before. All that is known for certain is that he was killed, and it is generally surmised that he practically committed suicide, plunging alone into the hostile ranks. But this is by no means certain. He at any rate survived the first charge and was later engaged in the French rear near the village of Ligny. Accounts of his death are also conflicting. He is variously described as being killed by grapeshot, struck down by three wounds, lying in a ditch with his throat cut – in a state of complete nudity,[2] while, according to Mrs Harcourt, 'A cannon ball carried off half his head'.[3]

Chappuis was captured, while his army streamed away to the rear and did not stop till it was once more safe in Cambrai. So ended what Fortescue calls 'the greatest day in the annals of the British horse'.

It was also a great day in the annals of the British commander. For he had fought the battle, as far as I can judge from all available evidence, impeccably. Consider the situation which greeted him that morning. Thanks to the fog, a great French

[1] I agree with Fortescue's siting.   [2] *Combermere*, I, p. 36.   [3] *Harcourt*, V, p. 430.

concentration had been carried out opposite his unsuspecting lines, and a great surprise had been achieved. Such a thing is, of course, not unusual in war, but what is unusual is that an army attacked by surprise should not only ward off the danger, but revert to the counter-offensive so speedily, so thoroughly and so successfully. The tables were turned with a vengeance, and in an almost unprecedented manner. The very extent of the victory deprived the infantry from playing more than a passive part in it; the horsemen had done their job so well that there was nothing left for the footmen to do. This fact forestalls the only possible criticism, namely that the Duke did not make use of his infantry arm. But I have not heard this charge explicitly made and there is no substance in it.

The Duke wrote from the field of battle that evening an exultant letter for communication to his Sovereign, strikingly reminiscent of that written by Marlborough on the field of a still more notable victory.

'Heights above Cateau,
'April 26, 1794.

'Sir,

'It is from the field of battle that I have the satisfaction to acquaint you, for His Majesty's information, with the glorious success which the army under my command have had this day. . . . The enemy's general Chappuis is taken prisoner and we are masters of 35 pieces of the enemy's cannon. . . .

'I shall not fail to send you a [? full] account at the first opportunity.'

In his letter to the King we get these interesting particulars:

'As soon as I determined to detach the Cavalry of the Right wing to turn the Enemy's Flank, I rode up to the head of these three Regiments [Blues, 3rd D.G.s, Royals] and told them that I had every reason to be displeased with their conduct two days before, but that they would now have an opportunity of regaining their credit, and that I trusted that they would that day behave in such a manner as to regain my good opinion. When the affair was over I went to each Regiment to return them My thanks for their conduct. Upon that a man of the Blues called out to me, We shall ever behave well, when we are well led on.

'With regard to poor General Mansel, I hardly know what to

think of his death. When the cavalry began to move I saw him at the head of his Brigade. I understand that he told his son, who was His Aide de Camp and a Captain in the 3rd Dragoon Guards, to join his regiment and not to come near him for the rest of the day. From that time he disappeared, so much so that upon some order being brought he was looked for and not being to be found, Colonel Vyse who was in the second Line was obliged to leave his own Brigade and to take the Command of the two Brigades of British. Some time after the affair was over his body was found by some of the Skirmishers considerably in front of the main body of the Cavalry with a musket shot through the breast and the throat cut. His epaulets were cut off and his pockets rifled. His son likewise who was a very fine lad is missing and no tidings whatsoever have been heard of Him.'[1]

The Duke published an order to his army in which he declared: 'His Royal Highness has at all times had the highest confidence in the courage of the British troops in general, and he trusts that the cavalry will now be convinced that whenever they attack with the firmness and order which they showed upon this occasion no [possible] number of the enemy can resist them.'

The Duke was generous in his praise of the British cavalry. Writing to the Prince of Wales, he declared that 'the Light Dragoons are really the astonishment of everybody, and all the foreigners allow that they had no idea of such a Corps'.[2]

But perhaps the best tribute comes from a French military historian (incidentally the one who has made easily the best study of this battle): 'The decisive day of the campaign: it shows an army, immobilized in front of a fortress, being out-manœuvred and turned by an active and enterprizing enemy, propelled by the invincible spirit of the offensive.'[3]

Thus was fought this strangely neglected battle. If Wellington defeated forty thousand Frenchmen in forty minutes at Sala-manca, it can be said with equal exactitude that York defeated thirty thousand Frenchmen in thirty minutes on the plains of Le Cateau.

This was a brilliant opening to the new campaign, and the British Commander basked in the sunshine of general approval.

[1] *Windsor*, 28.4.94. [2] Ibid., 5.5.94. [3] *Coutanceau*, II, p. 409.

'The Duke is well,' wrote Mrs Harcourt, 'and grows deservedly more popular every day.'[1]

*   *   *   *   *

What added to the success of the battle was that on Chappuis were captured Pichegru's orders for the campaign. These showed clearly that the main blow was to be delivered on the extreme northern flank. Fortunately Landrecies fell on April 29th, thus making the British army available to go to the help of Clerfait in the north. York announced his instructions thus: 'In consequence [of the fall of Landrecies] the Emperor has desired me to march this evening to St Amand and if necessary to Tournai, to the assistance of General Clairfait.'[2]

The army took three days to reach Tournai, averaging fourteen miles a day. Delay was caused both by bad weather and by the fact, noted before, that the Austrians would not allow the British troops to pass through the towns of Valenciennes and St Amand. 'An Officer of the Guards' draws a harrowing picture both by pen and brush of the plight into which the column was reduced as a result of this obstructionism.

'Our troops were compelled the *chaussée* to forsake
Malgré eux, to a miry deep road to betake.
Where the cannon so frequently stuck in the mud,
That night having harnessed her ebony stud,
O'ertook us, and frowning at this our intrusion,
Determined to throw us in horrid confusion.

Here a batt-horse was seen in the mud-holes to flounder,
There, with all its etceteras, a prostrate nine-pounder.
With soldiers and waggons the ditches were crammed,
With long-tailed troupees all the waters were damned.

Perceiving it totally fruitless and vain
To proceed midst the storm and the deluge of rain
Through the scattered mixed ranks it was soon understood
Each, dispersing, should shift for himself as he could.'[3]

Nevertheless, the army won through. Starting about midnight, and marching without a break, they covered a good

[1] *Harcourt*, V, p. 430.   [2] *W.O.*, I, 168, f. 821.   [3] *An Officer of the Guards*, II, p. 36.

eighteen miles to Famars, where they halted from 2 p.m. for
three hours. And then on once more, to meet the unpleasant
experience described above. The detour round Valenciennes
was about five miles. On the whole, therefore, they did well to
reach Tournai on 3 May.

Bad news greeted them. Pichegru had launched his long-
prepared attack in the north on 29 April; it extended from the
sea to the south of Menin. For the third time Menin was the
main target; for the third time it and Courtrai fell easily into
French hands; for the third time the French formed a great
salient on the axis Menin-Courtrai, and for the third time they
then obligingly sat down waiting for their opponents to mass
for a counter-attack.

But General Clerfait, after suffering defeat on the 29th at
Mouscron,[1] was almost as indecisive as his Gallic opponent;
indeed, it would be difficult to match two such uninspiring
generals pitted against one another.

For a week, then, there was practical stagnation on both
sides. By this time, if not earlier, the Duke of York had sized up
his Austrian colleague. On 6 May, he unburdened himself of
his feelings to the King. He had, he said, tried in vain to urge
Clerfait to action. The Austrian General wobbled painfully
and irresolutely. 'Having remonstrated with him', wrote the
Duke, 'on this change of sentiment, as much as possible, without
effect, I thought myself obliged to send our whole correspondence to the Emperor, who had sent him a peremptory order to
advance. No man on earth has more personal courage than
General Clerfait, but unfortunately his lack of resolution and
decision as a general is beyond all description and was the real
cause of the check which he received on the 29th.'[2]

BATTLE OF WILLEMS

On 10 May Pichegru at last resumed his offensive, attacking
between Courtrai and Tournai. The latter sector was held by
the British army, and an interesting battle developed. Bonnaud,
the French commander, advanced from Lille on Tournai with
30,000 troops. The clash took place midway between the two
cities, the main action being just to the south of the Lille road.

[1] Frequently mispelled Moucron in contemporary accounts.
[2] *Windsor*, 6.5.94.

At the outset the French captured the villages of Baisieux and Camphin, and were then brought to a halt. The Duke of York then, as so often before, made a close survey of the hostile line, assisted no doubt by that telescope of his. His keen eye spotted once more that the flank of the enemy was 'in the air'. Having located it, he arranged for it to be turned by a strong force of cavalry under the command of General Harcourt. Swinging round the French right flank, Harcourt wheeled to the north, and charged some squares of French infantry. Hitherto, such an operation against French revolutionary troops had always been successful, but this time, according to Stapleton Cotton (who provides much the most detailed account of the episode), though charged by nine regiments in succession, the infantry held fast. It was not till some guns were brought up that they broke.

However, the cavalry continued to make progress, and when they had almost reached the Lille road, the Duke, who had been waiting for the moment, unleashed a force of British infantry in a well-timed frontal attack. The French gave ground, and the battle swayed, surprizingly, in a northern direction; it eventually centred round the village of Willems (from which the battle takes its name). Meanwhile the Duke was urging forward his artillery, which ultimately came into action just south of Willems. The combined pressure of all arms thus directed upon them was too much for the French; they wavered and fled, hotly pursued by the British cavalry. 'The whole of Bonnaud's division recoiled in disorder to its point of departure,' writes a French historian.[1]

The French left thirteen guns and over 400 prisoners in our hands. Thirty thousand men had been decisively defeated by a very much smaller force; the victory was complete.

The dominating part played by the Duke in this battle speaks for itself. His tactical handling of it is beyond criticism. But he was modest about it; so delighted was he with Harcourt's skilful and vigorous leadership of the cavalry that in thanking him for it he presented him with his own sword. The Duke was unconventional and imaginative in the form of his awards, and recognition of meritorious service.

On the morrow of the battle the French again attacked

[1] *Coutanceau*, II, p. 224.

Clerfait, who had crossed to the north side of the river Lys, and drove him still further north, to Thielt, fifteen miles north of Courtrai. The Duke's observation on this to the King was: 'It was very much against my opinion that he undertook to cross the Lys with his whole corps in order to attack the enemy, as I was afraid, knowing his character, that he would never bring himself to act offensively, and unluckily I have been but too right in my conjecture.'[1]

After this, we can have no illusions as to the Duke's opinion of the Austrian Commander in Flanders. In the same letter York expresses his dissatisfaction with the Austrian conception of defence on the 'cordon' system, whereby the whole army was to be strung out in one thin long line of defence. The Duke, in company with all modern strategists, was in favour of concentrating the bulk of the army in strategical centres. It was at the bottom the same controversy that raged between Rundstedt and Rommel in Normandy in 1944.

'Tournai, 13 May, 1794.

'I humbly agree with Your Majesty that the system of Cordons, into which the Austrians have fallen ever since the beginning of this War is exceedingly pernicious as well as dangerous and has been the real origin of all the misfortune to which they have been subject.

'With regard to what Your Majesty is pleased to mention of General Clerfait having divided the Hannoverian troops so much that they in many places had no officers of their own at all. I shall take great care to inquire into it as it is very shameful of him, though I may venture to say privately to Your Majesty that the very high opinion the Austrians have of their own troops, and the sovereign contempt with which they speak of the others can not but make me believe that this story is true.

'I cannot help mentioning to Your Majesty how exceedingly well Ernest behaved on Saturday when he was left to cover the rear of the whole Column of Hannoverians when they retreated from their position at Coyghem. He was unfortunately forgot and was compleatly surrounded and however made his way with the whole Corps consisting of one Batallion of Hannoverian Guards and his own Regiment of Horse back to the

[1] *Windsor*, 6.5.94.

Main Corps. He has had the misfortune to have his arm hurt by the wind of (a) cannon ball which has swelled it very much.'[1]

BATTLE OF TOURCOING

It had now become clear to the British Commander-in-Chief that Pichegru, even though his methods were feeble, meant business in the north, and that the Allied forces were perilously weak in this theatre. He therefore wrote to the Emperor urging him to reinforce this sector, more especially as the strategical position into which Pichegru had got his army presented favourable possibilities. For the French were now sitting in a pronounced salient on a base about fifteen miles wide from Tourcoing to Messines, and fifteen miles deep.

After some hesitation, the Emperor decided to march north in accordance with the Duke's desire. But York was impatient, and without waiting to see what response his request might have, he resolved to attack on his own account. If he could induce Clerfait to co-operate, the strategical situation would be most favourable, for the Allies would then be enabled to operate on exterior lines against the French salient. We have already noted the Duke's predilection for such an operation. But Clerfait was not under his command; York could but plead. So he sent one of his most trusted staff officers, Major Calvert, to Clerfait, to inform him that he intended attacking on the 15th, and suggesting that he should co-operate. Unfortunately Calvert was so busy the next few days that he omitted to relate what passed between him and Clerfait. But the upshot can be given in the Duke's own words, writing on 16 May:

'To my great surprize I was awakened in the middle of the night before last, with the intelligence of the Emperor's march and that his army would be at St Amand in the morning [15th].

[1] Prince Ernest's own account to his brother, the Prince of Wales, makes good reading: 'Sadly have I got wounded, a strong contusion on my left arm occasioned by the wind of a 12 pound shot. My arm is quite dead except the elbow and fingers. When the Pitcher goes daily to the well at last it breaks. So is my arm with me, for three days running I have been in a fire. I had the command of a battalion and two squadrons to strengthen the outposts. They had forgot me, and by God j'etais prez d'etre entouré. However Goodwill and the determined bravery of my lads saved me. All went well till at last I got this contusion, had it been a lice nearer my arm was carried off and I a cripple the rest of my life. The Hanoverians as usual are gone to pot, in three weeks about a thousand are out . . . and among them many a brave officer.' (*Windsor, 28911. N.D.*)

I had before determined to attack the enemy, in spite of the great risk I must have run, yesterday; but upon this information I delayed my march till I had seen the Emperor, who immediately desired me to put it off till his army arrived. It is now determined to make a general attack tomorrow, in five columns. . . . I am also informed, as a great trust, that the whole blow of the campaign is altered, and that, should this attack succeeded it is the Emperor's intention to besiege Lisle.'[1]

The 16th was therefore a day of consultations and planning. The upshot of it all was that a battle was decided upon for the following day. The orders for this attack have never been published in England, so it may be worth while giving copious extracts. They are entitled 'Dispositions for the Attack', and are signed 'Frederick, Commander-in-Chief'; but it is evident that they originate from Mack.

They open in a very modern style, stating clearly the *Intention*. The *Method* is then given in outline, also with admirable clarity. The order then tails off into lengthy and diffuse advice, in quite a different style from the first part. In this, advice is given as to the method of employing the guns: they should be brought well forward in the column, and they should be prepared to use grape at a big range, in order to give support to their own infantry. (This sounds rather like the modern use of shrapnel shell to support troops in the open.) The important paragraphs of the order read as follows:

DISPOSITIONS FOR THE ATTACK

Tournai 16 May, 1794.

The intention of this attack is to act upon the enemy's communications between Lille and Menin and Courtrai, to defeat his armies that he has advanced upon the Lys and to drive him out of Flanders. . . .

CLERFAIT. On the 17th he passes the Lys above Menin, which he masques, and connects himself with the column that is acting on this side of the river.

The combined army will attack the enemy on the 17th in five columns, which must maintain the most uninterrupted connection with each other and must display in their attacks the utmost degree of vigour and resolution.

[1] *Windsor*, 16.5.94.

KINSKI. One battalion and two squadrons are to be further detached towards the right in order to keep up communication with the Duke of York and to cover His Royal Highness's left flank.

ARCHDUKE CHARLES. . . .

The principal part then of those two united columns [Kinski and the Archduke] marches with the greatest expedition towards Tourcoing, endeavouring to join the Duke of York and to assist him in forcing on towards the Lys. . . .

In the rather complicated battle which ensued it is impossible to divorce the part played by the Duke of York from any aspect of the battle. The details must therefore be given and must be grasped by the reader (sketch map 6 refers) if he is to form a just assessment of the Duke's conduct in the affair. The detail of the five columns referred to in the 'Dispositions' must therefore be given.

It will be as well to put them in tabular form. They were numbered in sequence from north to south.

No.	Commander	Strength	Place of Origin	Objective
1.	Bussche	4,000	Espierre	Mouscron
2.	Otto	10,000	Leers	Tourcoing
3.	Duke of York	11,000	Templeuve	Roubaix
4.	Count Kinsky	11,000	Froidmont*	Bouvines
5.	Archduke Charles	15,000	St Amand	Pont-à-Marque
	Clerfait	16,000	Thielt	Wervicq

* 3 miles S.W. of Tournai

Who was the originator of this plan? The matter is somewhat obscure, and the Duke's private letters to the King throw little light on the question. But it seems safe to accept the opinion of the accomplished French military historian, Colonel Coutanceau. Here is his verdict: 'The plan was the Duke of York's. . . . The author of the bold plan which, if it had been properly worked out, might well have punished Pichegru for the grave strategical mistake he had committed in forming a pronounced salient through Menin and Courtrai, was not the Austrian staff, but indeed the Duke of York himself.'[1]

The Duke had, in fact, as early as the 11th sketched out the germ of this plan to Clerfait, wherein he uses the words: 'To

[1] *Coutanceau*, II, p. 257.

envelop the enemy on all sides, and attack him everywhere.'
Note this wording closely. It is of the essence of operations on
exterior lines that the enemy shall be attacked *everywhere*. So
easy to say, but so difficult to do. The extent of the difficulty
the Duke probably did not fully appreciate, though he had
already had two disappointments of that nature.

Now turn to the wording of the 'Dispositions'. Here we find a
subtle difference in concept: the emphasis is upon *cutting the
enemy's communications*; the method of subsequently defeating
him is left completely vague. It is as if Mack imagined that the
threat to the communications would automatically induce the
enemy to quit Flanders. But cutting communications is only
a means to an end: that end, as the Duke of York appreciated,
is to defeat the enemy in battle; and he saw the way to do this –
by attacking him from all sides at once. Thus we see that half
the flavour of the Duke's original conception had been squeezed
out of it. It will be important to bear this point in mind when
we come to the crisis of the battle.

The First Day, 17 May

Clerfait, who should have moved off on the 16th in order to
get into position, was late in starting, and various delays, not all
his fault, occurred. Thus he did not reach Wervicq till the
afternoon of the 17th. Further delay in bridging the Lys
ensued, and only a few battalions were across the river by dawn
on the 18th; he was already twenty-four hours late.

No. 1 column, Bussche, captured Mouscron, but was driven
out again, and retired half-way to his starting-point. No. 2
column, Otto, captured Leers and Tourcoing, but failed to
establish communication with York on his left.

No. 3 column, the Duke of York, found Lannoy occupied by
the enemy. He carried out his usual manœuvre: holding the
enemy in his front with infantry, supported by artillery, he
sent some cavalry round the left flank, and the village was taken
without difficulty. He pushed on to Roubaix, which village
also fell to the Guards. So far so good. But though he sent
several patrols to the right and left, the Duke could get no
definite information about the neighbouring columns. If the
wind was in the prevailing quarter he would not be able to hear
the battle in Tourcoing, and, owing to the flat and enclosed

country, he would not be able to see what was happening on either flank. But if Kinsky was up, the sound of his battle should have been audible. York felt morally certain that Kinsky was *not* up. Nor was there news of Clerfait away in front. Cavalry patrols could find no sign of him. As we have seen, he had not yet reached Wervicq. The Duke therefore decided to hold Roubaix with his advanced guard and Lannoy with his main body, thus 'refusing' his left flank; for that was his dangerous one, Lille being only six miles distant. Orders to this effect had just been issued early in the afternoon when he received the unexpected order from the Emperor (who was following his column) that he was to continue as far as Mouveaux. The Duke tried to protest, but was overruled. Dutifully, therefore, he gave out fresh orders, the advance was resumed, and after another gallant action by the Guards, Mouveaux was taken with the bayonet. Cavalry reached Bondue, two miles farther west.

Before going farther with the narrative, we must consider whether the Duke was justified in protesting at the Emperor's order. In support of the Emperor, it is obvious that the farther the Duke advanced, the nearer he would approach Clerfait's column. If the primary object of the operation was merely to cut the enemy's communication, a continuance of the advance was indicated; and the Emperor's instructions made it clear that the cutting of communications was dominating his mind. But the Duke was, as we have seen, looking farther, and aiming at executing a proper exterior lines operation, i.e. a simultaneous attack by all the columns. Now, if he were to push on blindly at this juncture, without a semblance of any communication or co-operation with any of the other columns, the condition for the battle, as envisaged by him, would not obtain. By thrusting one column forward in advance of the remainder, the Emperor would be offering the enemy an opportunity to defeat the Allies in detail. To the objection that, for all he knew, Clerfait might be up to time and pushing forward rapidly and resolutely, we can put the Duke's correct reading of the character of his Austrian colleague; York had a shrewd suspicion that Clerfait would do no such thing until he was assured of strong support for his attack. But no word had come from him all day, and the Duke wisely 'wrote him off' so far as immediate co-operation was concerned. Moreover, the situation had altered since the issue of orders. York had been assured by Mack personally that he would be supported by Kinsky and the Archduke on his strategic flank; but no support had appeared. To push on blindly was to play the enemy's game, er – to alter the metaphor – to fire the gun at half-cock. I hold, then, that the Duke was amply justified in protesting at being forced forward beyond Roubaix, before his left flank was secured.

The British dispositions for the night were therefore as follows:

At Mouveaux, Guards Brigade.
At Croix (two miles south-west of Roubaix), Fox's English Brigade.
At Roubaix, four Austrian battalions.

The Duke was profoundly uneasy that evening. During the night he appealed to the Emperor to be allowed to withdraw from Mouveaux, but without avail. Obedient to orders, the Duke therefore held his ground. As Craig expressed it, 'His Royal Highness saw clearly the danger and remonstrated against it, but was directed to remain, and immediately determined upon that obedience to which he considered himself bound by his duty'.[1]

The night wore on and though the presence at Tourcoing of some advanced troops of Otto was at length established, still no news came in from the Austrians on the left flank.

We must now leave the Duke, passing a restless night in Roubaix, in order to see what was happening on his left, and also in the enemy's lines. Without going into details nor attempting to justify my conclusions, it must suffice to say that Kinsky had behaved extremely badly. His primary task was clear – to protect the left flank of the British column against an irruption from the direction of Lille. But he made little or no attempt to do this. Partly he was delayed by the Archduke, who, with more reason (for he had a long march to make), was eight hours late in reaching Pont-à-Marque. As a result of all this, no connection was established with the British column, and a gap four miles wide existed between the British and Austrians. Kinsky encamped with his main body near Bouvines, and the Archduke about seven miles south-east of Lille.

[1] *W.O.*, I, 169.

We must now cross into the enemy's camp. Here, the first thing to note is the absence of the French commander. Pichegru seemed to possess a knack of missing the battles in which his troops were engaged; on this occasion he had gone on a visit to the Army of the Ardennes. General Souhan was in temporary command of the *Armée du Nord*. His headquarters were at Coutrai, and he had under his immediate command 50,000 men. His army covered the area Ypres-Rousselare-Courtrai-Tourcoing-Menin. Clefait's 19,000 were to the north of him, and the Austro-British, 25,000 strong, were to the immediate south, reaching as far as Tournai.

When the battle opened he was occupied in pushing Clerfait westwards towards Ypres, but in the middle of this operation he suddenly learnt of the great Allied attack, and quickly sensed the import and importance of it. Hastening to Menin, he held a council of war in the middle of the afternoon, to decide what was to be done. Various plans were discussed; among them one by an anonymous colonel. The plan was bold enough to take his breath away; indeed, it was for the moment received in utter silence. Then Souhan rose and spoke: 'We should require better luck than we have a right to count on in order to save half my division and myself according to the plan that you propose; however, it is none the less the best available, and consequently it must be adopted.'[1]

Without delay he sent out orders to implement the colonel's plan, which we must now describe as Souhan's plan. The Archduke Charles's subsequent comment on this council of war was: 'One of the very rare examples in history where a conference of several persons has arrived at a vigorous resolution conformable to the end in view; it is a tribute to the spirit which at that time animated the generals of the French army.'[2]

What was this bold plan? A study of sketch map 6 will show that upwards of 65,000 Allies were in the act of what was meant to be a converging movement from north, east, and south against Souhan's 40,000.[3] Apart from the disparity in numbers, Souhan's line of retreat to Lille was threatened. By the common dictates of prudence his correct course was to slip out of the noose before it was drawn tight. But the imaginative colonel

[1] *Coutanceau*, II, p. 298.   [2] Ibid., II, p. 299.
[3] The remainder of his army was north of the Lys.

and the cool, courageous general cast their eyes farther afield. In the camp of Sainghin, a dozen miles south of his council chamber at Menin, was a large army of nearly 30,000 men, under the command of General Bonnaud. If co-operation could be secured from him, so far from retreating the prospect was held out of a successful blow against that portion of the Allied army that now lay between the two French armies. This portion, as we have seen, was the columns of Otto and York, 21,000 strong. Against these columns, it should be possible, if Bonnaud would play, to concentrate a force of nearly three to one. Instead of being crushed himself, Souhan would apply the same manœuvre against his nearest adversaries. The Allies would be 'hoist with their own petard': it would be a case of 'exterior lines turned traitor'.

That evening orders sped in all directions, changing the orientation of his numerous columns, and issuing to Bonnaud that all-important order, the non-delivery of which would spell disaster to his whole army. It was the risk that only a great general would face. Souhan faced it.

His messenger successfully eluded hostile intervention during his perilous evening ride: the message was delivered – and Bonnaud complied. The essential paragraph in this vital message ran: 'You must take the enemy in flank during their march and attack them sharply (*vivement*).' Foreseeing that Bonnaud might be fearful of denuding his own right flank facing Tournai during the attack, Souhan adds reassuringly: 'It is not necessary to leave many people in Sainghin Camp, some detachments at the bridges will suffice to prevent the enemy crossing or gaining information of our movements.' Bonnaud, who seems to have been another resolute soldier thrown up by the French Revolution, complied with this order to the letter. Zero hour for each advance was fixed at 3 a.m. on the 18th, and punctually the two armies set off to approach one another.

The Second Day, 18 May

The morning of 18 May dawned, and the first thing the Duke did was to dispatch another request to the Emperor for permission to retract his dangerously isolated position. Mack, however, assured him he would be supported by the Archduke, who, by a

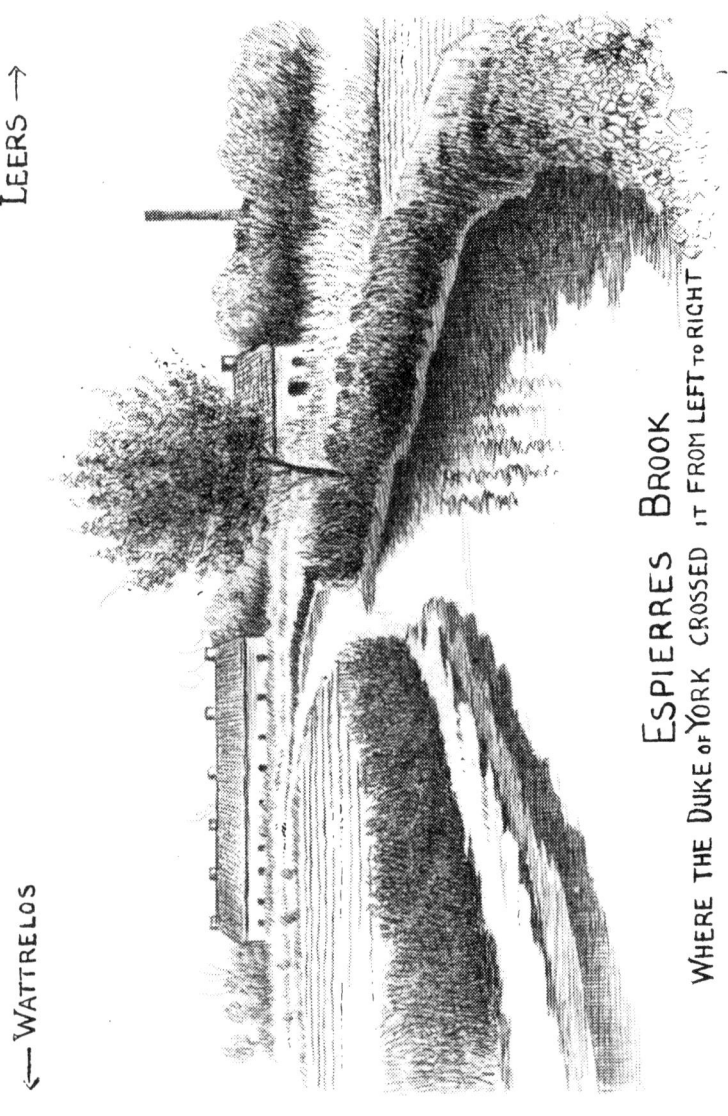

← WATTRELOS

LEERS →

ESPIERRES BROOK

WHERE THE DUKE OF YORK CROSSED IT FROM LEFT TO RIGHT

curious coincidence, had orders to set off for Lannoy at 3 a.m. – the same hour and the same destination as Bonnaud had received. The distance from the Archduke's main body to Lannoy was eleven miles and if the order had been carried out to the letter, no impediments being encountered, the Duke might reckon on seeing the white uniforms of the Imperialists looming out of the morning mist well before 9 a.m. But not a sign of their approach was visible. On the other hand, soon after 6 a.m. firing could be heard from the direction of Tourcoing, which was only lightly held by Otto's advanced troops. These called to the English for help, and the Duke, as was his nature and custom, loyally acceded to the request, in spite of his own obvious peril. He sent two Austrian battalions from his tiny reserve in Roubaix. He instructed them that if they arrived too late they were to return to him. This was followed a little later by a request for cavalry, but none were available. Shortly afterwards, probably 6.30 a.m. (but exact times are always difficult to ascertain in battle), danger threatened from the opposite flank: Bonnaud's attack struck a weak spot in the line and succeeded in penetrating between Mouveaux and Robaix, and into the suburbs of the latter village. In default of precise information, I make no doubt that the Duke had, ere this, taken up a position on the 'heights' (a misnomer for a gentle swell of ground) to the east of Roubaix. From here he could scan the skyline to the south. The area is now built over, so it is difficult to be positive, but Mr Hilaire Belloc says that from there he could see the French tents in their camp of Sainghin. As the distance is eight miles, he would require a very good telescope – which he may indeed have possessed – to pick out much detail, even if there had not been an intervening ridge.[1]

The double threat from the two flanks induced the Duke for the third time to apply to the Emperor for permission to withdraw from Mouveaux.

Next, he tried to organize assistance to the endangered Guards. But his resources were of the slightest. He sent off to recover the two battalions that he had so chivalrously lent to Otto; but in vain. He then set out to visit Abercromby in person, but found his route cut off by the enemy between the two villages. The situation had by now become extremely critical,

[1] See Note D on the battlefield, at the end of this chapter.

K

and, not waiting for a reply from the Emperor (who was still at Templeuve) he took it upon himself to order the Brigade of Guards back to the 'heights' behind Roubaix, and he sent off Craig to cover the retirement of Abercromby's brigade with the Coldstream Regiment. His next attempt was to ride to Fox's 'Little Brigade', near Croix. Again he found a solid wall of enemy blocking his path. What more could he do? Perhaps Otto would now return the compliment and send assistance. He would ride over to see him in person, with that object. Wattrelos, where he was believed to be, was two miles to the east, straight down the road. Off he galloped, and was just entering the village of Wattrelos when he discovered that place also was in the hands of the enemy, who now appeared to be everywhere. Otto had, in fact, abandoned both Tourcoing and Wattrelos and had fallen back on Leers, a further two miles in the direction of Tournai. In that direction York accordingly turned his horse, being fired at from Wattrelos at fifty yards range as he went. Drawing his sword, he galloped on towards Leers. Between the two villages there was a boggy brook (since canalized) called the Espierres brook. Riding full tilt across country, hotly pursued by French cavalry, rendered the more conspicuous by the Star of the Garter on his breast, the Duke was brought up sharply by this obstacle. He thrust spurs into his horse, intending to leap or ford the brook, but his charger reared up, declining to face the water. Retreat was cut off; there was only one thing for it – to dismount and wade across on foot. An undignified but ineluctable predicament. His Royal Highness waded across, accompanied by the faithful Calvert and the anonymous 'Officer of the Guards', to whom this was too good an opportunity to miss.

Thus did he describe the scene:
'We wheeled on a piece, no time to be lost,
And pushed t'wards a river, or ditch, which we crossed.
In the Duke's horse strong symptoms of madness appeared,
For at sight of the water he snorted and reared;
And kicked at the rowels, though often applied,
Till the spurs disappeared, buried deep in each side.
So his rider dismounted and plunged in the tide.
Like a second Leander he beat back the billows
And at length gained dry land by the help of the willows.

The Carmagnols,[1] judging pursuit was in vain,
Like Hell-hounds still eager our lives to obtain,
An eight-pounder planted and levelling well,
Each ball they dispatched from it close to us fell.
For the beautiful Star[2] they would fain have possessed
Which dazzled their eyes on His Highness's breast.'[3]

On the far bank another horse was obtained, some say a pack horse, some (more likely) a spare staff officer's horse. On his new mount York continued his journey without any more exciting adventures, and arriving at Leers, found General Otto in that place. The Duke afterwards frankly admitted that he owed his life to having a speedier horse than his French pursuers.[4]

But even at Leers he was still cut off from the British column, which had by now retreated to Lannoy, and the Duke spent the night with his neighbouring column commander.

Meanwhile the Guards had conducted their retreat with their traditional order and firmness, though not without some harrowing adventures, which do not concern us here. The 'Little Brigade' also came into its own in this battle, and got safely back to Lannoy with surprisingly small losses.

And what of the Austrians? A few words will suffice to chronicle their doings – or rather misdoings. The first setback was that when the Emperor's order for an immediate advance to the support of the English reached the headquarters of the Archduke, he was asleep, having had a fit that evening; and,

---

[1] The French.   [2] The Star of the Garter.
[3] *An Officer of the Guards*, II, p. 49. (See Note D.)
[4] Further interesting details are given by an officer writing to *The Times* a few days later: 'The Duke, accompanied by an Austrian general and two other gentlemen only, reached a village which had been the preceeding evening taken from the enemy . . . supposing it still in the hands of the Allies. They were riding in full gallop when, turning into one of the streets rather sharply they discovered that the village was in the hands of the French, and a column of the enemy facing them. The latter, supposing the Duke was heading a column of troops, at first fled, after firing a volley at them, which killed the Austrian general at the Duke's side. Recovering however from their error the French pursued the Duke and his two companions until they came near a river. The Duke threw himself off his horse and so did another gentleman and waded through the river; the third took the water with his horse. All this was done under the fire of the French who had brought a six-pounder to bear upon them. On the other side of the river the Duke fortunately met a led horse of Captain Murray's . . . The Duke's secretary had his hat shot through, and an orderly sergeant close to the Duke was killed.'

incredible though it sounds, his staff would neither awaken him nor read the order and act on it. Consequently his column made a very late start next day, and did not reach the Lille-Tournai road till 3 p.m., when the battle was over. Kinsky's conduct was even more extraordinary and inexplicable. He remained absolutely stationary from the evening of the 17th till 2 p.m. on the 18th, within five miles of the column which he had explicit orders to approach and support. Nothing was done by the Emperor to urge either of these columns forward, and it is the general opinion of both English and French (though not Austrian) historians that the Duke of York's column was deliberately abandoned to its fate.

Clerfait was almost equally inactive, but his conduct can be explained in a more creditable manner. He was not treacherous, but pusillanimous. The Duke of York had sized him up correctly a few days before: he would take no risks. He advanced with an excess of caution on the morning of the 18th. Even so, he reached Linselles, three miles short of Mouveaux, at 10 a.m., and if he had applied vigorous pressure even at that hour, he would at least have eased the situation of the Guards. The only sign of vigour on this occasion was performed by the 8th Light Dragoons, which had just arrived from England, and were temporarily attached to Clerfait's command. As British historians seem to have ignored the remarkable tribute to this Regiment paid by the French General Vandamme, I will transcribe it. 'At Bousbec the 8th Regiment of English Dragoons charged the infantry with the greatest impetuosity and broke up (*enfonça*) the battalions. They continued to charge with great temerity. They even reached the village of Halluin. They created havoc in the park near this village. The whole of the wagons, supply-vehicles and artillery fled in the greatest disorder along the Lille road'.[1] The 55th Foot also did good work.

It is now clear from Clerfait's inactivity that a big disaster to the British column was only averted by the resolute way in which the Duke had kept his column 'in depth'. If he had advanced his whole army to Mouveaux, or beyond, as the Emperor apparently wished, the whole force would probably have been surrounded and destroyed.

What are we to say of this remarkable battle and of the Duke's

---

[1] *Coutanceau*, II, p. 309.

conduct of it? Undoubtedly it was strategically the most interesting battle fought in either of the two campaigns. It exhibits from both sides the advantages and the difficulties of operations conducted on exterior lines. If successful, they are likely to be very successful. (But for the cool generalship of the Duke and the presence of the British Guards the French success would have been complete.) But it also illustrates the difficulties inherent in such operations. They demand an unusual resolution on the part of the subordinate commanders – the resolution to push forward vigorously 'into the blue'. This is where Souhan and Bonnaud shone, and where Clerfait failed. The Austrian had no communication with the other wing of the Allied army – a normal circumstance in such operations in the days before the invention of the telegraph and radio. This explains why such operations were so seldom successful in olden times; and we can join in the tribute of the Archduke Charles to the French generals.

It might on the surface be supposed that the same criticism should be applied to York as to Clerfait: namely, that he did not continue to push forward. But there was an essential difference. Apart from the fact that York knew his man, and rightly doubted Clerfait's will to push on, the essence of such an operation as he contemplated involved a *simultaneous* attack all along the line: his column was in position, ready to undertake it, but the main column on his left was not yet ready. The right policy was undoubtedly to wait a few hours till all the columns were in line. To attack a possible 28,000 with his own 11,000 in a piecemeal manner would have been unsound and indeed amateurish.

That this was the general opinion of the army we have ample evidence. When the Duke rejoined his troops after his humiliating and mortifying experience he was 'very cordially received'. It was recognized that he had been 'let down' by the Austrians. Colonel Calvert declared that 'my indignation is excited to a pitch I can hardly describe.'[1]

The French observer, Count Langeron, wrote: 'The English complained bitterly of the Austrians and were not wrong in complaining. The Prince of Coburg tried to attribute to them some of his own faults.'[2] Malone, writing to Charlemont ten

---

[1] *Calvert*, p. 217.   [2] *Langeron*, p. 81.

days after the battle, said: 'He (C. J. Fox) had a letter from his
brother, General Fox, dated between the two late actions [i.e.
between 18 and 23 May] and he told us that the Duke of York
before the unsuccessful action had strongly remonstrated with
the Emperor against it and particularly against the part assigned
to him in it. But afterwards, receiving orders, he thought it his
duty to obey. . . .' This third-hand account may be slightly
garbled; but Fox proceeds to make a shrewd and accurate criticism of Mack. 'The plan was General Mack's, and was, as some
of his are said to be, too "fine-spun" and without sufficient
allowance for unavoidable contingencies, for the time was so
nicely calculated that it was almost impossible that six distinct
columns widely dispersed, should be able to act in such complete
unison to the moment prefixed.'[1]

Another Frenchman at the Allied headquarters, Count
d'Arnaudin, was plainly suspicious of the Austrian good faith,
for he remarks prophetically: 'One would say this was the
plain beginning of the plan to abandon the Low Countries.'

Some of these murmurs reached the Austrian Court, and the
Emperor felt it incumbent on him to publish some sort of a
démenti. He therefore circulated an order to the effect that
York's column was in no way to blame for the lack of success
and commissioned Coburg to write a long personal letter to the
exasperated Duke, confirming it. This letter is quite unqualified
in its terms:

'His Majesty has enjoined me to give Your Royal Highness
the most positive assurances that not only is he perfectly satisfied
with the manner, ardent zeal, skill and valour in which Your
Royal Highness, the generals and the brave troops have executed all the movements which successively took place in the
battles of the 17th and 18th, but that he gives, by this letter, a
decided and unequivocal testimony that Your Royal Highness
has not made any manœuvre but what was essential to the
general arrangement, and which Your Royal Highness was not
enjoined to execute by regular messages received during the
whole affair from the Monarch himself.'

It was a handsome *amende honorable*. Moreover, the guilty
conscience of the Emperor seems to shine through every line of
the letter.

[1] *H. M. V. Charlemont*, p. 230.

But the Duke was concerned with something more important than his own *amour-propre* and reputation. The morale of his army seemed likely to be shaken by the late extraordinary proceedings. The troops were asking each other: 'Why? Why?' A general order to the army seemed to be indicated, but the wording of it would prove a delicate matter, for it was almost impossible to belittle the setback and to explain it away without exposing the glaring shortcomings on the part of his Allies. However, the Duke made the attempt:

'In noticing the event of yesterday, His Royal Highness the Commander-in-Chief, finds little to regret but the loss of brave men, which however appears to be less than from the nature of the action might have been expected.

'The proximity of the enemy's garrisons and armies, the want of that complete success in the other parts of the intended operations which would have secured the flanks of our position, and above all the nature of the country so favourable to the kind of attack which the enemy undertook, these will sufficiently account for what has happened, without any imputation on the conduct and bravery of our troops. With them His Royal Highness has every reason to be perfectly satisfied, and he doubts not that the enemy will feel to their cost, on the first occasion that may present itself, to what they owe the advantage that they have had the good fortune to obtain yesterday, over troops as much superior to them in bravery and discipline as is the cause we maintain to that for which they contend. . . .'

In the above order the Duke seems to have steered rather skilfully between Scylla and Charybdis. It is satisfactory to be able to record that, in the opinion of Colonel Craig, 'this affair has not made any impression on the spirits of the men'.

One further task remained – to inform the King and Government. Keenly aware of the advantage of getting in the first word, he took the unusual course of sending his own Adjutant-General home to explain the whole sorry affair *verbally*. Things could be spoken that it would be injudicious to put on paper. Thus we miss the customary candid letter to his father on this occasion.

On the morrow of the battle of Tourcoing the Allies withdrew their lines to a semicircle round Tournai, which city became the headquarters. As the Emperor rode into the town he was received in silence, but the populace loudly cheered the Duke of York. The latter was, however, secretly fuming. He had been badly 'let down', whether intentionally or not, and everyone in both armies was aware of it.

*   *   *   *

The French did not attempt to follow up their success, pending the return of Pichegru, which took place on the 21st. The French Commander-in-Chief thereupon decided on a counter-offensive, which he delivered on the next day – the 22nd. In this battle, generally known as Pont-à-Chin, the French were at first successful all alone the line. The British troops were held in reserve all day, till, on the fall of Pont-à-Chin (four miles north of Tournai), the Emperor called on the Duke for help. The latter sent Fox's 'Little Brigade'. Now, this Brigade had had a very hard time at Tourcoing, where it had distinguished itself in a very marked manner. Still, it was part of a tired and defeated force, and its vigour and morale might well be expected to have suffered. But, whether or not influenced by the Duke's 'pep' talk, it showed no signs of its recent ordeal, but most gallantly dashed at the village, which the French had captured, and ejected them at the point of the bayonet. The French retreated. The Little Brigade had saved the day.

But the Duke was not happy. The reasons for this he gave in detail in his next letter to the King. It is the last letter in the collection preserved at Windsor, and shall be given in full:

'I am sorry to say that ever since the battle [of Tourcoing] there has existed in the Austrian headquarters a degree of pusillanimity and allarm which still continues in spite of the success of yesterday, and which I am afraid will be productive of the very worst consequences. During the whole of the engagement yesterday they were talking of nothing else than of passing the Scheldt, and taking a position before Ath, in order to cover their magazines. I represented to them in the strongest terms I could how shameful such a project would be; but finding that I made no impression on them, I thought it my duty to say that, although I had no orders whatever from Your Majesty on that subject, yet I could not help telling them that England had as yet given them every assistance in her power, but that, as certainly one of the great objects of that assistance was to protect Flanders for the sake of Holland, should his Imperial Majesty choose to give up Flanders without attempting anything for its relief, he must not be astonished if Your Majesty employed those forces which you have in the country for the purposes most advantageous for yourself, and to your Allies the Dutch, without any regard whatever for Him [the Emperor].

'I have reason to believe that what I said had some effect, as this morning the Emperor called a Council of War, in which General Mack, in the Emperor's name, acquainted the general officers that as the victory was so considerable the Emperor had resolved not to abandon Tournai. . . .

'I have another very disagreeable subject to mention to your Majesty which is the very shamefull and insolent manner in which the Austrians behave to all the troops of whatever nation that are in Your Majesty's pay, which has so exasperated them that it is very much to be wished that we might form a separate army without being in the least mixed with the Austrians.

'Knowing of how much consequence it was to keep up a good harmony among the different troops I have done everything in my power to smooth and to keep everything quiet, but really the behaviour of the Austrians is such that it is my duty to represent it. They despise everything which is not their own, they are continually throwing every blame upon Your Majesty's Troops and accusing them of slackness when God knows they are infinitely braver than they are, and at the same time wantonly exposing them upon every occasion. Wherever I am they do not dare to do it, but I have received the strongest complaints on that account from the British, the Hannoverians and the Darmstadters who are now serving under General Clerfayt. I am informed that in the attack which General Clerfayt made upon Lincelles a French battery at a village near them having opened upon an Austrian Column, he had to send to another Column for an Irish and a Hessian Squadron to attack it, while he had in his own Column three Squadrons of Austrians whom he did not dare to employ. These two Squadrons succeeded in taking the battery, but the Irish squadron out of a hundred and forty two men only brought back thirty, and the Hessians Squadron lost seventy men. I therefore cannot help humbly entreating Your Majesty to allow me to form a Separate Army of the Troops in Your pay without the Austrians, and I have no doubt that we shall agree perfectly well together and being animated with the same spirit, we shall be able to be of much more use than we now are.'[1]

This last letter of the Duke's to be preserved is an important and significant one. It marks the turning-point in the campaign, and foreshadows the parting of the ways. Henceforth the Allies were to fall apart, literally and figuratively. York still advocated a forward policy with all his might, but the Emperor had made up his mind: the West had no further attractions for him; the East called. On 29 May he abruptly quitted the army, never to return to it. As a natural consequence Mack also left the army, and his place was taken by Prince Waldeck, an old officer, advanced in years, who also belonged to the 'Eastern school'.

In spite of the setback at Tourcoing, the impasse round Tournai, and the untimely departure of the Emperor and Mack, the Duke was rightly of opinion that the initiative must be regained, and that the Allies in concert must concentrate on expelling the enemy from Flanders. In this he was assured of the complete agreement of both King and Cabinet. Moreover, at a Council of War held on 25 May, the Emperor declared that he accepted the Duke's advice in this matter. Great things were expected from the co-operation of the Prussian army, 62,000 strong, under Marshal Mollendorf, which was already overdue in the field. Lord Cornwallis was dispatched to Mollendorf's headquarters to concert plans after consultation with York *en route*. The Government had been seized with the bright idea of attaching Cornwallis to the Prussian army, in command of a detachment of British troops, in order to ensure that the plans agreed to by the Prussians were actually carried out. Dundas, when informing York of the impending visit, made the broad hint that the Duke should seek the advice of the Marquis: 'Lord Cornwallis's presence will enable Your Royal Highness to have the benefit of his opinion (of which you will naturally be inclined to avail yourself).' But in a further letter, written the same day, Dundas states that Cornwallis will act 'under Your Royal Highness's orders'.[2]

Cornwallis reached the British headquarters on 4 June and

[1] *Windsor*, 23.5.94.   [2] *W.O.*, VI, II, f. 133.

had a series of talks with the Duke. This was, I think, their first
meeting since the old days in Hanover, when the Earl did not
seem to be very taken with the Duke. The result of the consultation is contained in a letter from York to Dundas on 6 June:
'In the various conversations that I had with his Lordship, we
thoroughly agreed in the great advantage which would arise
from the Prussian army being employed in West Flanders, in
preference to every other operation that has been pointed out
for it.'[1]

This plan was undoubtedly sound; it observed the principle
of concentration, and had the additional advantage that the
contiguity of the Prussian to the British army would give us
firmer control over its operations.

The Duke had also been enjoined by the Government to use
his utmost persuasive powers on the Emperor to dissuade him
from leaving the army. As these instructions arrived after the
Emperor's departure, all that York could do was to write him
a letter and entrust it to Cornwallis to deliver. In informing
Dundas of this, the Duke wrote a remarkably discerning letter
on the subject. 'With regard to the real motives which induced
Him to alter his intentions of staying with the army the whole
campaign, it is difficult for me to know them exactly . . . but
from what I could discover in a very long conference which I
had with General Mack before he left the army, as well as in a
subsequent one which I had with the Prince of Waldeck, it
appears to me to have been wholly contrived by M. de Thugut[2]
and General Rollin. . . .

'General Mack acquainted me that the very day before His
Majesty declared his intention of returning to Vienna, he sent
for him (Mack) and ordered him to explain in the presence of
Count Merci[3] and M. de Thugut, the whole of his plan for the
campaign. . . . General Mack added that at this conference
there had been a very warm dispute between M. de Thugut
and himself . . . in which the Emperor agreed with him
thoroughly, and declared with some degree of warmth to M.
de Thugut that he was now convinced from his own knowledge
of what General Mack said, that he had not sufficient troops in

---

[1] *Cornwallis*, II, p. 241.
[2] The Emperor's principal adviser.
[3] The Austrian Minister at Brussels.

this country, and that therefore he meant to bring part of the troops now acting on the Rhine to join him.

'This unexpected declaration of H.I.M. completely silenced M. de Thugut, for the moment, but at the same time showed him that it was not his [Thugut's] interest that the Emperor should continue longer with his army as he was able to judge for himself, and would not listen so implicitly to his advice as he had done till then.'

The Duke then adds: 'What makes me think that this surmise of General Mack may be well founded is that the Prince of Waldeck repeated to me two or three times that there were certainly people who had great weight with the Emperor and who were exceedingly anxious for His Majesty to give up the whole of Flanders. . . . I am likewise credibly informed, though I cannot assert it on my own knowledge, that M. de Thugut has declared openly that he has done everything in his power to persuade the Emperor to give up this country.'[1]

This admirably objective letter lays bare what history was to show to be the true story of the Austrian desertion of its Allies in Flanders. The German historian Sybel concurs in this. 'The Emperor's resolution to sacrifice his Allies and spare his own troops irrevocably turned the fate of the campaign.'[2]

Another disappointment was in store; Cornwallis continued his journey to meet Mollendorf, and with Malmesbury endeavoured to carry out his instructions.

In this he was singularly unsuccessful. The King of Prussia, like the Emperor of Austria, was more concerned with events on his eastern than on his western frontier. Poor Poland was at the root of trouble; she was at that time the 'sick man of Europe', and her three neighbouring powers, Russia, Prussia, and Austria, were, like vultures on a carcass, all intent on getting as large a portion as possible for themselves, and watching with suspicion and jealousy the efforts in a similar direction of their rivals. To Poland, in fact, Revolutionary France should have been grateful for the safety of her own borders during the year 1794. Though Cornwallis assured York that 'nothing shall be wanting on my part to impress him . . .' he left the persuasion to be done by Malmesbury.

[1] *Cornwallis*, II, p. 243.   [2] *Sybel* iii, p. 435.

*   *   *   *   *

During these anxieties and discords the Duke was suddenly confronted with a novel type of problem. The bloodthirsty National Convention issued a ferocious order directed against the English army. Here are some extracts from this extraordinary document:

'England is capable of every outrage on humanity, and of every crime towards the Republic. She attacks the rights of all nations, and threatens to annihilate liberty. How long will you allow to continue on your frontiers the slaves of George – the soldiers of the most atrocious of tyrants? . . .

'When therefore the results of battle shall put in your power either English or Hanoverians, bring to your remembrance the vast tracts of country English slaves have laid waste. . . . Do not trust to their artful language, which is an additional crime, worthy of their perfidious character and Machiavellian government. Those who say they abhor the tyranny of George, say, can they fight for him? No! No! Republican soldiers, therefore, when victory shall put in your power either English or Hanoverians, strike: not one of them must return to the traitorous land of England, or be brought into France. Let the British slaves perish, and Europe be free.'

The reaction of the Duke of York was typical of the man. He immediately penned another order to his army, and such importance did he attach to all his troops becoming fully acquainted with it that he ordered it to be read out 'and explained' at three successive roll-callings.

'His Royal Highness, the Duke of York, thinks it incumbent on him to announce to the British and Hanoverian troops under his command, that the National Convention of France, pursuing their gradation of crimes and horrors, which has distinguished the periods of its government as the most calamitous of any that has yet occurred in the history of the world, has just passed a decree, that their soldiers shall give no quarter to the British or Hanoverian troops. His Royal Highness anticipates the indignation and horror which has naturally arisen in the minds of the brave troops whom he addresses, upon receiving this information. His Royal Highness desires, however, to remind that, that mercy to the vanquished is the brightest gem in a soldier's character, and exhorts them not to suffer their resentment to lead them to any precipitate act of cruelty

on their part, which may sully the reputation they have acquired in the world.

'His Royal Highness believes that it would be difficult for
brave men to conceive that any set of men, who are themselves
exempt from sharing in the dangers of war, should be so base
and cowardly as to seek to aggravate the calamities of it upon
the unfortunate people who are subject to their orders. It was
indeed reserved for the present times, to produce to the world
the proof of the possibility of the existence of such atrocity and
infamy. The pretence for issuing this decree, even if founded in
truth, would justify it only in minds similar to those of the
members of the National Convention. It is, in fact, too absurd
to be noticed, and still less to be refuted. The French must
themselves see through the flimsy artifice of an intended assassi-
nation, by which Robespierre has succeeded in procuring the
military guard, which has at once established him the successor
of the unfortunate Louis, by whatever name he may choose to
dignify his future reign.

'In all wars, which from the earliest times have existed
between the English and French nations, they have been accus-
tomed to consider each other in the light of generous, as well as
brave enemies, while the Hanoverians, for a century the allies
of the former, have shared in this reciprocal esteem. Humanity
and kindness have at all times taken place, the instant that
opposition ceased; and the same cloak has frequently been seen
covering those who were wounded and enemies, whilst indis-
criminately conveying to the hospitals of the conquerors. The
British and Hanoverian armies will not believe that the French
nation, even under their present infatuation, can so far forget
their character as soldiers, as to pay any attention to a decree,
as injurious to themselves as it is disgraceful to the persons who
passed it. On this confidence, His Royal Highness trusts that the
soldiers of both nations will confine their sentiments of resentment and abhorrence to the National Convention alone; persuaded that they will be joined in them by every Frenchman
who possesses one spark of honour, or one principle of a soldier;
and His Royal Highness is confident, that it will only be on
finding, contrary to every expectation, that the French army
has relinquished every title to the fair character of soldiers and
of men, by submitting to and obeying so atrocious an order,

that the brave troops under his command will think themselves justified, and indeed under the necessity of adopting, a species of warfare for which they will then stand acquitted to their own conscience, to their country, and to the world: in such an event, the French army alone will be answerable for the tenfold vengeance which will fall upon themselves, their wives, their children, and their unfortunate country, already groaning under every calamity which the accumulated crimes of unprincipled ambition and avarice can heap upon their devoted victims.'[1]

Not content with ensuring that his own men should all be aware of the contents of this order, he arranged to have copies of it captured by the French patrols, so that the French army should also be aware of it. This action had its due effect; the French army quietly disregarded the bloodthirsty order of their own government.

*   *   *   *   *

The month of June opened gloomily for the Allies. The superiority of the French in numbers had by now become marked, and was increasing daily. The efficiency of the Allies was at the same time decreasing: the Austrians had lost all heart in the war, and with the departure of the Emperor and Mack, more than 50 per cent of their officers were trying to resign, and it seemed only a matter of time before the Austrian army would follow them. On the first of the month Pichegru struck his blow. Ypres was the target. Concentrating 35,000 men against it, 15,000 of them besieged the town whilst the remainder took up a position at Passchendaele.[2]

Clerfait called for reinforcements, which Coburg sent. But even so, Clerfait made no real attempt to relieve the beleaguered city, and at last the Duke of York impatiently suggested that he might be entrusted with the task.

'Let what will happen,' declared Craig, 'I am sure the Duke is not to blame. He has even offered to go with the British and attack if Clerfayt would not.' And to Cornwallis he wrote that 'the Duke is urging day and night that something may be done'.[3] On 6 June and again on the 11th he made this offer,

[1] *Watkins*, p. 265.   [2] On the ground occupied by the Germans in 1914.
[3] *Cornwallis*, II, p. 247.

repeating it in writing on the 12th. In this letter he added an
alternative suggestion: 'Or perhaps Your Royal Highness could
take command and do it.'[1] Coburg, acting on this suggestion,
himself set out to relieve Ypres on 18 June, but on the next day
the town fell. Simultaneously, on the other flank, the French
under General Jourdan, crossed the Sambre at the sixth attempt,
and laid siege to Charleroi. Thus was Carnot's great plan of
operating on both flanks at once at last taking shape.

It is of interest to note that the Duke and Craig were anxious
for the Allies to adopt the opposite strategy, that of interior
lines: their plan was to march the whole army to the Sambre,
and after striking a blow there, march rapidly back to Flanders.
The shape of the line facilitated such an operation, for, after
taking a fairly straight course from the sea to Quesnoy, it
swung round in a great arc to Charleroi. Thus the Allies,
marching across the arc of the curve, would have about thirty
miles shorter distance to cover than the French opposed to
them. But Coburg would not listen to it. What, then, was to be
done? The French were now in overpowering numbers in
Flanders; between Ypres and the sea they had over 80,000
men, whilst their army on the Sambre was little if anything less
numerous. The problem was admittedly a difficult one for the
Allies.

Two days after the fall of Ypres Coburg marched away in
the opposite direction towards the Sambre, leaving York with
a pitifully weak force to hold the centre of the line round
Tournai. But reinforcements from England were at last on
their way, and indeed began to arrive at Ostend on the very day
that Coburg marched inland. They consisted of about 7,000
(nominally 8,664) men under Lord Moira, whom we last met
on Wimbledon Common five years before. His troops were
intended primarily for the defence of Ostend, but were to act
under the Duke of York 'in any measures he decided on'.
Events were now moving fast. Each day brought some change
in the situation. On the fall of Ypres, Clerfait had fallen back
to Deynse on the Lys, a retreat of thirty miles. Pichegru followed him up and defeated him there on the 23rd. Clerfait, in
semi-panic, thereupon retreated still farther, through Ghent, to
a position on the canal to the north of the city. Thus the old

[1] *W.O.*, I, 169.

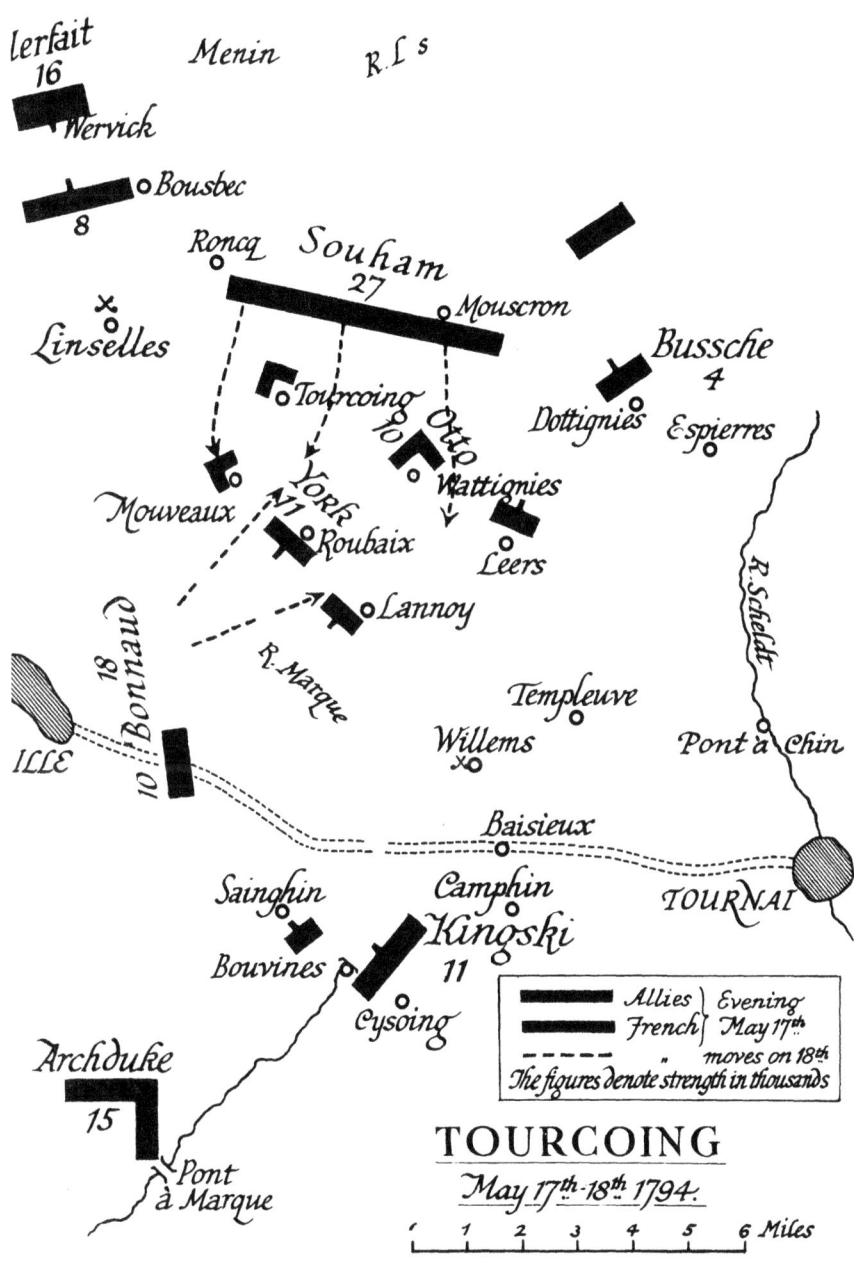

lerfait
16
Wervick

Menin

R. L s

Bousbec
8

Roncq

Souham
27

Mouscron

Linselles

Tourcoing

Otto
10

Bussche
4

Dottignies

Espierres

Mouveaux

York
17

Wattignies

Leers

Roubaix

Lannoy

R. Marque

Templeuve

Willems

R. Scheldt

Pont à Chin

18
Bonnaud
10

ILLE

Baisieux

Sainghin

Camphin
Kingski
11

Bouvines

Cysoing

TOURNAI

Archduke
15

Pont
à Marque

| | Allies ⎱ Evening |
	French ⎰ May 17th
	moves on 18th

The figures denote strength in thousands

TOURCOING

May 17th–18th 1794.

0   1   2   3   4   5   6 Miles

HOLLAND.
Dutch Fortresses in Red

Nº 7.

Ostend

Sluys

Bruges

Ghent

Menin

Lille

Courtrai

R. Lys

R. Schelde

Oudenarde

Renaix

Tournai

Mons

Alost

Lombeek

BRUSSELS

Waterloo

R. Dyle

Malines

Lierre

ANTWERP

Bergen-
op-Zoom

Rosendael

Helvoet

Rotterdam

Dort

Breda

Oosterhout

R. Meuse

R. Waal

R. Lek

Boxtel

Bois-le-Duc

R. Aa

Grave

The
Peel

Eindhoven

Louvain

Tirlemont

Namur

Liège

Maastricht

R. Meuse

Roermond

R. Roer

Venloo

Nimeguen

Arnhem

R. Rhine

0   10   20   30 Miles

Lys salient, that the French had made in the Allied lines no fewer than three times, reappeared in an aggravated form. A mere glance at the map (No. 1) will show what a precarious position the Duke of York's army had suddenly become involved in. Direct communication with Ostend was already cut off, and if Pichegru followed up Clerfait again, as must be assumed, even Antwerp would be threatened; for Ghent was almost exactly half-way between Tournai and Antwerp. Theoretically it should be possible to mount another combined operation against the French Lys salient; but that would involve the co-operation of Moira from Ostend, and it was doubtful if the Government would allow him to leave the vicinity of that port.

A second possible course for the Duke of York was to burn his boats altogether and march off in the opposite direction to join Coburg on the Sambre. Such had been his plan a fortnight ago; but the situation was now entirely changed; things were too far gone for that to offer any attractions. To sit still where he was, waiting to be surrounded, was out of the question. There only remained one possible course – to fall back towards Antwerp. The Duke did not take long to make up his mind. Directly he learnt of the upshot at Deynse he issued orders to fall back to Renaix, fifteen miles away, and seven miles short of Oudenarde. On the same day a French force was marching in the opposite direction from Deynse towards Oudenarde. It reached the outskirts of the town that evening. Thus York was practically cut off from the direct approach to Antwerp. The distress of the inhabitants of Tournai, who had come to look upon the Duke as their natural protector, as the British army marched away, was touching to behold.

On that eventful 24th of June, when news reached the English army that Clerfait had been sent reeling back on Ghent, news also reached Tournai of the arrival of Moira's force at Ostend. Now, as we have seen, the Government had sent out this force primarily for the defence of Ostend. But the Duke of York had different ideas on the subject. His mind was soon made up, and he wrote simultaneously to Dundas and Moira, indicating pretty plainly that the only sound course was for the latter to abandon Ostend and join forces with the main army. To Dundas he was almost curt, declaring that it was 'absolutely necessary that the force under Lord Moira

L

should join me';[1] while to Moira he wrote: 'A junction with your Lordship seems to be the most advisable and proper measure.' He went on to 'earnestly recommend' him, in concert with the Navy, to take ship for Antwerp and thence join him overland. Assuming that the shipping which brought Moira's force to Ostend was still available, this advice was obviously sound, as a glance at the map will show. However, Moira, accepting the Duke's letter as an order, decided to adopt the more hazardous expedient of an overland march through Bruges and Ghent. In this he was somewhat surprisingly successful. But this is to anticipate.

Disaster piled on disaster. Scarcely was the Duke settled in at Renaix than he heard that Coburg had engaged Jourdan in battle at Fleurus, just north of Charleroi and had been obliged to fall back on Brussels. On the battlefield-to-be of Waterloo Coburg made his headquarters.

The only bright spot in the picture was the direction of Coburg's retreat – north instead of east; towards the British army, and not away from it. There might yet be a chance of holding the line Waterloo-Ghent.

Meanwhile, on the 28th, the pressure on Oudenarde from the north increased. This was in accordance with the Carnot plan of campaign: Pichegru was to wheel to his right through Oudenarde, while Jourdan pushed north to meet him, what in modern parlance is called 'a pincers movement'.

Craig declared dolefully that 20,000 enemy troops were massed in sight of Oudenarde. This may not be an exaggeration if for 'Oudenarde' we read 'the heights to the east of Oudenarde', those same heights from which Marlborough's sweating columns descended to defeat Vendome in the valley below. The sluggish River Scheldt divided the two armies. It must have been almost as short of water as it was at the same spot 146 years later (when it again separated British troops from the enemy), for Craig describes it scornfully as 'a ditch that no foxhunter would pull his horse up at'. As the river was at the very least forty yards wide, Craig must either have been trading on Dundas's ignorance or meant that a fox-hunter would swim or ford it. At the end of this very despondent letter. Craig paints one pleasant picture: it is of the English Commander-in-Chief:

[1] *W.O.*, I, 169.

'The Duke has been out of order, but is perfectly recovered again. It is impossible to conduct himself [sic] with more temper and resolution than he does in a situation so critical, and in which he feels his responsibility to be so great. His Royal Highness is perfectly aware of all the danger, and feels every anxiety incident to it, but is neither cast down nor negligent of the precautions which are necessary. The greatest unanimity prevails among us which in our present situation is of some consequence.'[1]

But war is full of surprises, and now came a big surprise. Instead of attacking Oudenarde, Pichegru, on 30 June suddenly retraced his steps and disappeared. The explanation of this sudden change was that the National Convention had decided on the invasion of England and had directed Pichegru to capture some bases for this purpose – Ostend, Nieuport, and Walcheren. Thus the civil Government interfered, with unhappy results, in military strategy.

That same day, not knowing of the French change of plan, the Duke rode over to Braine-l'Alleud, a forty-mile ride, much of it in the night, for a conference with Coburg. At this important war council, held on 1 July, it was decided that Clerfait's force should be moved south of the British army, ostensibly in order that the latter might be closer to its line of communications with England; but the move may have had a sinister significance – it may have been the first step towards concentrating the Austrians in a position from which they could the easier shake free from their Allies. Already the English staff was talking openly of treachery, and confidence in the good faith of the Austrians had completely vanished. And one can feel little surprise at this attitude when one reads the terms of the agreement reached at Braine-l'Alleud.

To the question propounded by York and Prince Frederick of Orange: 'What are the Austrian intentions regarding the Low Countries?' they received the following written declaration: 'The Archduke Charles and the generals pledge their word of honour that they have no orders from His Majesty to quit the Low Countries, and in consequence they feel, as honourable men, obliged to defend the country as long as human force will allow them, and to all extremities.'[2]

[1] W.O., I, 169, f. 653.   [2] W.O., I, 169 f. 727.

But scarcely was the ink dry on this precious document, and the Duke back with his own army at Renaix, than an express letter arrived from Coburg, making nonsense of it. For the letter announced that Coburg had been obliged to fall back again, and the Duke was advised to do the same.

Meanwhile Pichegru was marching on Ostend, whilst Moira was marching from Ostend in almost the opposite direction. The two armies did not quite clash, and Moira by a rapid and skilful movement managed to make his way to Ghent, and a few days later to Alost, where he placed himself under the Duke's immediate orders.

And now things went from bad to worse with the ever-increasing speed of water approaching a waterfall. During the first three days of July, Tournai, Oudenarde, Ghent, and Mons fell, and the whole line of the Scheldt was in French hands except for the fortress of Valenciennes. This place, Condé, Landrecies, and Quesnoy alone remained of all the frontier fortresses. Ostend was (on orders from home) evacuated, but Nieuport retained. Urged to it by Coburg, the British army fell back to Grammont on 3 July, and Lombeke, midway between Brussels and Alost, next day. But there was no rest here; for Coburg had again, after a trifling action, fallen back to Waterloo, and thence in an easterly direction to Ramillies, flitting shamefully from a future to a past battlefield of renown. The Austrian Commander-in-Chief had at least shown his hand: Flanders was to be abandoned, the Allies were to part company, in spite of the reiterated protest of the Duke both to Coburg and to the Archduke Charles. Finally, on 7 July the Duke was stung into writing a blunt and bitter letter to Coburg – described by General Harcourt as one of the finest he ever read. In it he wrote: 'I own I am at length driven to the necessity of openly stating to Your Serene Highness that the opinion which the British nation must have on the subject cannot be other than that we are betrayed and sold to the enemy, and Your Serene Highness knows that in a country such as Great Britain popular opinion is not to be despised.' But all was of no avail, and with a heavy heart York fell back, as suggested by Coburg, in the direction of Malines and Antwerp.

Calvert[1] draws a harrowing picture of the dismay of the

[1] Calvert, now a lieutenant-colonel, remained on the Duke's Staff to the end.

inhabitants as the retreat became more and more pronounced; and his pen becomes almost vitriolic when he refers to the Austrians. Lord Cornwallis spent a few days with the army on his return from his abortive negotiations with the Prussians. His account is as depressing as Calvert's: 'Cornwallis goes to England without a plan, and declares he knows not what can be done. He is miserable and says the provoking part is that the Austrians have fled from shadows and that this campaign is absolutely given away – *given*, not lost.'[1]

From the same source we also learn that 'The Archduke (Charles) openly talks of treachery.'

On the other hand, 'the Duke of York rises daily in esteem, keeps up no state, has no unnecessary people with him, sometimes hardly a servant, and generally wears a plain coat'.[2]

Truly the Duke's position was a painful one. I have already quoted a passage showing by implication that Cornwallis was in agreement with the Duke at this stage. This is corroborated by Calvert, who writes to his sister on 10 July: 'I have the great happiness and pride in believing that the conduct of the Duke of York under these arduous circumstances has been such as to do honour to himself and to his country. His sentiments have been expressed with candour and firmness, and they have always tended to give protection and support, and to abandon nothing till driven to that sad necessity by irresistible force. I look upon Lord Cornwallis's presence at this critical period as one of the most fortunate circumstances of the Duke's life; for I had rather that he should have the approbation of that great and good man than of any other on this side of the grave.'[3]

What need, after this, to give in meticulous detail the marches and movements of the Duke's army? The British army was now to experience once more the questionable pleasure of the companionship of the Dutch army. For while the British held from Antwerp to Malines, the Dutch continued the line to Louvain, beyond which, to the south-east, lay the Austrian army, stretching through Tirlemont and Landen to Liége.[4]

These dispositions were taken up without molestation by the French. Like the British Government in 1793, the French Government was interfering in the province of strategy, with

---

[1] *Harcourt*, V, p. 480.   [2] Ibid., V, p, 483.
[3] *Calvert*, p. 274.   [4] See sketch map No. 7

harmful effects. Their strategy on exterior lines had worked admirably, and Brussels was entered by both armies almost simultaneously, though without managing to encircle many of the enemy. But instead of pursuing their advantage and pressing the Allies' retreat relentlessly, they turned away to invest Condé, Valenciennes, Landrecies, and Quesnoy. However, on 15 July Pichegru did make an attack on Malines, which was held by some Hessian and Dutch troops, who offered feeble resistance. The Duke did not for the moment attempt to retake it, but drew back his line slightly to the River Nethe. On the 18th he intended to counterattack, but in the meantime the Dutch had lost Louvain and the Austrians had fallen farther back towards Liége. The two armies were thus entirely separated, and so far from counterattacking the Duke was compelled to make a further retreat over the border into Holland.

Thus the British and the Austrians, after fighting side by side for two campaigns, parted company. Fortescue's verdict on the last sorry two months is that the Austrian operations were 'deliberately contrived to hasten the evacuation of the Netherlands'. Sybil's verdict is not quite so sweeping: 'The conclusion of the whole matter was that though the Emperor neither determined upon nor ordered the evacuation of Belgium he abandoned all the measures that were necessary to defend that country.'[1]

The net result, as regards the English army, was the same in either case. This being so, it would be idle to examine the Duke of York's conduct of operations for good or bad points: he was not a free agent, and as Lord Cornwallis remarked, it was utterly impossible to make any plan, for there was no prospect or possibility of carrying it out. We can thus pass on without more ado to the next phase of the campaign where the Duke was, in a sense, a free agent.

NOTE B. VAUX BATTLEFIELD

The course of events is very easy to follow, the ground not having altered in essentials. The ridge on which the cavalry demonstrated and the guns came into action is clearly defined, on the ground

[1] *Sybil*, III, p. 449.

(though not on the map). It runs north-west from Molain village, parallel to and distant 700 yards from the French ridge on which was situated the windmill and the Star Redoubt. The foundations of the mill are still visible, thirty yards to the south of the road. All traces of Star Redoubt have vanished, but it must have been on the crest about point 147 on the 1/40,000 map. Just behind it is an old barn, which still bears bullet or shell-splinter marks, but whether these date from 1793 or 1918 I do not know. The line of the 'woods on the right' which marked the French position can still be seen; there were a few redoubts along it, and as viewed from the Duke's command post on the ridge it must have looked, as he said, very strong. Finally, the forming-up point, in the dip behind Molain, is obvious, and also the route taken by Abercromby's column. It must have turned off the road in Molain to the left, have threaded its way along the valley of the Selle (here a tiny stream) till opposite the Star Redoubt, and then turned sharp to its right and charged up the hill. Thus it would be under cover from the French till about 100 yards from the redoubt. Evidently the guide, whoever he was, was a capable man.

NOTE C. BATTLEFIELD OF BEAUMONT

This battlefield produces no difficulties; the ridges are so well defined and the villages so numerous that there is not much scope for error. Nor is it difficult to site the Duke of York's command post fairly closely, whether it be in mill or redoubt. It was in either case obviously on the ridge-top, whence he would see the French left flank 'in the air' to the north-east of Audencourt. If we assume that he came out of Le Cateau up the Cambrai *chaussée* – a reasonable assumption – and if we follow that course ourselves, it will naturally take us to a view-point midway between the *chaussée* and the northern edge of the straggling village of Troisvilles. Probably mill and redoubt were contiguous (just as they had been at Vaux). The panorama that I have sketched is taken from this point. It shows the French left flank; the hollow where the cavalry formed up for the charge is naturally out of sight, dead behind Beaumont.

To reach this spot the cavalry had to cross over the Troisville ridge on the north side of the Cambrai *chaussée*. But at this point they would be concealed from the French by the buildings of Inchy and Beaumont villages, if the movement was skilfully carried out, which no doubt it was. Sinking the hill, they would then follow the course of the present light railway, skirting round the villages of Inchy and Beaumont. The obvious forming-up point is the hollow which crosses the Cambrai road exactly 1,000 yards west of the centre of Beaumont. This hollow runs askew to the direction of advance, so it must have been difficult to marshal the long lines of the great cavalry force in the correct dressing. Praise must be accorded to the Austrian leadership. Their cavalry were at this epoch considered the best in Europe. The charge was slightly uphill for about 1,000 yards, and thereafter downhill. The whole affair, in conception, execution, and aftermath was impressive to a degree.

NOTE D. THE BATTLEFIELD OF TOURCOING

The 'heights of Roubaix' are evidently situated at La Justice, which is still in open country. Hilaire Belloc in his *Tourcoing* (p. 84) claims that 'once Roubaix was captured the English commander could see across these fields, a couple of hours' march away, the tents of the great French camp at Sainghin, under the walls of Lille'. Actually the view in this direction is limited by a ridge extending from Lannoy to near Croix. I have verified this fact from both ends. Even from this ridge it is doubtful if much could have been seen. Mr Belloc seems to have ignored the existence of trees; presumably the present ones had ancestors. Incidentally Sainghin is a good five miles from the walls of Lille. But Mr Belloc is apt to be inexact in his statements; he makes the Duke two years younger than he was; and he asserts that Linselles is visible from Mouvaix, whereas two ridges intervene.

Though all the country between Roubaix and Wattrelos is now built-up the ground between Wattrelos and Leers is fortunately still under cultivation. Consequently it is still possible to trace the course of the Duke's 'death ride' with some precision and certainty. It was evidently parallel to the Wattrelos road, and within sight of it (else the French six-pounder, which cannot have been far from the road, would not have spotted the Duke). Moreover, it must have been within sight of the road bridge, which was held by some Hanoverians. Thus I place it about 200 yards from the road. At this point it still runs within its natural channel, is eighteen feet wide, and had a muddy bottom. The willows have disappeared. There is a steep five-foot drop into the stream, which would deter most horses, and make the willows a welcome assistance in getting out on the far side.

HOLLAND

7

When, on 24 July, 1794, the Duke of York fell back across the frontier into Holland, a new phase of the campaign opened. Hitherto he had been acting under the orders both of the home Government and of the Austrian Commander-in-Chief – though the latter relation was a nebulous one. Now he was to treat with the Austrians as equals, while the Dutch acted with him (for Clerfait and the Prince of Orange had changed places), in as nebulous a position as he had recently been in with the Austrians. The farther the Austrians fell back, the greater would become the gap between the two Allies, and the less the chance of co-operation between them. This weakness of divergent lines of communications is common to all armies operating on exterior lines when they are obliged to retreat. On the other hand, hopes were held out that the 62,000 Prussians in our pay, in spite of past disappointments, would still eventually join up with the British army in Holland. The first and immediate object was therefore the defence of Holland; the second, a resumption of the offensive, with the help of either the Prussians or the Austrians, or both. Little was to be expected from 'our treacherous allies, the Austrians', as Mrs Harcourt pleasantly called them; and the Prussians were far away. The defence of Holland therefore was for the moment all that could be hoped for, and the problem that confronted the Duke of York can best be understood by a glance at sketch map 7. From this it will be seen that Holland was defended by a line of four fortresses in a straight line, about twenty miles apart – Bergen-op-Zoom, Breda, Bois-le-Duc,[1] Grave – with a fifth – Nimeguen – refusing the left flank.

[1] The modern Dutch name of this ancient town is 's Hertogenbosch. I avoid this uncouth word. Similarly I deplore and eschew the modern Dutch spelling of Nimeguen.

For the time being there was little danger of the line to the east of Bois-le-Duc being threatened; so the Duke arranged to fill the interval between that fortress and Breda with the Dutch army, while his own army took up position at Rosendael, midway between Breda and Bergen. To judge from the map, this was the best and obvious method of defending the frontier, but Craig had misgivings, and as this is the first occasion of a sign of difference of opinion between the Duke and his Adjutant-General, it is worth while quoting from the remarkably interesting letter that the latter wrote to Nepean on arrival at Rosendael:

'We have two entrances into Holland which equally require our attention, that by Bergen-op-Zoom, and that by Breda, widely separated and totally unconnected with each other. By covering one we leave the other open. By putting ourselves between both, as we have done – and as indeed seems the most natural way – we leave both open. . . . But the reasoning would only be applicable supposing we were in sufficient force to defend either position by a battle, which in fact we are not. What can be expected for 35,000 men, which will be the outside of our numbers even joined to the Dutch.[1]

'I cannot but admire the Duke, particularly on one point of his conduct just now. I see clearly the reluctance with which he has given way to the circumstances which have so considerably compelled him to retire day after day for the month past. In spite of himself he eagerly seized every [illegible], however slight, for halting, and I am sure his first emotion would be that of the highest pleasure were it reported to him that the enemy were within a mile of us. Yet with all this we see him bend to the necessity of the situation. . . .

'The moment the Austrians retire over the Rhine the Frenchmen have sufficient force to attempt all these three passages at once [Bergen, Breda, Grave] and *it will be utterly impossible for us to resist them.*'[2]

Craig precedes to outline his own plan, which was to form an entrenched camp under the walls of Breda.

[1] Dundas queried this figure, pointing out that on paper the army was 36,349 strong without the Dutch; but Craig evidently allowed for sick, detached men, etc. The exact figures for the Dutch are vague – and unimportant. Taylor estimates that they never exceeded 15,000 men in the field.
[2] *W.O.*, I, 170, f. 45.

Which plan was the better? To arrive at the correct answer it is always as well to view the problem from the enemy's aspect. Now there can be no doubt that the French, as their recent conduct had shown, were more intent on taking fortresses than on defeating the British army in the field. Since the battle of Beaumont they had not once initiated an attack on the Duke's army. The first fortress in their path was Bergen. Would they not rather that the British army should be twenty-five miles distant from this fortress – at Breda – rather than ten miles distant – at Rosendael? For the moment, then, though its flanks were in the air, the British army was better situated at Rosendael than anywhere. Unfortunately, subsistence was difficult round Rosendael, and water was scarce: moreover, the Austrians were continually falling back, till on reaching Maastricht they were eighty-five miles from Rosendael, thus making an attack on the eastern end of the Dutch line increasingly feasible. After a few days, therefore, the Duke made a new plan, and after some difficulty he persuaded the two Princes of Orange to agree to it. In his letter to Dundas he describes it as 'entrusting the defences of the fortresses to the Dutch troops, and taking up some central position with the whole of my corps, in order to be able to move immediately to any point which the enemy might appear to threaten. . . . It was agreed that the Dutch troops should undertake the defence of Bergen and Breda and that they should furnish part of the garrison of Bois-le-Duc, whilst I should march as soon as possible . . . and take up a position behind the River Aa, having my right to Bois-le-Duc and my left to a great morass called the Peel.

'From this position I shall be enabled to move immediately to the assistance of any of the fortresses in Dutch Brabant, should the enemy choose to attack them, and I shall effectually cover the province of Guelders and hinder any attempt of the enemy upon Grave or Nimeguen.'[1]

Thus the Duke in clear, concise terms expounded his plan. Was it sound? I think so. It avoided the weakness of the cordon system, whilst it did not go to the other extreme, advocated by Craig, of practically shutting himself in an entrenched camp. He preserved his mobility, and to that extent kept the enemy

[1] Ibid., f. 53.

guessing, which under Craig's plan he would not have done.

Before, however, he had time to put the plan into effect, the Prince of Orange took fright at the thought of the British army being so distant from Bergen (fifty miles), and in order to appease him York consented to go no farther for the present than Oosterhout, eight miles beyond Breda. To Oosterhout, therefore, the army marched on the last day of July.

Meanwhile the British Government was getting increasingly and naturally apprehensive about the conduct of the Austrians. Constant behests were sent by Dundas to York to urge closer co-operation on the part of the two armies; but all to no purpose. The Duke strove manfully to carry out these instructions. As late as 14 July he had essayed to ride over to see Coburg at Tirlemont, but according to Calvert: 'The extreme badness of the roads and other obstacles prevented him prosecuting his journey, and I understand from Colonel Craig that His Royal Highness was so ill on the road with the spasms he was subject to last year that he was very glad to return.'[1] The Duke had only mentioned these 'spasms' to the King when he applied to come home in the winter.

A pause in the operations now set in, due to the fact that the French army, 80,000 strong on paper, was engaged in lapping up the Dutch fortresses along the coast – Nieuport, Ostend (which was evacuated), and Sluys. Thus the British army had a peaceful interlude throughout the month of August. This was so pronounced that the Duke's birthday was celebrated by great festivities, amongst which was a dinner given to 150 persons by ten general officers, the share of each coming to £40. No doubt there may have been a few sycophants among these generals, who desired to curry favour with His Royal Highness, but even so, one could hardly picture them going out of their way to this extent if they were lacking in confidence and genuine regard for the Commander-in-Chief, though probably there were one or more malcontents.

In desperation Pitt now sent a mission to Vienna consisting of Lord Spencer and Thomas Grenville, to plead for a more active conduct of the war and for closer co-operation with the British army. The mission was fruitless in this respect; but it did achieve something that was eventually to have a profound

[1] *Calvert*, p. 277.

influence upon the Duke's career. They persuaded the Austrian Government to dismiss the Prince of Coburg. Unfortunately, a satisfactory successor could not be found, so Clerfait was given the temporary command. This was a very unsatisfactory appointment, as the Austrians themselves recognized, and Count Mercy, the Austrian Minister at The Hague, suggested – in Pitt's words to Cornwallis – 'He is persuaded that if *you* had the command of our army with the local rank of field-marshal there would be no difficulty in so arranging it that you might have the virtual command of the whole army, Austrian as well as British.'

An obvious objection to this project was then dealt with by Pitt. 'I am fully aware of the apparent difficulty of superseding the Duke of York's command. But on thinking over the subject I think that difficulty not insuperable. He has, I believe, good sense enough to feel that his having the command of the whole combined army is out of the question. His being under the command of Clerfait, or the two armies remaining independent of each other, I think he must feel to be equally inconsistent with any plan that can be useful; and I do not at all despair that by stating these circumstances to him distinctly . . . he may be brought freely to acquiesce in such arrangement, and continue to serve under you.'[1]

In other words, the Government jumped at Mercy's proposal. Cornwallis replied that he, though with reluctance, was prepared to assume the post. His reluctance was natural: only a month before, on his return from the front, he had spoken highly of the conduct of the Duke[2]. Pitt then approached a very delicate task, that of broaching the matter to the King. He did it by first drawing up a lengthy paper, bulging with circumlocutions, to which he received the assent of the Cabinet. This paper starts off by stressing the importance of establishing an undivided command. After asserting that the Austrians would not consent to placing the Duke over Clerfait, Mercy's proposal is then mentioned. Then comes a sop for His Majesty in the following cumbrous sentence: 'The situation in which His Royal Highness would stand might indubitably be so arranged as to afford him an immediate command and a field for the exercise of military talent not less extensive than that which

[1] *Cornwallis*, II, p. 257.   [2] *Calvert*, p. 425.

has been allotted in the greatest part of the time since the com-
mencement of the war. . . .'[1]

Pitt, in a covering letter, stated that Windham (who had
just been made Secretary at War) had offered to go out and
explain the situation to the Duke, and try to gain his acquiescence in the project.

The King promptly replied, in somewhat acid terms, that he
would not withhold his consent, adding: 'But I own, in my
Son's place, I should beg my being allowed to return home if
the command is given to Lord Cornwallis. . . .'[2]

But now a hitch occurred. After writing his letter of consent
Cornwallis began to hedge. He came up to Town and had an
interview with Pitt on the 27th, the day after Pitt had written
to the King. At this interview he declared that he could not
possibly consent to serve *over* the Duke of York, and that the
only possible way would be for York 'to ask a temporary leave
of absence' while he, Cornwallis, assumed the command.

However, the King had already approved of Windham going
out, so out he went, and Pitt wrote again to the King – acting
on Cornwallis's hint:

'In consequence of Your Majesty's gracious permission Mr
Windham left Town yesterday. . . . Your Majesty's servants
flatter themselves that His Royal Highness's zeal for the service
will lead him to consent to act under the command of Lord
Cornwallis . . . though upon consideration, it has been
thought probable that even on that supposition His Royal
Highness may wish for a short leave of absence which may
perhaps be a more eligible mode of making the arrangement
than transferring the command on the spot.'[3]

The result of this mission was surprising, not to say dis-
concerting, to the Government – for the Secretary at War
'went to curse and remained to pray'. In other words, after
putting the proposition to the Duke and pressing the matter
'with greater pertinacity than I can ever bring myself to use',
Windham veered round to the Duke's own opinion that no
change ought to be made. He wrote to Pitt to this effect on
4 September and again on the 10th. This was tiresome for the
Prime Minister, and necessitated a further carefully composed

[1] *Windsor, Pitt to the King*, 26.8.94.
[2] *Cornwallis*, II, p. 261.   [3] *Windsor, Pitt to the King*, 30.8.94.

letter to the King. Out of another lengthy epistle this is the salient passage:

'Mr Pitt thinks it his duty to submit to Your Majesty a letter which he has had the honour of receiving from His Royal Highness the Duke of York, and also one from Mr Windham, which he ventures to submit to Your Majesty though written entirely as a private letter. The same messenger brought the account of the unfortunate and inexplicable surrender of Valenciennes and Condé. This event so far changes the face of affairs, and the considerations arising out of it, as well as those suggested by Mr Windham's letter, are so many and important that Mr Pitt feels unwilling, without more consideration, to submit to Your Majesty any sentiment which presents itself to his mind, except the impression which it is impossible not to feel of the very honourable manner in which the Duke of York postpones every personal consideration to whatever may be deemed most advantageous for Your Majesty's Service.'[1]

The letter from the Duke to which Pitt refers has been preserved in the *Chatham Papers*. In it the Duke wrote:

'Whatsoever my present sentiments may be on this occasion I should feel myself exceedingly unhappy at the idea that any measure that His Majesty's Ministers might judge conducive to the advantage of His Majesty's affairs or to the better carrying out of the war, should be given up for any personal consideration for me. I am at the same time thoroughly conscious of the Marquis Cornwallis' merit and of the gracious partialty that was shown by His Majesty towards me in His appointment of me to the command of the British troops in Flanders last year. I shall in silence submit to whatever His Majesty's determination may be.

'Should His Majesty be pleased to appoint Lord Cornwallis to the command, as it is now proposed, I trust that His Majesty will graciously consent to my request for permission to return to England. Howsoever anxious I may be to continue to serve, I foresee how very unpleasant it would be to Marquis Cornwallis if I was to remain with the army as a Volunteer,[2] and the regard I must naturally have for my own honour as an officer

[1] *Windsor*, 9.9.94.
[2] The practice of serving 'as a volunteer', in an unofficial capacity, was common in those days.

would never permit me to serve in any other capacity under a person who is junior to me in military rank in His Majesty's service.'[1]

Windham's comment on this letter was as follows: 'The King has sent me a letter from His Royal Highness which has struck me very much, both from its manliness and liberality.'[2]

But Weathercock Windham, having blown hot, then cold, three days later blew hot once more. In a letter to Lord Spencer at Vienna of 13 September he speaks of 'my own wrong judgment.[3] I certainly yielded more in my own opinion to the difficulties and risks of sending over Lord C. [Cornwallis] immediately than I now wish I had done.' Another three days, and he writes in the same strain to Pitt.[4] But much had happened in those three days. We must therefore return to the Front.

* * * * *

We left the army comfortably installed at Oosterhout. Here it was unmolested, but its patrols ranged far and wide. On one occasion they captured twenty-seven prisoners a good twenty miles distant from the camp. In the middle of the month of August, however, both Landrecies and Quesnoy fell, and Pichegru prepared to resume the advance into Holland. On the 28th he attacked the British outposts, apparently heading for Bois-le-Duc. This would threaten the British left, as the Dutch were rapidly falling back in that quarter. That night the Duke assembled a council of war. We have not heard him doing such a thing since that held at Thorout nearly twelve months before. What was the reason for this reversion to an old policy? Was it that he was now losing confidence in himself? Or was it perhaps explained by the presence of Windham? From what happened a few days later I am inclined to believe that Windham's presence was the direct cause.

The council came to the obvious conclusion that it was time to fall back to the prepared position on the River Aa, and this conclusion was put into effect next day. This decision seems to have met with the approval of the army. Captain Jones notes that the army was now in the same camp as that occupied by the Duke of Cumberland in 1747, in the War of the Austrian

---

[1] *Chatham Papers*, Vol. 106.   [2] *Windham*, I, p. 232.
[3] *Cornwallis*, II, p. 267.   [4] *Windham*, I, p. 239.

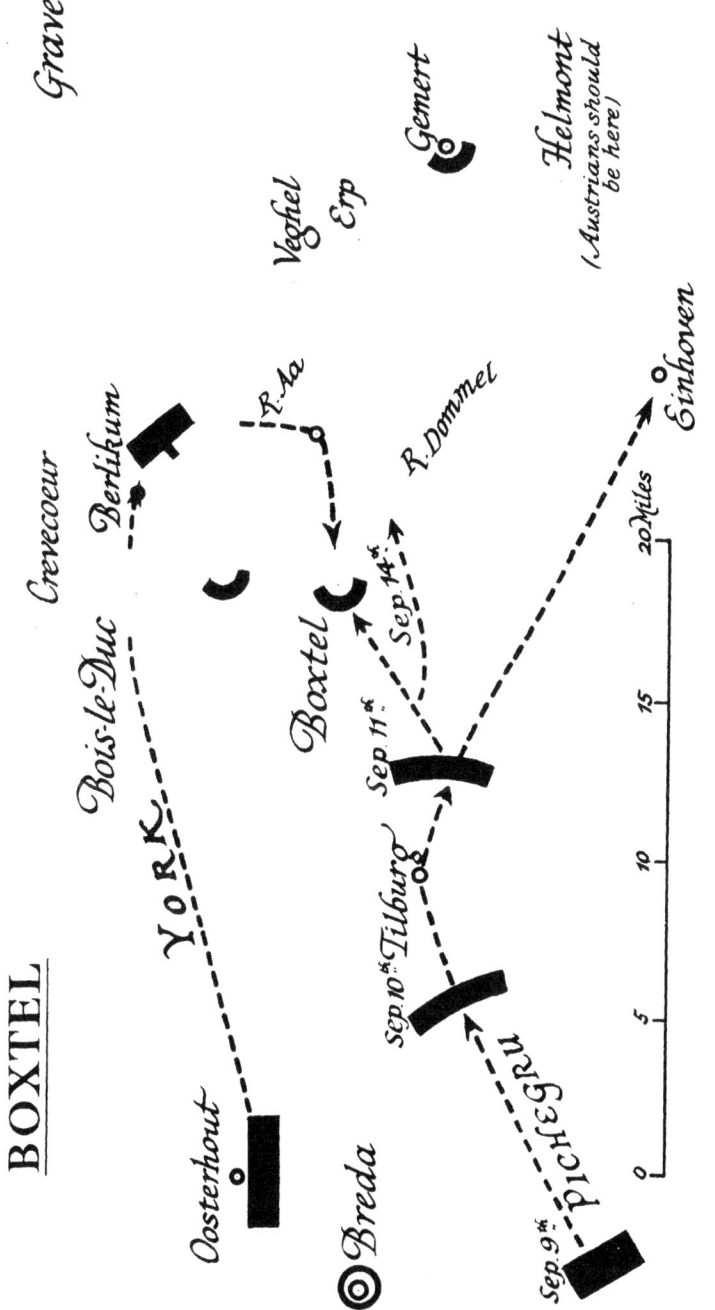

BOXTEL

v. Meuse

Grave

Gemert

Helmont
(Austrians should
be here)

Veghel
Erp

Crevecoeur

Bois-le-Duc

Bertikum

R. Aa

R.Dommel

YORK

Oosterhout

Boxtel

Sep 11ᵗʰ

Sep 14ᵗʰ

Einhoven

20 Miles

Breda

Sep 10ᵗʰ Tilburg

Sep 9ᵗʰ PICHEGRU

0   5   10   15

The Helder

THE HELDER
CAMPAIGN

0   ½   1 Mile

THE LANDING

Schage

Petten

ZYPE LINE

Camperdown   Oudkarspel

o Schoorl

o Bergen   Hoorne

Egmont   ALKMAAR

P O L D E R S

Akersloot   ZUIDER

o Kastrikum

o Uitgeest   ZEE

Wyk   Beverwyk   Permerend

HAARLEM

AMSTERDAM

Succession, and he adds: 'There was much judgment, and generalship in that timely retirement to Bois-le-Duc, without the loss of a man, as there might have been in any action.'[1]

The new position lined the River Aa from Bois-le-Duc south-eastwards to the Peel Morass, with a line of outposts on the River Dommel, eight miles in front. The chief of these posts was at Boxtel.[2]

While Pichegru with 68,000 men followed up this withdrawal and sent a large force to take Eindhoven (twenty miles south of Bois-le-Duc), Jourdan drove Clerfait's army back towards the Rhine. Simultaneously the two remaining Flanders fortresses, Condé and Valenciennes fell. Clerfait seized this moment to propose to the Duke a general advance and the recapture of Antwerp.

On 1 September a conference was held between the Duke, Beaulieu (for the Austrians), and the Prince of Orange, at which this proposal was considered. The Duke warmly embraced this first sign of a renewal of co-operation and offensive spirit on the part of the Austrians, but the news of the fall of Condé and Valenciennes dashed hopes to the ground. Craig, always inclined to take the pessimistic view, now for the first time openly differed from his chief, as a letter he addressed to Nepean shows. (It is significantly marked 'Private and Confidential'.)

After pointing out that the fall of Condé and Valenciennes had altered the position, he writes: 'I had a good deal of conversation with His Royal Highness whilst he was writing his dispatch last night and it was impossible not to subscribe to his argument of the importance which it must be to England in particular to prevent the French obtaining the permanent possession of Flanders, as well as of the greater facility that we shall find to drive them out now, instead of waiting till next campaign, and thus affording them the opportunity of fortifying the passes of the Scheldt. But as His Royal Highness's extreme condescension permits me to give you my opinion, and as between ourselves I am too little of a courtier ever to conceal it, I could not help differing from His Royal Highness in one respect, which is of being able to take up our winter quarters in Brabant and Flanders. . . .'

[1] *Jones*, p. 119.　　[2] See sketch map No. 8.

M

He then expatiates on the impossibility of attacking an army of 80,000 men. In this matter, he magnifies the strength of the enemy and minimizes his own. Moreover, the French were of poor fighting quality, whilst the English, despite their long retreat, were in good heart, and longed to have a chance of battle. 'In all our distresses we have the comfort of seeing our troops in health and spirits and ready to undertake any service.'[1]

Such was the situation on 14 September, when Pichegru attacked and captured the outpost position on the Dommel at Boxtel, taking prisoner two battalions of Hessians almost without resistance. The events of the following twenty-four hours were so critical in the military life of the Duke of York that I shall devote considerable space to them.

First I will give the story in the Duke's own words, in his dispatch of 17 September. It was evidently carefully worded and merits equally careful reading.

'On Sunday afternoon, a sudden attack, in which it appeared that the enemy were in great force, was made upon all my posts of the right; and that of Boxtel, which was the most advanced was forced, with considerable loss to the troops of Hesse-Darmstadt who occupied it. As the line of my outposts upon the Dommel could not be maintained while the enemy were in possession of Boxtel, it appeared necessary to regain it; at the same time the degree of resistance that the enemy would make would serve to ascertain whether this attack was supported by their army, with a view to a general attack, or was merely an affair of outposts. I therefore ordered Lieut.-General Abercrombie to march with the Reserve during the night, with directions to reconnoitre the post at daylight, and to act as he should judge best, from what he should discover of the force of the enemy. Lieut.-General Abercrombie having advanced as directed, found the enemy in such strength as left little room to doubt of the proximity of their army,[2] and he accordingly retired, but in such good order as prevented the enemy from making any impression, although they followed him for some distance.

'About this time I received private information, upon which I could rely, and which was confirmed by the observation of my

<hr/>

[1] *Harcourt*, V, p. 510.
[2] Shown by a dotted line on sketch map No. 8.

patrols and the reports of deserters, that the enemy had been reinforced by the troops which had hitherto been acting in West Flanders, as well as by a column of the army which had been employed before Valenciennes and Condé. The same information assured me also that the column which had been marching towards Maestricht had suddenly returned towards us. From these accounts and from what I knew from the previous strength of the enemy, it appeared that the actual force now advancing against me, and whose object could only be an attack upon my army, could scarcely be less than 80,000 men. The hazard of an action with such a very great disparity of numbers could not but become a matter of the most serious consideration; and after the most mature deliberation I did not think myself at liberty to risk, in so unequal a contest His Majesty's troops or those of his Allies serving with them. I had the utmost reliance on their courage and discipline, and I had no doubt that these would have enabled me to resist the first efforts of the enemy; but it could scarcely be expected that even with the utmost exertion of their qualities they would be able to withstand the reiterated attacks which the vast superiority of the enemy would enable them to make, and which we knew from experience it is a general principle on which they act. Actuated by these reasons and the further information which I received about noon, that the enemy were marching considerable columns towards my left, in which part my position was most vulnerable, I determined upon retreating across the Meuse.'

There is a good deal below the surface of this dispatch that does not meet the eye. It will be well first to outline events from the British point of view, and then to go over into the enemy's camp and relate the story from his point of view.

Abercromby's orders were not merely to reconnoitre and 'act as he thought best', as stated in the dispatch, but to retake Boxtel.[1] Abercromby marched during the night with ten battalions and ten squadrons, including the pick of the English troops, and reconnoitred the position at dawn. The Guards were ordered to attack, but Abercromby, impressed by the apparent strength of the position, held up the attack whilst he referred back to the Commander-in-Chief for instructions. The

[1] *An Officer of the Guards*, II, p. 72.

Duke replied that he was to persist in the attack, but not to proceed farther than he thought prudent. Abercromby, by some curious reasoning, interpreted this to mean that he need not attack at all, promptly called off the Guards, after about thirty casualties had been suffered, and returned to camp, unmolested by the enemy.

How Abercromby discovered that the enemy were in such strength it is hard to say. There are normally two methods of ascertaining this: by fighting or by ocular methods. Abercromby did no fighting, and his blindness prevented him using ocular methods. Moreover, the ground was flat, and being in the leafy season of the year, most of the enemy troops must in any case have been invisible. However that may be, Abercromby on his return to camp made his report: a conference was held, and in view of all the reports received, it was decided to fall back to the line of the Meuse about Grave.

Let us now enter the French lines, and view the affair from that side. The first surprise that greets us is to find that Pichegru had no immediate intention either of attacking or of outflanking his enemy. He wished merely to secure the line of the Dommel in order to cover his right flank whilst he turned to besiege Breda, which was then on his left rear. For this purpose he sent forward a force variously described as 'a force of one division'[1] and 'a strong party of observation, which fell in with their troops and defeated them, without the army being informed of it'.[2]

If the army was not aware of it, it cannot have been in sight of Boxtel, and therefore Abercromby (who did not get within a mile of the place), apart from other disabilities, could not possibly have seen it. A French division might be just under 10,000 men – that is about the same size as Abercromby's force – but it would be of vastly inferior quality to the British Guards. Nor could it in the short time available have done much to fortify its position. It seems probable that, isolated as it was, it would have received a reeling blow from our Guards had Abercromby allowed them to attack, and the timid Pichegru, who was, according to Jomini, advancing 'avec circonspection', would have fallen back. Moreover, he had available not 80,000, but only 56,000 men.

[1] *Victoires*, p. 161.   [2] *David*, p. 80.

But, it may be asked, how are we to account for the numerous reports as to an outflanking movement round the British left? These reports came from three sources: spies, prisoners, and patrols. As regards spies, they may have been in the pay of France (a large portion of the population was ill disposed to the Allied cause). As regards prisoners, such persons have been known to tell misleading stories. As regards patrols, we can believe their stories; the explanation is that the French bodies they saw on their left flank were there by mistake: they were lost! We have several sources for this assertion. David writes: 'But the troops were greatly fatigued by their march, and besides our knowledge of the country was very imperfect as it was not described in any of M. Ferari's charts. We were in the greatest want of good maps which occasioned several columns to mistake their route, and prevented them from reaching the places of their destination. The army was so dispersed by mistakes of this sort, that it was obliged to halt on the 15th and 16th.'[1] (The Germans, in two of the battles in the Ardennes in 1914, stumbled upon victory owing to some units losing their way.)

Finally the dispatch of the force to Eindhoven was for the obvious purpose of connecting with Jourdan's army on the Meuse. It had no intention or thought of turning the British left flank. We see, therefore, the value of that semi-divine gift of the great commander, that of 'seeing the other side of the hill', and rightly sensing the plans and dispositions of the rival commander. In short, I consider this the greatest – in fact, the only great error – made by the British Commander-in-Chief in the course of two campaigns.

The result was that at the moment when at last the Austrians were showing some faint signs of co-operation in an advance, the British army allowed itself to be turned out of a specially selected and prepared position of considerable natural strength – not even by bluff, but by a *mistake*! Pichegru was so surprised that he was not prepared to follow up his unlooked-for success. Moreover, his lethargy, timidity, and lack of spirit were so ingrained that he did not attempt to take advantage of this favourable situation, but turned aside to besiege the fortress of Breda.

[1] Op. cit., p. 85.

Up to date the morale of the British troops had been unimpaired; all their objurgations were directed at their perfidious Allies. But there were no Austrians or Dutch at Boxtel: it was a British paid army that had been apparently outgeneralled and forced back to the River Meuse, leaving the fortresses of Bergen, Breda, and Bois-le-Duc to their fate. Who was to be blamed if not their own general? It must now have seemed to many of the troops that success under such a commander was no longer likely. But are we to put all the blame on to the shoulders of the Duke of York for this humiliating affair?[1]

It will be noticed that I mentioned (what the Duke in his dispatch omitted) that a conference was held before it was decided to retreat. Who was present at this momentous conference, and how was the disastrous decision to retreat arrived at? Windham, though a civilian, was certainly present at it, also Craig and Abercromby. These were probably the essential members. Now, we have seen that Craig was inclined to see the gloomy side of things; Abercromby's future career was to show that he could almost be described as 'a defeatist'.[2] There remains Windham, the weathercock. It might be supposed that a civilian who happened to be present at Headquarters during the battle, would either not be present at the meeting of senior officers, or would keep his own counsel at the meeting. For Windham, though a fine scholar – described by Lord Rosebery as 'the finest English gentleman of his or perhaps all time' – was no soldier and had no military knowledge. We have already seen how his opinion veered, and it is interesting to note that he afterwards earned the nickname of 'The Weathercock'. This Windham, then, what part did he play at the conference, in the formation of the decision to retreat? According to his own account, a big, possibly a decisive one. In a private letter to Pitt, written the very next day, he specifically states: 'I certainly took all pains to make him adopt that resolution (to retreat).'[3]

---

[1] The fact that Fortescue only devotes eighteen lines to this affair must be accounted for by the fact that he accepted the dispatch at its face value, and even writes: 'Abercromby only just missed falling into the midst of Pichegru's main army.'

[2] I would refer those who object to my using this term about that fine old man, but bad general, to an article by me in *The Fighting Forces*, February 1947.

[3] *Windham*, I, p. 242.

What an astonishing situation does this confession disclose! The main reason why the Duke should be recalled is given in the same letter as the 'lack of confidence' felt in his leadership by the army – a lack that was stimulated by the very efforts of the writer himself!

Further light is thrown on the proceedings of the council by various passages in two of Windham's letters to Pitt on the 16th, the public and the private one. These letters, though full of interest, are too long to quote in full here. (They are both printed in the *Windham Paper*.) From them it is clear that the Duke opposed a retreat, but that the senior officers present were practically, if not quite, unanimous in favour of it. Nor need this occasion surprise when we consider that the most influential of them were Craig and Abercromby. 'He yielded more to the opinions of others than followed his own,' admitted Windham.[1]

So it comes to this, that the Commander was drawn into a false move as the result of assembling a council of war, probably at the request of a civilian politician. Yet it is to be noted that in his dispatch he makes no reference to this council; he does not attempt to shelter himself behind it, but boldly assumes all the responsibility and odium that the receipt of the news in England will be bound to produce. In the same manner his dispatch throws no blame on Abercromby's action; or rather lack of action. He glosses over the failure to carry out his orders; he shields his subordinate, just as the Duke of Wellington afterwards did in the Peninsula. Incidentally the Iron Duke, as Colonel Wellesley, was present at the action, and must have taken note of the way the dispatch dealt with this faltering general.

As for Windham's pretensions to form military judgments, the following passage from his 'public letter' is illuminating. 'The recovery of the Scheldt . . . has been for a great while out of my hopes; and it was very much from that consideration that I shared, less than I should otherwise have done, in the desire of the Duke to maintain his late position, and to take the chance of an action. It seemed to me that even a complete victory . . . as could possibly be looked to, would have given

[1] Ibid., I, p. 241.

us after all no very confident hopes of being able to effect a great deal in that quarter.'[1]

If I appear to have laboured this subject it is because I feel the more convinced, the further I study the question, that failure to 'take the chance of an action' made inevitable what before was only probable, namely the loss of the campaign – and the downfall of Frederick, Duke of York.

To resume the narrative: on 16 September the whole army retreated through Grave to the River Meuse. The army proceeded to line the north bank with headquarters at Wychem, a short distance north of the town. The French followed very slowly, only occupying the Allies' old camp near Bois-le-Duc three days after the engagement, after which Pichegru turned off to besiege Breda. Losing not a moment, the Duke sent off Colonel Calvert, together with Thomas Pelham, who had accompanied Windham to the Front, on a mission to Clerfait. Before these two reached his headquarters however, the Austrians also had fallen back, and were occupying a position on the River Roer, to the east of the Meuse. (Sketch map 7.) Thus the two armies were still separated by a gap of about sixty miles. Clerfait had no intention of resuming the offensive, but undertook to connect up with the British army at Venloo on the Meuse, thirty miles south of Grave in a straight line. Though this meant that the British army would have to cover a front of about nintey miles with a force of 27,000 men, the Duke agreed, and duly carried it out. His right now rested on the Waal to the north of Bois-le-Duc, and his left at Venloo.

*   *   *   *   *

We now return to the manœuvres to get rid of the Duke of York. In his private letter of 16 September Windham had suggested that York might be made Commander-in-Chief at home and replaced by Cornwallis in the field. But he continued his wobbles. Having given it as his opinion on 16 September that the change must be made at once, he wrote three days later to tell Pitt that it would be much better to defer it till the next year. Another two days elapsed, and he writes to say that the

[1] Ibid., I, p. 236.

Duke, whom he has been 'sounding' would probably be willing to go 'at this moment', which he maintains was to be desired; but he immediately qualifies this with a final wobble: 'At the same time I don't say that the measure would be desirable if the army was at this moment in the most difficult situation.'[1]

That vacillating and veering weathercock of a Windham continued to wobble. Just before departing for home, on 23 September, he threw out two different suggestions in the same letter; one that the Duke should be immediately made Commander-in-Chief at home, the other that Cornwallis should command the British contingent, 'leaving the Duke to have the (nominal) command of the whole'.[2]

On setting foot in England, at Deal, Windham sent Pitt another, and it is to be hoped final, suggestion: 'Why might it not be possible to give him a command nearly equal to that he has at present?'[3] On this vague and unhelpful note we will take our leave of this egregious Secretary at War.

Pitt, on receiving these confused but startling letters, after consulting Portland and Grenville, replied with guarded approval of the project. On receipt of Windham's third letter on 25 September he wrote asking permission to show the letters to the King. Now, Dundas had not been present at these consultations, since he was at Walmer Castle, having 'left his pen in Pitt's hands', and his part in the 'Business' has hitherto been obscure. But perhaps it is fortunate for the historian that he was at this moment absent from his office, for it necessitated a letter to Pitt. This letter has lain for 150 years neglected and unprinted – probably because it is undated (marked '? 1794') and is consequently slightly out of place in Pitt's papers. From internal evidence it can with confidence be assigned to 27 September, 1794. Not only does this letter fill a gap in our knowledge, but it throws a light on the character of Dundas: in short, it is an important and a revealing letter.

Pitt had written to Dundas, and had stated that he proposed approaching Cornwallis to take the command in Flanders. Dundas replied to it the same day.

'I shall be in Town on Monday (the 29th) forenoon. I would set out immediately, but I am sure on recollection, you must

---

[1] *Windham*, I, p. 250. [2] *Chatham Papers*, Vol. 190. [3] Ibid., 30.9.94.

be satisfied it is totally impossible for anybody to go down to Lord Cornwallis till once you have seen the King, and if the Business is considered by you in so pressing a light either Lord Cornwallis or you must go to Windsor; but how is this to be done before you have Mr Windham's permission to show the origins of this new proposition in his letters?

'But be that as it may I am positive, on reconsidering the Business you must be satisfied nobody can go to Lord Cornwallis without the King's previous *knowledge*, I had almost said *special request*.

'All this to the preliminary part; but your difficulty is not then over, I do not think the proposition to send Lord Cornwallis a fair one, or one that you can expect him to accede to; nor am I aware of the necessity of it, for if the Austrians are hearty in acceding to our wishes there can be little doubt that General Clairfait and the Duke are able, by a vigorous measure, to raise or prevent the siege of Maestricht. If the Austrians do not accede you cannot think it possible to desire Lord Cornwallis – or any other man – to undertake the business with the Duke of York's army alone.

'As to the expedient of pleasing the Duke of York by making him Commander-in-Chief at home, it will not have the effect; and placing him in that situation will entail a deal of uncalculable trouble upon you during the whole of the King's life. I do not feel this as strong as other points of the Business because perhaps with a friendly Secretary at War there are considerable advantages to be got from a Prince of the Blood being at the head of the army. It was so felt in the Duke of Cumberland's time.

'It would not be right in me to keep back one circumstance from your consideration, but I declare to you most solemnly I do not state it as an objection, for I feel it the reverse. It would enable you by constant intercourse with him [The Duke] to prevent the delays that at present arise from Lord Amherst's not having strength or resolution enough to stand to points after we have settled them with him. All this would be prevented by an efficient Commander in Chief acting in concert with a vigilant Secretary at War. How far it would answer as to the immediate business of employing Lord Cornwallis I confess I have my doubts; that would depend upon the Duke of York having manhood and true spirit sufficient to prompt him to act as he ought to do.

'Having stated all this to you, you will anticipate the point I told you that I could not with propriety keep back. You must feel that the late Judge Advocate General's office must be the office of the Commander in Chief. Dont (?) at it for you must on a moment's reflection be satisfied not only of the necessity but of the propriety of it, for any other person acting in that office would be a real incumbrance in business in place of commanding it. Even as it now is, I think that is sometimes the case, but with such a Commander in Chief as I am supposing, and such a Secretary at War, I am positive it could never answer to keep any Person *whatever* in the situation I now hold. I state this with reluctance in case it should give you a moment's uneasiness, but I am sure it should not, and your understanding must perceive the justice of what I say upon it. In plain words, the Duke of York and Mr Windham acting in the same Department together would never submit to the official orders and business that I am in the daily Routine of doing.

'You will not impute to me a desire to avoid difficulties. I cannot state that stronger than by saying that if your Brother's mind could bring itself to view the Idea in the light I mean it, I shall without any reluctance agree *while the war continues* to act with him as a Puisne Lord of the Admiralty.'[1]

Apart from the curiously dictatorial tone of this letter addressed by a Cabinet Minister to the Premier, and the cool manner in which Dundas indicated the particular post that he would be pleased to accept, the letter shows that his main motive was one of jealousy – the fear that the replacement of the old Baron by the youthful Duke at the War Office would 'cramp his style'. It also throws a light upon the manner in which the Government regarded Lord Amherst, whose work as the head of the army has gone almost unrecorded by historians.

It is difficult to see how Dundas can really have supposed that his letter would not give the Prime Minister 'a moment's uneasiness'. He was in effect holding a pistol at his Chief's head – and his Chief submitted. The Cornwallis project was

---

[1] *Chatham Papers*, Vol. 157.

dropped, and Pitt was reduced to falling back upon the alternative of putting forward the name of the Duke of Brunswick.

The curtain now rises on the correspondence between the Prime Minister and the Sovereign. Having taken a fortnight to think things over, and after consulting Windham on his return from the Front, Pitt at length screwed himself up to the ordeal of tackling the King. On 11 October he wrote him another of his lengthy letters. Starting by stressing the necessity for 'one uniform direction of the war', he presently comes to his proposal, which is 'to propose to the Dutch government to offer the Duke of Brunswick the joint command of both Your Majesty's forces and theirs, and of any other which may serve within the Republic. Mr Windham seems confident, from the result of his conversations with the Duke of York, that His Royal Highness would feel no difficulty in acting under the Duke of Brunswick.

'It will be impossible for the Dutch to refuse the proposal if insisted on in Your Majesty's name. Should the Duke of Brunswick decline (which seems unlikely) the only alternative which has occurred is to endeavour to establish some council of war, which might direct the general operations of all the troops in Holland according to some uniform plan.'[1] This last remark is typically vague and amateurish – coming from the head of the Government after two years of war. The Royal reply came with the greatest promptness. Here it is in full:

'Windsor, 12 Oct., 1794.

'Mr Pitt's letter has been this instant received, but as the state of public affairs, I may say, fills up every crevice of my mind, I am able instantly to answer its contents: I entirely agree with him in opinion that, even should the Dutch be roused to suitable exertions, no great hope of success can be expected unless they will consent to be directed in the mode of employing those efforts suitably. I know I can answer for the zeal and good sense of my son, the Duke of York, that, to obtain so desirable an event, he will gladly consent that the Duke of Brunswick should be invited to come and take the supreme command of the allied army in the same manner the late

[1] *Windsor*, 11.10.94.

Prince Ferdinand of Brunswick stood in the last German war, which gave no interference in the interior arrangements of the separate troops that composed his army: thus my son's commission for commanding the British and Hannoverian troops would not be infringed on, and the Hereditary Prince of Orange would still be at the head of the Dutch. Should the Duke of Brunswick decline, I do not see any other mode of forming a Council of War than the offering the Prince of Orange himself to be at the head of it, which (though the natural place of the Stadtholder in time of danger) he will decline; then I must insist on my son holding that situation with such men as Gen. Walmoden, Sir William Erskine, Lieut.-Gen. Abercrombie, and such other foreign, as well as national officers, as it may be thought right to place such trust in, with perhaps the assistance of some civil man for conducting the arrangements with the Dutch. It occurred to me that Mr Windham might be one of the properest persons for such a commission.'[1]

The Duke of Brunswick declined the post, and there the matter for the moment came to a standstill.

The King's letters to his son at this time are full of interest, judging by the rather rare examples that have survived. Writing on 3 October he gave some good advice: 'I trust . . . you will collect your whole force together, not throw small parts of it into those fortresses which must reduce your army to nothing, and prevent your being in a situation to carry sufficient force to repel the attacks that may be made at any given point. . . . It is by experience of former error that we can alone guard against the renewal of them. . . . Keep up your spirits, remember that difficulties are the times that show the energy of character; and as the rest of Europe seems blind to the evils that await the unprosperous conclusion of this business, it is my duty and that of my country by the greatest exertion to attempt to save Europe and society itself.'[2]

* * * * *

On 2 October Clerfait fell back across the Rhine, and prospects of co-operation between the two armies appeared more remote than ever. To add to the Duke's worries, the state of the army was deteriorating. Fresh units were sent out, consisting

[1] *Rose*, p. 229. The original is in the *Chatham Papers*, Vol. 103.   [2] *Taylor*, p. 49.

of green troops, inadequately trained, equipped and disciplined, and badly officered; some of the new colonels were youths scarcely out of their teens. This disgraceful state of affairs was directly due to the system devised by Dundas and Pitt, whereby anyone who was prepared to pay for raising a regiment might have the privilege of commanding it in the field. There is no need to expatiate here on the viciousness of this system – if it can be dignified with the name. The artillery was, above all, in a parlous condition. To Windham the Duke wrote, pleading for help in this matter: 'For God's sake press for the sending out of more artillery, men and of drivers . . . as we shall have many batteries to defend along the Waal, and as we have a great many horses without any persons to take care of them.'[1]

On hearing of the proposal to place the Duke of Brunswick over his head he assured Windham: 'I cannot hesitate a moment in acquiescing cheerfully in it, and I need not, I know, add that I shall continue to serve with equal zeal under the Duke of Brunswick.'[2]

The retreat of the Austrians across the Rhine necessitated the Anglo-Dutch conforming by lining its continuation – the Waal – with forward posts still maintained at Grave and Nimeguen. But hope flickered on that the Prussians would at long last co-operate in this campaign, and on 20 October York sent Colonel Don to see Mollendorf with the suggestion that the Prussians should defend the line of the Rhine as far as Bonn, and that a continuance of the British subsidy would in that case be granted. But Mollendorf told Don bluntly that the Treaty was 'at an end and that he had nothing to do with any plan of co-operation with the Duke of York or Clerfait'.[3]

About this time the faithful Calvert writes to his uncle: 'General Balfour is returning to England in a few days . . . and if I mistake not, returns with strong favourable impressions of the Duke of York, which I dare affirm will be the case with all liberal, candid men, who have intercourse with His Royal Highness.'[4]

Unfortunately, it was not every officer then serving in the army who was liberal and candid. Calvert evidently had these persons in his mind as he wrote on, his pen almost spluttering

[1] *Add. MSS.*, 37842, f. 78.   [2] Ibid., f. 95.
[3] *Malmesbury*, III, p. 144.   [4] *Calvert*, p. 367.

with rage, in an incoherent passage: 'Much do I fear that, in spite of the most damning evidence, there still remain in certain quarters grains of confidence (which bear in them the ruin of our country) in the most unprincipled and deceitful and now most ineffective imbecile Cabinet that ever disgraced the political annals of Europe.'

Meanwhile the military prospects became steadily, even rapidly worse. Bois-le-Duc was shamefully surrendered by the Dutch on 10 October, and the Dutch garrison and defences of Nimeguen were so weak that the Duke was obliged to use some of his own exiguous forces to strengthen this vital town. The fortress lies on the southern bank of the River Waal, here about 400 yards wide. There was no permanent bridge, but the Duke's engineers threw a bridge of boats across it in twenty-eight hours – a remarkable achievement.

As the month of October drew to its end the days of Nimeguen seemed numbered: the French had reached its outskirts, and soon they would have the bridge of boats under the fire of their guns.

The Duke of York had by this time removed his headquarters to Arnhem, where 260 years previously the Earl of Leicester and Sir Philip Sidney had also established their headquarters. Nimeguen had also historic connexions for the English army, for it was from that town that the Duke of Marlborough had set out on his ten years of victories at the other end of the century.

On 28 October affairs took a sudden turn for the better. York's patient wooing of Clerfait seemed about to produce some result. At a conference at Arnhem, General Clerfait unexpectedly promised direct assistance to the Duke in the shape of a corps, 7,000 strong, under the command of General Werneck. The British Government was still paying out large sums to its Austrian allies, and the fruits were at last becoming visible. Werneck's corps was approaching along the eastern bank of the Rhine, via Wesel (forty miles higher up the river than Nimeguen). Clerfait undertook that Werneck's troops should arrive on 1 November, in time for a combined offensive by the Allies from Nimeguen on the 3rd.

The Duke was naturally delighted, and hastily began concentrating his troops and strengthening the garrison of Nimeguen. He calculated that he would be able to concentrate 30,000 troops for the battle, whereas the French opposite Nimeguen were, on Craig's estimate, about 25,000.

But now an ominous fissure in the structure of the Duke's army began to appear. Hitherto the Hanoverians, though they had often caused anxiety, had fought tolerably well, and, compared with the Austrians or Dutch, had been a very bulwark of strength.[1] But on the very day of the conference with Clerfait the Hanoverian generals held a meeting of their own, at which they decided to press for the evacuation of Nimeguen. And Craig remarks to Nepean: 'The Duke trusts Walmoden (the Hanoverian commander), but recently he has been leaning one way.'[2]

We shall very shortly see what this 'way' was. On 1 November Werneck's corps was due to arrive, but it was still reported to be ten miles distant, and Werneck gave a series of unconvincing reasons why it could not arrive till the 5th, in time for a battle on the 6th or 7th. He rode forward himself, on the 1st however, to Nimeguen, where the Duke called a conference to concert plans for the coming battle.

Let Craig (in a letter to Nepean) relate the doings of this momentous day.

'His Royal Highness desired me to ride over to Nimeguen with him, where there was to be a conference to be held to determine on the outline of the plan of attack.' Together, therefore, they galloped along the dozen miles of road that separated these two famous towns, along the selfsame road that British troops trod so painfully in the opposite direction in the same month of 1944 – one hundred and fifty years to the month later.

'Generals Walmoden, Werneck, Prince Frederick of Orange and His Royal Highness were the persons present, and it is necessary to observe that I considered myself only as an officer attendant upon His Royal Highness to give him any information that might be necessary, or to obey any commands that he might have to give.

'It was proposed to go to the church to view the enemy's camp, and in a conversation previous to leaving the room, His

[1] The Hessian mercenaries had already cracked, as the affair of Boxtel had shown.
[2] W.O., I, 170, f. 885.

Royal Highness observed that General Hammerstein must be acquainted with the country, upon which General Walmoden said he would send for him. General Hammerstein joined us at the church and accompanied us home, as I supposed by accident. During the conversation which ensued I could not refrain from making a few observations. . . . To my surprise, as soon as the paper was drawn up by General Walmoden [this was a statement opposed to the proposed battle] I found myself called upon to sign it. I did not hesitate an instant in declaring that I could not put my name to a paper by which would be implied my assent to the contents of it. . . . What I said appeared to me to give offence both to Walmoden and to Werneck. . . .

'His Royal Highness was of my opinion, and is so still, yet I cannot but think that he acted wisely in adopting the movement proposed by General Werneck in preference to it, for otherwise we should have run the greatest risk of not attempting anything at all.

'The whole will depend upon Nimeguen being able to hold out till the 8th or 9th.'[1]

General Werneck's proposal was that, instead of joining the Allies at Nimeguen and co-operating in an attack from there, as proposed by the Duke, his own corps, reinforced, should cross the Rhine at Wesel, over a bridge to be thrown by him (and paid for by the British) and attack the enemy from the east. There was no talk of co-operation by the British army from Nimeguen in this attack.

Craig's letter concludes: 'The position which (the French) have taken offers in my opinion, every hope, if the attack was managed in the way proposed by His Royal Highness, of gaining their right flank upon a range of heights which entirely commanded the position of their whole army.'

The probable explanation of this conduct on the part of Walmoden is that the strain of the war was becoming too much for him: he was visibly wilting. We have evidence of this in an unlooked-for quarter. The young Prince Ernest showed by his letters to his eldest brother (written sometimes under a pledge of secrecy) that he had a keen eye and shrewd judgment. About this time he writes to the Prince of Wales: 'The troops

[1] *W.O.*, I, 171, f. 11.

N

look wonderfully ill. As for Walmoden, he is so altered. I never saw the like.'[1] These few short words explain a good deal.

In an undated letter, but probably written on 2 November, and marked 'Private and Confidential', Craig tells the same story. 'There is an invincible repugnance in all our Foreigners to charge themselves with the defence of Nimeguen. The Duke was there today, but as I went there at 5 o'clock in the morning, I was just come back and did not attend him. I was told that he was under a necessity of speaking pretty plain before he could get them to consent to stay. I own I have no great opinion of the Austrian movement by Wesel. . . . I by no means like Werneck. However, if the town can hold out for five days, by his accounts he will be ready. If it can hold out ten days the weather will probably relieve it.'[2]

'The paper' that Craig refused to sign is an astonishing document. It trumps up every possible specious objection to an attack by the British army; one of the objections being: 'That supposing the success of the attack, the difficulty of subsistence would render the results absolutely fruitless.'

As a sop to the Duke the past paragraph of this egregious paper hints that, if Werneck's plan fails the Duke's attack might be tried after all! This was a tolerably safe hint, for the signatories had a pretty shrewd suspicion that Werneck's attack would not take place at all.

And that is precisely what happened. Werneck eventually constructed his bridge (near the spot where the British crossed the Rhine in the opposite direction on 24 April, 1944), but he only passed two battalions across; Pichegru concentrated a force against them and threw them back again without difficulty. The bridge was dismantled, and the operation was over.

The operation was over, and so was the command of His Royal Highness the Duke of York. For the one event led directly to the other. As long as there remained a reasonable chance of returning to the offensive, in co-operation with the Austrians, hope 'sprang eternal' in the British breasts. But all chance of that seemed now over; the Austrians, Dutch, Hessians, and Hanoverians had already lost heart; and now, last of all, the British looked like following suit. Everything that might maintain or

[1] *Windsor*, 6.11.94.   [2] *W.O.*, I, 170, f. 921.

repair the waning morale was lacking; a shiftless, helpless, incompetent Government was depriving the troops of the very vitals of life. Craig, pleading bluntly: 'I wish to God you would send us, but it must be immediately, 20,000 pairs of good shoes', was reduced to adding: 'We will pay for them.'[1]

The situation was one of unrelieved gloom. When such a situation supervenes on a long retreat there is not an army in the world that will not have its morale impaired – even a British army. There will be a keen search for a scapegoat – on the part of the troops to relieve their feelings, on the part of the Government to save their own skins. The miserable physical conditions in which the army now found itself, with the prospect of their further deterioration as winter drew on, was bound to exacerbate this feeling. There were two possible scapegoats: the Commander-in-Chief and his Adjutant-General. So we need not be surprised to find Prince Ernest telling the Prince of Wales: 'From all that I can find out here, the whole army is enraged at Craig and Fox.'[2] (The reason for the animus against Fox, who still commanded a line brigade, is not obvious.)

In a letter of a later date Prince Ernest again girded at Craig and Fox. It happened this way. General Werneck, evidently anxious to rehabilitate himself in the eyes of the British after the Nimeguen fiasco, seems to have hoodwinked the future Duke of Cumberland, pouring into his ears a multitude of excuses, complaints, and wanton accusations. These were swallowed by the young and gullible Prince, who wrote to the Prince of Wales in blunt terms: 'The Duke has lost all his reputation with the Austrians', but he goes on to qualify it: 'They do not attribute it to him, but Craig and Fox are looked on, and *with right*, as two blockheads.'[3] It should be noted, however, that the headstrong and impulsive Prince Ernest was embittered against his brother for refusing him a higher command.

So much for the Austrians. To discover any outward word of complaint against the Duke on the part of the troops is difficult. No one would be anxious to commit himself to paper on such a dangerous subject. But the disheartening events of the fiasco of the great attack, followed a few days later by the unavoidable sequel, the evacuation of Nimeguen,[4] induced at least one

[1] *W.O.*, I, 171, 3.11.94.   [2] *Windsor*, 6.11.94.   [3] Ibid., 1.12.94.
[4] The evacuation of Nimeguen on 9 November was a military event of the greatest interest, involving exciting scenes on the bridge of boats and the flying bridge, and

officer, at or near headquarters, to write to an important personage at home, expressing his opinion – in very guarded terms – that there should be a change in the command.

The important personage was no other than Lord Cornwallis. The name of the writer has never been disclosed; evidently Cornwallis took appropriate steps to confide it to oblivion. Here is the portion of the letter which Cornwallis decided to send on to the War Secretary, at the same time enjoining him not even to attempt to guess the name of the author.

'Despised by our enemies, without discipline, confidence or exertion among ourselves, hated and more dreaded than the enemy, even by the well-disposed inhabitants of the country, every disgrace and misfortune is to be expected. You must thoroughly feel how painful it must be for me to acknowledge this, even to your Lordship, but no honest man who has any regard for his country can avoid seeing it. Whatever measures are adopted at home, either removing us from the continent or remaining, something must be done to restore discipline, and the confidence that always attends it. The sortie from Nimeguen on the 4th was made entirely by the British, and executed with their usual spirit; they ran into the French without firing a single shot, and consequently lost very few men; their loss was afterwards when they were ordered to retire; Yet from what I have mentioned in the first part of my letter, I assure you I dread the thought of these very troops being attacked or harassed in a retreat.'[1]

Before relating the sequel, let us examine a few points in the subject-matter of this letter. In the first place, it should be observed that the opening statement was much too sweeping and unqualified. Relations with the inhabitants varied considerably from place to place. Shortly afterwards Mrs Harcourt wrote: 'As to the English cavalry, they are so beloved that the people are as glad to have them as they are desirous of being rid of other troops.'[2]

typically cool behaviour on the part of the British troops trying to restore the situation and avert a panic; involving also strenuous efforts on the part of the French artillery to destroy the bridge, and of the British artillery to counter them. These little-known events belong to the history of the army and not of the Duke of York. They are contained in *W.O.*, I and VI.

[1] *Cornwallis*, II, p. 274.   [2] *Harcourt*, V, p. 557.

The first sentence of this letter does not give a true picture of the state of the troops, if credence is to be accorded to a description of the state of the army given by a regimental officer, Captain L. T. Jones, of the 14th Foot. 'There was no duty, be it ever so fatiguing or dangerous, but was done with cheerfulness and pleasure; there was a wonderful good understanding between all ranks, from headquarters down to the lowest; and one circumstance is to be mentioned, and which perhaps never happened before, nor ever will again in any army, that is, that there was not a tattler, or tale-bearer, in the whole army, or even a person suspected.'[1] Such a distinguished and experienced officer as David Dundas wrote that 'our late operations certainly do not tend to raise our spirits, but I do not think they have much damped them.'[2]

This first sentence, in fact, sounds a trifle hysterical; possibly the writer's nerves were giving way, like those of Walmoden. Then the phrases seem to come too trippingly: 'Honest man', 'regard for his country' – what have these expressions to do with seeing the facts correctly? The author is naturally sick of the campaign – as who was not? – and hints at the desirability of throwing up the sponge, and leaving the Dutch, for whom we had gone to Holland in the first instance, in the lurch. He is anxious to show everything in as gloomy a light as possible, but he has to get over the awkward fact that, in spite of being 'despised by our enemies', our troops had just soundly trounced that enemy in a brilliant sortie; so he is reduced to throwing out vague fears that in some future contingency (which, in fact, never arose) the result would be to make him shudder. He also admits farther on in the letter that he is speaking only for himself. In short, when examined closely, it is not a very impressive document.

Why, then, did Cornwallis decide to communicate it to the Government? It would be easier to answer this question if we knew the identity of the writer. But the implication seems clear, that he was a person whom Cornwallis had up till then held in high regard.

This brings us back to the problem, who was the writer of the fatal letter? Since the editor of the Cornwallis correspondence in 1859 could find no trace of his identity, it is unlikely

[1] *Jones*, p. 144.   [2] *Windsor*, 38955.

that his name will ever come to light. Cornwallis seems to have covered up the tracks too effectively. But from a number of indirect pointers, both in the letter itself and in Cornwallis's letter to Colonel Ross[1] we can, I think, get tolerably close to the author. He was evidently either at or in close touch with Headquarters, and had had personal dealings with the Duke. (Personal rancour cannot therefore be entirely ruled out as a motive, though not necessarily the dominant one.) He had been present with the army for some time; he had been in the habit of writing to Cornwallis prior to the war: he was a fairly intimate friend of the Marquis. From all this it would seem that the writer of the letter was either a member of the Headquarter Staff or a general officer. A further possible indication is that Cornwallis evidently had two correspondents at the front whom he indicates in a letter to Colonel Ross by the initials P. and D. I can trace no member of the Duke's 'family' under either of these initials except Colonel Don, who is not mentioned in the Cornwallis correspondence; moreover, there is not the faintest trace of any criticism, or lack of faith in the Duke on the part of the 'family'. What, then, of the generals? The initial P. (assuming it to be a surname) draws a blank. There were two generals with the initial D, namely David and Ralph Dundas. David was a level-headed officer, who a few years later consented to serve under the Duke on active service; further, he had just written an admirable appreciation of the situation to the Prince of Wales, which showed not the faintest trace of criticism of his chief. I think we can safely rule out David Dundas, as also Ralph Dundas, for the latter had no particular connexion with Cornwallis, and his name also never appears in the Cornwallis correspondence.

One more point about this letter should be noted. It does not explicitly advocate the recall of the Duke, and it is possible that the writer merely intended to put forward the idea once more of the selection of Cornwallis as Supreme Commander of the Allies. Certain it is that when the writer learnt of the result of his letter, he became 'a little frightened at the consequence of his letter', from which it would appear that he did not anticipate affairs taking the course they did. And finally he made it clear that it was in no sense a plot to get rid of the Duke; he had

[1] *Cornwallis*, II, p. 273.

not discussed it with his friends. The authorship must remain a historical mystery.

Cornwallis may have mistaken the import of this letter, and his action on it may have been hasty; but the Marquis was the soul of honour, and there can be no question of an intrigue on his part to supplant the Duke.[1] On the contrary, he feared rather than coveted the post, remarking to his friend, Colonel Ross, that it was in any case too late to save the campaign. That being his view, it must always remain a bit of a mystery what induced him to forward a large portion of the letter to the Government without even asking the consent of the writer.

This is not to suggest that under no circumstance is a subordinate justified in reporting home material facts which may be adverse to the commander in the field, but which will not otherwise come to the notice of authority. Nor is any blame to be imputed to Cornwallis for forwarding them. The cause is greater than the individual, however highly placed he may be, and governments are perforce dependent to some extent on the opinions of subordinate commanders when they decide to replace the commander in the field. It is a difficult, delicate matter for all concerned. It is analogous to the problem: 'Quis custodiet custodes?'

To resume the narrative. Dundas duly received Cornwallis's letter, but for several days he did not reply to it. He was busy conferring with his friend and chief, William Pitt. In the nature of things these two would not be likely to commit much to paper, and we are left to guess at the trend of their discussions. Eventually Pitt's mind was made up. The Duke must be recalled. He thereupon sat down one Sunday to indite to the King what was probably the longest and most difficult letter he ever wrote to His Majesty. Most of his letters were short to the verge of abruptness. Yet he had already sent three bulky envelopes to the King, containing letters on the subject of his son, and when George III saw the size of the new envelope he must have had a pretty shrewd idea as to the nature of its

---

[1] Only a few weeks before he had written to the Duke disclaiming any idea of what he called 'a dirty intrigue' in the controversy about the supreme command; to which the Duke magnanimously replied: 'I need not I trust, assure you that I am not of a suspicious disposition, and at the same time I have too high an opinion of your character to think that you are capable of any low or dirty intrigue.' (Cornwallis, II, 276.)

contents. Dundas, at any rate, was full of admiration for the letter, describing it as 'a very long and dutiful letter, but at the same time a very honest and firm one'. Let the reader judge for himself. Here is the momentous letter *in extenso*:

'Hollwood, Sunday, Nov. 23, 1794.

'Mr Pitt trusts Your Majesty will do him the justice to believe that he can never have a more painful task to execute than when he finds himself under the necessity of submitting any opinion to Your Majesty which is likely to create the smallest uneasiness and anxiety in Your Majesty's mind. On the present occasion he is aware that the subject to which he wishes to solicit Your Majesty's attention, is one of the greatest delicacy, and the most interesting to Your Majesty's feelings. But it appears to him to be at the same time too nearly connected with Your Majesty's service to make it possible for him to suppress his sentiments upon it without proving himself unworthy of the confidence with which Your Majesty has so long condescended to honour him and without sacrificing his duty to Your Majesty and the Public.

'It is hardly necessary to state how much the interests of Your Majesty's dominions and of all Europe depend upon the issue of the present crisis in the situation of the United Provinces. It is obvious, too, that, supposing the negotiation between the Dutch Government and France to proceed, the chief hope of their obtaining the terms which have been held out to them, or any others, consistent even with their temporary safety, must depend on effectual steps being taken during the negotiation to show that, in case of its failure, they are prepared to defend themselves with vigour. On the other hand, if the negotiation is broken off, the utmost exertions are evidently indispensable both with a view to their immediate safety, and to any plan of operations in the next campaign. Nothing, therefore, can be of more pressing necessity than to take every measure which can be likely to encourage such exertions.

'The languour and indifference of a great part of the [Dutch] nation, and the disaffection of others towards the subsisting Government are obstacles which, perhaps, cannot be entirely overcome. But their effect is certainly heightened by other causes. It is too evident how little harmony subsists between

Your Majesty's troops and those of the Republic. The inhabitants at large, instead of looking at the former as their protectors, have conceived an impression of their want of discipline and order which is represented to make their approach as much dreaded in many places as that of the enemy. These sentiments are not confined to the lower orders of the people, but are entertained in a greater or less degree by persons of the first weight and consideration.

'It cannot be disguised (however painful it is to be under the necessity of stating it) that these impressions with respect to the army affect in some degree the public opinion with respect to the commander. It is indeed impossible that the zeal and meritorious exertions of the Duke of York should be disputed by anyone who has the opportunity of being accurately informed of his personal conduct. But the general impression is formed on other grounds; and even those who know in how many respects he is entitled to praise, are not without apprehension that the want of experience and of habits of detail may have made it impossible for him to discharge all the complicated duties of his situation, and effectually to prevent or remedy the abuses and evils which have crept into the service. In addition to these circumstances, which relate to the interior management of the army, it is also evident that the relative situation of the Duke of York and of the Prince of Orange too naturally leads to occasions of jealousy and misunderstanding. There exists nowhere a sufficient confidence in the general direction of military operations. This circumstance would of itself be sufficient to check and discourage effectual exertions, and the Duke of York is left to contend with these disadvantages, in a situation which would of itself be difficult and arduous to the most experienced general possessing the most unlimited confidence of those with whom he is to act.

'Under these circumstances Mr Pitt is reluctantly compelled to submit to Your Majesty his deliberated opinion that the continuance of the Duke of York in the command can be attended only with the most disadvantageous consequence to His Royal Highness himself; and that, considering the prejudices which he has to encounter, there is little prospect of his having the benefit of that hearty co-operation on the part of the Dutch which is so necessary at the present crisis. On these grounds alone Mr Pitt would humbly implore Your Majesty to put an end to the Duke of York's command for the sake of His Royal Highness as well as that of the country.

'But it is not in Holland only that the public impression is to be considered. It is impossible to say how far this impression, if it is not removed, may operate in Parliament and in the Public [*sic*] to the disadvantage of Your Majesty's Government, and possibly to the obstruction of the vigorous prosecution of the war. At all events Mr Pitt ought not to conceal from Your Majesty that it will be impossible to prevent this subject from being brought into Parliamentary discussion; and he need not observe how much that circumstance would augment the difficulty either of His Royal Highness retaining or of his relinquishing the command. Mr Pitt has, in one respect, the less regret in finding himself obliged to state these considerations at the present moment, from a persuasion that, even if they were out of the question, the course of the war would of itself probably prevent the Duke of York's command from being of very long duration, at least to its present extent.

'It seems every day more and more evident that the period is approaching when a junction may be attempted with the royalists in the maritime provinces of France, and that the only chance of any decisive success from active operations will arise from directing the principal exertions of Your Majesty's arms to that quarter. If this opinion should, upon due consideration, appear to be well founded, Mr Pitt knows that Your Majesty feels too much the importance of all the interests which are at stake, to suffer any considerations of a personal nature to interfere with so essential an object; and he cannot doubt that the Duke of York's magnanimity and his zeal for Your Majesty's service, would make him enter warmly into the same feelings.

'Mr Pitt trusts the importance of the occasion will be an apology for his trespassing so long on Your Majesty's indulgence. He is aware of the repugnance which Your Majesty may naturally feel in the first moment to a measure which nothing but a sense of indispensible duty and the most anxious concern for Your Majesty's service would have led him to propose. If, on considering the reasons which he has taken the liberty of urging, Your Majesty should be pleased to approve of the Duke of York's withdrawal from the command, it will remain to consider in what manner the measure may be adopted with the greatest attention to the wishes and feelings of the Duke of York. If the armies on each side should soon take up their winter quarters, or if events should lead to dividing Your Majesty's force according to the plan lately transmitted by His Royal Highness, either of those circumstances might naturally furnish an opening for His Royal Highness coming home on leave of absence; in which case the command of the Hanoverians would probably devolve upon Gen. Walmoden, and it might perhaps not be difficult to manage that the British should be placed under the command of Gen. Abercrombie, who seems to stand higher than any other officer in general opinion.

'Mr Pitt would have performed but in part the painful duty which he has undertaken if he omitted to state that in this country many persons, the most attached to Your Majesty's Government, and the most eager for the vigorous prosecution of the war, cannot suppress their anxiety on this subject. It seems generally felt that, when the Duke of York was originally appointed to the command, it was under circumstances in which he would naturally act in conjunction with officers of the first military reputation, with whom the chief direction of operations would naturally rest.[1] But by the course of events he is now placed in a situation where the chief burden rests upon himself, and where his conduct alone may decide on the fate of Holland, and perhaps on the success of the war. Such a risk appears to be too great to remain committed to talents, however distinguished, which have not the benefit of long experience, and which cannot therefore be expected at such a time to command general confidence.'[2]

How are we to assess this letter? What were the dominant motives that decided Pitt's course of action? Let it be granted at once that there might appear to be a *prima facie* case for a change of commander. Now, practically every step in war (and

---

[1] In the original draft of this letter, preserved in the *Chatham Papers*, this passage runs (portions excised denoted by brackets): 'It was under circumstances in which he would naturally act in conjunction [if not under the direction of] officers of the first military reputation [and in which the want of military experience in himself might be productive of no material inconveniences] with whom the chief direction of operations would naturally rest.' (Op. cit., Vol. 101.)

[2] *Rose*, p. 230. The original is at Windsor, No. 7659.

for the matter of that in peace) is the resultant of divergent motives and considerations; it is a balance of pros and cons. It is not an absolute, but a relative consideration. It is not sufficient to say 'X has his failings as a general, therefore we will replace him by another general', but 'Can we find a better man for the job here and now?' Unless the answer to this question is a clear affirmative, a change in the command in the field with all the inevitable dislocations and frictions that must accompany it, is not justified. Before changes of high command were made in the Great War, the Government were satisfied that they had immediately available a better commander in a Haig, an Allenby, a Maude. The same was true of the World War. But this was emphatically not true of 1794. Pitt hinted vaguely that Abercromby might eventually be given the command of the British portion of the army, but even if that were fixed (and it never was), there would remain two equal commanders side by side, a British and a Hanoverian – a nonsensical arrangement. How could Pitt or anyone really suppose that the military operations would be executed more effectively with this divided command than under the single command of the Duke?[1] Pitt seems in his letter to have toyed with the argument that it did not really matter, for the campaign was practically over. But this was a contradiction of thought unworthy of the Prime Minister, for, if it were true, there was no overruling necessity to remove the existing commander, even though a suitable replacement were possible. Pitt was trying to have it both ways: in one sentence he hints that the campaign is over; in another he speaks of the fate of Holland being decided unless the Duke is removed. This line of argument is unconvincing, if not specious and insincere. It gives the impression that Pitt is trying to snatch at any argument and build up a case without proclaiming his real reason for the change.

What, then was his real motive? Is the clue to it contained in the hints thrown out in the course of the letter that political trouble would ensue unless something was done? Was the Duke, in fact, to be made a scapegoat? For several weeks the Government had been anxious to change the command, and their

---

[1] As a matter of fact, it was *less* effectively executed; the Allied generals, after the departure of the Duke, fell to quarrelling among themselves.

first attempt was described by Windham, in an unguarded phrase, as a 'stratagem'. As the British military fortunes became progressively worse, the need for a scapegoat became the greater. The Opposition would soon be on the warpath, and the Government would be fatally discredited. Such considerations can be attributed to the Prime Minister and at the same time he can be absolved of any unworthy motives or intrigues. He no doubt believed implicitly what he wrote to the King, that if the Government was discredited it would possibly militate against 'the rigorous prosecution of the war'. Pitt's patriotism cannot therefore be impugned, however much we may recognize and regret that the removal of the Duke of York was mainly occasioned by political considerations, based on an anonymous letter.

Be this as it may, the letter was dispatched and duly received. As usual the King was prompt with his reply. Here is the salient passage:

'Having no longer a son at the head of the army on the Continent, I shall certainly not confer the command of the Hannoverians on any other general than Gen. Walmoden; and if there is any intention of drawing from the army on the Continent troops to embark for France, Mr Pitt must remember I from the beginning of the war declared my Hannoverians could not be employed on that service. They must therefore either remain to defend Germany against the French, if this country will keep up an army on that side, or be allowed to return home. I own(e) from this hour I despair of any effectual measure against France; for if our attention is only taken up to the North and West, or that only on the East the appearance, not an efficient army, is kept up, I fear no good will follow such an half measure.'[1]

Two days after inditing this reply the Sovereign met his 'confidential advisers' in the Closet. With some trepidation they must have approached the council chamber. What would the King say? The King said – nothing; absolutely nothing! And Pitt did not venture to broach the subject, though several essential arrangements remained to be discussed and settled. That evening Dundas, having returned to his own office, wrote to the King, and simultaneously Pitt did the same.

[1] *Stanhope*, II, App. xxi.

'Nov. 26 1794.

'Mr Pitt did not trouble Your Majesty this morning on the subject on which he had so lately submitted his opinion to Your Majesty, conceiving from the answer which Your Majesty honoured him with that Your Majesty did not wish to enter into any particular description of it. Mr Dundas now submits to Your Majesty a draft of a despatch to the Duke of York conformable to that opinion. On the subject itself it is impossible for Mr Pitt to add anything to what he has already stated except to express the satisfaction he derives from observing that Your Majesty does justice to the motives which led to the representation which he humbly submitted to Your Majesty.'[1]

The King's reply:

'Queen's House, Nov. 27, 1794.

'There could have been no advantage in discussing with Mr Pitt yesterday the subject of his letter, as I had, though reluctantly, assented to his proposal. I have written to my son simply that the present complication of affairs required his presence here, but thought it more advisable not to enter any farther as to the end this business may take.'[2]

Dundas's letter of recall was framed as follows:

'Horse Guards, Nov. 27, 1794.

'Sir,

'The present very extraordinary and critical situation of Holland, and the state of the combined forces employed for the protection of that republic, render it extremely desirable that His Majesty's confidential servants should as soon as possible have a personal communication with Your Royal Highness upon those important subjects, and I am commanded to signify to Your Royal Highness, His Majesty's pleasure that you should take the earliest opportunity of returning to England, leaving the command of His Majesty's British forces in the hands of such British officer as may be next in seniority to Your Royal Highness, after furnishing him with such information and instructions as Your Royal Highness may judge to be necessary for his guidance.'[3]

Apart from the glaring *suggestio falsi* of this epistle, the extraordinary ignorance and apparent indifference of the War

[1] *Rose*, p. 234.   [2] Ibid., p. 234.   [3] *Cornwallis* ii, 275.

Secretary as to who was to succeed to the acting command should be noted. It is even worse than it appears, for though Harcourt was the second senior, Dundas assumed that it was Erskine, and wrote instructing him to open the Duke's correspondence during his absence.

The Duke, acting on his instructions, handed over the temporary command to Generals Harcourt and Walmoden, made a brief leave-taking, and on 2 December departed from his army – never to return.

The simple-hearted Jones records: 'Here the British army lost a father and a friend, who had endeared himself to them by his humanity, justice and benevolence. The army felt themselves very much obliged to their commander.'[1]

The Duke's departure was a sudden one. Mrs Harcourt wrote: 'I am sure you will be as much surprised as we were at the Duke's sudden journey; he got orders suddenly and unexpectedly. The command of all the British devolves on General Harcourt. . . . He therefore most anxiously wishes the Duke's speedy return.' And next day she adds: 'All here are puzzled and uneasy at the Duke's being sent for to England. I hope he will not be ill-used there for he does not deserve to be so. God grant that he may soon return.'

A few days later she writes: 'The Duke of York has been cruelly dealt with: he had every impediment to success when here, and ill-usage from home to encounter.'[2]

Colonel Calvert also had his misgivings: 'If the Duke's stay in England is protracted beyond a very short period we expect his orders to follow him. I am patriotic enough sincerely to wish that His Royal Highness's immediate return may render this measure unnecessary, for I am persuaded his presence will remove many difficulties to which the service is subjected.'[3]

Chesterfield's cynical saying that no man is a hero to his own valet (read 'staff') was untrue in the case of the Duke of York.

That he did not himself expect recall is shown by his last letter, written to the Prince of Wales on 29 November, in which, after detailing the best route to England for Princess Caroline, he concludes serenely: 'We are strongly upon our guard.'[4]

[1] *Jones*, p. 144. [2] *Harcourt*, V, p. 570.
[3] *Calvert*, p. 410. [4] *Windsor*, 29.11.94.

As far as his personal feelings were concerned, it must have been with a sense of relief that the Duke stepped on board the ship that was to take him to England. For eight months continuously he had borne upon his shoulders the immense responsibility of a protracted and unsuccessful campaign, replete with defeats, disasters, disappointments – but not despair. With none but Colonel Craig to whom he could look for sound advice – his English generals being undistinguished and his Allied generals unreliable – he was a lonely figure, a Royal Prince, the second subject in the Realm, beset with a sea of difficulties – and enemies. Badgered by an inquisitive and interfering Government, he scarce could call his soul his own. Yet not a word of public complaint escaped him, as far as I can ascertain – though he probably privately unburdened himself to the King, his father, in those lost letters. To his favourite brother, George, he made the studied understatement: 'I certainly have not passed a pleasant time.' And in moving, simple words he wrote: 'I have gone through a great deal indeed in this campaign; those who wish me well and are fully informed will do me justice.'[1]

On arrival in England the Duke went straight to Oatlands, where he found his Duchess well, and then on to Windsor. The details of what occurred at his first interview with the King, we naturally do not know. But he assured Calvert that the King received him 'most kindly', and we may be sure that he was shown Pitt's letter and the King's reply. Did he also see the fatal letter from Cornwallis's unnamed correspondent?

A surprising and curious development arose. Something went wrong with Pitt's calculations. No steps were taken to give the command to Abercromby, nor to attempt to unite it once more; Cornwallis, who had rather expected, and feared, a further invitation from the Government to assume the command, was kept out of touch with Ministers. The Cabinet were finding that it is not the easiest thing to sack a Royal Commander-in-Chief, and carry on as if nothing very particular had happened. They were still fencing about to find the best way out of a difficult situation. One project was to make the Duke Commander-in-Chief, with a seat in the Cabinet, and Cornwallis Master-General of the Ordnance, also (like his predecessor Richmond)

[1] *Windsor*, 4.11.94.

with a seat in the Cabinet. When Cornwallis heard of this he did not relish the idea, as he would be junior to the Duke, both being in the Cabinet. He therefore contemplated resignation.

Meanwhile the days and weeks were passing, and the farce of pretending that the Duke was merely on leave was kept up. Thus, when in December it was decided to remove seven battalions from Holland for service in France with the Royalists, orders were sent both to Harcourt and to York. What confusion there must have been! As late as 5 January 1795 we find the Duke writing sagaciously to the King, suggesting that his Ministers at Hanover should be asked to help in the provision of food and ammunition when our troops crossed the Yssel, as they were about to do, on their long retreat to Bremen.

Throughout this period the Duke was metaphorically in a state of 'suspended animation'. On 22 December he told Calvert briefly: 'Nothing is as yet settled concerning me, but I think a very few days will determine my fate.'

Finally Pitt addressed to the King a definite proposal. He writes of the present Commander-in-Chief, Lord Amherst, that 'his age, and perhaps his natural temper, are little suited to the activity and the energy which the present moment calls for'. He suggests that he should be given 'honourable retirement', and adds: 'Mr Pitt believes that, if it should be consonant to your wishes to place the Duke of York at the head of the army, such an arrangement would be very gratifying to Your Majesty's servants, though they do not presume to form any opinion . . . till they know that it is conformable to Your Majesty's sentiments.' Then the Prime Minister goes on, rather surprisingly: 'If Your Majesty should not incline to this proposal, it is humbly submitted to Your Majesty's consideration whether, with Lord Cornwallis in the Cabinet, as Master-general of the Ordnance, the Details of the army may not be conducted through the war office, without any commander-in-chief, more expeditiously than at present.'[1] This letter from the Windsor Archives clears up the doubt expressed by Fortescue as to who was responsible for this selection, though he believed it to be the King himself.

To Pitt's proposal the King agreed, but without specifying a date for the appointment to take effect. On 9 February Pitt

[1] *Windsor*, 28.1.95.

o

wrote again, suggesting that the appointment might well be made at once. The same day the King notified Pitt that he intended to make both Amherst and the Duke of York field-marshals,[1] and on the morrow the following letter to the Secretary at War ushered in a new chapter in the career of Frederick, Duke of York.

'George III to William Windham
'Queen's House, February 10, 1795.

'Mr Windham is to notify my son the Duke of York as Field Marshal and insert it in this night's Gazette besides sending the usual notification to the Secretary of State's Office.

'At the same time he is to have a letter of Service placing him on the Home Staff, which will give him naturally the command, which has till now been entrusted to Lord Amherst.

'I suppose Lord Amherst's Situation ceasing, it will be proper that (it) should be notified to him by Mr Windham, who, I am persuaded, will express it in terms of my approbation of his Services, both when commanding in North America and since I have called him into Succession to the head of the British Staff.

'George R.'[2]

[1] Lord Amherst declined the honour.
[2] *Windham*, I, p. 286.

8

Having reviewed and examined the Duke of York's generalship in his first campaign, we will here confine ourselves to the question: Did his generalship develop or deteriorate in his second campaign? It will be convenient to consider this from three points of view, that of the Government, that of the general public and lastly that of the historian.

Taking the Government first: there can be no doubt that in the eyes of Pitt and Dundas the Duke was a disappointment. They were civilians, and did not understand war; they judged purely by results – not a bad method in some circumstances, but particularly dangerous and misleading in the present case. They placed an exaggerated value on the ability of the general to decide the issue of a campaign. When his strategy is decided for him, either by his own Government or by his allies; when those allies prove themselves treacherous or devoid of the will to fight; when he has had no say or hand in the training of his troops; when the majority of them are foreigners whom he has not met face to face till the eve of the battle; when, as happened in his second campaign, he is consistently outnumbered; when he is provided with an improvised and inadequate staff; when he is allowed too few generals, and when those few are for the most part, of second-rate quality; when he has thrown at him a number of newly formed regiments, recruited from the dregs of the population, ill armed, ill equipped, ill trained and ill clad, and commanded by youths who are themselves totally devoid of training – when the commander-in-chief is confronted with all these adverse factors, it is idle to judge him by results, or to express surprise when he fails to produce victories 'out of his hat'.

Yet such was the position of the unfortunate Duke of York, and the wonder is that he did not throw up the sponge long before the end of his second campaign. Only a high sense of duty deterred him from this course.

In the previous chapters his difficulties with his allies have
only been lightly touched on; these details pertain rather to the
history of the army than to that of the Duke of York. Those
who are interested will find the subject excellently dealt with
in Fortescue's admirable *History of the Army*. But, in this connexion, it will be as well to insert here a paper drawn up under
the direct supervision of the Duke of York, if not actually
written by him, in November, setting out the main headings of
his trouble with the Dutch. It is doubtful whether the Cabinet
gave much heed to it, or even read it, for by the time they
received it they had made up their minds to recall their
Commander-in-Chief. Yet it contains valuable information, not
obtainable elsewhere.

The Duke's covering letter to Windham and the paper can
now be given.

'20 Nov. 1794.

'I at last send you enclosed the paper which you wished to
receive containing a short account of the many subjects of
complaint which I have against the Dutch. The continual
hurry and press of business since you left me have delayed my
drawing it up since, nor indeed have I had time to correct it.
It would have been impossible to specify every instance of want
of foresight, of energy, of faith which I have met with during
the course of this campaign from the Dutch nation. . . . I
have therefore only mentioned the principal ones. At this
present instant every effort is making to throw the whole
blame for the evacuation of the Netherlands on me, and they
even go so far as to say that it is owing to my having evacuated
the Netherlands that the Austrians could not act.

'They at the same time refuse us quarters and even places to
put the magazines in. . . .'[1]

The paper referred to in the above letter (*Add. MSS. 37842*
f. 97, extending to twenty-one pages of foolscap) is as follows:

'From the moment the Austrians abandoned the Scheldt, it
was easy to see that they had resolved to retire behind the
Meuse and that the whole Dutch frontier would be open to the
attack of the enemy, having no other protection than their
fortresses and their army in His Majesty's pay, which did not
at that time exceed 23,000 fighting men, and which certainly

[1] *Add. MSS.* 37842, f. 95.

was not strong enough to cope with the armies which the enemy could bring against it.

'In different conferences held during the time the army covered the dykes, the Hereditary Prince of Orange was repeatedly entreated to press the putting the Dutch fortresses into a perfect state of defence, which he as often promised.

'When the British retired from Antwerp to the camp of Rosendael, the governor of Bergen-op-Zoom sent to acquaint the Duke of York that his garrison consisted only of 400 men, and that he required 2,000 merely to secure the place from being taken by a coup de main, adding at the same time that he had no artillerymen and was exceedingly deficient in arms and provisions.

'Under these circumstances the Duke of York thought himself obliged to give him two British and two Hessian battalions for the immediate protection of the Place, but under the most solemn promises of both the Princes of Orange that they should be immediately relieved by Dutch regiments, as it was directly contrary to His Majesty's instructions that any of his troops should be placed in the Dutch fortresses.

'This promise was again repeated at a conference held at Breda on 27th July.

'On 8 August, in consequence of the news of the enemy having forced the passage of the island of Cadzand, and having invested Sluys, the Prince of Orange proposed to make an expedition in order to attempt the relief of the Place for which purpose he desired the Duke of York to leave the 2 British and 2 Hanoverian battalions (which were to have quitted Bergen the next day) till after the expedition, giving his most solemn promise that whether the expedition succeeded or not, these battalions should be relieved within 12 days, and Prince Frederick acquainted the Duke of York at the same time that even if the expedition proved successful it was the Prince of Orange's determination to remove the artillery and ammunition from all the fortresses in Flanders and to evacuate that country.

'Induced by these assurances, by which at any rate 4 out of the 6 Hanoverian battalions, near 5000 troops, and 300 pieces of cannon, would be saved, the Duke of York agreed to leave the battalions at Bergen till the expedition was over. The Dutch troops were accordingly sent over to the island of Axtel, and the day fixed for this attack. But before it took place, accounts were received of His Majesty's gracious intention of sending Lord Mulgrave with 4000 British troops to Flushing, upon which the expedition was put off till their arrival and never could afterwards be attempted with any possibility of success: as at the time of its being first proposed the enemy had invested Sluys with only 8000 men, but upon receiving intelligence that the Dutch had sent a corps of troops to the island of Axtel, they immediately reinforced their army to the number of 20,000, which totally prevented any further attempt.

'Having waited till every idea of this attack was avowedly given up, the Duke of York reminded the Prince of Orange of his positive promise to relieve the troops in British pay at Bergen; when he received for answer that his Serene Highness had determined not to evacuate Flanders and that it was impossible to relieve the British troops in that Fortress.

'During the time that the British troops were encamped at Berlikum, the Duke of York repeatedly pressed Prince Frederick of Orange and Colonel Bentinck, the Dutch Q.M.G. to put Fort Crevecoeur into a proper state of defence, and to provide it with a sufficient garrison, as it was allowed by them both to be the key of Bois-le-Duc. Colonel Bentinck insisted that it was provided with everything except a garrison. However when it was attacked it was found by woeful experience that the Place was not only totally unprovided with ammunition and provisions but that there was not a single traverse in all the works and that the inundations which form its principal defence, not having been begun till after the retreat of the enemy from Berlikum, and therefore not being completed, the enemy was enabled to wade through the water and to come actually upon the glacis.

'On the day that the British army retreated across the Meuse the Prince Frederick of Orange begged the Duke of York to send a detachment of 300 men into Fort Crevecoeur, promising to relieve it within three days, to which the Duke of York (knowing the importance of that Place) felt himself obliged to consent, and he immediately sent them three companies of the Hesse Darmstadt Light Infantry. The Prince of Orange's promise, however, was not kept, and though the Dutch battalions which were destined to be thrown into Bois-le-Duc, arrived opposite to the Fort, upon finding that communication was cut off between that place and Bois-le-Duc, they retreated without relieving the Hessian garrison which was accordingly taken in the Fort; and they have been obliged to be sent back to their own country as they are not allowed to soldier again till exchanged.

'Prince Frederick of Orange undertook the same day to provide the artillerymen necessary to defend the island of Bommell, as well as Fort St Andrew, and insisted on entrusting the construction of the batteries to a Dutch engineer. These works, however, were not begun for a week after the troops destined for the defence of the island arrived in it and were carried with the greatest slowness in spite of the repeated representations of the Duke of York, nor was half of the cannon necessary for the defence of the work sent there for above a fortnight which obliged the Duke of York to give them one battalion of the Hessian Reserve artillery, and when the Dutch artillery did arrive no artillerymen came with it so that the Hessians were obliged to lend their artillerymen to work the Dutch guns nor was this neglect remedied during the whole time that His Majesty's troops occupied the island of Bommell which was till 25th October, as in spite of every representation of the Duke of York and of Lieut.-General Abercromby there never came more than two Dutch artillerymen per gun.

'On 23rd September at a conference held at Nimeguen at which the two Princes of Orange, the Duke of York and Mr Windham were present, the Hereditary Prince of Orange proposed to the Duke of York that in case either the passage of the Meuse was forced or that the Austrian army abandoned its position on the Roer, which would equally oblige the Duke of York to cross the Waal, that he should take upon himself the defence of that river and keep as long as possible Nimeguen, engaging on the part of Holland to put that town into the most perfect state of defence and to make the batteries along the river, as well as to furnish the artillery and artillerymen necessary for these batteries, to which the Duke of York consented. The Hereditary Prince added that the artillery necessary for the town of Nimeguen and for the batteries of the Waal was already embarked, and was hourly expected to arrive. However, on 7 October when His Majesty's army was obliged to

retreat to Nimeguen in consequence of the Austrians army
having abandoned the Roer, and crossed the Rhine, the Duke
of York found that nothing had been done to put the forts of
that town into a state of defence, except palisading a small part
of the outwork, that no artillery whatsoever was arrived, that
not even a platform was laid nor was a single battery begun
upon the Waal.

'Grave had been equally neglected, in the same shameful
manner in spite of the repeated entreaties of the Duke of York
and of promises as frequent on the part of the Prince of Orange.

'On 7 October there was not a morsel of provision in the
town, neither did the Dutch garrison consist of more than 800
men, though the place required at least 1800 to defend it.

'Under these circumstances and knowing the extreme importance of making every effort to save them, the Duke of York
thought himself obliged to remain as long as possible in front
of Nimeguen with that part of his force which was not detached
for the defence of the island of Bommell and of the banks of the
Waal and Rhine, in order to keep up the communications with
Grave and to give as much time as possible to throw the necessary succour into it as well as to cover the works carrying on at
Nimeguen to put it into some state of defence. After the most
pressing entreatie, the Duke of York at last obtained a reinforcement of 400 men and 30 artillerymen for the defence of
Grave but the remaining 400 which were equally promised
were never sent. The necessary provisions for the place were at
last with great difficulty thrown in. In order to expedite as
much as possible the repair of the work at Nimeguen the Duke
of York furnished 800 workmen per day from the troops encamped before the town, and at the same time employed the
battalions cantoned along the northern bank of the Waal, to
make all the batteries along the Dykes, and which were finished
without receiving the least assistance from the Dutch, though
they undertook the whole work.

'As for the artillery and ammunition both for the town of
Nimeguen and for the batteries along the Waal which the
Hereditary Prince of Orange had declared on 23 September
was already embarked and coming up to Nimeguen, no tidings
whatever could be heard of it except that three days after the
troops retreated to the camp before Nimeguen, it had arrived

at Bommell. But as the enemy were at the moment in possession of St Andrew, Major General Balfour had been obliged to send it back and order it to come round by the Issel lest it should fall into their hands.

'Finding that no one of the Dutch officers knew anything of this artillery the Duke of York was obliged to send four officers of His Majesty's troops to seek after it and to hasten its arrival, but unluckily, in spite of all their endeavours, so many difficulties were thrown in the way by the shameful negligence and want of foresight of the Dutch, in not providing horses or ropes to draw the boats up the Issel, which the Duke of York was obliged to send detachments of cavalry, that it did not arrive at Nimeguen till the night of the 18 October when all the outposts had been driven in and a part of the troops had already crossed the Waal, in order to strengthen the cordon upon the river. It was likewise so divided in the different boats and without any specification of the freight of each that it was found impossible to disembark it and it was obliged to be sent back to Pannardin and to be there examined and put into order.

'However defenceless a state of defence the town of Nimeguen was in yet, sensible of its importance as being the only passage over the Rhine except Mayence which the Allies could command, the Duke of York was anxious to make every effort to save it, and therefore left in it a corps of above 8,000 men with all his field artillery which he thought he could do without much risk, as long as he was able to preserve the bridge over the river.

'As however it was impossible to know how long the troops would be able to hinder the enemy from advancing sufficiently to endanger the bridge, and being thoroughly convinced by the report of the chief engineer as well as of all the general officers that the town could not be defended four days after the bridge should be destroyed the Duke of York thought it necessary for his own honour and vindication to acquaint the Prince of Orange with the real state of the Place and with the utter impossibility of defending it should it be seriously attacked.

'It is not necessary in this paper to enter into the transactions which passed concerning Nimeguen: suffice it to say that His Majesty's troops kept that place till every chance of succour from the Austrians was over, and till the bridge was considerably damaged.

'They at last evacuated the town without the least loss and the Dutch troops might have done the same if it had not been for the shameful neglect of their commander General Hache, and their own fears which prevented them from following the directions given them for making use of the flying bridge.

'Having thus briefly stated the material causes of complaint which His Majesty's troops have against the Dutch it is but right to add that the ignorance and want of activity of all the Dutch officers are such as to impede every operation in which their assistance is necessary. Even the inundations, which being the great feature of the defence of the country they ought particularly to have studied, have in every instance yet been misrepresented.

'At the same time the ill-will manifested upon all occasions and the want of energy in the Government to counteract the impediments arising from the claims of rights and privileges of towns and nobility, make it extremely difficult to conduct the necessary movements of an army.'[1]

It is a sad, sorry story, and one puts the paper down with the strong conviction that the Duke's problem was quite insoluble, that whatever steps he took or attempted the die was cast: the Dutch nation had no stomach for the fight, and was looking for the first opportunity to get out of the war. This, indeed, it succeeded in doing one month after the departure of York from the army.[2]

But not only did the Government judge by results: they, to some extent had their minds poisoned against the Duke by a 'whispering campaign' directed from the front by well-born but ill-disciplined officers, civilians of yesterday, who had got into uniform solely by the power of the purse. It is difficult to trace the details of this poison-talk: it is in the very nature of the case that it should be so; these disgruntled officers took good care to cover up their tracks, but there is no reason to doubt Fortescue's assertion that the Government did lend a ready ear to such tales. The irony and the tragedy of it is that the Government were themselves the authors of the egregious scheme which produced such insubordinate and harmful

---

[1] *Add MSS.* 37842, f. 95.
[2] It is sad to read in a modern Dutch history that the Dutch were left to their own resources, their allies only affording them 'token' support.

officers. The fact is, the army at the outbreak of the war was in as bad a state as it had even been in, and the ill-considered steps devised by the Government to increase its size tended to make it worse rather than better. Not even Lord George Sackville in the War of the American Revolution was more inept in his efforts at strategy and administration than was Dundas in the opening years of the War of the French Revolution.

It will have been observed that Pitt in his search for reasons for recalling the Duke had instanced his lack of experience. There might have been some substance in the 1793 campaign, but by November 1794 York had been continuously directing an army in the field for over a year and a half. Moreover, lack of practical experience is not necessarily an insuperable handicap to a general. The great Jomini dealt with this matter in an illuminating passage in his *Précis de l'Art de la Guerre*. 'One is often asked: Is it preferable to appoint a general of long experience in command of troops or an officer of the staff with little experience in the handling of troops. Without a doubt, war is a distinct science, and it is quite possible to be able to concert operations skilfully without having ever led a regiment against an enemy. Peter the Great, Condé, Frederick, Napoleon furnish examples of this.'

The Duke's knowledge of staff-work was, of course, confined to what he learnt during his seven years' tuition in Germany, which probably amounted to a good deal more than was possessed by the average English officer whose experience was confined to fighting in North America. Pitt also hinted in his letter to the King that he had hopes the Duke would consent to be guided by General Abercromby, of whose qualities as a general, he, in common with many others of his day, had formed an exaggerated notion. Though Abercromby had grown grey in the service and had not an enemy in the world, he had, contrary to general belief, seen no more field service than the Duke. Though he had served on the staff during part of the Seven Years War in Germany, he did not, according to his biographer, 'smell powder' till May 1793, three months after the Duke. As for listening to Abercromby's counsel and being actuated by it, the Duke's mistake was not that he ignored it, but that he did *not* ignore it. For Abercromby was, I regret to say, what would be now termed a 'defeatist', and his reports and counsel at Boxtel were, as we have seen, disastrous.

The Duke was handicapped, rather than helped, by the Government at home. The most apt criticism came from, of all people, Mrs Harcourt (no doubt echoing her husband's views), who wrote: 'Why will they not satisfy themselves with forming the general outline of the campaign, and supplying men and money, without attempting to direct particular military operations, having no knowledge of the art of war, being ignorant of local circumstances and at too great a distance to know the important and sometimes very sudden changes that arise.'[1] How the Duke of York would have enjoyed writing in these terms to Dundas! The latter implicitly admitted the interference of the Government in military operations when he wrote to Pitt: 'The operations of War are canvassed and adjusted in the Cabinet.' This he wrote in July 1794, when opposing the institution of a separate Secretary for War – an appointment which he considered superfluous! George Rose, writing to Lord Auckland in November, provides another example: 'Mr Pitt is to see Lord Grenville today, when the fate of the expedition will probably be finally settled.'[2] The propriety of taking expert military advice in these military matters does not seem to have occurred to the politicians.

A further difficulty against which the Duke of York had to contend was the inadequacy of his staff, and bad intelligence service. Bunbury states explicitly that 'every department of the staff was more or less deficient'.[3]

This shortage of staff reacted directly upon the Duke's control and influence on his army, for he was obliged to spend long hours at his headquarters inditing letters with his own hand to a multitude of correspondents of the various nationalities with whom he had to deal. The inevitable result was that he could not get abroad among his troops in the way that a Montgomery could. In the days before typewriters, stenographers, duplicators and motor-cars, such activity among the troops was impossible unless the army was concentrated, which it seldom was. Towards the end of the campaign it was strung out on a line ninety miles long. Under such circumstances it was physically impossible for the Duke, with the best will in the

[1] *Harcourt*, V, p. 418.   [2] *Auckland*, III, p. 140.
[3] *The Great War with France*. p. xxi.

world, and despite his well-known physical energy, to exercise personal influence on the discipline and morale of his troops. All he could do he did do, which was to issue strong disciplinary orders. These could not, however, be expected to have great effect.

And as regards intelligence, Captain Crauford of his staff wrote to Lord Auckland: 'The cause of failure in many instances in the last campaign was the want of good intelligence.'[1]

We deal next with the view of the Duke in the eyes of the general public. This is at once difficult and easy. Difficult, inasmuch as it is always difficult to generalize, and because there is little direct evidence: easy, if we confine ourselves to London Society, which led public opinion and which was very limited in extent. Roughly speaking, the public formed its assessment from three sources of information: first, the record of events at the Front, and the progress of the army; second, the stories and tales received from individuals at the Front, and third, cartoons and caricatures in the Press. As regards the record of events, the public saw, after a promising opening to the campaign, a great defeat, followed shortly afterwards by a long retreat which had not apparently been stemmed at the moment when the Commander of the army was recalled. As regards the tittle-tattle – for that is about what it amounted to – we are in the same difficulty as in the case of the Government: absence of documentary evidence. But caricatures usually reflect public opinion fairly accurately, and caricatures were not very kind to Frederick, Duke of York, during the campaign, as we have seen.

At the very moment when the Duke was marching with his army throughout the night, in his successful operation against the Camp of Famars, an infamous caricature was circulating through London from the pen of James Gillray, portraying life at the Duke's headquarters. He and his officers are sitting, carousing, the Duke with a girl on one knee, and a glass in his hand. His arrival in England in February for the conference with Mack was heralded with another disgraceful cartoon, in which the Duke, in a tipsy condition, is hiccoughing his greetings to the King, who is seated on his throne in hunting kit, and many other details of a like nature. It was on such things that the public was fed. Parliament was not much better.

[1] *Auckland*, III, p. 182.

Malone wrote to Lord Charlemont: 'The Opposition, of course, when there is the least disaster, are clamorous against him. . . . But they have been greatly supported by some of the fine gentlemen of St James's Street, who having gone into the army merely for pastime, as soon as the war came on most shamefully sold out; but now endeavour to screen themselves from disgrace by saying that they were driven out by the Duke's imperious and unpleasing manners.'[1]

And this brings us to the third point of view – that of the historian. In the first place, can the historian detect any difference in calibre, in method, in maturity, between the Duke of York at the beginning and at the end of his campaigns in the Low Countries? And if there was change, was it for the better? Let us consider first his mental approach to his task. Compare his actions in his first and in his last engagements. At Raismes we saw him rushing forward very largely in order to 'see the fun' for himself. At Caesar's Camp he led his advanced guard in person. At Boxtel, on the other hand, he kept back at his headquarters whilst awaiting a report from his advanced guard commander – Abercromby. From a technical point of view the latter was the correct action; in that respect he had learnt his lesson. At the same time it prompts the question: Was he losing his fire, his ardour for battle, his intense belief in the virtues of the offensive? Had the high living at headquarters about which there were so many whispers and tales sapped his vitality? It is the type of question to which it is impossible to give a positive and unqualified answer. All I confine myself to is to avow that I can find no direct evidence of it. No doubt, he, like everyone else, was, towards the end of the campaign, becoming depressed and even despondent. But there is no sign that he had lost faith in the offensive and was not, up to the last, constantly devising ways and means of carrying it out. No one surely can read Craig's account of the abortive war council at Nimeguen without realizing that the Duke, almost alone, was still adamant for the fray, while those around him had lost heart. Yet Sybel could write of him at this time (no doubt following Ditfurth): 'The Duke of York saw the growing evil with dull, hopeless despair.'[2]

Allied with the offensive spirit, and indeed a necessary con-

[1] *H. M. C. Charlemont*, p. 230.   [2] *Sybel*, IV, p. 127.

comitant with it, is the readiness to take risks – a military virtue for which British generals have not invariably been conspicuous. This virtue the Duke possessed to the full, and never was it more marked than in his last attempted operation, the abortive offensive from Nimeguen. The risk was certainly great, and was unduly harped upon by the Austrians and Hanoverians. There was but one bridge over the Waal with which to feed and support the attacking army. Yet the Duke, with his eyes open to the risk, did not flinch from it. David Dundas was explicit on the point in a letter to the Prince of Wales: 'Believe me, the Duke of York was determined to risk much, if the co-operation of our allies could have been brought into effect.'[1]

Our conclusion, then, must be that the Duke had matured since the outset of the campaign, and that his ardour and resolution were unimpaired at the time when he was recalled.

On what specific counts, then, can he be condemned – or even accused? Our difficulty in dealing with this question is that critics have been singularly vague in their accusations. Where a specific accusation is made, it can be investigated and either endorsed or refuted. But though I have searched every source of which I am aware in the English language, I have yet to find a specific charge (except in the case of Dunkirk) that at any period of his operations he took one course whereas he should and could have taken another. The absence of this form of criticism is most noteworthy. The fact is, he was so 'cribbed, cabined and confined' by his instructions that he seldom had the power to decide for himself in strategical matters. Thus there is little evidence on which to judge his operations. It was only in the little-known post-Dunkirk Campaign of 1793 that he was allowed any initiative, and here, by rapid marching, he was able to influence operations favourably.

On the other hand, we have ample evidence as to his strategical *ideas*. They are contained in his invaluable letters to his father, and again and again in his public letters and at councils of war. In this matter, we can find no trace of abandonment of the broad principles of strategy, which we noticed as being very much in evidence in his first campaign: the principles of the offensive, of co-operation, and of concentration. At Nimeguen he was still trying to bring about a great CONCEN-

[1] *Windsor*, 38970.

TRATION, by means of CO-OPERATION with his Allies in order to
take the OFFENSIVE against the French. The will was there: the
power was not.

To what extent was the Duke responsible for the lack of
effective co-operation on the part of his Allies in the field?
Just as it takes two to make a quarrel, so it requires two to
produce co-operation in the field; if one of the parties 'will not
play', there is little to be done. Yet the Duke of York seems to
have been uniformly on good personal terms with the generals
of the Allies. Here, no doubt, his position as a Prince of the
Blood helped him, and helped to justify his selection. He never
outwardly quarrelled with them, any more than did the Duke
of Marlborough with the Dutch generals. Nor were the ultimate
results of his patient endeavours to achieve co-operation with
Clerfait entirely fruitless. Though the fact is slurred over by
Fortescue, there is good evidence that Clerfait was beginning
to respond to the Duke's entreaties and overtures in the last
weeks of his command. The Duke had given pecuniary assistance to Clerfait and had provided Werneck with bread and
forage. St Helens, British ambassador at The Hague, wrote on
27 October: 'Clerfait continues to co-operate with us.'[1]

But, ironically, the full co-operation was only reached a few
days before the Duke's recall, when St Helens again wrote to
Paget: 'He (the Duke) has been actually joined by 32,000
Austrians under General Alvinzy, who has been directed to
put himself under H.R.H.'s command.'[2] The United Command
at last! Over 60,000 British, Hanoverian, Dutch, German, and
Austrian troops under a British commander – the largest army
to be commanded by an Englishman between Marlborough and
Wellington! Thus had the Duke's army grown from 2,000 to
over 60,000. And then he was recalled!

After strategy, tactics. We noted York's eye for country at
Famars and at Caesar's Camp. This essential quality of a general
was again demonstrated strikingly at Vaux, at Beaumont, and
probably, but not certainly, at Willems.

Moreover, his tactical combinations in these battles seem
beyond criticism – certainly I have not heard any of them criti-
cized. But this brings us once more up against the difficulty that
I have mentioned, that critics refrain from specifying what

[1] *Paget Papers*, I, p. 80.   [2] Ibid., I, p. 89.

alternate action to that taken should have been adopted. In the only case where I personally feel he was open to criticism (namely at Boxtel), his critics have endorsed his action: and in this case I believe that Windham and Abercromby were the evil geniuses. I think his real failing here was that he misrated the military judgment of Abercromby, and accepted his appreciation of the situation from a distance, whereas he should have gone forward to see for himself (though technically correct in remaining at his command post), when his eye for country and his resolution and his readiness to take risks would probably have resulted in the attack being carried out. Abercromby was his personal friend and was old enough to be his father, and the Duke was not firm enough with him.

This brings us to a point which I consider a real flaw in his quality as a general: he was too lenient with his subordinates. I think he lacked, or was averse to applying, the driving power that was necessary in the case of 'sticky' generals such as Abercromby. But there is not much evidence to go on. Boxtel is the only glaring example of it. We do know, however, that right through life he was kindly disposed to all, and consequently, like Abercromby, he had scarcely a genuine enemy in the world. The question is: Can a man be a really great general and yet have no enemies? It is doubtful. General Fuller probably has hit upon Robert E. Lee's weakness as a general when he asserts that he was 'too much of a gentleman'. The Duke of York was perhaps too much of a gentleman.

This leads on to the final point to be examined – the growing indiscipline in the army in Holland. Largely it was the fault of Dundas, who sent indisciplined soldiers to the front. When such folk join an army in full retreat, and never see it advance a single yard, when, in addition, they are stinted for food and clothing, and see quantities in the farms around them, while the inhabitants seem sour and hostile, the sequel is almost inevitable – pillage. The question is: Could the Duke have prevented it? We have seen the energetic steps he took to put it down early in the campaign and what complete success attended them. Did he later in the campaign become inured to such excesses or too lazy to exert himself to suppress them? Again one would like more evidence than is available. He certainly issued some

P

very stern orders of the day, reprobating such conduct and threatening sharp punishment; but these orders seem to have had little effect. Could he personally have done more? In the absence of specific evidence I am inclined to think that he was slightly remiss in this respect; that he did become partially resigned to what appeared to him almost unavoidable. The conduct of a majority of the Dutch inhabitants was so despicable and roused his ire to such a pitch that he would have been less than human if he had not been tempted to turn a blind eye to all but the worst excesses. Courts-martial, and punishments, however, did go on, and officers were not exempt from them. The truth is, many of the officers set such a bad example that discipline became doubly difficult to enforce.

Linked with discipline is morale. The one reacts upon the other. A prolonged retreat, such as that in North Africa in the summer of 1942, is bound to lower morale, and discipline is thereby endangered. But morale is an elusive thing to assess; it fluctuates rapidly on active service, and sometimes bursts unexpectedly into flame. In the very last engagement fought under the Duke – the action at Nimeguen on 4 November – the morale of the English troops engaged was to all appearance as high as it ever was. It is safe to say that excesses and indiscipline are not absent from any long retreat in any army. They are afterwards forgotten when the retreat ends in victory, such as did Sir John Moore's terrible retreat to Corunna; but if Moore had been recalled before he had had time to fight the battle of Corunna, more would have been heard of the bad conduct of the retreating troops.

If it was, under these circumstances, difficult for the Duke to curb the excesses of the British soldiers, how much harder it must have been to control disgruntled foreigners in British pay? The problem could only be solved in one way, and that way the foreigners practically refused to take – namely a resumption of the offensive.

The conclusion therefore seems to be, to put it into a nutshell, that impossible things were demanded of the Duke of York, and that he did as well as humanly could be expected of any English general. But if he had been less of a gentleman he would have been more of a general.

AT THE HORSE GUARDS

9

It must have been with mixed feelings that Frederick, Duke of York, took his seat for the first time in the Commander-in-Chief's chair at the Horse Guards.[1] On the one hand, he was keenly conscious of the shortcomings of that institution: who more so, considering that he had suffered so acutely under its vagaries and vacillations during two long campaigns? On the other hand, though he was itching to remedy these short-comings, he found himself handicapped and circumscribed by civil interference at every turn. In order to explain this we must glance at the structure of army command and control. The civil head of the army, with a seat in the Cabinet, was the Secretary of State for War and Colonies, Henry Dundas. His functions were much the same as those now possessed by his successors in that office, except that there was also a Secretary at War, William Windham, who controlled finance and expenditure in the army. These two civilians between them practically ran the army; since the Seven Years War the office of Commander-in-Chief had been either in abeyance altogether or almost a dead letter. The last holder of the office was, as we have seen, the veteran Lord Amherst. After acquiring an easy and exaggerated reputation as general in Canada (where he is still held in esteem), he continued to rise, owing to the favour of the Sovereign. He first held office as General on the Staff from 1778 to 1782, and even in those early days he had been scathingly described by Horace Walpole as 'that log of wood whose stupidity and incapacity are past belief'. After a short tenure of command by General Conway the office lapsed altogether till the outbreak of the war in 1793, when Amherst was brought back. In this office he was a complete nonentity and the army continued to be run by the civilians during the next two years. By 1795 Amherst was 79 years of age. The Dictionary

[1] In the room over the archway, and probably at the office desk that is still there.

of National Biography is very severe on him. 'He allowed innumerable abuses to grow up in the army. . . . He kept his
command, though almost in his dotage, with a tenacity that
cannot be too much censured.' Writing privately to Lord
Grenville shortly after the change, Dundas said: 'The mischief
he [Amherst] did in a few years will not be repaired but by the
unremitting attention of many.'[1]

The principal subordinate of the Commander-in-Chief was
the Adjutant-General, but his duties were confined to matters
of discipline. Promotions and appointments of officers were
vested in the civilians.

Hence the Duke, on taking office, resembled a highly bred
horse champing at the bit, but confined by the restraining reins
of his rider. Both the King and his Ministers, however, were
prepared to ride him with a light rein, that is to say – to extend
the powers of his office, but the sage monarch gave him the
sound advice not to be a 'new broom', but to carry out the
reforms on which he had set his heart gradually, starting slowly.
The Duke was sensible enough to heed this advice, and the
reforms that we are about to summarize extended over the next
decade. Consequently they met with but little opposition. Perhaps York or his father had read Bacon's advice to copy the
methods of time, which 'innovateth greatly, but gradually and
by means scarcely to be perceived'. Or perhaps he remembered
Queen Elizabeth's famous 'Festina lente' – 'Make haste slowly.'

This is not a history of the army, and a detailed account of
the reforms carried out during the next ten years would be out
of place. Moreover, although it is customary to connect the
name of the Commander with any reform or instructions issued
under his name, it is tolerably certain that a large proportion of
them have been devised by subordinate staff officers. On the
other hand we have the best possible evidence – that of Sir
Herbert Taylor, his Military Secretary for many years – that
the Duke was himself the initiator and inspirer of the majority
of the reforms that marked his tenure of office. Sir Herbert
wrote as follows: 'H.R.H. had been at the head of the army
more than thirty-two years; during that period various officers
were successively employed by him in the situations of military
secretary and at the heads of departments at the Horse Guards,

[1] *H. M. C. Dropmore*, IV, p. 264.

and they possessed his confidence and exerted themselves zealously. But the merit of rescuing the army from its impaired condition, of inspiring, establishing and maintaining its system; of introducing that administration in every principle and every detail, which has raised the British Service and promoted its efficiency, belongs exclusively to His Royal Highness.'[1]

The Duke's first step was to appoint a Military Secretary through whom officers could correspond instead of approaching the Secretary at War. Promotions and appointments were also vested in this officer. The sphere of the Adjutant-General was also extended, and the drill and efficiency of the army became his concern. Further, the Commander-in-Chief gradually got into his own hands the financial powers that had hitherto resided in the hands of the Secretary at War – not without a struggle on the part of William Windham.

The Commander-in-Chief was now in a position to launch his reforms. It will be convenient to list the principal of these without strict regard to chronological order. We will take first the case of officers. Here laziness, ignorance, incompetence, and indiscipline reigned supreme. Commissions were granted by influence or purchase, and promotion was almost entirely by purchase. This system has no defenders nowadays, but it had some redeeming features. It made possible rapid promotion for keen young officers such as Arthur Wellesley. But for this system we might never have known a Duke of Wellington. Some of the most enlightened officers of the day were against its abolition, and indeed it existed till mid-Victorian days. The new Commander-in-Chief did not attempt to abolish the system, but he increased the number of unpaid promotions, and he also firmly suppressed the scandal of commissions being granted to those of tender years and unsuitable quality. John Watkins relates that 'boys on the lower forms at school, and even infants in the nursery were gazetted as lieutenant-colonels of regiments to the detriment of veterans grown grey in the service of their king and country'.[2]

Colonel Willoughby Gordon testified at the Investigation in 1809 that 'prior to his being appointed Commander-in-Chief, an officer who had money could purchase up to the rank of

[1] *The Last Illness . . . of the Duke of York,* by General Sir Herbert Taylor (p. 73).
[2] *Watkins,* p. 308.

lieutenant-colonel in three weeks or a month'.

The Duke, in order to prevent such scandals, enacted that no officer should be promoted captain without at least two years' service, or field officer with less than six years. He next turned his attention to the professional education of officers. The Artillery and Engineers already had the Royal Military Academy for the instruction of cadets, but the rest of the army possessed no such institution. The Duke rectified this by establishing a military school at Great Marlow for cadets between the ages of 13 and 16. After a four years' course these cadets were granted commissions in the infantry or cavalry. This school became known later as the Royal Military College, Sandhurst. Previous to this he had instituted at High Wycombe a school for officers who hankered after staff employ. This school blossomed into the Staff College of a later date. He also formed a library, the nucleus of what he called, in a letter to Pitt 'the formation of a deposit for military knowledge'. This is now the War Office Library. And for their improvement and uniformity in the field he promulgated some 'Instructions for field exercises and evolutions', which had been composed by General Dundas.

Not only was the professional knowledge of the officers catered for; their discipline was also vastly improved, as they could no longer take their grievances to Cabinet Ministers.

An insight into the lines adopted by the Duke in his manipulation of the immense patronage at his disposal in the case of senior officers is provided in a letter from the Commander-in-Chief to the King in 1797: 'The only officers with any length of service who have applied for governor (of Quebec) are Generals Morris, St John, and Lieutenant-General Dalrymple. As I am not aware of any distinguishing features of military merit among these three Your Majesty may possibly prefer the oldest and poorest of them, which is General Morris, and promote him to be Governor of Quebec.'[1]

To modern eyes the system whereby anyone could obtain a commission merely by the recommendation of someone of influence seems utterly reprehensible. But we must remember that, except in the case of the Artillery and Engineers, there was no qualifying examination before the granting of commissions,

[1] *Windsor*, 14.12.97.

and it is difficult to see any satisfactory alternative to a nomination by the Commander-in-Chief on the recommendation of someone whose judgment he respected. It was indeed preferable that the Commander-in-Chief, a soldier, should have this patronage rather than the civilian head of the army, as at one time had been the case. It proved not so easy to obtain favours from the Royal Commander-in-Chief as it had from the easygoing Amherst or through members of the Cabinet.

Thus, even so influential a personage as Sheridan could only obtain a captaincy for his son through the combined solicitations of the Dukes of Norfolk and Devonshire, Lord Moira, and the Prince of Wales himself. It is, of course, true that any system of patronage lays itself open to abuse and suspicion of abuse, but this was less so in the case of a Royal Commander-in-Chief whose income was assured throughout his life than in the case of a commoner whose temptation and liability to corruption and bribery would naturally be greater. Dundas recognized the practical advantage of having a Prince of the Blood as Commander-in-Chief in a letter to Lord Grenville in 1798.

I stress this point for a reason that will transpire in due course. In order to assist him in assessing the recommendations for promotion presented to him, the Duke instituted a system of annual confidential Reports on Officers, which have subsisted to the present day.

So much for the officers. When we come to the other ranks the list of reforms is even longer. The principal of them are as follows: The pay of privates was increased by about 80 per cent. Their rations were increased, too. They were to be provided with comfortable quarters or barracks. Their clothing was improved, the long skirt being done away with. The pigtail or queue was done away with in two steps: first the white powder was abolished; when this reform had been thoroughly digested, as it were, the pigtail followed. Greatcoats were provided for all; doubtless his sad experience in Holland had impressed on the Duke the importance of this step – as also of the next – the thorough reform of the medical service. Hospitals were established, including a lying-in hospital for soldiers' wives; an extremely thoroughgoing set of rules for medical officers, many of them with a distinctly modern sound, was drawn up under the Duke's directions. In this matter we see the practical advantage of appointing a Commander-in-Chief who had had recent experience of active service. The medical shortcomings in Holland had made a painful but fruitful impression on the Duke. Mindful of his own early experience at the hands of Dr. Jenner, he also enjoined vaccination upon all ranks. Understanding the character of the British soldier, the Duke issued the following sensible order on the subject: 'H.R.H. requests that you will require commanding officers to give this order all possible effect . . . by explaining to the men the beneficial consequences resulting from the introduction of the cow-pock which have now been proved to the entire conviction of those who have the best opportunity for noting the progress of this important discovery.'[1]

The general orders and circular letters issued by the Duke of York in his early years at the Horse Guards testify still further to his interest in and care for the welfare of the rank and file. He put a stop to the scrubbing of barrack-room floors, a practice which was reintroduced and survived within the memory of soldiers still serving. If the following General Order had been kept in mind the retrograde practice would never have been reintroduced. 'The general practice of washing the floors of barrack-rooms having been found very prejudicial to the health of the soldiers, by exposing them to a damp atmosphere, H.R.H. the Commander-in-Chief is pleased to direct that this pernicious custom shall be discontinued, and that dry scrubbing shall be instituted in its place.'

Soldiers on furlough were also catered for. 'Soldiers requiring a prolongation of furlough shall apply to the nearest officer, or failing him to the civil power.'

Instances have occurred within living memory of trouble being caused owing to troopships being in an unsatisfactory state when taken over by the troops. The Duke of York had thought of this, too, as the following circular letter will show: 'It being considered expedient, with a view to the health and comfort of the troops embarked on board transports that the ships shall be regularly and carefully inspected by an officer of the medical staff, I have received the Commander-in-Chief's command that whenever troops shall be embarked . . . you will immediately direct . . . a senior officer of the Medical

[1] *General Orders and Circular Letters* (Horse Guards, 17 February, 1804).

Corps to report on board, and make a most minute and particular inspection.'

As for the payment of the troops, 'The Commander-in-Chief desires that you should strongly recommend the custom of the officers personally paying the balances due to their men, with a view of their becoming acquainted with their characters and habits and as a sure means of detecting any abuse or irregularity which may exist in the mode of furnishing them with necessaries or provisions.'

But the service performed for the soldiers with which the Duke's name is most prominently connected is the institution of the Duke of York's School. It was described as 'an Asylum for educating one thousand children, the legal offspring of British soldiers', and was sited in the country midway between Chelsea village and London. At the opening in 1803 there were only 150 inmates, but competition to get in was tremendous, and the numbers were rapidly raised to 1,250, with a branch establishment at Southampton in buildings now occupied by the Ordnance Survey. The Duke from the first took the deepest interest in the school which bore his name, frequently visiting it, sometimes as often as once a week. In 1909 the school was removed to Dover, its old premises being taken over by the London District.

As a final example of the deep humanity of the Duke, and of his care for the welfare of the rank and file, the story may be mentioned of how when the King ordered him to place a certain unit in the barracks at Dorchester, Frederick flatly refused to do so, the barracks being in his opinion unfit to house troops.

In another respect the Duke of York was in advance of his time, i.e. in his measures for the proper compiling of regimental records. If these measures had been properly carried out they would have earned the lasting gratitude of historians. It was entitled a 'National Military Record' and it comprised the following particulars:

1. An account of all battles in which units have been engaged.
2. Paintings of the colours and trophies captured by units.
3. Names of officers killed and wounded in each action.

4. Names of officers, N.C.O.s and men who have particularly distinguished themselves.

5. A list of units engaged in each action, 'together with paintings of such badges and distinctions as H.M. may have been graciously pleased to authorize to be borne on their standards, colours, and appointments, in commemoration of their distinguished conduct and signal intrepidity.'[1]

It was the opinion of officers competent to judge at the time that the general effect of these reforms was that the wave of discontent and mutiny that swept over the Navy in the critical year 1797 did not pervade the Army. Fortescue considered that the decade with which we are dealing was the most fruitful in reform that the Army has ever experienced. The historian of the Army concludes as follows: 'In 1795 he took over a number of undisciplined and disorganised regiments, filled for the most part with the worst stamps of man and officer, and in less than seven years he converted these unpromising elements into an army.'[2]

An unexpected tribute to the Duke at this period comes from the French General Foy: 'Seeing much for himself, being personally acquainted with the chiefs and a great number of the officers, he led and administered the army as a good colonel governs his military family.'

But perhaps the most comprehensive and impressive testimony came from Sir Arthur Wellesley, who spoke thus at the Clarke Investigation in 1809: 'I can say from my own knowledge, as having been a lieutenant-colonel in the army when H.R.H. was appointed to command it, that it is materially improved in every respect; that the discipline of the soldiers is improved; that under the establishments formed under the direction of H.R.H., the officers are improved in knowledge; that the staff of the army is much better than it was; and much more complete than it was; that the cavalry is improved; that the officers of the cavalry are better than they were; that the army is more complete in officers; that the system of subordination among the officers of the army is better than it was; and that the whole system of the management of the clothing of the army, the interior economy of the regiments, and everything that relates to the military discipline of the soldiers and the

[1] *Watkins*, p. 511.   [2] *History of the Army*, IV, p. 929.

military efficiency of the army has been greatly improved since
H.R.H. was appointed Commander-in-Chief.'[1]

When the Duke of York took up the arduous duties of Commander-in-Chief he was in his thirty-second year and in the
prime of his natural faculties. In a pregnant phrase Thackeray,
who as a boy may have seen the Duke, describes him as 'big,
burly, loud, jolly, cursing, courageous; he had a most affectionate and lovable disposition, was noble and generous to a
fault, and was never known to break a promise' – a description
that might do duty for the traditional John Bull. The Duke was
certainly John Bullish in figure and appearance.

His methods of business soon became an orderly routine. He
would arrive at his office shortly after 9 a.m. and remain till as
late as 7 p.m. His correspondence was enormous, sometimes
amounting to the almost incredible number of 300 letters per
day, which, we are assured, he answered promptly. Most of
these would concern the patronage side of his work, for he
centralized this function in his own person. This involved not
only written communications, but personal interviews. He made
a point of being accessible to all officers, and set apart definite
days, Tuesday and Friday in every week, when Parliament was
sitting, and once a week for the remainder of the year, when any
officer who had a grievance or a request to make could be sure
of an attentive hearing. He was also accessible to the other ranks,
and the tradition, at a general's inspection, of asking if any
soldier has a complaint to make to the general may date from
his régime. At the same time he was particular as to the observance of the outward forms of etiquette and decorum; he was
punctilious in acknowledging salutes and insisted on his officers
being so too. During the week he lived in a house in Piccadilly
that he had acquired from Lord Melbourne. It is now known as
'The Albany' in memory of the Duke of York and Albany. In
1807 the Duke moved to the Stable Yard St James's Palace.[2]
At week-ends he would repair to Oatlands Park, the country
house near Weybridge that he had bought soon after his
marriage in 1791. Here his placid but barren wife had her permanent abode, surrounded by her pet dogs and parrots.[3] In the
beautiful grounds surrounding the house was the famous grotto

[1] *A Circumstantial Report, etc.*, p. 516.   [2] It is still so called.
[3] The D.N.B. is in error in stating that the couple had separated.

constructed by the Duke of Northumberland in the early eighteenth century, which once had the reputation of being the largest and most curious in the country. It took ten workmen six years to build, the materials being collected from all over the country. The Duchess also made a large collection of shells to add to it. In a much-quoted passage Greville describes it, and the great bath of ice-cold water that he partook of, and how the Prince Regent used to play cards in it with his brother till the small hours of the morning.[1]

Life might have been pleasant enough had it not been for the anxious situation of the country. In the year 1795 after the failure of the Allies in the Low Countries, an invasion of England was generally expected. Against this it fell to the Duke to prepare an army. Unfortunately the bulk of the trained soldiers were abroad – freezing to death in North Holland and Germany or rotting with fever in the West Indies. Including militia and Fencibles (regulars enlisted for home defence) there were but 60,000 troops at home, and it was calculated that 77,000 were required as an absolute minimum. Such troops as did exist were in a most backward state of training, many of them being in new and untrained regiments. One of the first steps the Duke took was to reduce many of these corps and to draft the personnel into existing units. He also endeavoured to gain control of the militia which for some absurd reason was technically under the Home Secretary. Here there were powerful vested interests to be overcome. The principal obstacle was the Earl of Buckinghamshire, a conceited and egotistical militia-man, who caused the long-suffering Commander-in-Chief a deal of trouble. It was indeed some years before the Duke had full control of all the forces of the Crown (except the Artillery and Engineers, which continued to be under the command of the Master-General of the Ordnance). The Duke also aimed at establishing two battalions per regiment and placing them on a territorial basis – an arrangement that later became normal. He also increased the strength of Light Dragoons, no doubt influenced thereto by his experience in Flanders, where they had shown their value, and their general superiority over the heavy cavalry in that country.

[1] Alas, this unique erection was demolished as 'unsafe' in the year 1948, despite vehement protests of the Georgian Group.

Thus by slow degrees and 'by steps scarce to be perceived' he welded the home forces into a machine that was capable not only of defending its own home, but of taking the field in an expeditionary force on the Continent.

The first of those duties seemed the most likely to be required in those end-of-century years. We are apt to connect the invasion peril solely with the years 1803–1805, but the danger was very present throughout the period 1795–1801. One of the Duke's first acts as Commander-in-Chief was to impress on Pitt the urgency of hiring camping grounds for the troops on coast defence. There is an illuminating illustration of the ever-present danger in the Royal Archives. One day in February 1797 the Commander-in-Chief was seated placidly in his chair at the Horse Guards when he was astonished to receive the following letter from the Prince of Wales, who was down in Dorsetshire at the time:

'Captain Seymour from Windsor has this instant reported to me that the enemy's fleet is off the coast, and I am instantly joining my regiment where I shall wait the arrival of the General of the District, and in the meantime I shall make such arrangements as I may think necessary. . . .'

To this his brother was able to send a reassuring reply to the effect that his letter was 'the first account I received of an enemy's fleet being upon our coast. From intelligence, however which has been received since, we have every reason to think that the fleet seen off the Start was not an enemy but one of our own.' He adds, very prudently and tactfully: 'Captain Seymour was notwithstanding perfectly right in making that report immediately as we cannot be too much upon our guard.'[1]

The Duke's official title was constantly changing. In 1795 he was appointed Field-Marshal on the Staff, which automatically made him head of the army; on 3 April, 1798, he became Commander-in-Chief in Great Britain; on 4 September, 1799, Captain-General of the Forces (an interesting revival of an old title); and on 9 June, 1801, Commander-in-Chief of the forces in Great Britain and Ireland.

As Commander-in-Chief the Duke of York executed the duties of what we should now call the Inspector-General. In this capacity he made long journeys and carried out prolonged

[1] *Windsor*, 21.2.98.

inspections all over the coastline. One of his first acts had been to appoint Calvert to his staff as D.Q.M.G.[1] In the summer of 1795 Calvert accompanied the Commander-in-Chief on a long tour of the coast defences from the Isle of Wight to Sunderland and Tynemouth; and later in a tour to Plymouth.

By July the Duke had grown so sure of himself that, in agreement with the Cabinet, he embarked 3,000 troops for Quiberon without first asking the King's permission. The same month we find him writing to the King requesting his approval of an order to the troops: 'Not to wear their powder till further order. I am sensible that this would be but a trifling saving in the consumption of flour, but it would have at the moment a good appearance.'[2]

The reference is to the shortage of corn in the country pending the harvest, and the Duke cannot have guessed that 'till further orders' would mean for ever and that this letter marked the first step in the abolition of the obnoxious pigtail.[3]

In September the Duke was again on the south coast, seeing to the embarkation of Abercromby's expedition to the West Indies. This was one of Abercromby's abortive operations, the sequel of which can be read in the Duke's letter to the King of 30 January, 1796.

'The fleet after persevering for seven weeks has been obliged . . . to return to St Helens. As it is absolutely necessary that the troops should be disembarked as soon as possible and as many arrangements must be made previous to it for the removal of the regiments which occupy the barracks and quarters round Portsmouth, which may be made much easier upon the spot than they could be from London, I mean to set off immediately for Portsmouth.'[4] He encloses a letter received from Abercromby written on the previous day – quick work! Thus did the pleasure-loving but duty-bound Duke quit his beloved London in the depth of winter in order the better to attend to the wants of his 'family'.

The defence of the coast necessarily devolved largely on the artillery, of which the Marquis Cornwallis was then the Master-

[1] In 1796 this admirable officer became D.A.G., and in 1800 Adjutant-General.
[2] *Windsor*, 18.7.95.
[3] On another occasion the Duke gave orders that one-third of the officers and men should assist the farmers in the harvest.
[4] *Windsor*, 30.1.96.

General. In an interesting correspondence between the two the Duke gives expression to some views on defence which have a distinctly modern ring:

'Your Lordship knows that the establishment of fixed batteries along the coast, except in some very particular situations, is perfectly contrary to my notions and that I am of the opinion that the coast can be infinitely better and more efficiently defended by a moveable artillery stationed at certain centrical situations in each district which can be brought expeditiously to the point of attack.'[1]

Inspections continued during the next few years to take up much of the Duke's time, and it may be of interest to read a specimen report that he made of one such inspection to the King.

'The Hampshire Fencible Cavalry are a very pretty corps, exceedingly well mounted, particularly the bay troop, and rode very well except that their stirrups are too long. The Royals are in the highest order possible: they ride perfectly well and have strictly kept their stirrups to your Majesty's orders with regard to the length of stirrups. The only error I found in them was that they rode too much by the snaffle. The troop of the Horse Artillery and the park are in very high order and exercise perfectly well.'[2]

By the turn of the century the Duke's reforms were having their effect, and we find the *British Military Journal* declaring that 'We no longer hear of captains at the boarding school, of majors spinning their tops, and of beardless lieutenant-colonels lording it over veterans. . . . An officer cannot now obtain rank but by actual residence with his regiment and he is prevented from skipping from one step to another by being obliged to serve a certain time in each previous to his promotion.'[3]

After the Helder campaign (which will be described in a separate chapter), the Peace of Amiens in 1801 brought a temporary relaxation of strain to the army and to its Commander. But it was to be of short duration. On the resumption of the war in 1802 the old 'invasion scare' was revived, and the Windsor Archives swell with letters and memoranda on the subject of

[1] *Chatham Papers*, Vol. 106, 20.12.96.
[2] *Windsor*, 16.8.97.   [3] *British Military Journal*, II, p. 9.

home defence. For the renewal of the war made the chances of invasion greater than ever and the Commander-in-Chief correspondingly busy.

Before describing the works that he set in motion we must record some important changes on his staff at the Horse Guards. Old David Dundas, who for some years had been Q.M.G. to the forces, was promoted General on the Staff, and succeeded by Major-General Brownrigg, the Military Secretary. His place in turn was taken by Colonel W. H. Clinton, whilst our old friend Harry Calvert had been promoted Adjutant-General, in which capacity he rendered distinguished services.

Altogether the team was a strong one; and it had need to be, for the danger of invasion was a very real one. We are too apt, profiting by after-knowledge, to belittle this risk and assume that Bonaparte was bluffing. Even now historians are not unanimous on this point, but the general tendency nowadays is to credit the Corsican with the serious intention of invading England, and that the concentration of troops in and near Boulogne was no bluff. We are not concerned here with the causes which led to the invasion being cancelled, but the steps taken to counter the threatened invasion, under the supervision of the Duke of York, not only are relevant, but, in view of a similar invasion threat in 1940, are of exceptional interest.

There is preserved in the Windsor Archives a voluminous report by the Commander-in-Chief, presented to Lord Hobart, the Secretary of State for War, dealing with the general defence of Great Britain. It was founded on the basic principle of concentration, one passage reading: 'Too great a division of force is what an enemy has most to desire, and innumerable instances occur in war where the stakes contended for have been lost from arrangements aiming at universal protection.'[1] This practically echoes a precept laid down by Jomini, but it is more likely that it had been inspired by Frederick the Great in his youth, who declared concisely 'He who tries to protect everything protects nothing.'

This defence report incorporated a plan of defence which the Duke had presented to the Government on 29 June, 1803, and which had been approved by them. Working on the above-mentioned principle of concentration, the Duke laid down that

[1] *Windsor*, 25.8.03.

AT THE HORSE GUARDS, 1807, AGED 44

*From the painting by Sir William Beechey
painted for the Duke of York's School*

IN GERMANY, 1781, AGED 18
From the painting by A. Ganz

COLONEL OF THE FIRST GUARDS, 1787, A(
From the bust by J. Lochee, in possession of Lord S

!MANDER-IN-CHIEF, 1822, AGED 59
From the painting by J. Jackson

AT NEWMARKET, 1826, AGED
From the drawing in the Royal Library, Windso

the first object of the new disposition was 'to collect the disposable force for the immediate defence of the capital, even to the prejudice of more distant though important points'. These forces were in turn replaced by an 'army of Reserve', totalling 56,000 men, who were responsible for the coast from Hythe to Brighton.

The credit for the construction of the famous Martello towers is attributed by Fortescue to Pitt, but it was recommended by the Duke before ever Pitt came back to office in 1804. 'I strongly recommend the Master-General the principle of armament defences in the shape of towers proposed by Colonel Twiss . . . from Eastern Bay to Selsea Island.'[1]

A further defensive measure to which he directed his attention was that of inundations. 'I have directed measures to be prepared to ensure the inundations . . .' in the neighbourhood of Pevensey. On July 2 he sent orders to David Dundas to strengthen the lines of Chatham, and three days later he wrote to Craig, who was now a general in command on the East Coast, concerning the construction of field works at Colchester and Chelmsford.

The Duke then turned his attention to the immediate defence of the capital, or rather he put into effect a plan made under his direction in 1801. This took the form of two lines – an outer or outpost line, extending from Deptford by Shooter's Hill to Blackheath; and an inner line running from Sydenham to Wandsworth. North of the Thames it took the line of the River Lea to Stamford Hill, Hampstead, Willesden Green, Holland House, and Little Chelsea. He estimated that the garrison for the whole line would require 180,000 men. In addition to the field works, sluices were constructed on the River Lea for the inundations. The Duke adds: 'The preparation of the River Lea and the works upon Shooters Hill is what I think most important to be undertaken previous to the landing of an enemy.'[2]

A few days later he reported that 'The only considerable field works at present carrying on under my authority are: the entrenched camp at Chelmsford, the construction of three re-

[1] *Windsor*, 44417.
[2] Traces of the works on Shooter's Hill are still discernible and it is possible that they were renovated in 1940.

Q

doubts in the neighbourhood of Plymouth and the preparatory measures for inundating the River Lea.'[1] He awaits the approval of the Cabinet before proceeding further. From the above letters it is clear that the burden and responsibility for the defence of the country fell directly and principally upon the Commander-in-Chief.

A small but significant matter, showing how meticulously the Duke thought out every contingency and everything for the benefit of the army, is contained in a letter he addressed to Addington, the Prime Minister in October 1803, pointing out that in the event of an invasion paper money might depreciate and that consequently specie should be made available for the use of the army.

To the manifold cares and anxieties that assailed the Commander-in-Chief during these fateful years was added an utterly unnecessary but tiresome one – a quarrel in the Royal Family. It came about in this way. On the resumption of the war in May 1803 a surge of patriotism swept the country. The whole nation sprang to arms, and the King himself was prepared to march at the head of his army and drive the insolent foe back into the sea, should he dare to land. His second son, the Duke of York, was Commander-in-Chief of the Army, his younger sons were admirals or generals. Only the first-born, the Prince of Wales, could boast of no higher rank than that of colonel. Back in 1793 he had been given the rank of lieutenant-colonel, and appointed to the command of the 10th Light Dragoons, which was stationed at home. In 1795, 1796, and 1799, becoming restive at the absence of further promotion, he applied to the King for higher rank, and indeed for foreign service, but his request was always refused. The reasons advanced by the King for this refusal remained in dispute, as the correspondence will show; but it may throw some light on the problem if we look back to the King's own experience when himself Prince of Wales, in 1759 – in the midst of another war and of another invasion scare. He then applied for a military command, only to meet with a brusque refusal from his grandfather, George II.

And now, forty-four years later, George III was exhibiting

[1] *Windsor*, 44418.

the traditional Hanoverian suspicion of his heir, and he became as adamant as his grandfather had been.

But the Prince of Wales was set on getting promotion; the question was how best to go about it. Mindful of the past two rebuffs, he ultimately decided to approach the Sovereign through the medium of the Prime Minister. On 18 July, 1803, therefore, he wrote a personal letter to Addington, preferring his request, and ending cordially: 'I remain, Sir, very sincerely yours, G. P.'

A week went by without any acknowledgment. The Prince returned to the charge, but this time a certain coolness entered into the letter. It was written in the third person, and began: 'A week has now elapsed . . .' and it requested a reply.

Addington replied the next day, the 27th, also in the third person. He had laid the Prince's letter before the King 'and the letter is still in his Majesty's possession'. The King had, however, merely referred him back to his previous answers on the subject.

This elicited a curt and peremptory reply from the Prince, who 'requires Mr Addington to submit to his Majesty his last note of the 26th'. Addington hastened to assure the Prince the same day that he 'will not fail to lay the letter before his Majesty'.

He was as good as his word, and on 1 August the Royal answer came. It was to the effect that the King 'again referred Mr Addington to the order he had before given him', with the addition that 'the King's opinion being fixed, he desires that no further questions should be made to him upon the subject'.

This was unpropitious; indeed, it looked as if the Prince was up against a stone wall. He went down to Brighton and spent the next three days deep in thought. Then his mind was made up; he would write direct to the Sovereign. Several individuals have been claimed as the composer of the resulting letter, including Sheridan and Sir Philip Francis. A recent writer states unequivocally: 'It is known that these letters were written for the Prince by Sir Philip Francis', but as far as I can discover the only reason is that Francis's family afterwards came to believe he was the author, probably because a copy of them was found among Francis's papers. The truth, no doubt, is that the Prince conferred with his boon companions at Brighton (where he indited the letter) and that each of them afterwards was only too glad to have the authorship ascribed to himself. In 1798 the Prince had written a similar letter in the same style, and I am satisfied that the letter was essentially his own composition. In this remarkable epistle he addresses His Majesty '. . . . with the sanguine hope that the ears of an affectionate Father may still be opened to the supplications of a dutiful son'. He soon comes to the point that rankles: 'The highest places in your Majesty's service are filled by the young branches of the Royal Family; to me alone no place is assigned – I am not thought worthy to be the junior Major-General of the Army. . . .'

He ends on a curiously mixed note of resignation and challenge: 'Should I be disappointed . . . I shall lament in silent submission . . . but Europe, the World and posterity must judge between us.'

The letter must have been sent post-haste to Windsor, for the very next day the King penned his reply.

'My dear Son,

'Though I applaud your zeal . . . yet, considering the repeated declarations I have made of my determination on your former supplications to the same purpose I had flattered myself to have heard no farther on the subject. Should the implacable enemy so far succeed as to land, you will have an opportunity of showing your zeal at the head of your regiment. . . .'

But this letter – as implacable as the foe – did not produce the 'silent submission' that his son had promised – though a fortnight's silence may have caused the King to flatter himself that such was the case.

'Brighton, August 22nd.
'Sir,

'I have delayed thus long an answer to the letter which your Majesty did me the honour to write, from a wish to refer to a former correspondence which took place between us in the year 1798. These letters were mislaid, and some days elapsed before I could discover them. Allow me then, Sir, to recall to your recollection the expression you were graciously pleased to use, and which I once before took the liberty of reminding you of, when I solicited foreign service, upon my first coming into the army. They were, Sir, that your Majesty did not then see the opportunity for it, but that if anything was to arise at home I ought to be the "first and foremost".'

This was clearly a 'bull point' and the Prince makes the most of it, going on:

'There cannot be a stronger expression in the English language and one more consonant to the feelings that animate my heart. In this I agree most perfectly with your Majesty. *I ought to be "first and foremost"*. It is the place which my birth assigns me. . . .

'After such a declaration I could hardly expect to be told that my place was at the head of a Regiment of Dragoons. My next brother, the Duke of York, commands the army. The younger branches of my family are either General or Lieut.-Generals and I, who am the Prince of Wales, am to remain a Colonel of Dragoons. . . .'

With rising anger, he, who a few days before had spoken of 'silent submission', now boldly proclaims:

'I pledge myself never to desist till I receive that satisfaction which the justice of my claim leads me to expect. . . . Reason and honour forbid me to yield . . .' and so on.

But before closing he evidently reads the letter through and becomes a trifle uneasy as to the heat that has gradually entered into it. So he ends up:

'In this candid exposition of the feelings which have agitated and depressed my wounded mind, I hope no expression has escaped me which can be construed to mean the slightest disrespect to your Majesty. . . .'

To this *cri du coeur* the King vouchsafed no reply. It is impossible not to feel some sympathy for the genuinely distressed Heir Apparent. By the public he was looked upon as a mere hedonist – a role that was singularly inappropriate in the perilous times through which the country was passing. How was he to show that he was a reformed character (at least *pro tem.*) unless he was given some command in which he could prove himself? To us it must seem curious that he should assume that he was qualified for high military rank, since he had only played at soldiering in a dilettante fashion. But it was the custom of the age to appoint Royal princes to high command, even though they had not gone through an apprenticeship;

their staffs were expected to see them through. Moreover, the Prince was a soldier at heart, and was aflame for military glory.

So far there had been two rounds, and the Prince had been worsted in both. Should he hazard a third round? He gave the matter five weeks' anxious thought, and then his mind was made upon. He would make one more approach – this time through his younger brother, the Commander-in-Chief – unless the next *Gazette* should show that his appeal had been heard. On 1 October the eagerly awaited *Gazette* was published. It contained a long list of promotions, but the name of the Heir Apparent was not in it.

That decided him; he would play his last card – an appeal to the Commander-in-Chief of the Army.

His letter was dated from Brighton, 2 October, 1803. It read with some slight omissions, as follows:

'My dear Brother,

'By the last night's *Gazette*, which I have this moment received, I perceive that an extensive promotion has taken place in the Army, wherein my pretensions are not noticed; a circumstance which, whatever may have happened on other occasions, it is impossible for me to pass by, at this momentous crisis, without observation. . . .

'In a moment when the danger of the Country is thought by Government so urging as to call forth every arm in its defence, I cannot but feel myself degraded, both as a Prince and a Soldier, if I am not allowed to take a forward and distinguished part in the defence of that Empire and Crown, of the glory, prosperity, and even existence of that People, in all which mine is the greatest stake. . . .

'To be told, I may display this zeal solely and simply at the head of my regiment is a degrading mockery. . . .

'It is for the sake of tendering my services in a way more formal and official than I have before pursued, that I address this to you, my dear Brother, as the Commander-in-Chief, by whose councils the Constitution presumes that the military department is administered. If those who have the honour to advise his Majesty on this occasion, shall deem my pretension, among those of all the Royal Family, to be the only fit one to be rejected and disdained, I may at least hope, as a debt of justice and honour, to have it explained, that I am laid by in virtue of that judgment, and not in consequence of any omission or want of energy on my part.'

This letter placed his younger brother in a cruel quandary. In the midst of his pressing duties, with an invasion of the country looming, he found himself involved in a dispute between the Sovereign, his father, and the Heir Apparent, his elder brother. He was the favourite son of the King, and he knew it; he was the favourite brother of the Heir, and he knew it. At the moment he was the commanding officer of his brother, but any day (if the King went mad again or died) that brother might become his Sovereign. He therefore had to walk delicately. The letter that he composed is so admirable in tone, feeling and substance, and so perfectly meets the case, that Dr Johnson himself might have been proud to claim authorship. As a matter of fact, there can be no doubt that it was the unaided composition of the harassed Commander-in-Chief. It merits quotation in full:

'Horse Guards, October 6, 1803.

'Dearest Brother,

'Nothing but extraordinary press of business would have prevented me from acknowledging sooner your letter of the 2nd instant, which I received, while at Oatlands, on Monday evening.

'I trust that you are too well acquainted with my affection for you, which has existed since our most tender years, not to be assured of the satisfaction I ever have felt, and ever must feel, in forwarding, when in my power, every desire or object of yours, and therefore will believe how much I must regret the impossibility there is, upon the present occasion, of my executing your wishes of laying the representation contained in your letter before his Majesty. Suffer me, my dear Brother, as the only answer that I can properly give you, to recall to your memory what passed upon the same subject soon after his Majesty was graciously pleased to place me at the head of the army; and I have no doubt that, with your usual candour, you will yourself see the absolute necessity of my declining it.

'In the year 1795, upon a general promotion taking place, at your instance, I delivered a letter from you to his Majesty, urging your pretensions to promotion in the army; to which his

Majesty was pleased to answer, that before he had appointed you to the command of the 10th Light Dragoons, he had caused it to be fully explained to you, what his sentiments were with respect to a Prince of Wales entering into the army, and the public grounds upon which he never could admit of your considering it as a profession, or of your being promoted in the service; and his Majesty, at the same time, added his positive command and injunctions to me never to mention this subject again to him, and to decline being the bearer of any application of the same nature, should it be proposed to me; which message I was of course under the necessity of delivering to you, and have constantly made it a rule of my conduct ever since; and indeed, I have ever considered it as one of the greatest proofs of affection and consideration towards me, on the part of his Majesty that he never allowed me to become a party in this business.

'Having thus stated to you fairly and candidly what has passed, I must trust you will see that there can be no grounds for the apprehension expressed in the latter part of your letter, that any slur can attach to your character as an officer, particularly as I recollect your mentioning to me yourself, on the day in which you received the notification of your appointment to the 10th Light Dragoons, the explanation and condition attached to it by his Majesty; and, therefore, surely you must be satisfied that your not being advanced in military rank proceeds entirely from his Majesty's sentiments respecting the high rank you hold in the state, and not from any impression unfavourable to you.

'Believe me ever, with the greatest truth, dear Brother,

'Your most affectionate Brother,

'Frederick.'

The Prince of Wales received this letter the next day (it must have gone by special messenger) and wrote a lengthy reply. This letter also must be given in full (the italics in this case are mine):

'My dear Brother,

'I have taken two days to consider the contents of your letter of the 6th inst., in order to be as accurate as possible in my answer, which must account to you for its being longer, perhaps than I intended, or I could have wished.

'I confide entirely in the personal kindness and affection expressed in your letter, and am, for that reason, the more unwilling to trouble you again on a painful subject, in which you are not free to act as your inclination, I am sure, would lead you; *but as it is not at all improbable that every part of this transaction may be publicly canvassed hereafter*, it is of the utmost importance to my honour, without which I can have no happiness, that my conduct in it shall be fairly represented and correctly understood. When I made a tender of my services to his Majesty's ministers, it was with a just and natural expectation that my offer would have been accepted in the way in which alone it could have been most beneficial to my country, or creditable to myself; or, if that failed, that at least (in justice to me) the reasons for a refusal would have been distinctly stated, so that the Nation might be satisfied that nothing had been omitted on my part, and enabled to judge of the validity of the reasons assigned for such refusal.

'In the first instance, I was referred to his Majesty's will and pleasure, and now I am informed by your letter, that before "he had appointed me to the command of the 10th Light Dragoons, he had caused it to be fully explained to me what his sentiments were with respect to a Prince of Wales entering into the army".

'It is impossible, my dear Brother, that I should know all that passed between the King and you; but I perfectly recollect the statement you made of the conversations you had had with his Majesty, and which strictly corresponds with that in your letter now before me; but I must, at the same time, recall to your memory my positive denial, at that time, of any condition or stipulation having been made upon my first coming into the Army; and I am in possession of full and complete documents, which prove that no terms whatever were then proposed, at least to me, whatever might have been the intention; and the communications which I have found it necessary subsequently to make, have ever disclaimed the existence of such a compromise at any period, as nothing could be more averse to my nature, or more remote from my mind.

'As for the conversation you quote in 1796, when the King

was pleased to appoint me to succeed Sir William Pitt, I have not the most slight recollection of its having taken place between us. If your date is right, my dear Brother, you must be mistaken in your exact terms, or at least in the conclusion you draw from it; for in the intimacy and familiarity of private conversation, it is not at all unlikely that I should have remembered the communication you made me the year before; but that I should have acquiesced in, or referred to a compromise which I never made, is utterly impossible. Neither in his Majesty's letter to me, nor in the correspondence with Mr Addington (of which you may not be fully informed) is there one word, or the most distant allusion to the condition stated in your letter; and even if I had accepted the command of a regiment on such terms, my acquiescence could only have relation to the ordinary situation of the country, and not to a case so completely out of all contemplation at that time, as the probable or projected invasion of this kingdom by a foreign force sufficient to bring its safety into question.

'When the King is pleased to tell me, "that should the enemy land, he shall think it his duty to set an example in defence of the country", that is, to expose the only life which, for the public welfare, ought not to be hazarded; I respect and admire the principles which dictate that resolution, and as my heart glows with the same sentiments, I wish to partake in the same danger, that is, with dignity and effect. Wherever his Majesty appears as King, he acts and commands; you are Commander-in-Chief; others of my family are high in military station; and even by the last brevets a considerable number of junior officers are put over me. In all these arrangements, the Prince of Wales alone, whose interest in the event yields to none but that of the King, is disregarded, omitted, his services rejected; so that, in fact, he has no post or station whatsoever in a contest on which the fate of the crown and kingdom may depend. I do not, my dear Brother, wonder that, in the hurry of your present occupations, these considerations should have been overlooked; they are now in your view, and I think cannot fail to make a due impression. As to the rest, with every degree of esteem possible for your judgment of what is due to a soldier's honour, I must be the guardian of mine to the utmost of my power. I have, etc.,   'G. P.'

York evidently found his brother's letter very tiresome. He had no intention of going back on his first *non possumus*, but he was anxious to avoid any appearance of cavalier treatment of his brother's request. He solved the problem – for the moment – by drawing a red herring across the trail, and ending with a delicate hint that the correspondence should cease:

'Horse Guards, Oct. 11th 1803.

'My dear Brother,

'I have this moment, upon my arrival in town, found your letter and lose no time in answering that part of it which, it appears to me highly necessary, should be clearly understood.

'Indeed, my dear Brother, you must give me leave to repeat to you, that, upon the fullest consideration, I perfectly recollect your having yourself told me, at Carlton House, in the year 1793, on the day on which you was informed of his Majesty's having acquiesced in your request of being appointed to the command of the 10th regiment of Light Dragoons, of which Sir William Pitt was then Colonel, the message and condition which was delivered to you from his Majesty, and which his Majesty repeated to me in the year 1795, as mentioned in my letter of Thursday last, and I have the fullest reason to know that there are others to whom at that time you mentioned the same circumstance; nor have I the least recollection of your having denied it to me; when I delivered to you the King's answer, as I should certainly have felt incumbent on me to recall to your memory what you had told me yourself in the year 1793.

'No conversation whatever passed between us, as you justly remark, in the year 1796, when Sir William Pitt was promoted to the King's Dragoon Guards, which was in consequence of what was arranged in 1793, upon your first appointment to the 10th Light Dragoons; and I conceive that your mentioning in your letter my having stated a conversation to have passed between us in 1798, must have arisen from some misapprehension; as I do not find that year ever adverted to in my letter.

'I have thought it due to us both, my dear Brother, thus fully to reply to those parts of your letter in which you appear to have mistaken mine; but, as I am totally unacquainted with the correspondence which has taken place upon this subject, I must decline entering any further into it.

'I remain ever, my dear Brother, with the greatest truth,
'Your most affectionate Brother,
'Frederick.'

Only twenty-four hours later the Prince's reply was on the way. (The Brighton road must have been getting hot with galloping hooves.) The Prince had spotted the red herring, and was giving nothing away.

'Brighton, Oct. 12th 1803.
'My dear Brother,

'By my replying to your letter of the 6th inst., which contained no sort of answer to mine of the 2nd., we have fallen into a very frivolous altercation upon a topic which is quite foreign to the present purpose. Indeed, the whole importance of it lies in a seeming contradiction in the statement of a fact, which is unpleasant even upon the idlest occasion. I meant to assert that no previous condition to forego all pretensions to ulterior rank, under any circumstance, had been imposed upon me, or even submitted to me, in any shape whatever, on my first coming into the service; and, with as much confidence as can be used in maintaining a negative, I repeat that assertion. . . .'

After recapitulating a few dates and facts in support of his contention, he ends somewhat unexpectedly, on another note:

'The only purpose of this letter, my dear Brother, is to explain, since that is necessary, that my former ones meant not to give you the trouble of interceding as my advocate for mere rank in the Army. Urging further, my other more important claims upon Government, would be vainly addressed to any person who can really think that a former refusal of mere rank, under circumstances so widely different, or the most express waving of such pretensions, if that had been the case, furnishes the slightest colour for the answer which I have received to the tenders I have now made of my services.

'Your department, my dear Brother, was meant, if I must repeat it, simply as a channel to convey that tender to the

Government; and to obtain either their attention to it, or an open avowal of their refusal.

'I am, etc. etc.,

'G. P.'

The next letter from the Duke is difficult to assess. Either it is extremely shrewd or it is rather obtuse. He seizes on a somewhat ambiguous sentence in the Prince's letter, and misconstrues it. It seems to be a palpable attempt to 'pass the baby' to the political side whence it had come.

'Horse Guards, October 13, 1803.

'Dear Brother,

'I have received your letter this morning, and am sorry to find that you think I have misconceived the meaning of your first letter, the whole tenor of which, and the military promotion which gave rise to it, led me naturally to suppose your desire was, that I should apply to his Majesty, in my official capacity to give you military rank, to which might be attached the idea of subsequent command.

'That I found myself under the necessity of declining, in obedience to his Majesty's pointed orders, as I explained to you in my letter of the 6th inst. But from your letter today, I am to understand, that your object is not military rank, but that a post should be allotted to you, upon the present emergency, suitable to your situation in the State.

'This I conceive to be purely a political consideration, and, as such, totally out of my department; and as I have most carefully avoided, at all times, and under all circumstances, ever interfering in any political points, I must hope that you will not call upon me to deviate from the principles by which I have been invariably governed.

'Believe me, my dear Brother,

'Frederick.'

This letter seems to have brought the Prince back to London, whence his final letter is addressed, only twenty-four hours later. In the opening section of it he certainly establishes his point with force and clarity.

'Carlton House, October 14, 1803.

'My dear Brother,

'It cannot but be painful to me, to be reduced to the necessity of further explanation on a subject which it was my earnest wish to have closed, and which was of so clear and distinct a nature, as, in my humble judgment, to have precluded the possibility of either doubt or misunderstanding.

'Surely there must be some strange fatality to obscure my language in statement, or leave me somewhat deficient in the powers of explanation, when it can lead your mind, my dear Brother, to such a palpable misconstruction (for far be it from me to fancy it wilful) of my meaning, as to suppose, for a moment, that I had unconnected my object *with efficient military rank*, and transferred it entirely to the view of a *political station*, when you venture to tell me, "my object is not military rank, but that a post should be allotted to me, upon the *present* emergency, suitable to my situation in the State". Upon what ground you *can* hazard such an assertion, or upon what principles you can draw such an inference, I am utterly at a loss to determine; for I defy the most skilful logician in torturing the English language, to apply *with fairness*, such a construction to any word or phrase of mine contained in any one of the letters I have ever written on this, *to me*, most interesting subject. . . .'

The letter (and the correspondence) ends on a dignified note which could hardly have been more felicitously phrased:

'. . . Feeling how useless, as well as ungracious, controversy is upon every occasion, and knowing how fatally it operates on human friendship, I must entreat that our correspondence on this subject shall cease here; for nothing could be more distressing to me than to prolong a topic, on which it is now clear to me, my dear Brother, that *you* and I can never agree, etc. etc.

'G. P.' [1]

The Prince of Wales had lost his battle – but he fired the last shot. He published the correspondence with the King in the public Press – an action clearly hinted at in the passage I have italicized in his letter of 9 October.

For some months after this the two brothers were estranged,

[1] This correspondence was printed originally in the *Morning Post* and reprinted as a pamphlet the same year. The originals are in the Windsor Archives.

the Prince of Wales going so far as to write to Frederick in the third person. It was the only really serious quarrel (and a very one-sided one) that the two brothers ever had. Farrington notes in his diary with satisfaction that in the following February the Prince of Wales and Duke of York shook hands.

The climax of the invasion scare came in August 1805, Napoleon's army lay massed at Boulogne, awaiting the advent of Villeneuve's fleet. Its appearance in the Channel would be the signal for the invasion to commence. Napoleon ordered the Imperial Guard from Paris to Boulogne, whither he himself set out. Intimation of these happenings reached the British Government, and Pitt sent off an alarmist dispatch to the Duke of York, who was then at Weymouth. In reply the latter wrote:

'I take the earliest opportunity to . . . assure you how thoroughly I co-incided with your opinion concerning the necessity of taking at this moment every precaution against invasion in consequence of the very (?) intelligence received; though it certainly would have been one of the rashest attempts, in my opinion that Bonaparte ever made. I have in consequence written by this days messenger to order the necessary orders to be immediately circulated. . . .'[1] On the very day the Duke penned these words Napoleon counter-ordered the march of his Guard from Paris. The threat of invasion passed.

No sooner was the danger of invasion over than the Government began to lay plans for the recovery of Hanover in conjunction with Russia, Sweden, and Prussia. Prussia had not then declared war on France, but Pitt was optimistic, and in October 1805 a force under General Don was dispatched to the Elbe. In November, without waiting to see whether Prussia would come in, Pitt ordered a reinforcement under General Lord Cathcart to join Don's force. As soon as York heard of Pitt's intention he sat down and wrote a letter which if heeded by the Prime Minister might have had important consequences, and avoided or at least mitigated what Fortescue designates as 'an egregious farce'.[2]

The letter, which seems to have escaped the notice of historians, is marked 'Most Private and Secret', and it has the

: *Windsor*, 8.7.05.   [2] *Fortescue*, V, p. 297.

melancholy distinction of being the last letter that the Duke of York ever wrote to William Pitt. It is dated 27 November, 1805, and the salient passages are as follows:

'The proposed expedition under Lord Cathcart has been determined upon, if I am not mistaken, under the supposition that Prussia will join heartily in our cause, and that the Swedes and Russians, joined by the corps under General Don, are advancing towards the Ems; then with the addition of the troops under Lord Cathcart it is deemed possible that the whole may be able to advance to the Yssel and perhaps even occupy Holland as far as the Waal.

'The first supposition, that Prussia will enter heartily into the cause I shall not touch upon, as I consider it is a *sine qua non* without which the whole plan must at once be given up. I shall therefore confine myself to stating to you the real situation of the troops and the probable consequences that are, in my opinion, to be apprehended.

'With regard to the corps under Lt. General Don, I am perfectly sure that they cannot be in a state for active service, that the British not having a single horse for means of conveyance of artillery or baggage of any kind with them, the artillery horses not yet being enlisted and the major part of the artillery ammunition and even artillerymen now lying in the Downs.

'The German Legion, except the artillery, is in my opinion in a still less state of preparation for taking the field as each battalion is intended to receive an augmentation of 300 men.

'I therefore think it impossible for General Don, however anxious he may be to comply with the wishes of the Russians and Swedes, to move forward with his corps, though he may be perfectly able to take up the position on the left bank of the Weser or even to blackade Hameln.

'The corps intended to sail under Lord Cathcart, though supplied with everything in our power to give them, for immediately taking the field (particularly at this inclement time of year) therefore must trust to the country they land in to supply the rest of their wants. This the country about the Ems, being fertile and full of horses, can certainly do with the concurrence of the Prussians (unless Prussia has herself looked to the requirements of her own cavalry for supplying her own armies) but still some time will be required for this operation.

'Supposing however all these difficulties surmounted and the troops in a state to move forward, the country in which operations must be undertaken is so deep as to be utterly impassable at this season of the year (except in frost) for either artillery or carriages, and there is little or no covering for the troops till they arrive at the towns upon the Yssel, which are all to a degree fortified. And though probably the fortifications may not be in the best state, yet if they do not open their gates of themselves and if any armed men (it need not be trained soldiers) oppose them, it will be utterly impossible for the allied army to take them (the towns) by force, as the corps cannot have a battering train with it; nor indeed would the season of the year admit of trenches being opened. Still less could this corps contrive to pass the Yssel; and even if it had the means of carrying a train of pontoons with it, leaving detachments sufficiently strong to mask each of these respective towns, the corps even at its fullest strength would weaken itself so much. It would therefore be under the necessity of effecting its retreat back to the Ems, which would be a complete failure of the plan.'[1]

The foregoing letter might be taken as a classic example of how the military advisers of the Government should approach and report on such a contemplated operation. Observe, the Duke does not venture an opinion as to the prospects of Prussia coming into the war; he leaves that to the politicians. His letter is confined to purely military considerations. It is packed with military factors. All the difficulties inherent in the proposed operation are succinctly but forcefully set out. Here speaks the practical soldier. The Duke had had experience of winter operations in the country round the Yssel; none knew better than he what those conditions were. He foresaw military disaster, and he did all that a soldier could do to prevent it before it was too late. So far as one can assess it at this distance of time, his judgment in this matter was sound, and had an attempt been made to cross the Yssel and recover Holland, disaster would probably have ensued. As he rightly apprehended, the plan could not be carried out without Prussia's adherence, and Prussia did not adhere. It is likely that the Duke, having closer knowledge and experience of the Prussians than

[1] *Chatham Papers*, Vol. 106, 27.11.05.

R

most Ministers at home, guessed that this would be the out-
come. Nevertheless, he was right to act on the assumption that
she would come in, and confine his letter to purely military
considerations. His letter might with advantage be pinned up
on the office walls of every War Minister.

We must now go back to the Helder Campaign of 1793.

10

As a result of the 1793–5 campaigns, France had overrun Holland, ejected the Prince of Orange, and set up a Batavian Republic, with a French army of about 15,000 men, under General Brune, occupying the country. For a few years Great Britain was reduced to the defensive, but after overcoming the perils of 1797 Pitt began to consider possible theatres for offensive action. Holland was naturally the first theatre considered.

The project was born in November 1798. The Duke of York then wrote to the King:

'I have the honour to report to Your Majesty that I met Mr Pitt this morning by appointment at Mr Dundas's, where he mentioned to me that account had been received from Holland which could be relied upon that the French troops have been for the most part removed out of Holland into Brabant on account of the insurrection and that the Dutch are so exceedingly discontented with the French that if a body of troops could be sent there it could be easy to seize upon Flushing.'[1]

He goes on to ask the King's permission to use the Foot Guards for this purpose.

Nothing came of this for the time being, but the project was revived in earnest next January, when it was decided to offer subsidies to Prussia and Russia if they would join in an attempt to recover Holland. All through the summer negotiations proceeded, with the result that, though Prussia would not move, Russia promised to send a force 18,000 strong for a combined campaign.

By coaxing men out of the militia into the regular army Pitt managed to raise an army of 30,000 good-quality troops. At the head of the combined force was to be placed the Duke of York.

The reason for his selection sounds slightly quaint to modern ears. Dundas explained it in a letter to Pitt:

[1] *Windsor*, 18.11.98.

'Our idea was that the Duke of York should sail as soon as the Russian troops arrive at Yarmouth. The Duke of York is ready to go at an hours notice. Independent of the Russian troops we shall have in Holland an army of 24,000 British infantry. . . . This is certainly a command fit for the King's son, and I cannot help thinking that with a view to future connection it is desirable that a Prince of the Blood should have a chief part in the deliverance of Holland and the re-establishment of the House of Orange. Besides, H.R.H. being on the spot and having influence which it is said he has with the Prince of Orange may be of essential use in the further details we talked over the last time Lord Grenville, you and I met together.'[1]

Thus the Duke of York was given supreme command largely upon political grounds. It was felt, and probably rightly, that he was the best man to keep harmony in a force of mixed nationalities – British, Dutch and Russian. It is noteworthy that he had been sent on a mission to the Prince of Orange immediately after his recall from Holland in 1794. The Czar of Russia was also anxious to have a Royal Prince at the head of the combined army. The Duke himself seems to have interpreted his appointment in this light, and it was almost certainly conveyed to him that he should defer to the military opinions of Sir Ralph Abercromby, who was put in command of the advanced guard of the Expeditionary force. It was, of course, to be an amphibious operation, and the Fleet was put under the command of one Admiral Mitchell.

The method by which the orders for the expedition were drawn up is instructive. A passage in the above letter from Dundas hints at it – 'the last time Lord Grenville, you and I met together'. Grenville was Foreign Secretary, and Dundas still Secretary for War. Further letters from Dundas confirm the impression that these three civilians formed a 'triumvirate' which decided on an important military operation without taking, or even hearing, the advice of military experts.

Thus on 28 August, 1799, when the expedition had already sailed, we find Dundas sending the King a copy of a letter he had written to Pitt, 'as it contains the outlines of what occurs to Mr Dundas to be the best plan for future operations. It will afford Your Majesty an opportunity of correcting any of Mr Dundas's

[1] *Windsor*, 28.8.99.

ideas which may not meet Your Majesty's concurrence.'[1]

The same day he writes to Pitt: 'In the course of the night I have been ruminating upon what directions it will be necessary to give (to the Duke of York).' And he adds that he is also writing to Lord Grenville 'in case he has any suggestions'.

Thus the unhappy results of civilians trying to run the military operations had been forgotten. Verily this 'triumvirate' reminds one of the Bourbons.

On the other hand, Fortescue is less than fair when he accuses the Government of vaguely telling Abercromby to 'land somewhere and do something'. They gave him the 'intention', or objective, namely to land on the coast of Holland and eject the French; and they gave him the choice of two landing-places, Zeeland or the Helder. The real criticism of Dundas is that he ordered any operation at all without consulting the experts as to its practicability.

Abercromby set sail from the Downs on 13 August, and, in agreement with Admiral Mitchell, decided to make the Helder his objective. 'The Helder' is the name of the Dutch naval base on the tip of the peninsula which divides the North Sea from the Zuider Zee. It is, as Fortescue observes, 'no ordinary country'. Apart from the strip of sand dunes, averaging about one and a half miles wide, along the western shore, it is as flat as a pancake and below sea level. In order to keep out the sea a system of dikes had been constructed, great earthen banks, with roads running along them. The intervening ground is cut up by innumerable canals and ditches, so that vehicular movement is confined to the roads.

The point selected for the landing was a few miles to the south of the Helder. Owing to bad weather it did not take place till six days after the appearance of the expedition off the coast. Despite this delay and warning, there was only a weak force of Dutch troops under the command of General Daendels in position on the dunes to oppose it. The whole Dutch army was only 20,000 strong and the French occupying army 10,000, and owing to the destination of the expedition not being known the defending army had to spread over the whole coastline. Consequently it was weak everywhere.

At dawn on 27 August the landing took place, covered by a

[1] *Windsor*, 28.8.99.

barrage from the naval guns. It was completely successful. After fighting on the dunes for some hours the Dutch drew off hastily to the south in the evening, and the British troops bivouacked on the ground they had won. No attempt was made to pursue the enemy in this flight, or to cut off the garrison of the Helder, which escaped during the night under the very nose of the invaders.

Three days later Mitchell's fleet sailed past the Helder and received the surrender of the Dutch fleet without firing a shot.

There was consternation in the Franco-Batavian ranks. Appeals were made to Paris for help, but no more than 13,000 troops could be spared, and they could not arrive for five weeks. Meanwhile the loyalty of the Batavian Republic to their French masters was doubtful. A bold and immediate advance by the invaders would indubitably have met with little opposition short of Amsterdam. Abercromby had recognized this need for prompt action before ever he set out. 'The advanced season of the year,' he had written, 'demands the greatest promptitude and vigour.' Yet for four days he did nothing and when he ultimately moved forward it was not with any offensive intent, but in order to maintain his troops the better. He described it as 'a matter as much of necessity as of choice. A better country is now open to us and we have found some horses and wagons and a plentiful supply of fresh provisions.'[1]

In a private letter on the day after the landing he used some expressions remarkable in the mouth of a victorious general.

'This expedition has hung heavy on my mind ever since it was thought of. The risk was far too great, and (even) now all is not daylight.'

There can be no doubt that Abercromby was speaking the exact truth when he declared to Dundas: 'I trust the Duke of York will soon join us; it is my wish. I shall serve with more zeal than if acting for myself.'[2] Yet he was aware that it was not Dundas's intention that he should hold up his advance till the arrival of the Duke, for he wrote on 4 September to the War Minister: 'I know you will say why is Sir R. A. so long inactive, but I am prepared for that.'[3] He proceeds to excuse himself, ending up with a request for reinforcements. It is true that the longer he delayed the stronger he would become, but the same

[1] *W.O.*, I, 179.   [2] *Dropmore Papers*, V, p. 338.   [3] *W.O.*, I, 179.

might be equally true of the enemy. It *was* true. In General Brune the Franco-Batavian forces[1] possessed a strong and vigorous commander-in-chief.

By almost incredible exertions he managed to amass a force of 21,000 men, one third of whom were French, and to attack Abercromby on 10 September. The British held a strong position along the Zype dyke, twelve miles long and stretching from shore to shore (see sketch map 9), and they repulsed the attack with heavy losses. The Dutch troops fled even more rapidly than they had done on the first day, many of them not halting till they reached Alkmaar. But Abercromby again did not pursue. The comment of Baron Jomini on this is caustic: 'Failure will always be the lot of maritime expeditions when, instead of pushing the invasion rapidly, one confines oneself to acting pusillanimously, leaving time to the enemy to manoeuvre.'

Meanwhile the Navy was equally inert. With the command of the sea, and with the Dutch fleet in our possession, there were great possibilities for co-operation with the Army both on the North Sea coast and in the Zuider Zee. But Mitchell did practically nothing. He made no attempt to co-operate, and Abercromby complained to Dundas that for three days he had heard nothing from the admiral. Thus both on land and on sea affairs had reached stagnation-point right up to 13 September. On that day Abercromby received a welcome reinforcement; the Duke of York had landed.

Though the Duke of York was to command the combined expeditionary force, Dundas had not deemed it necessary to take him into his confidence or to discuss the operation even as much as he had with Abercromby. The Duke therefore continued to transact his ordinary business at the Horse Guards till the last minute. It was not till 7 September, when the approach of the Russians was signalled, that the Duke embarked at Walmer. Even then there was a delay of two days owing to the wind being foul. The Duke utilized it to write to his father, and in a postscript immediately before sailing he discusses the question of filling a majority in the Queen's Dragoons. He then handed over to his deputy, General Sir W. Fawcett, and set sail.

When Frederick, Duke of York, stepped ashore at the Helder

[1] Hereinafter described as the French.

on 13 September, 1799 he was thirty-six years old, exactly the same age as his French opponent. Five years' sedentary work in an office and the same period of good living had made its mark on the Duke – at any rate a physical one – he was becoming corpulent. His pristine vigour was evaporating. It may also very well be that the opprobrium that had been so unjustly heaped upon him for the disastrous termination to the Flanders campaign had to some extent impaired his self-confidence. Instructions from the Government that he should be guided by the opinions of his senior generals in important decisions would scarcely be calculated to lessen this feeling.

The Duke's staff contains some names already familiar to us – Clinton, Henry Taylor (afterwards his private secretary), and Colonel Brownrigg, his Military Secretary at the time. It was evidently 'hand-picked'.

His landing at the Helder coincided with that of a Russian division, and the Duke paid them the compliment of staging a march past, before riding off to his headquarters. These were situated in the tiny village of Schagen Brug, about one mile behind the centre of the line and a dozen miles south of the Helder.

His first letter to the King strikes an ominous note. In it he explains his delay in writing by the fact that he had had to go to headquarters 'in order to obviate anything unpleasant that might have happened had the Russian general joined Sir R. Abercromby's corps while I was not present'. Evidently there were already misgivings in his mind as to the degree of co-operation that might be expected from our new allies. The letter also betokens a quiet confidence in his own competence to smooth over any difficulties. He also tells the King that he is only awaiting the arrival of the 1st Division, 'when I mean to lose no time in moving forward, which I hope to be able to do on the 18th or 19th at furthest. I yesterday reviewed the whole of our position from Hollendam upon the German Ocean to Colhorn upon the Zuider Zee. It is astonishingly strong. The Hereditary Prince of Orange accompanied me and I was rejoiced to see him so well received by the country people. . . .

PS. I beg pardon for troubling Your Majesty with this postscript, but it slipped my memory to beg Your Majesty to grant the local rank of general to Sir R. Abercromby upon the Continent of Europe, and if Your Majesty is graciously pleased to approve of this suggestion and to order the commission to be dated from the day on which he sailed from England I believe it would obviate all difficulty with the Russian general who would find that Sir Ralph had the rank before he joined the army.'[1]

The Duke had not forgotten the petty jealousies that had existed in the higher ranks of his polyglot army in Flanders. He correctly assumed that one of his most important functions was to preserve the peace and ensure harmonious dealings and smooth co-operation between the three nationalities in his army. (We have had recent experience of the practical value of such a commander.)

The Duke did not mention that in addition to riding right along the line (twelve miles in extent) he had climbed the church tower at Schagen Brug in order to obtain a general view of the enemy. Though the ground is so flat and cumbered with dikes, trees, and villages that it is to be feared he did not see much, it at least witnesses to a certain physical activity on his part.

After reconnaissance comes plan. Now, it had been discovered that the French had an 'open' right flank: Major-General John Moore's brigade had been able to advance on the left up to the very gates of Hoorne without opposition. The Duke therefore conceived the idea of turning the hostile right. But he went further than this: he resolved to earmark for the purpose four of the best brigades in the British army, amounting to over 10,000 troops, and to send them round the French right by a wide turning movement. They were to capture Hoorne in the night preceding the battle, and when the action was well under way next day to turn the right of the enemy, taking advantage of whatever success the other columns met with. The rest of the army was to make a frontal attack in three parallel columns. By a tactful gesture the Duke gave the Russians the place of honour on the right of the line – an empty honour in reality, for the main work was to be done by the British on the far left. Two central columns, the right under David Dundas and the left under James (Murray) Pulteney, completed the order of battle.[2]

This plan was indeed a bold one, and it is surprising that the

---

[1] *Windsor*, 16.9.99.   [2] Pulteney's column was to capture Oudkarspel.

Duke secured the agreement of cautious generals like Abercromby and Dundas. But we have the explicit statement of the
former in a letter to Dundas, that 'the plan of attack was, I am
persuaded, the best that could be devised. It was laid by H.R.H.
before General Hermann (the Russian commander) myself and
General Dundas and it met with our united approbation.'[1]
The Duke corroborated this in his official report after the
battle.

The plan was essentially an operation on exterior lines, and
depended for its success on initiative and determination on the
part of the detached column. It is therefore difficult to comprehend why the Duke selected for this command General Abercromby, who had displayed a lack of these qualities at Boxtel,
(as well as after the recall of the Duke). Nevertheless the plan
was a sound one, provided the requisite leadership was forthcoming. A French account, translated into English in 1801 as
The History of the Campaign of 1799, agrees that the plan was
indeed a 'bold but also a just, extensive, and skilful application
of the principles and rules of the art of war'.

There is a curiously worded passage in the orders which probably indicates that the Commander-in-Chief was not unaware
of the congenital caution in his Second-in-Command. 'If the
attack of the right proves successful Sir R. Abercromby risks
nothing in pushing every advantage to the uttermost.'

At the last minute General Hermann complained that he
would not be ready to attack on the 19th, and York thereupon
offered to postpone the attack till the 20th. Hermann accepted
this alteration, but again changed his mind and agreed to the
19th.

BATTLE OF BERGEN, *19 September, 1799*

No two battles are alike, but few can have been so indivi-
dualistic as that of Bergen. 'Zero Hour' was to be at daybreak,
and Abercromby's column marched out at 6 p.m. the previous
evening in order to be in position betimes. Two hours before
zero hour the Russians, without warning, began their advance.
The extraordinary reason given for this was that their troops
were hungry. (Incidentally the Duke had allotted them an
extra pound of bread per head.) The probable reason was that

[1] *W.O.*, I, 179.

they wished to take the French by surprise. In this they were successful. Sweeping down the road to Bergen in a single massed column, they crashed without much difficulty through the French outposts and, without pausing, pushed straight on through the night till their leading troops found themselves in the village of Bergen. Their units in rear had stopped to pillage the villages through which they passed. The leading troops followed suit in Bergen. Very thorough was their work; muskets were fired into door-locks, and the church was burnt down. (It still stands in ruins, a mute witness to Russian barbarism.)

This enjoyable work went on for some hours, till at last the French recovered from their surprise, and by counterattacking, inflicted the surprise in turn on their opponents. General Herman himself was captured. A retrograde movement set in, while the French who had been swept aside on to the dunes during the night attack advanced once more and peppered the Russians in both flanks. The retreat became a rout, and eventually the whole Russian column fell back into their old lines, and proceeded to disperse. An ugly gap in the Allied line would thus have been formed had it not been for the foresight of the Duke, who had detailed a British brigade to march in support of the Russians. This brigade was thus able to fill up the gap in the line and hold the French at bay.

Meanwhile Dundas's column, which started off at the correct time, advanced cautiously – perhaps too cautiously – till it found the Russians on its right in retreat. Dundas sent some troops to their support, and fell back slowly himself in conjunction with them.

Still farther to the left Pulteney had had a brilliant success. Overcoming the water obstacles, he at 2 p.m. rushed the Dutch position and drove the enemy in panic before him half-way to Alkmaar. This victory of Pulteney's has been slurred over in all except an unpublished Dutch account in The Hague Archives, which concludes as follows: 'The English continued their pursuit, firing blindly into the bunched-up mass and advanced with fixed bayonets. The retreat of the Batavians developed into a flight. Daendels himself was dragged along, lost his horse and escaped capture only by a trumpeter offering him his own. The idea of making a stand had to be given up; the troops standing in reserve were unable to hold up the fleeing troops, and themselves joined in the flight. The flight became general.'[1]

The moment was ripe for the intervention of the Abercromby columns. But there was no sign or sound of it. Where was it and what was it doing? The answers are that it was still at Hoorne and that it was doing – nothing. A few hours later it moved – back to the British lines!

This sorry incident, so humiliating to our military record, must be examined in detail. The column had moved out punctually at 6 p.m. on the previous night, but a heavy rain delayed the march, and it was not till between 3 a.m. and 4 a.m. that it reached Hoorne. The Dutch garrison surrendered the town, and their column halted to rest, the men lying down by the roadside. Next morning the battle could be heard raging a dozen miles away, but Abercromby did not deem it prudent to approach it any nearer till he had news as to how it was going. This news would manifestly take several hours to reach him and even if it were fully satisfactory it would require some further hours before he could obtain contact with the enemy.[2] At an early hour Sir Robert sent off his A.D.C., Captain Bunbury, to report to the Duke on the tired condition of his troops and the difficult nature of the country in his front. Bunbury was also to inquire how the battle was going. Abercromby then sat down once more patiently to await news. The hours passed. Noon arrived, and at last came welcome intelligence. Dundas had stormed the first French line; no news of the Russians. Still Abercromby did not move – not even an approach march to diminish the big gap between his column and Pulteney's. The afternoon wore on. Evening came. The troops had now been stationary for about sixteen hours. Now at last a messenger had arrived. He reported that Pulteney's column had been successful, but that the Russians had failed. In consequence the column was to return to our lines, while Abercromby himself was to go on ahead to report at headquarters, where the Duke wished to consult him. Abercromby complied, but evidently he lost his way, for he did not reach headquarters till 2 a.m. next morning. Pulteney had also been recalled and obeyed with the greatest

[1] *MSS. of General G. J. W. Beinen. G. S. Archives, The Hague.*
[2] A statement that Daendels had detached a battalion to delay Abercromby's march was incorrect – Daendels was not even aware of the capture of Hoorne.

reluctance. The attack had failed. The army had been defeated by an inferior army of French and Dutch.

Who was to blame? It seems certain, humanly speaking, that if Abercromby had observed the hint of the Duke to push every advantage, the success on our left would more than have cancelled out the failure on our right; Alkmaar would have been captured and the retreat of the French left wing should have been jeopardized. A glance at the map will show this. Had the column resumed its advance from Hoorne after, say, six hours' rest, i.e. at 8 a.m., it could have been in touch with Pulteney's column soon after noon, in time to share in his success and make it still more decisive by cutting off the Dutch retreat, for it had no troops opposed to it. A force of about 15,000 British troops would then be almost astride the line of retreat of 8,000 Frenchmen. If Brune, instead of retreating, then fell back on to the Dunes, he would soon have run short of water, and found himself hemmed in between the navy on the sea and the army on land. The campaign would have been brought to a conclusion by the first general action. The reasons for Abercromby's inaction must therefore be carefully scrutinized.

Sir Ralph Abercromby's apologia was given in his own words: 'The state of the roads, the fatigue of the troops, the broken nature of the ground, above all, the uncertainty of events on the right made (an advance) impossible.'

Let us take these, point by point. *The state of the roads* did not prevent movement; there is no evidence that his roads were worse than those used by the other columns; moreover, he could not be aware what their state might be in the course of his further advance. As to *fatigue of his troops*, they had had several hours' rest before it was necessary to resume the march. He must have known, when giving his adhesion to the plan, the distance his men would have to cover and the approximate conditions that might be encountered (though the rain would admittedly make conditions slightly worse). The possibility of rain should be reckoned with at the Equinox. They were not so fatigued that they could not do another fifteen miles back to camp that night. Captain Bunbury, who was with them, considered that they would be quite fit to march by noon. The *'broken nature of the country'* presumably means that it was cut up by dikes and canals. But what else did Sir Ralph expect when he agreed to the plan? The terrain was normal for that theatre of war. Abercromby complained that he found two canals in his front. So did Pulteney, but he took the precaution of carrying small boats with him which helped his progress.

But the proof that the above handicaps were not considered vital by the General comes out of his own mouth, and is contained in the words 'above all': the chief reason for his inactivity, in other words, was *not* the physical difficulties but the moral – the deadening effect of uncertainty – '*uncertainty of events on the right*'. But here also an examination of the map before he set out should have shown him that news of the result of the Russian attack was not likely to reach him till the afternoon, for the messenger would have about twenty miles to cover. There was bound to be uncertainty. What was the use of sitting down a dozen miles away from the battlefield, and even more from the enemy's line of retreat, until he received any news of what the Russians were doing? Even if he had moved when he heard of Dundas's success, he might have been in time to make his presence felt to a slight degree. John Moore, who was present in command of a brigade, declared it as his conviction that the column 'might have profited by the advantages gained by Sir J. Pulteney and at least have made it possible to reach Oudkarspel'; which implies that Abercromby did have some intelligence of Pulteney's progress that has not been recorded in histories of the battle. Others, including Bunbury, were of the same opinion.

We are therefore still probing for the real reason of Abercromby's abject failure. Bunbury probably adds some light when he observes mildly: 'Abercromby was a little too old for hard service.' He was over 65 years of age. He had had a fatiguing and trying night march, with little or no sleep. He was physically at a low ebb. It is well known that the physical reacts intimately on the moral: the general's morale was low. But the operations of a detached column during a battle require a high morale in the commander; the sense of isolation has a deadening, even paralysing effect. As a natural result military history shows time and again that the detached column fails to intervene in the battle, or that it intervenes too late. Abercromby threw up the sponge; he gave up. All through his life he had been in the habit of giving up. He early gave up his practice at the Bar; he gave up the chance of fighting in America; he gave up the West Indies Command; he gave up the Army; he gave up the Irish Command; he thankfully gave up the command to the Duke of York; he gave up nearly every operation in the field of which he held the command. He might be described as 'the give up' general.

But though the failure was directly due to Abercromby's culpable inaction, some blame must be imputed to the Duke of York, who knew, or should have known, this military failing in his understudy, and should have refrained from employing him on a mission of such a nature.

This brings us to a consideration of the generalship shown by the Duke in the battle. He seems to have remained during the action at or near his headquarters. This was probably a right decision, for there was no point of vantage from which he could have observed more than a minute portion of his wide-flung battle-line, and for a general to interest himself too closely in events near at hand is to become parochially-minded. A general cannot influence such a battle to any extent. He can only take decisions on *faits accomplis*, and it is to be feared that the Duke took one vital and disastrous decision in this battle. In the middle of the afternoon (it is impossible to fix the time more precisely) the situation had become an anxious one in the centre of the line. The bulk of the Russians had already retreated behind the dike and dispersed, and Manners's Brigade of semi-trained militiamen was hard at it defending the dike. Immediately to the front of the Duke's headquarters Dundas's column was slowly falling back, owing to the retreat of the Russians on its right. The sound of firing drew nearer and nearer. Bunbury, who having arrived with Abercromby's message was retained at headquarters, reports that the Duke became anxious at the near approach of the French. The situation looked ugly and the Duke sent off Bunbury to obtain troops to hold the village of Krabbendam, which formed a sort of Hougoumont in front of our lines. Bunbury succeeded in this and the position was stabilized. Indeed, the French drew back as soon as they saw our troops re-entering our lines. It seems likely that at this juncture the Duke or his staff, or both, temporarily lost their heads, and decided that the battle was lost. Accordingly the fatal message was sent to recall Pulteney and Abercromby. Bergen should, in fact, go down in history as one of those battles in which the commanders, not the troops, were defeated.

There may have been extenuating circumstances of which we know nothing. We are reduced to judging by results. The result of the recall order was that the battle was lost, and the Duke, as Commander-in-Chief, must take the blame for it. One cannot picture a Wellington or a Lee issuing such an order. But then they were not saddled with War Councils and Abercrombys.

An anonymous poem published a few months later sums up the battle in caustic but merited terms:

'Ten thousand troops to scatter wild dismay,
Were marched to Hoorne, wisely detached by night.
To stop the hostile army in its flight;
That when they shrunk from Russia's conquering spear,
This corps might charge them on the flank and rear.
But when, alas, the fatal mine was sprung
And the sad news confirmed by every tongue . . .
They beat to arms, pursued their former track,
Rejoined the Prince – and to a man came back.'

Significant actions on the part of the Duke followed next day. In his General Order on the battle he whitewashed Abercromby. 'The column under General Sir R. Abercromby . . . from the doubtful situation of affairs upon the right could not in prudence advance further.' His other action was to write a graceful letter of condolence to General Essen, on whom the Russian command had fallen, and to send him some of his own surgeons to attend to the Russian wounded. Essen did not requite this action; but according to Bunbury 'held himself as much as possible aloof from the Duke's society and councils'. The Russian troops Bunbury reports as 'angry, sullen and scarcely to be counted as allies'. Some of their little ways surprised our troops. When issued with grease for their vehicles they spread it on their bread and ate it. Months later the Duke returned good for ill. Hearing that the Czar of Russia was displeased with the conduct of his troops and had broken the regiments concerned, York wrote him a long letter in which he warmly defended specific regiments, adding: 'I have been a witness of the order and bravery with which all these corps fought against the enemy, and have always testified to them my satisfaction.'[1]

In an endeavour to improve relations between the Russian and British soldiers the Duke also took the responsibility, without first consulting the Government, of issuing extra pay to our allies in order to bring theirs on a level with ours. This action showed his understanding of soldiers' characters. Its example might with advantage have been followed in a subsequent war where we have had allies.

Meanwhile what was the British fleet doing? One might suppose that, having the command of the sea on both flanks, it could do a great deal, by attacking the enemy's flanks and by threatening landings in his rear. (The possibility was very similar to that utilized by our fleet at Gallipoli, when it landed an army at Suvla, behind the enemy's lines.) Yet, strange to say, most of our naval histories pass over this part of the campaign in silence, seeming to imply that, after their bloodless victory in acquiring the Dutch fleet, no more was to be expected from it in this amphibious campaign! As a matter of fact, a few small gunboats were employed on the canals in co-operation with the troops, and some gunboats shelled French reinforcements moving up the coast. But naval action was practically limited to this and Admiral Mitchell seems to have become as passive and defensively minded as General Abercromby. For nearly three weeks after the surrender of the Dutch fleet inertia reigned, explained probably by the fact that Admiral Duncan, under whose eagle eye the first operation had been carried out, had gone to England on sick leave.

His return seems to have galvanized the fleet into some sort of activity. On 21 September Mitchell at last sailed into the Zuider Zee with four bomb vessels and a few lighter craft. They effected some desultory landings by the ships' crews at various points and interrupted traffic between Amsterdam and Friesland, but they did not threaten Amsterdam itself, nor did they have any direct influence upon the land operations. Guiot, the French representative at The Hague, was fearful of an attack on Amsterdam and wrote to Talleyrand: 'I fear that the English will fit out a flotilla of light boats to attack Amsterdam by the Zuider Zee. Its inhabitants in general are well disposed, but it

[1] Watkins, p. 385.

s

is none the less certain that a few bombs directed against so populous and so rich a town would cause it to capitulate. This would be the coup de grace of the Dutch government; it would have no more money or resources to pay its forces.'[1]

The French historian of the campaign, Gachot, writes in terms that must be humiliating to our navy: 'Whilst the English, masters of the sea, could have thrown a few regiments on shore, occupied the Hague and Amsterdam, overturned the Batavian government, cut off the retreat of the soldiers who were on the Bergen front – they contented themselves with tacking about at cannon range from the shore. A flotilla formed on the Zuider Zee advanced timidly towards the south, disembarked feeble contingents at Medemblick and Eckhysen, but their crews did not dare set foot in Hoorn, which was so close to Alkmaar that a column of troops could have reached it in the rear of the French in a few hours.'[2]

It is to the Duke of York's credit that he wished and proposed to employ the fleet in this way. One of his proposals was that it should convey a portion of the army to the Yssel, utilizing its command of the sea. Another was 'to detach from our present position a strong corps upon our left to threaten the enemy's right, and possibly with the assistance of the admiral, to threaten Amsterdam'. Clearly he had in his mind co-operation between the two services. Unfortunately 'I thought it my duty to ask the opinion of Sir Ralph Abercrombie and General Dundas upon these plans but they deemed it infinitely too dangerous to be adopted.'[3] Thus the opportunity was lost and the Duke was forced to fall back upon a mere repetition of the plan already tried at Bergen (cutting out the fourth column).

The greatness of this opportunity was disclosed at the time in a letter from Guiot to Reinhart: 'If the Anglo-Russian expedition had been better concerted and if the enemy had attacked this country at the same time at several points it is almost certain that they would have been master of it today. . . . If the English had disembarked only 3,000 men here (Scheveningen), the garrison of the Hague only consisting of 200 French and about 1500 other troops, the Batavian Repub-

---

[1] *Guiot to Talleyrand, The Hague Archives.*
[2] *Brune en Holland*, by E. Gachot, p. 243.   [3] *W.O.* I, 180.

lic would have experienced the fate of the Italian Republics.'[1]

It is to be noted that the naval commander was little more optimistic about the campaign than his original army colleague. On 10 October he wrote a long, incoherent letter to Lord Spencer at the Admiralty, in which occurs the passage: 'I have, ever since the 19th had my doubts of success.' He states that he cannot understand Abercromby's failure at Hoorne, and adds: 'I have another idea to say: according to the nature of the country the army has always been too much collected together, when they have moved forward to attack, as they could only move in close or narrow columns along the Dykes, the right excepted, as it had the beach to extend, and without the assistance of the Navy and gunboats, and they of the smaller force, comparatively speaking, they could not have got in at all: therefore, my Lord, the length of the column the men in the rear be of little service, as the ground was [illegible] by the front of the column.'[2]

What my Lord made of this, if he made anything, history does not relate, possibly because Admiral Mitchell was almost immediately recalled to England and replaced by Admiral Dixon.

Bad weather now set in again, and large quantities of fresh stores and ammunition had to be accumulated. The new attack could not in consequence be launched till 2 October. By that time Brune had inundated a large area covering his right flank. The size of the two armies was but little altered. The Dutch were diminishing in numbers, largely from desertion, at the same rate that the French were increasing.

Bad weather has a tendency to depress the spirits, and it did nothing to reduce the pessimism of Sir Ralph Abercromby, who wrote home two days before the attack in which he was allotted an important part: 'We must expect sickness . . . and I wish the nation may prepare itself for a disappointment. . . . In short my reason does not tell me we are to have any success.'[3]

It was perhaps as well for his peace of mind that the Duke of York was unaware of what his naval and military advisers were

[1] *Gedenkstukken der Algemeene Gescheidenis van Nederland*, by Dr Colenbrander, p. 79.
[2] *Spencer Papers*, III, p. 195.
[3] *Life of Sir Ralph Abercromby*, by Lord Dunfermline, p. 203.

writing home. Whether or not he had any suspicions, he persevered with his task and issued orders for battle.

BATTLE OF EGMONT, 2 October[1]

For this battle the Duke of York reversed his plan. Abercromby's corps was transferred from the left to the extreme right, and given orders to advance along the seashore. Next to it on top of the dunes came Dundas, with the Russians on his left. Pulteney was ordered merely to hold his position opposite Oudkarspel. The main blow was again to be struck by Abercromby's corps. It is difficult to decide whether the Duke still reposed confidence in him or whether he felt he must defer to general opinion, for Sir Ralph's reputation was tremendously high. Short of sending him home after his failure at Hoorne the Duke probably felt he had no option but to give him a prominent command.

To mark the importance he attached to the task of this column, the Duke turned out to watch it file past him at dawn at Petton on the seashore. Then he turned to Dundas's column, which he followed in its attack.

Abercromby met with only slight opposition until the French main position was reached on the dunes one mile north of Egmont. Here a stiff fight ensued in which Sir Ralph displayed great personal bravery, having two horses shot under him. The French were defeated and fell back to their second position south of Egmont. The time was about 5 p.m., and meanwhile Dundas and the Russians had met with greater resistance on the dunes. The Russians refused to advance beyond Schoorl, in spite of two requests from York. General Essen merely replied: 'We do not move from here.' (The Duke was so disgusted that he next day asked the Government to induce the Emperor of Russia to replace Essen.) However, York sent up Chatham's brigade from his reserve to reinforce Dundas and progress was resumed. But Bergen had not been captured when Abercromby's battle was over. He thus found himself in a somewhat similar position to that at Hoorne, being to the flank and in rear of the French position. The smoke from the Bergen battle, three miles away, could be seen from the dunes (though Abercromby himself was too blind to see it), and an opportunity

[1] Sometimes misleadingly called Alkmaar.

presented itself to strike a decisive blow, but Sir Ralph decided that his troops were too tired, and as at the Helder he put them to bivouac on the battlefield.

It is hard to blame the general for this decision, for his troops were really tired and his ammunition supply had run low. At the same time it must be noted that similar conditions obtained in the hostile army, and Brune was only too glad, as soon as darkness fell, to abandon his whole position and retreat south. Nor can the Duke be blamed for not ensuring that his right column should co-operate in the attack on Bergen, for communications were so primitive in those days and in that terrain, that he was completely in the dark, even though he kept his A.D.C.s galloping all over the country. The heavy sand, after the rain, made going very difficult and slow, while the dunes denied him a sight of what was proceeding. The Duke, in fact, increased his reputation by his conduct of this battle. 'In this engagement the judicious disposition of the combined force, made by the special direction of the Duke of York, appeared conspicuous and attracted general admiration,' writes Watkins.[1]

Writing to his father, York modestly ascribes the victory to the valour of his troops: 'The conduct of Your Majesty's troops is worthy of Y.M.'s approbation. It is to their steadiness and galantry alone that through Divine Providence the victory was gained.'[2]

Brune fell back to a line stretching from Wyk on the coast, through Kastrikum to the flooded polders on the east, and on 7 October the Allies advanced through Alkmaar and Egmont to regain touch.

BATTLE OF KASTRIKUM, 6 October, 1799

Resolved to maintain pressure on the defeated enemy, the Duke of York ordered an advance on the 6th, in order to obtain contact with the new French position, with a view to an attack on it next day.

But Brune decided to make a partial counterattack on that day. Thus an encounter battle resulted, both armies being somewhat surprised at the action of their opponents.

General Brune, impulsive as ever, rushed forward in person

[1] Op. cit., p. 362.   [2] Windsor, 6.10.99.

with his reserve to the assistance of his advanced posts at Kastrikum, where the battle became general. Each side in turn poured in fresh troops. Once again Abercromby on the extreme right had advanced with little opposition far ahead of the rest of the line. In response to an appeal for help from the Russian troops in Kastrikum he marched with four of his battalions to their aid, whilst on the opposite side of the village Coote, who had captured Limmen, was also approaching. The combined attack succeeded. On the left flank Dundas had captured Akersloot and advanced to the outskirts of Uitgeest when darkness fell. Further east, Pulteney had not been engaged.

The French resistance had been surprisingly strong, and our casualties were very heavy, but we had gained a good deal of ground and taken 500 prisoners, and that without intending to fight a battle at all. The French losses also were heavy. The verdict of Richard Surtees on the day's work was: 'No army ever got a more complete drubbing than the French did before the business terminated'[1], an excusable exaggeration on the part of this great-hearted soldier.[2]

The Duke of York on the morning of the battle was rightly at his headquarters, which he had established in the town of Alkmaar. Kastrikum is a good six miles to the south-west, and out of sight and sound. He, however, sent Bunbury up the lofty church tower to report what could be seen. Unfortunately, to add to the fog of war, heavy rain was falling and visibility was very bad. The Duke was therefore reduced to sending out orderlies and A.D.C.s. But the reports they brought back were meagre in the extreme. Short of getting on his horse and riding about, there was little that he could do. The control of events was completely out of his hands. The position was a mortifying and frustrating one, and the Duke cannot have cut an impressive figure. It was probably this experience that gave Bunbury a poor opinion of the Duke's capacity as a commander in the field. But worse was to follow.

An official sent by the French Government to ascertain the reason for the French retreats reported back to his Government:

[1] *Surtees: 25 Years in the Rifle Brigade*, p. 28.

[2] Bunbury's assertion that the officers 'had lost all confidence' probably means that he had himself, and other staff officers in contact with Abercromby and Dundas.

'I found Brune very dissatisfied. He supposes that the Dutch Government are not only little disposed to make sincere efforts for the common cause but that they are so arranging things that they may not be on bad terms with which ever side wins.'[1] This accurately sizes up their attitude. Difficulties were also experienced in supplying the troops owing to the fact that the bread wagons had to be used to transport the wounded. It is clear that Brune expected the attack to be continued on the 7th, but the British rested on their arms – much to the relief of Rostolland, Brune's Chief-of-Staff, who wrote that day to the Batavian Government: 'Aujourdhui l'ennemi nous laisse tranquille.'[2] We hear of 'lassitude extrême' among the French troops and on 3 October Rostolland wrote of their being 'harrassés de fatigue'. On the 7th Guiot was writing to the French Government: 'Supplies of all natures are becoming exhausted, and it is to be feared that if circumstances remain the same the funds and credit will in about one month fail to provide the requirements of the army.'[3]

The General Staff Archives at The Hague also contain an interesting document in the form of a report drawn up by a deputy of the Batavian Government to explain why supplies failed after the battle of Egmont. The first reason given by this report is the precipitation and haste of the retreat from Alkmaar, whereby large quantities of bread and flour were abandoned (and consequently captured by the Allies). There was also a lack of transport. 'The commissary has only 24 wagons whereas 100 would not suffice. On the retreat from Alkmaar the commissaries left without orders, abandoning their stores.'[4]

Two battalions of French reinforcements had just arrived, but no more were immediately expected. Approximate numbers of the two armies were now:

Allies	British	28,000	Total 42,000
	Russian	14,000	
French	French	14,000	Total 24,000
	Dutch	10,000	

Putting all these facts together, it is apparent that the French army was in a parlous state, and that continued pressure,

[1] *Alkmaar Archives.* [2] *Rijks Archiefs, The Hague.*
[3] *Alkmaar Archives.* [4] *G.S. Archives, The Hague.*

especially if combined with demonstrations or landings upon
the unprotected coast by the navy, would have led to a head-
long retreat, and the probable liberation of Holland from its
French captors.

A French comment on this lamentable affair, though humiliating to us, cannot be gainsaid: 'French generals would have
tried again before retreating, but the English, *whose caution in
war has always been remarkable* . . . renounced their project of
conquest, thinking only of extricating themselves from the bad
position into which they had got.' A still greater Frenchman
once said: 'A battle gained is one in which you refuse to
recognize defeat.'

As the battle died down that night, the British remaining, as
the Duke justly observed, 'masters of the ground', a doubt
arose in his mind as to the best course to pursue next day, and
he asked the lieutenant-generals for their opinion. They evidently held a concerted meeting late that night and drew up a
lengthy document which they submitted to the Commander-
in-Chief. The details of the whole affair are obscure, but there
are indications that the generals gave their advice orally in the
first instance, and that the Duke, recognizing the gravity of it,
told them to go away and commit it to writing. As this document was destined to have a big influence on the upshot of the
campaign, and as it has never been printed, it deserves detailed
attention. It might be described as an 'appreciation of the
situation' and consists of a long catalogue of the difficulties that
now faced the Allies: hardships due to the wet weather, difficulty of supplying troops owing to bad roads, paucity of horses
and barges, heavy losses in the recent battle without any
balancing advantage, sickness owing to exposure, absence of
good billets, the difficulty of the terrain in their front, the
strength of the French position at Haarlem, the fact that the
farther they advanced the greater would become their difficulties, whereas the French were being reinforced by 6,000
fresh troops; finally the great fatigue of the troops who had been
out in the rain for several days. Then comes their conclusion:
'From what we see, and what we feel we are humbly of opinion
that however we might have given efficacy to a revolution in
Holland we are not at this moment equal to the conquest of
the country or of remaining (even if it was an eligible one) in

our present situation and that any further advance affords no prospect of decided advantage but on the contrary is fraught with much difficulty and dangers should we fail; that therefore we should return to the position of the Zype which we quitted and then await more favourable change of circumstances.'

Quite apart from the errors of fact with which this precious document bristles, two points are deserving of notice. The first is that all the adverse factors except the losses suffered in the late battle and the subsequent rain were equally present three days before, when no question was raised of retreat. (The losses were almost balanced by the enemy's losses, and the rain which falls upon 'the just and the unjust' fell in equal measure on the enemy.) The truth is that Brune's brusque and timely counter-attack had had an effect out of all proportion to its weight.

The second point is that none of the factors affecting the enemy's situation was considered – thus making it a singularly incomplete and unbalanced appreciation of the situation. As a matter of fact, and as we have seen, practically all the difficulties listed in this document were common to both armies. The enemy had equally bad roads, and we had considerable local supplies of food at hand. A week earlier Lieutenant W. Gomme was writing home: 'We live upon beef and mutton and so cheap that we cannot spend our pay.'[1] Apart from a certain amount of colic, sickness had not started to make itself felt. The French had not fortified Haarlem; their numbers were, and were likely to remain, greatly inferior to those of the Allies; prisoners had reported 6,000 reinforcements, but they had probably been in-structed to spread exaggerated reports; the Russians might be unreliable allies, but they could hardly be more unreliable than the allies of the French; a further advance increases supply difficulties in nearly all campaigns, by its very nature, but it is offset by the supplies that will be captured in the course of that advance; moreover, in this campaign it might be hoped that the navy would at last bestir itself and effect some fresh landings.

War is a tug-of-war. You cannot assess the chances of your own side without examining the state of the enemy. Your own team may appear to be in the last stages of exhaustion. But have a look at the other end of the rope. There you see similar agonized expressions, but in addition one man has twisted his

[1] *Life of Sir W. Gomme.*

knee, another has slipped and is sitting on the ground, a third
has quit the rope in sheer exhaustion and despair. Go on! One
more pull, and you will have them over!

On the morning of 7 October the Army Commander sat
down to study the Abercromby memorandum, if we may so
describe it.[1] He seems to have been perturbed by its conclusion, but having asked for and received the unanimous opinions
of his lieutenant-generals, he did not feel strong enough to
turn it down completely: he however resolved to put off retreat
as long as he could. He wrote all this in a long letter to Henry
Dundas. Scarcely had he finished it than he was visited by
Abercromby and Dundas. The two Scots were more than ever
impressed with the imprudence of remaining any longer in
their present position. They made use of remarkably emphatic
and peremptory terms for subordinates to employ, according to
the Duke's report to Dundas: 'They stated the impossibility of
remaining longer in the position we were then in, the certainty
of being under the necessity of fighting two severe actions
before it would be possible to get possession of Haarlem, without which town no secure position could be taken . . .' and so
on. The Duke concludes: 'I found myself under the necessity
of complying.'[2]

Weak, no doubt: one cannot picture a Wellington or a
Bonaparte 'complying'. Still, we must not forget the hampering
restrictions on his own freedom of action that the Duke, rightly
or wrongly, felt were imposed upon him. He had been so consistently adulatory of his two cautious subordinates in his letters
home that he could not suddenly ignore their combined advice.

Orders were accordingly issued for the retreat to commence
that afternoon. These orders caused 'surprise and disappointment' among some at least of the troops. But the bad state of the
roads, of which we have heard so much, did not prevent a
fairly speedy and orderly withdrawal unmolested by the enemy,
and on 9 October the old position along the Zype dike was
again taken up. The French followed slowly and cautiously.

Communications between London and the army took on an

[1] Abercromby wrote a long letter to Huskisson in such similar terms that there
can be little doubt that he was the principal author of the document.
[2] *W.O.*, I, 180.

average four days. Colonel Brownrigg, who had been entrusted with the Duke's letter announcing his intention to withdraw, reached London on the 14th, and Brownrigg did not get back with the Government's approval of York's action till the 18th.

By that time fresh developments had occurred. The Commander-in-Chief had been favoured by yet another visit by the twin pessimists on the 12th, when they gave it as their opinion that the Helder could not be held through the winter, and that therefore evacuation should take place at an early date.[1] On the same day a letter arrived from Dundas promising between 4,000 and 5,000 reinforcements.

York now did the sensible thing; he called for a report both on the practicability of holding the Helder and also of fortifying his position on the Zype. His two senior Engineer officers drew up these reports, one being as gloomy as the other. It is impossible to tell whether these reports were accurate or whether they had been tinged with the prevailing pessimism that seems to have spread from the top downwards. The final blow was delivered by the navy, who suddenly discovered that it was 'very difficult for fleets to enter the Helder after the middle of November'.[2]

On the face of these reports the Commander and his generals decided that there was no time to be lost, and that evacuation should be attempted as speedily as possible. Here the French came unexpectedly to his aid. Abercromby wrote home: 'The first hint came from the French army, which was taken up by the Duke's État Major. When proposed by them to me I desired them to put it into writing. I heartily concurred with them and desired them to carry it to Lord Chatham [who was sick], which was done.'[3]

A correspondence lasting from the 15th to the 18th ensued. General Brune secretly jumped at the opportunity of ridding the country of his enemy without further fighting, but he naturally dissembled his eagerness, and made certain stipulations. The

[1] Abercromby was continuing to write home in his usual strain: 'My mind always went in opposition to the undertaking. . . . As yet the army is not sickly, but sickness must necessarily come.' This was his second prophecy of sickness. Both were falsified. The weather improved, 'and continued fine during my stay in the country, and so warm that I several times enjoyed sea-bathing.' (Lieutenant Hunt, *R.U.S.I. Journal*, April 1914.)
[2] *W.O.*, I, 180.   [3] *Dunfermline*, p. 201.

chief of these were that the Dutch fleet should be handed back, that the allies should fall back to a position on the dunes, pending embarkation, and that 15,000 prisoners in England should be restored. To the first the Duke returned a firm and dignified refusal. 'His Royal Highness will on no account treat upon this article.' And he meant it. He announced privately that he would abandon the whole convention sooner than hand back the Dutch fleet.

Nor would he abandon his present position on the Zype. He recognized the reasonableness of handing back some prisoners in consideration of the saving in casualties to his own army, but he cut the figure down to 5,000. Eventually the figure of 8,000 was agreed upon and the convention was signed on 20 October.

All this time the Duke was, of course, completely in the dark as to how the Government and King George would take this action of his, especially the restoration of prisoners, which he was utterly unentitled to do. It was therefore with great feelings of relief that he learnt a few days later that a Cabinet meeting had been held simultaneously with the negotiations, at which the very step that he was taking was decided on.

Hostilities ceased on 29 October, and the embarkation commenced shortly afterwards. It was carried out without incident, and when the number of troops left was not considered equal to a field-marshal's command the Duke was ordered home, leaving the rearguard to be evacuated by a subordinate.[1]

The one pleasing feature of the whole sorry affair from the Duke's point of view was the unswerving support he received throughout from Henry Dundas, the Cabinet, and (what meant infinitely more to him) from his own father. King George made out a draft with his own hand (still visible in the Public Record Office) completely exonerating the Duke.

'To H.R.H. the Duke of York. 27th Oct. 1799.

'The situation of [sic] the army under the command of my dearly beloved son the Duke of York was placed by the supreme strength of the country and the difficulty of getting off the troops without the loss of the rearguard fully exculpates him for the steps he has taken of negotiating and concluding a suspension of hostilities without previous directions from Hence,

---

[1] The same principle was observed at Dunkirk in 1940, though whether this precedent was consciously followed I cannot say.

and on these grounds I fully give my sanction and approbation for that measure. George R.'

Pitt's letter was positively jubilant in tone, and must have rather surprised the worthy Duke. He assures him that 'every part of the transaction is marked with Dignity, Firmness, and Wisdom, and as far as Y.R.H. is personally concerned must entitle you to the confidence and gratitude of the country in at least as great a degree as the most splendid and prosperous issue which would ever have attended our enterprise.'

It is impossible to assess the powers of generalship of the Duke of York from this, the Helder campaign. It was too short: the Duke only took over the command in the middle of it; his hands were from the outset so tied that he can hardly be judged by the same tests that one would apply to a normal commander in the field. If his chief *métier* was to cultivate harmonious relations with the Russians, he must be adjudged to have failed. But Russians are perhaps not the easiest of allies. Our men looked upon them as only half civilized – which many of them were. After being evacuated they 'astounded the good people of Yarmouth by drinking the oil from the street lamps'. The Duke did what he could for them on several occasions, but General Essen proved himself a surly brute whom it was quite impossible to placate.

Nor were the Duke's relations with Admiral Mitchell much more close; but that again was scarcely his fault, and it is to be noted that he got on well with the Naval liaison officer (as we should now call him), Captain Popham.

It is clear that Abercromby was York's 'evil genius' during the Helder campaign. The universally beloved Sir Ralph was one of the most lion-hearted (physically) and most chicken-hearted (morally) generals who ever led a British army to failure and defeat. It is no pleasure to depict the military failings of a man possessing such a grand moral character and lovable nature as Sir Ralph, but it has been necessary to do it in order to re-establish the military reputation of the Royal Duke whom he 'let down'. The Duke's reputation has suffered far too long for the sins of others.[1]

[1] *The Dictionary of National Biography* sums up his Helder campaign in this sentence: 'From the moment that the Duke landed disaster followed disaster – an outrageously incorrect statement.'

As for the tactical handling of the army the Duke showed sound sense. Failing co-operation in turning movements with the navy, he was confined to turning movements on land, with what result we have seen. A passage by Bunbury that is almost invariably quoted in accounts of the campaign has done much damage to his military reputation in the field. The chief counts in his A.D.C.'s indictment are: 'He had little quickness of apprehension, still less of sagacity in penetrating designs or forming large views; painstaking yet devoid of resources and easily disheartened by difficulties. . . . To these defects must be added habits of indulgence and a looseness of talking after dinner about individuals which made him enemies and which in this unfortunate campaign probably incited, or inflamed the rancour of the Russian generals.'[1]

We should know better how to assess this judgment if young Bunbury had indicated more precisely what the Duke omitted to do, what faults he committed, and what designs he failed to penetrate. I can only think of one unpenetrated design – that of Brune on 6 October – not that it made much practical difference. What 'large views' should he have formed? What resources should he have conjured up? Disheartened by difficulties we can well believe of him – or of anyone who had as his immediate subordinates two such consistently cautious and almost 'defeatist' generals as Ralph Abercromby and David Dundas. Who would be proof against such a numbing influence? 'A looseness of talking.' Ah! We shall meet this again. But whether in this campaign it did practical harm there is no evidence or indication. The Duke certainly had the moral courage to take an unpleasant and prompt decision, whether we approve of it or not. A fair conclusion would probably be that he did as well as could be expected from a normal general under the peculiar and cramping position in which he was placed.

[1] *The Great War with France*, Sir H. Bunbury, p. 44.

MRS CLARKE

II

It is a lamentable trait in human character that we are more prone to remember persons in lofty stations by their foibles and follies than by their virtues. The case of Frederick, Duke of York, is no exception to this general rule. The two episodes by which he is chiefly connected in the public mind are his alleged march up a hill and subsequent countermarch and his supposed sharing of the command of the army with his mistress, Mrs Mary Anne Clarke.[1]

The Clarke affair, though it held the attention of the whole country to the exclusion of everything else for some weeks, died down speedily, and left no permanent traces. I would willingly pass it over cursorily, were it not that it had direct concern with the Duke's military career, and also had the incidental effect of throwing more light on the administration of the Horse Guards than the ordinary course of events would have done.

In or about the year 1776 a daughter was born to an obscure journeyman printer named Thompson. A young man who was interested in the girl placed her for two years in a school at Ham in Essex, thus providing her with an education above her station, of which she took full advantage. At the age of about 16 she formed a connexion with a stonemason of the name of Clarke, and shortly before bearing him her third baby she married him. Not long after this they parted, and she subsequently formed a series of irregular connexions, eventually meeting the Duke of York in the year 1803. He took her 'under his protection', as the current phrase was, and next year set her up in a house in Gloucester Place, and in addition granted her £1,000 per annum.

But Mary Anne had incurably expensive tastes, and she

---

[1] Even a historian of the calibre of Sir Charles Oman could write of 'the days when the Duke of York, with the occasional assistance of Mary Ann Clarke [*sic*], managed the British Army.'

rapidly piled up a formidable mass of debts. In order to meet this unsatisfactory state of affairs, she decided to make use of her wits – with which she was bountifully endowed. She reckoned that it should prove possible to influence the Commander-in-Chief in the course of his patronage, or if she failed in this, that she might at least be able to persuade applicants for patronage that she had the requisite influence for the purpose. She therefore set about acquiring military knowledge and plied the Duke with seemingly artless questions concerning persons and posts. Frederick was madly infatuated with the woman, and was the possessor of an incautious tongue, as we have already noted. The rest was easy. Mary Anne was able to wheedle out of the Commander-in-Chief sufficient information on military matters to enable her to approach various officers on the look-out for promotion, exchanges, etc., and to persuade them that she could obtain them their desires – at a price, adding carefully that this price must be paid in advance. By this means she became enriched to a considerable extent during the next two years. Whether the Duke shared in these pecuniary matters or was even aware of or suspected them we must leave an open question for the time being. Suffice it that rumours of these matters began to circulate in London during the next few years, and anonymous broadsheets, hinting at corrupt dealings, made their appearance. To all these York paid no attention.

Meanwhile in May 1806 the Duke parted company with Mrs Clarke, having discovered that she was pledging his credit with tradesmen, and was boasting of her influence in the distribution of patronage. He however agreed to pay her £400 per annum so long as she behaved herself. This she could hardly be expected to do, and early in 1808 he discontinued the allowance.

Mrs Clarke, in keeping with her character, then exhibited 'the fury of a woman scorned'. She threatened to publish his intimate letters to her unless he resumed the payments. This threat of blackmail the Duke coldly ignored.

Next, Mrs Clarke, aiming high, approached the Prime Minister, the Duke of Portland, for 'protection', if her own account is to be believed. But it is not easy to piece together the story, for there was a deal of hard swearing and false testimony in regard to the matter. A regular war of pamphleteers was waged, in which it is difficult to separate truth from falsehood. Meanwhile Mary Anne Clarke settled down in the arms of another lover, an official in the Commissariat named Dowler, and bided her time.

She had not long to wait. There were others besides the artful courtesan on the track of the Commander-in-Chief, but for very different purposes. A certain Pierre McCallum, who seems to have been a particularly odious creature,[1] had, whilst living in S Domingo, considered himself unjustly treated by General Picton. Failing to get satisfaction from the General, he applied to the Commander-in-Chief, with a like result. McCallum vowed vengeance on the Duke.

We pass on to the third person in the hunt. The Duke of Kent had not been very friendly disposed to his elder brother for some years. Kent had been recalled from his command at Gibraltar in 1803, owing to some mutinous proceedings that had taken place under his command. The recall emanated from the King, but the Duke suspected that it really originated with brother Frederick. There had been a further cause of estrangement between them, for much the same reason that had occasioned the trouble with the Prince of Wales; Kent was clamouring for another active appointment, but he found himself relegated to the shelf, and again Frederick got all the odium for it. Now, the Duke of Kent had a faithful and assiduous secretary, one Captain Dodd, who had been with him in Gibraltar. Dodd in due course obtained an inkling of the Clarke affair, and scented danger for the Commander-in-Chief. If he were driven from office the reversion to the Horse Guards might be expected to fall upon his (Dodd's) master, the Duke of Kent. If the Duke were exalted to this high office Captain Dodd would scarcely fail to rise in comparable degree. He had visions of the Secretaryship at War. His course of action was thus plain; he must encompass the fall of the elder brother.

The part played by the fourth party in the hunt is rather obscure. Captain Glennie had been dismissed from the Royal Artillery by the Master-General, the Duke of Richmond, many years before, and was embittered against the whole military hierarchy. He was the friend and confidant of Dodd.

[1] He was afterwards pleasantly described by an acquaintance as 'a convicted swindler'.

T

The fifth member of the pack was a retired Militia Colonel, one G. L. Wardle, who, possessed of a wealthy wife and a large family, had recently become a Member of Parliament. He had joined the extreme Opposition, led by Whitbread and Burdett, and he calculated that if the fall of the Commander-in-Chief could be brought about, that of the Government might be expected to follow. This would probably lead to preferment for himself, whilst his attack would in its nature be bound to bring him favour with the mob. He seems to have been inspired by McCallum, who assured him that he would become the most popular man in the Kingdom – an idea that was not unpleasing to the aspiring Militia Colonel. Lord Folkestone, a prominent member of the Opposition, was also induced by the Jacobin William Cobbett – ever ready for mischief – to take up the cudgels against His Royal Highness.

Thus for quite different reasons a small but keen-witted party was united in a conspiracy for the downfall of the Commander-in-Chief.

The male conspirators may be described as inspired either with a desire for revenge and self-advancement, or with a self-effacing zeal for purity in public life, according to one's point of view. Of the woman in the case it is easier to speak with certainty: she was out for revenge and for pecuniary gain, *pur et simple*.

But however diverse and obscure might be the motives of the various conspirators, there can be no question but that the coalition was a formidable one.

It required considerable time to get all the parties together and to spin the web. The following seems to have been the order of events. Mrs Clarke sent her blackmailing letter in June 1808. Glennie already knew Dodd and McCallum, whom he introduced one to the other. McCallum's next step was to get to know Mrs Clarke. After lengthy and assiduous efforts, he succeeded in this in the early autumn. Then he sought out a convenient M.P., and his choice fell upon the right man – Wardle. Glennie also got to know Wardle. Thus the four men were all now in touch with one another, and it only remained to introduce the lady in the case. This was duly effected by the persevering McCallum on 18 November, after a meeting of the four male conspirators on the previous evening.

It would probably be necessary to bribe Mary Anne to give evidence which was bound to disclose her own obliquity, but this Wardle, who had married a wealthy wife, seemed ready to do. He opened with a douceur of £100, and promised to furnish a new house for her if she would move to an empty one in Westbourne Place (near Eaton Square) which was handily near his own abode. To all of this the lady agreed. The next thing to be done was to compile a dossier of evidence. It so happened that Dodd and Glennie had arranged to visit the coast defences in Kent, with a view to exposing any weakness in their design (for which the responsibility could be placed upon the Commander-in-Chief), and the happy idea was conceived of taking Mary Anne with them. There, out of sight of prying eyes, they could 'pump' her at their leisure. Mrs Clarke was willing, and Wardle, having equipped himself with a large notebook, they all set out together early in December.

The trip lasted four days and was a vast success. They visited the Martello towers and the Royal Military Canal. Glennie jotted down their criticisms while Wardle questioned Mrs Clarke and plied his pencil as diligently as Boswell ever did. By this means a formidable dossier was compiled. The hunt was up!

The next two months were busy ones for the conspirators, who neglected no trail in order to amass a foolproof body of evidence. In the course of time they succeeded by means of questionable subterfuges in collecting upwards of fifty witnesses in the case.

It is hard to say which member of the party was most venomous towards the Duke. Mrs Clarke (who did quite frequently speak the truth) afterwards quoted Dodd as saying 'Nothing could be dirty enough or low enough to employ against the Duke.'[1]

'The Press was now set to work and with matchless cunning the conspirators, instead of making a direct attack on the Duke of York, began by setting forth in elaborate detail the hard case of the Duke of Kent. . . . Pamphlets and paragraphs appeared, pretending to be vindicatory of the Duke of York, whereas in fact they came from his confederated enemies, for

[1] *The Rival Princes*, I. p. 114.

the purpose of placing him in a light requiring an apology.'[1]

The stage was now set for proceedings in the House of Commons. On 20 January, 1809, Colonel Wardle gave notice from his seat in the House that he intended proposing a motion on the subject of the conduct of H.R.H. the Duke of York. True to his word, he did so on 27 January, calling for a Committee of Investigation of his charges. In the normal course a specially constituted committee would have been appointed for the purpose, but so confident were the Government in the integrity of the Commander-in-Chief that Spencer Perceval, Chancellor of the Exchequer and Leader of the House, insisted (with the concurrence of the Duke) on a public committee of the whole House. Sir Arthur Wellesley, who as Irish Secretary was a member of the Government, warmly supported the Chancellor, and testified to the thoroughness and fairness with which pro-motions, etc., were now conducted. It was accordingly agreed that an Investigation before a committee of the whole House should open on 1 February.

It should be observed from the outset that evidence was not taken on oath before this committee, nor were the normal rules of procedure and of evidence customary in a court of law observed; most strikingly of all, the accused was neither present nor officially represented. Confident in his complete innocence, the Government were indifferent to these anomalies.

The charges brought forward by Wardle were, in the first instance, five in number, though others were later added. They may be stated succinctly as follows:

(1) Captain Tonyn had paid Mrs Clarke to be promoted Major.

(2) Mrs Clarke was paid to hasten the exchange of Lieutenant-Colonels Brooke and Knight.

(3) Major Shaw paid Mrs Clarke to be appointed barrack-master at the Cape of Good Hope. Later, as he only paid up half the agreed fee, he was placed on half-pay.

(4) Mrs Clarke obtained for Colonel French the right to raise a levy of troops in Ireland, in return for a complicated scale of payments to Mrs Clarke.

[1] *Watkins*, p. 452.

(5) Captain Maling had obtained a commission and rapid promotion to Captain, whilst a clerk in the office of the army agent, Greenwood.

The chief additional case was that of Samuel Carter, Mrs Clarke's footman, who, by her influence was granted a commission.

Mrs Clarke, by exerting influence on the Commander-in-Chief, had all these requests granted, and the Duke was aware that she had been paid for her services, and must indirectly have benefited thereby: thus he was himself guilty of corruption. Such was the charge brought forward by Colonel Wardle.

It will be convenient to anticipate the unfolding of the story to the extent of recording the actual facts, as established at the time or accepted at the bar of history – for there was no specific 'finding' on any of the charges, such as would be the case in a court of law.

The essential facts concerning the six above-mentioned charges were found to be as follows. The case of Captain Tonyn was a simple one (apart from an incident arising out of it which will be mentioned presently). It was established ('proved' would be an inappropriate word to use where evidence was not taken on oath, nor legal procedure observed) that Tonyn had already been selected for promotion before the date on which Mrs Clarke alleged she interceded for him.

The exchange between Colonels Brooke and Knight had followed the normal procedure; it had been under consideration for some time, and was eventually promulgated on a Saturday, only forty-eight hours after Mrs Clarke asserted that she had applied for it.

Major Shaw was appointed barrack-master on the recommendation of General Sir Harry Burrard. He obtained the appointment on the express stipulation that he would be placed on half-pay, this being the normal procedure.

Colonel French had had a previous levy, and it was quite natural to employ him again. He was allowed to keep on with it, despite slow results, for some time, but when the Duke received a definitely adverse report on him he withdrew the letter of service within twenty-four hours.

Captain Maling was a right and proper person to receive a commission, and his rapid promotion was the result of a personal application by General Fraser, who selected him as his own A.D.C.

In none of these five cases was the promotion, exchange or appointment due to solicitation on the part of Mrs Clarke.

In the case of Samuel Carter, the original recommendation for him had been made three years before Mrs Clarke met the Duke. Carter was represented as being the son of an officer who had died on active service. For the time being no commission was awarded, because the army was in that year being reduced. But with the rapid expansion of 1804 Carter received his commission. In this case Mrs Clarke may have drawn the Duke's attention to the case; but whether or not, it was generally considered a deserving case for a commission; moreover, there was here no question of Mrs Clarke being paid for her recommendation. It is a curious fact that at the investigation this case caused more odium against the Duke than probably any of the others, the heinousness of the offence being that he should grant a commission to a mere footman!

Another case that aroused much odium, although it had nothing to do with the army, was that, at Mrs Clarke's request, the Duke forwarded to the King a petition from a divine of the name of Dr O'Meara to be allowed to preach before him. Here also no money passed, and it is difficult to understand the feeling aroused in the public mind by this recommendation, though it seems that the Doctor was a bit of an impostor.

This disposes of the charge of corruption against the Commander-in-Chief. There remains to consider whether he connived at, or suspected, these nefarious machinations of his mistress. A word must, however, first be said on the procedure of this curious Investigation, and the general course of events during the hearing of evidence.

We will first take a bird's-eye view of the proceedings, which, as has been said, lasted for seven weeks. During the whole of this time the interest and attention of the country was concentrated on the case to the exclusion of practically everything else. We were in the midst of a life and death struggle with France, our arms had recently met with something like disaster at

Corunna, where we had lost our best general. The transports carrying the survivors came limping back to home ports utterly ignored by the populace in general, who were all agog to learn the latest tale that fell from the lips of the mistress of the Commander-in-Chief. One would have to go back to the Parliamentary inquiry on the Duke of Marlborough to find anything approaching a parallel. But even that parallel was but a faint one: Marlborough was a commoner; York was the second subject in the Realm, the favourite son of a loved and revered Monarch, and a Commander-in-Chief who during the last fourteen years had, by general consent, reformed the army out of all knowledge. With a handsome income voted to him by Parliament he might be supposed to be above the pecuniary temptations of less fortunate mortals. Moreover, the Duke was accused of the very evils that he had been striving to root out of the army. Indeed, there could hardly be an individual in the country less amenable to the charges propounded by an obscure Member of Parliament than Frederick, Duke of York.

It certainly required nerve and courage on the part of Wardle to tilt at such a windmill of a man as the Duke. But the Colonel was playing for high stakes – nothing less than the post of Secretary at War when the Opposition should come into power.

Three weeks were consumed in taking evidence. These three weeks presented a spectacle never before witnessed in the House of Commons, or repeated since. The lobbies were thronged with some of the most shady and disreputable characters in the Metropolis, headed by a harlot. Each in turn appeared at the bar of the august chamber once or oftener. Mary Anne appeared twelve times. She was recalled on the smallest excuse: it would almost seem as if Honourable Members, so far from feeling their precincts desecrated by the presence of such an abandoned creature, actually revelled in it. 'The idlers at Whites, and the frequenters of the opera – whom at other times it had been found difficult to drag from the claret bottle or the ballet – were now unfailing in their Parliamentary attendance.'

The centre of attraction was the inimitable Mary Anne Clarke. Upon the whole she was undoubtedly one of the cleverest courtesans of her century and among the most remarkable women of her generation. In spite of her squalid early years she had acquired a marked gift of the pen; her handwriting was of an educated type, and her boast that she was interested and widely read (for a woman) in history was justified by her aptitude for historical allusions. It is easy to sneer at her literary effusions as does Mr Huddleston, who remarks of the famous *The Rival Princes*, that she might have had the help of the gentleman who later became editor of the *Eatonswill Gazette*,[1] but this book is a unique example of utterly fearless writing, libels abounding on every page, but uttered in such an adroit and pertinent fashion that she 'scored many a bull's eye' against anyone who chanced to cross her literary path – notably the hapless Wardle. But this is to anticipate.

It took no less than three weeks to get through the evidence. This was in part due to the fact that there were no recognized and agreed rules of procedure, and whenever a question was objected to the witness was ordered to withdraw while the House gravely debated whether the objection should be allowed or not. This was an egregious method of proceeding and it is particularly exasperating to modern readers because the subsequent debate on the point was seldom reported.

When the investigation opened sentiment was on the whole on the side of the Commander-in-Chief. Wardle had contrived to make himself look ridiculous by uttering vague accusations against others besides the Duke, including the Prime Minister and the Lord Chancellor. But little by little, as the evidence was unfolded, opinion began to veer. So much mud was thrown that some of it stuck. Nor was it by any means all mud. Wardle and Mary Anne became the heroes of the mob; men ran behind the carriage of Mrs Clarke, and collected in the portals of the House in order to gape at her going in to give evidence. Mary Anne had gained an astonishing hold on members by her air of assurance, her flashing wit, her ready retort, and her pert and saucy manner. Her conduct lends credibility to the assertion of her friend, Miss Taylor, that she once played the part of Portia at the Haymarket with great *éclat*. She openly revelled in the proceedings and was usually the first to see and laugh at a joke. Even the stern moralist Wilberforce found himself attracted to her. The *Annual Register* for 1809 gravely records that 'she carried her ease, gaiety and pleasantry to a degree of pertness which was very reprehensible.'[2]

[1] *Warriors in Undress*, p. 47.   [2] Op. cit., p. 144.

As an example of her artfulness and guile, when she was unexpectedly called upon to give evidence in a matter where she had not been 'briefed', she pleaded 'extreme fatigue', and got away with it. On another occasion, on instructions from Wardle, she pleaded illness and took to her bed.

As for Colonel Wardle, even before the proceedings were ended the city of Glasgow presented him with an address in which the M.P. is described as 'one of the most Magnanimous, Patriotic, Firm, and Candid men of His Majesty's Dominions'.

The course of the proceedings from day to day can most clearly and accurately be followed in the daily reports from Spencer Perceval, Leader of the House of Commons, to the King, which are now happily preserved in the Royal Archives at Windsor. Perceval was a man of the highest principles and of unblemished integrity, and his reports can be unreservedly relied upon. They open in a quietly confident vein, but gradually a note of anxiety can be detected in them, till eventually we find expressions such as 'Mr Perceval feels that he cannot disguise it from Your Majesty that the situation has become serious'. On the completion of the evidence he even hinted to the King that it might involve the Duke being put on his trial. He despaired of his obtaining a fair hearing in the existing excited state of the House.

The cause of this change of tone is mainly due to an unexpected development in the case, one which surprised both sides equally. Early in the proceedings a certain Captain Huxley Sandon, of the Royal Waggoners Corps, landed from abroad, and learnt that his name had been mentioned in the case. He had, as a matter of fact, been one of Mrs Clarke's chief go-betweens or 'contact men'. Worried about this, he consulted his commanding officer, Colonel Hamilton, who enjoined him (Sandon) to tell him the whole story. Sandon accordingly related how Captain Tonyn had become impatient and suspicious of Mrs Clarke as his promotion was so slow, and how Mrs Clarke had given him (Sandon) a letter from the Duke to show Tonyn, as his name was mentioned in it, and it indicated that the Duke was concerned in his case. This Sandon had done, but instead of handing back the letter to Mrs Clarke, he had kept it and still had it in his possession. Colonel Hamilton informed the Government of this, and Perceval at once decided that whether the letter were a forgery or not, it must be produced before the Committee. Sandon, for some reason becoming alarmed, prevaricated, first stating at the bar of the House that he had destroyed it, then that he had mislaid it, and finally, after being placed under arrest for prevarication, admitting that he still possessed the letter. It was produced before the Committee. More than this; with it were found a regular 'cache' of letters – forty-one in all – written by Mrs Clarke to Sandon, which that foolish officer had kept. These letters were read at the bar of the House and produced a profound impression opon both sides, for they disclosed the ramifications of Mrs Clarke's machinations, and seemed to show that the Duke was privy to them.

It was this double discovery that caused the sudden turn in opinion in the House and in the populace in the street. In point of law, these letters were not evidence that the Duke was privy to what was going on, but merely that Mrs Clarke wished Sandon to believe that he was. They need not therefore be referred to again.

The case of the single note, however, is different, for it purported to emanate from the Duke himself. It was described at the time as a 'mysterious letter' and it still remains mysterious. Was it a forgery? I confess that in the course of prolonged ruminations on the question I have veered to and fro in my opinions. Let the reader therefore judge for himself!

The letter or note was addressed on the outside to George Farquhar Esq. (an address used by the Duke in his correspondence with his mistress) and it bore his own seal. The terms of the letter were as follows:

'I have just received your note, and Tonyn's business shall remain as it is – God bless you.'

First, as regards the handwriting. Many witnesses examined it and two other letters that were admittedly in the hand of the Duke. They were asked to say if the handwriting of all three was the same. Their opinions differed. One stated positively that the handwriting was different. The remainder, though agreeing that it was very similar, were not prepared to state positively that it was the same, though in varying degree they showed that they all believed that it was at least possible that it was the same. On the other hand, most of them detected a slight difference between the note and the two letters – the note being in smaller characters. Thus the matter was left in doubt, though it should be recorded that the one witness who was positive that they were different made a poor showing in cross-examination. It transpired that he had not noticed that in all three the letter 'i' was usually undotted. This was characteristic of the Duke's writing at the time, and if the letter was forged the forger had evidently made a very close study of his hand.

As for the difference in size of the writing, 'the prosecution' pointed out that a normal man's writing does often vary in size, and even in style. This, of course, is true, but here I would interpose the remark, as one who has perused well over one hundred of the Duke's letters, that I can testify that his writing was unusually consistent both as to size and style. Unlike that of his brother, it was not the 'sprawl' that it has been described by a modern writer. Even when writing in an uncomfortable billet in Flanders in the evening after an action this consistency is in evidence. Thus the argument as to difference in size and style must carry some weight.

When the Duke and Mrs Clarke were informed of the letter both outwardly reacted to it in the same way – each was emphatic that they could not remember the letter. This is one of the baffling aspects of the case. Of course, if it was a forgery the Duke would not remember writing something that he had not written, but Mrs Clarke would remember such a proceeding vividly, and it would be part of her case to declare that she remembered the letter, whether true or not. Mary Ann Clarke was a confirmed and unshamable liar, but even liars sometimes speak the truth, and she may well have blurted out the truth when first unexpectedly confronted with the letter in the witness-box, not realizing at the moment its bearing on the case.

The case of the Duke's denial is different. Frederick, Duke of York, was the soul of honour and I cannot find that at any time in his public life he ever affirmed anything that he did not believe to be the truth. On this occasion he behaved exactly as an innocent man would. Directly he heard of the proceedings in the House he went in a state of great indignation straight to the house of his military secretary, Colonel Gordon (whom he found getting into bed), and he burst out at once 'This is most extraordinary: it must be a forgery.' At the time and afterwards he affirmed and repeated unwaveringly: 'I have no recollection of it; it must be a forgery.' So convinced was he that he requested Perceval to have the letter brought before the committee and examined.

On the other hand, it should be recorded that he was never confronted with the actual note; it is possible to forget that one has written something till one comes across the actual document. It is therefore conceivable that the Duke's memory failed him here. If the letter had an innocent import he would be all the more likely to forget it.

The next difficulty concerns the terms of the note. Its meaning is not clear, and it is not such as one would expect a forger to concoct if his sole object was to convince Tonyn of the Duke's intention to promote him. It might indeed be taken in an opposite sense – that he was leaving the matter alone. On the other hand, forging handwriting is a slow and difficult operation, and the forger would keep the letter as short as possible; the shorter the safer.

The next question to consider is, if forged, who was the forger? Now, Mrs Clarke herself confessed that she had at times imitated the signature of the Duke, and there was an independent witness to this fact. From what we know of the character of the woman she was utterly unscrupulous and would not hesitate to forge anything if she was capable of so doing and if it was calculated to benefit herself. In this case it did benefit her: Tonyn was reassured. It is also a fact that her bosom friend, Miss Taylor, was also addicted to this curious pastime of imitating other people's writing. According to McCallum, she forged a letter in order to extract £10 from the Duke of Kent.[1] One cannot help regretting that the letter was never produced for the Duke's scrutiny, and that it has not been preserved for future generations and experts to give an opinion on.

Assuming for the sake of argument that the note was a genuine one, what deductions can we make from it? It is difficult to say. Even Whitbread, Leader of the Opposition, confessed in the House that it did not connect up with other events in the case. All that it seems safe to deduce from it is that Mrs Clarke had mentioned Tonyn's affairs to the Commander-in-Chief. She may have pointed out to him that Tonyn's promo-

[1] *The Rival Queens*, p. 130.

tion was very slow, and the Duke may have told her that he would look into it. But this is mere conjecture. What is certain is that Tonyn was in fact promoted in the normal course; he was one of a huge batch of fifty-two, thirteen of whom were his juniors.

There we could leave the matter were it not that the rabble quickly decided that the letter was genuine and that the Duke was as good as convicted of the charges. The Government became gravely concerned, and the Lord Chancellor, Lord Eldon, was deputed to write to the King, breaking the seriousness of the state of affairs to him as gently as possible. His letter (still preserved at Windsor) is a model of what such a letter should be, though he wrote rather helplessly that it was difficult to see what could be done about it.

There were two other causes for this revulsion of feeling against the Commander-in-Chief. One was the evidence of Miss Taylor in conjunction with the French case. According to her, she had been present at dinner with the Duke and Mrs Clarke when the following conversation had taken place:

The Duke: I am continually worried by Colonel French. He worries me continually about the levy business, and is always wanting something more in his own favour. How does he behave to you, darling?

Mrs Clarke: Middling; not very well.

The Duke: Master French must mind what he is about or I shall cut up him and his levy, too.

The second item is a passage in a letter from the Duke to Mrs Clarke, dated 24 August, 1804, which runs as follows:

'Clavering is mistaken in thinking that any new regiments are to be raised; it is not intended; only second battalions to the existing corps; you had better therefore tell him so and that you were sure there would be no use in applying for him.'

Both these items made a deep impression against the Duke as proof that Mrs Clarke did interfere in military matters. Since the only other evidence (other than her own) was contained in the 'mysterious letter' which we have already dealt with, these two items deserve close examination.

As regards the conversation about Colonel French, the first thing is to examine the credibility of the witness. Miss Taylor, the illegitimate daughter of a man named Chance, was the bosom friend of Mrs Clarke. In her cross-examination she showed herself an unsatisfactory witness. For the most part she put up a stonewall defence of invincible ignorance. Here are some typical passages:

Q. Where was your boarding-house?
A. At Kentish Town.
Q. What part of Kentish Town? What street?
A. It had no name.
Q. Can you tell us what number?
A. No, it was neither a number nor had the place a name.
   A little later:
Q. Where did your father live?
A. I must appeal to the indulgence of the Chairman.
   (She was told she must answer.)
A. I cannot recollect just now.
Q. Why did you wish to be excused answering that question, when you only did not recollect where your father lived?
   A. For that reason.

There was also grave suspicion that she had been 'trained for the part'. It was stated by a contemporary, and possibly an eye-witness, that 'her evidence was manifestly the effect of tuition'.[1] Though she could give a precise report of a conversation that took place five years before, she expressed forgetfulness of any conversation only five weeks old. Her studied profession of ignorance or of forgetfulness aroused the natural suspicion that she feared to tell a story that might not tally with Mrs Clarke's evidence.

Moreover, she admitted that Mary Anne had reminded her of the conversation about Colonel French and induced her to come forward with it. But perhaps the most suspicious point of all was that Mrs Clarke's butler stated that Miss Taylor never dined with Mrs Clarke when the Duke was present. The butler was cited as a hostile witness to the Duke, so this statement was very upsetting to Wardle. He accordingly visited him outside the court, with the result that the butler recanted next day, explaining that he had had a headache that had caused him to be forgetful.

Apart from the credibility of the witness, the very terms of the

[1] *Memoir of Mrs Mary Ann Clarke*, p. 51.

conversation are incredible if the Duke was 'in the know', for it would obviously be to his advantage to keep on good terms with French, and not to take the line he took in the alleged conversation. Nor would Mrs Clarke be likely to reply that French treated her 'middling'. He had already paid her £1,300, and she was hoping for the balance of £700. She would therefore stand up for him with the Duke. Under the circumstances no law court would have credited Miss Taylor's testimony. I am disposed to credit the allegation that Wardle paid her £10 for her evidence.

There remains the case of General Clavering. This case, unlike most of the proceedings, is crystal clear. It proves that in one case at least Mrs Clarke did discuss the interests of military persons with the Commander-in-Chief, though it is, of course, not evidence that he was aware that the General had paid Mrs Clarke £1,000 for 'favours to come' – favours which incidentally never did come.

'One swallow does not make a summer'; the fact that the Commander-in-Chief did once discuss or disclose military matters to his mistress is not evidence that he made a practice of it, but it does render it more conceivable that in the cases of Tonyn and French he may have referred to their affairs or military prospects with his mistress. There for the moment we will leave it.

What of 'the prisoner at the bar'? That was the trouble: the 'prisoner' was *not* at the bar. While accusations were mounting up against him, while insinuations, rumours, gossip – both inside and outside the House – were besmirching his name, the Commander-in-Chief was sitting at work in his office at the Horse Guards, picking up what he could about the proceedings, and discussing the case with his friends – but out of all official contact with proceedings that so vitally affected himself. The first account he received of the opening day's proceedings came in this letter from the Prince of Wales:

'27 January 1809. I congratulate you most truly on the turn that the whole of this infamous business has taken in the House of Commons this day. Tyrwhitt is this moment come in and gives me the whole detail. The indignation general in the whole House against Mr Wardle. . . . None found to defend that villain but Sir Francis Burdett.' To this the Duke replies that this is the first intelligence he has had of the matter, and goes on: 'I am not at all surprised at the Trio that stand forward upon this occasion. On the contrary I rather glory in it, as I think every honest man ought to be ashamed of their praise.'[1]

Presumably the Trio were Wardle, Burdett, and Mrs Clarke; the machinations of Dodd and Glennie and McCallum were not known to the Duke at this time. The situation was an extraordinary one – blatantly unfair to the Duke.

The hearing of the evidence was not completed till 22 February. There was then a lull of a fortnight while the evidence was being printed. A lull in the House, but not in the country. Excitement was rapidly rising; it seemed to be forgotten that the accused had not been present at his 'trial' and had had no chance to confront and refute his accusers face to face. He had, of set purpose, maintained a dignified silence whilst the evidence was being taken, but the moment it was completed he wrote the following letter to the Speaker:

'Horse Guards, Feb 23rd, 1809.

'Sir,

'I have waited with the greatest anxiety until the committee appointed by the House of Commons to inquire into my conduct as commander-in-chief of his Majesty's army, had closed its examinations, and I now hope that it will not be deemed improper to address this letter through you to the House of Commons.

'I observed, with the deepest concern, that, in the course of this inquiry, my name has been coupled with transactions the most criminal and disgraceful; and I must ever regret and lament, that a connexion should have existed which has thus exposed my character to animadversion.

'With respect to any alleged offences connected with the discharge of my official duties, I do, in the most solemn manner, on my honour as a prince, distinctly assert my innocence, not only by denying all corrupt participation in any of the infamous transactions which have appeared in evidence at the bar of the

[1] *Windsor*, 27.2.09.

House of Commons, or any connivance at their existence, but also the slightest knowledge or suspicion that they existed at all.

'My consciousness of innocence leads me confidently to hope, that the House of Commons will not, upon such evidence as they have heard, adopt any proceedings prejudicial to my honour and character; but if, upon such testimony as has been adduced against me, the House of Commons can think my innocence questionable, I claim of their justice, that I shall be not condemned without trial, nor be deprived of the benefit and protection which is afforded to every British subject, by those sanctions, under which alone evidence is received in the ordinary administration of the law.

'I am, Sir, yours,
'Frederick.'

There are conflicting accounts of how this famous letter came to be written. The *Morning Chronicle* of 24 February wrote: 'A consultation was held at the Queen's House[1] in the Park, on Wednesday morning (Feb. 22nd), at which His Majesty, the Prince of Wales and several of the Royal Dukes were present, where it was resolved that H.R.H. the Duke of York should address to the Speaker of the House of Commons a letter. . . .' On the other hand, Walpole avers that it was drawn up as a draft by Perceval and that the Duke made certain alterations before consenting to sign it.[2] This account is supported by the statement of Temple to the Duke of Buckingham that the Cabinet had written a letter for the Duke of York to sign, notifying the House of his resignation, 'which the Duke had positively refused to sign'.[3]

Neither of these accounts is quite correct. It is clear from Perceval's correspondence with the King that the Duke of York wrote the first draft himself and submitted it to Perceval for his comments. Perceval wrote to the King: 'It was not till after a very full and deliberate examination for some hours in the Cabinet this morning, of every sentence in the letter, and approbation of its contents, that Mr Perceval submitted to H.R.H. the few alterations which appeared in it from the draft as first proposed by H.R.H.'[4]

[1] Now Buckingham Palace. [2] *Life of Spencer W. Perceval*, I, p. 319.
[3] *Courts and Cabinets of George III*, IV, p. 326. [4] *Windsor*, 23.2.09.

U

The letter was duly read out to the House by the Speaker. It met with a curious reception on the part of the Opposition, who tried to maintain that it infringed the privileges of the House. It seems, however, to be the simple and obvious act of an innocent man to demand a trial. However that may be, the matter ended in smoke, and the House for a few days turned its attention to the matter of the Corunna campaign.

The debate on the evidence commenced on 8 March. It was carried on day after day, or rather night after night, with un-flagging intensity, the House seldom rising before 4 a.m., and on one occasion not till 6.30 a.m. Spencer Perceval bore the brunt of the defence, and it is impossible not to feel amazed at the strain he must have been put to during those anxious days and nights, constantly in his place throughout the sittings, frequently intervening in the debates, and, when everyone else had trooped off to bed, repairing to his writing-room and inditing a long, clear, and fair report of the proceedings to the King. Next morning he might have a Cabinet meeting or consultation on the case; then he would attend to his duties as Chancellor of the Exchequer, and perhaps prepare a speech for the ensuing sitting, and be in his place when the House sat. In all this he seems to have received no help from the nominal Prime Minister, the aged Duke of Portland, whose correspondence with the King during those critical weeks for the Government was confined to forwarding two notes that he had received from a member of the Commons – without comment!

The debate on the evidence, one of the longest that the Commons had ever known, was discursive, and much of it took the form of a discussion on the form of procedure, whether by reso-lution, or by an address to the King, or both. Perceval drew up a form of address, and obtained the King's approbation of it before proposing it to the House, which seems a curious pro-ceeding. It is not, however, necessary to examine the arguments on this head. As regards the main point at issue – whether, and if so to what extent, the Commander-in-Chief was guilty, three outstanding speeches were delivered, all from the Government side of the House. The first was that of Perceval himself. Rising late at night on the opening day, he gave a masterly exposition of the case, pleading powerfully for the Duke of York. At 3.30

a.m. he confessed to the House that 'he felt rather exhausted but had not nearly finished', and shortly afterwards the House agreed to adjourn. The speech was therefore finished on the following day, and it earned the congratulations of Whitbread, Leader of the Opposition.

But the speech which most affected the House was that of Francis Burton, the blind judge. This truly remarkable man (who died at the age of 87 in 1832) had been blind for ten years. Yet such was the acuteness of his memory that he was able to follow the detailed and lengthy proceedings, and after having them all read over to him twice, and part of them a third time, he was able to rise and hold the House in a long and brilliant exposition of the case which made a profound impression on those who heard it.[1]

Judge Burton began by admitting that he had started with a prejudice against the Duke (the judge was a stern moralist); but after a careful scrutiny of the evidence he had come to the conclusion that there was no ground for any of the charges, and that the testimony of Mrs Clarke was 'a tissue of falsehoods'. He computed that she was guilty of at least twenty-eight falsehoods. He also made the point that if the Duke were a corrupt man he would have surrounded himself with corrupt subordinates, not the officers of unblemished integrity who in fact composed his staff; to disguise his nefarious dealings from them would have been difficult, if not impossible.

But easily the most outstanding speech was made by John Wilson Croker. After analysing the relevant times and dates, thereby demolishing most of the evidence of Mrs Clarke, Croker explained her method of procedure by an ingenious analogy.[2] 'She tells you she had hundreds and hundreds of applications, and her instances of alleged successes are four or five. Like insurers in the lottery, she took her chance of what might turn up; in the thousands of names that are annually gazetted some

[1] A full report, nineteen pages in length, appears in a *Biographical Sketch of Francis Burton*, by O. B. Cole. The Albion Press report of the proceedings compresses it into five and a half pages. The rather odious Cobbett, in his *Political Register*, which had great influence on public opinion, omits it altogether.
[2] This passage appears only in the full report of Croker's speech which was printed separately, over ninety pages in length. The Albion Press report accords it only one page, while Cobbett, of course, omits it altogether.

tickets might be drawn. The shortest time that anyone appears to have been on her books . . . is six months, and with all this delay and all these chances, what success had she to show? In August 1804 at the height of her favour and traffic a *Gazette* came out containing upwards of 200 promotions; and fortunately for her Tonyn's name was in it. That, to be sure, was a prize of £500, but unfortunately for her purse then, and her credit now, a greater prize – viz. Spedding – lay undrawn at the bottom of the wheel.'[1]

The chief speeches from the Opposition side of the House came from Whitbread (its Leader), Wilberforce, Lord Folkestone (who had actively espoused Wardle's cause), with a violent outburst from Sir Francis Burdett, the Jacobin. But it is significant that no one attempted to answer the arguments put forward by Croker; they all fell back on sweeping assertions and general abuse.

As the long debate dragged on Perceval became more cheerful as to the issue, but he still was doubtful whether it would be possible to avoid an address to the King for the removal of the Commander-in-Chief. On 5 March he screwed up his courage to hint fairly plainly to the King that the Duke should voluntarily resign his office in order to avoid the embarrassment of an Address for removal. The King, who had hitherto agreed with the views and the steps of the Leader of the House, now asserted himself. In a letter full of dignity and power he declined absolutely to countenance any action which might have the appearance of 'compromise'. An absolute and unconditional acquittal was his demand. He did, however, towards the end of his letter seem to drop a hint that after obtaining acquittal the Duke might on his own initiative resign his office, and it is more than likely that he quietly suggested this move to his son. Unfortunately, the Duke's letters at this epoch do not seem to be extant.[2] In any case, anything that may have passed between the Sovereign and the Duke was probably verbal only. The King, who was now completely blind, and employed Sir Henry Taylor to write his letters in the cheapest possible ink, did not stir from Windsor during the crisis. Once at least during this

[1] *Speech of John Wilson Croker, Esq.*, by an eminent Reporter (1809), p. 52.
[2] They were almost certainly destroyed by his executor, Sir Henry Taylor.

painful period Perceval went to Windsor for an interview.

The further the debate proceeded the more frequent became the allusions to opinion outside the House. Members of the Government deprecated this attention to uninstructed outside opinion on what was essentially a legal matter to be decided on the evidence. The Opposition conceded that outside 'clamour' should not be heeded, but contended somewhat flabbily that 'feeling' as opposed to 'clamour' was deserving of attention. One Member even went so far as to suggest that the Duke should be removed else the public would make his life a burden to him.

On 16 March the House at length divided on Wardle's cele-brated motion. This took the form of a long-winded address, the governing sentence of which affirmed that various specified abuses could not have existed 'without the knowledge of the Commander-in-Chief' and that the House was of the opinion that 'the Duke of York ought to be deprived of the command of the army'.

At this point, while Honourable Members are trooping through the division lobbies, it will be as well to form our own opinion on the points at issue. It will have been observed that Wardle's motion, whilst not ruling out corruption on the part of the Duke, does not explicitly charge him with it. This was prob-ably an artful attempt to attract the greatest possible number into the Aye lobby. As a matter of fact, no evidence leading to the Duke's participation in the financial transactions of Mrs Clarke had been produced, and it is doubtful if even a handful of Members really believed that charge. History has pronounced him innocent of it and there is no need to go over the evidence again. But the question of connivance or knowledge, still more of suspicion, is not so susceptible of disproof. Documentary evidence would be unlikely to exist, so that it becomes a ques-tion of pitting against one another the word of the Duke and of his mistress, and of assessing the probabilities of the case.

As regards trusting the word of a Duke, the testimony of his contemporaries is emphatic: he never broke his word, he never promised what he did not try to his utmost to perform, when he made a statement 'on the word of a prince'[1] this was

---

[1] Cobbett, of course, jeered at this, declaring truculently that *he* would not trust the word of a prince. But Cobbett was a Republican.

for him as solemn an oath as the famous oath of the Black
Prince: 'By the soul of my Father.'

Next, let us examine the Duke's general attitude throughout
the business. It was that of an innocent man; of a man who had
a clear conscience. In the first place a man who had something
to hide would scarcely ignore the threats of blackmail on the
part of a discarded mistress. When he heard of the charges that
were being preferred against him he asked Perceval to accord
them an open hearing in the House in order that his name
might be cleared of all slander; so serenely confident was he,
that he infected all those in touch with him, officers and politicians alike, with complete faith in his integrity and innocence.
The officers on his staff were gentlemen of the highest honour
and probity; he could scarcely – as Burton had pointed out –
have been guilty of the charges levelled against him without
some knowledge or suspicion on the part of his subordinates. A
shady individual would have collected shady individuals around
him, in order to shield himself and make easier his crook-deal-
ings. The uncompromising manner in which he dismissed his
mistress was not that of a man who conceives the merest possibility of being blackmailed; and when two years later she
threatened, he defied her.

As for conniving at abuses of the promotion system: if guilty
of the very offences which he had fought against so hard in
others, he must have been the most double-faced of men and
contemptible of hypocrites. But nowhere else in the whole
course of over forty years' service in the army did he show the
least sign of this failing. It is an ironical fact that only forty-eight
hours before Wardle was charging him in Parliament of bending
to improper pressure regarding the requests of officers, he
should be writing a letter (unbeknown to Parliament and to
posterity) to his brother, the Prince of Wales, refusing a request
made by him on behalf of an officer in his own regiment. In the
course of his reply the Duke writes: 'I am under the painful
necessity of expressing my regret that it is not in my power
consistently with my duty to the interests and welfare of the
army to consent to a proposal that is contrary to all regulations,
and that, I am sure you will concur with me, if granted in any
instance would be exceedingly injurious to the service.'[1] Con-

---

[1] *Windsor*, 25.1.09.

sider the pressure thus resisted – that of his own brother, Prince of Wales, and later to be his sovereign! Incidentally the Prince, rather surprisingly, complimented the Duke on his firmness, and admitted he was right. There is also convincing evidence that if his mistress did intercede with the Commander-in-Chief for her friends he was inflexible, for one of the first persons she would try to obtain rapid promotion for was her own brother, Captain Thompson. But Thompson remained a Captain.

Taking all the above considerations into account, it is difficult to believe that the Duke of York, who, in the words of Sir John Fortescue, 'fought manfully against all traffic in commissions', should have connived at these very abuses on the part of anyone. Perhaps the best possible evidence that he was unaware of what was going on behind his back is the extreme anxiety Mrs Clarke evinced to keep this knowledge from him. Why was she so anxious? Obviously because he had expressed himself strongly to her in the matter. How then, it may be asked, are we to account for the fact that he had, at least on one occasion, and probably on more, referred to military matters, especially as he had denied disclosing military matters to her? The simple answer is that the passage relating to General Clavering was not a 'disclosure of secret information' by which he might perhaps benefit, but a purely negative statement to remove a misconception under which Clavering was labouring, and which it would be only kindness to clear away. It is unlikely that the Duke gave the matter a moment's further thought, and that if taxed five years later with writing that letter he would have denied all recollection of it – as he did in the case of the Tonyn letter. This brings us back to this 'mysterious letter'. Judge Burton showed conclusively by a study of dates that whatever it did refer to (assuming that it was genuine) it did not refer to Tonyn's promotion, for he had been promoted five days previous to the date on which it must have been written. It must have been on some insignificant matter, such as might well cause the Duke five years later to exclaim that he 'had no recollection of it'.

The degrees of guilt can be stated in this order: Corruption, connivance at corruption, knowledge of it, suspicion of it. Having shown that there is no evidence for the first three, we come to the last and most difficult of these – suspicion or doubt in the mind. Most difficult, because if a man searches his own mind in some matter where he has eventually come to suspect a person of something, he will generally find that doubt arose gradually, like a 'tiny little seed' in his heart, with intermittent growth. It is thus possible that some questions put by Mrs Clarke dealing with officers might at first appear to have sinister implications, only to be dismissed from his mind. For when a man is blinded by infatuation, as the Duke undoubtedly was, reason and clear perception go by the board. So far from being the artless plaything that the Duke fondly imagined, Mary Anne Clarke was about the most artful female of her generation. Instead of flinching from the fearsome prospect of facing the House of Commons and having her nefarious actions brought into the fullest publicity, she remarked gaily on the Sunday before the Inquiry began that she would make half the members of the House fall in love with her. And it appeared that she did – up to and not excluding the austere Wilberforce. It was reminiscent of the story of Samson and Delilah, or of Lohengrin and Elsa.

But there might be other grounds for suspicion. An argument employed to the full by the prosecution was that the lavish extravagance of Mrs Clarke must have caused the Duke to wonder where she obtained the necessary money. This argument sounds impressive and must be examined carefully. We do not know how much money Mary Anne extracted from her dupes, but it may have been as much as £5,000. This seems a large sum till we consider how much she received from the Duke. She alleged that he paid her £1,000 per annum to start with, but that it fell into arrears. On the other hand, Perceval established that York paid her at least £5,570 in cash and £16,751 in settling her tradesmen's bills, making a total of over £21,000. The addition to this figure of a few thousands from other sources might escape the notice of anybody, unless they made a careful check of her expenses. This the Duke was hardly likely to do. He was much too engrossed during that hectic two years in preparing to meet the invasion of the country by Napoleon. Moreover, he had given her the house, furniture, and a good deal of wine. Finally, why should he assume that all the extravagance he witnessed had been paid for? He might argue rather the contrary, considering how he had paid a succession of bills for her. How could he be sure that all the others were paid? Bills have an awkward way of being presented after we have forgotten about them and have balanced our accounts. Taking everything into consideration there is no ground for supposing that the Duke suspected that his mistress's lavish display was paid for in part from improper sources.

The Duke of York from his early days exhibited an absence of comprehension in money matters. His tutor complained of this weakness to Judge Burton at the time. It clung to him all his life. Hopelessly and mercifully unconscious of his financial position, he bequeathed in his will the residue of his property to his favourite sister Sophia, but when his assets were realized and his estate came to be proved, he was found to be heavily in debt. It is quite a common though curious failing for people who are normally intelligent in other matters to lack this sense of values and balance where money is concerned. When a lightning conductor was placed at the summit of his Column in London unkind persons suggested that it was to take his unpaid bills. We have also seen how his tutor complained that the young Duke would leave his personal letters and papers lying about open, in an utterly careless and irresponsible way. He undoubtedly was careless and happy-go-lucky throughout his life, incapable of harbouring suspicion against anyone. Indeed, Mary Anne Clarke herself probably gave the clue to his confiding, imprudent conduct when she declared, one third contemptuously, one third pityingly, and one third lovingly that the Duke was a 'great big baby'. This is probably the clue to his conduct throughout the affair: he acted towards his mistress like a great big baby.

Our finding must, then, be that Frederick, Duke of York, was innocent of all the charges.

To resume the narrative. All through the night of 16 March, 1809, the debate had dragged on, and it was not until 6.30 a.m. on the morning of the 17th that, amid tense excitement, the division on Wardle's motion was taken: The figures were announced as: For the motion, 123; Against, 364. The motion was therefore lost by 241 votes.

In the days that followed 'the 125' (including the tellers)

were toasted up and down the country. But Perceval, writing to the King that morning, confessed that no clear conclusion could be drawn from the figures, presumably because in drafting the motion Wardle had deliberately excluded all direct reference to corruption or connivance.

So the debate was resumed the same afternoon, on the direct issue. Eventually a motion (technically an amendment to Perceval's motion) was proposed by Sir Thomas Turton, declaring that 'there were grounds from the evidence at the bar to charge H.R.H. with a knowledge of these practices, with connivance at them, and consequently with corruption'. The curious phrasing of this motion betokens another ingenious attempt to induce members who only believed the Duke guilty of knowledge to vote for corruption. The amendment was defeated by 334 votes to 135. This was the large majority that Perceval had hoped for and expected.

The House then voted on Perceval's original motion which reversed the sense of Turton's, stating that there was no ground to charge H.R.H. with personal corruption or connivance. The voting was as follows: For Perceval's motion, 278; Against, 196; Majority for, 82. The Duke was cleared, but by a smaller majority than Perceval had calculated on. History, curiously enough, does not relate how the result of the division was received by the different parties in the House, but we know its effect on Perceval, for he went away and wrote his report on it to the King. But before the House adjourned the Opposition wished to proceed with a motion calling for the resignation of the Commander-in-Chief. This was just what Perceval did not want. He feared that the temper of the House was such that the motion would be carried. It was a Friday; the House would not be sitting again till Monday. Perceval had planned to hold a Cabinet meeting on the Saturday, and, as he confessed to the King in a very candid letter, 'to submit to Your Majesty their humble opinion upon the subject of the continuance of the Duke of York in his present position'.[1]

Fortunately for the Duke and for everyone, Perceval was able to prevail upon the House to adjourn till Monday.

The Cabinet meeting never took place. On Saturday morning the Duke of York, 'of his own immediate and spontaneous

[1] *Windsor*, 18.3.09.

motion, waited upon his Majesty and tendered to him the chief command of his Majesty's army'. Thus apparently ended in gloom, disaster, and disgrace the military career of Frederick, Duke of York and Albany.

THE AFTERMATH

12

The Duke had bent to the storm that was sweeping the country – even more than it was the House of Commons. Indeed, the voting of the Commons, strictly speaking, exonerated him.

Historians are, however, in general agreement that the size of the adverse vote was almost equivalent to a condemnation. We must therefore analyse this vote. Perceval, writing to the King before repairing to bed the same morning, declared that he could not understand why the majority in the case of his motion was smaller than in the case of Turton's. This failure to comprehend the difference is clear indication of the extreme state of mental and physical exhaustion poor Perceval had been reduced to by the end of the debate. For Turton's motion was not a mere reversal of the Chancellor's. Strictly speaking, only those who believed in corruption could vote for it. But those who voted against Perceval's motion might (and probably did) believe only in connivance, not corruption; yet it is generally represented that no less than 196 voted for corruption. Nor does it follow that they necessarily believed even in connivance: some of them may have been influenced by the final passage in the motion – the demand for the Duke's removal.

'The 125' were probably influenced by widely differing considerations. United in the same lobby were members of many different factions. There were Jacobins and Republicans, who saw in this case a grand opportunity to aim a blow at the throne. There were the less extreme partisans of the Opposition, who, when they saw the Government ranged on one side, instinctively favoured the other. There were persons of the strong Puritan strain who felt that they were striking a blow for morality. There were those whose legal faculties were not strongly developed and who were swayed by sentiment and the strong effect of a mass of apparently incriminating evidence, in the absence of the Duke's own testimony. Finally, there were those

316

who were frankly swayed by the popular clamour outside, and either by fear or by favour of the mob voted in the way that they hoped would render them popular with that mob – as it did.

When we have taken all the above into account the residuum who conscientiously believed that the Duke of York was guilty of corruption was probably exceedingly small – a mere handful of misguided men.

But the damage was done. The Duke was 'finished', and the man who had done more than anyone living for the army he loved retired to ruminate over the 'slings and arrows of out- rageous fortune' and to gain such solace as he could in the beautiful gardens and grotto of Oatlands. There for the moment we will leave him, while we attempt a final appraisal of the affair.

When all is said and done and assuming the Duke innocent of corruption, connivance, knowledge, and even suspicion, is there any other impropriety with which he can be charged? There is. The question of the morality of keeping a mistress was not relevant to the case. Among his defenders were men of the strictest morality, such as Judge Burton, and Spencer Perceval – a good family man with thirteen children, who had even attempted to introduce a Bill making divorce illegal. More- over, we must maintain a sense of proportion, and assess matters and morals by the custom and spirit of the age. It is a fact that the keeping of mistresses was customary among our Hanoverian kings, George III being the single bright exception to this rule. It is also probable that there was scarcely a com- mander-in-chief either in England or on the Continent in the eighteenth century who did not keep a mistress. The Duke's offence was even palliated by an Opposition speaker in the course of the debate, who pointed out that Royalty is more tempted in this respect than the commonalty of mankind, inas- much as a Royal prince could seldom marry the lady of his choice for political and dynastic reasons, and that consequently a 'working arrangement' whereby he had an official wife and an unofficial one was condoned or winked at. But this does not quite dispose of the matter. It may not on moral grounds be less defensible for the head of the army to keep a mistress than any- one else, but it has grave practical objections, especially when the paramour is a woman of wit, intelligence, and interested in

military affairs. Such objections may not be applicable to the
present day, when 'patronage' in military appointments and
promotions has been superseded by the examination system;
but they were very applicable in 1804, in spite of the efforts of
the Duke himself to eradicate the most objectionable features of
the practice. Indeed, until the institution of competitive examinations, such abuses as those which the Inquiry disclosed were
inherent in the system that obtained, not only in military affairs,
but in all walks of official life. Of this the Duke must have been
aware, and it therefore behoved him as long as he held the
position, under the King, of being the very fount of military
patronage and honour, to take meticulous care that not only
did he not lend himself to abuse of it, but that there could be
no possible suspicion of it. As a Member said during the debate,
the Commander-in-Chief should be like Caesar's wife – above
suspicion. This is where the Duke failed. Either by a too easygoing lack of responsibility or an utter want of elementary dis-
cretion and *savoir-faire*, he was guilty of the gross impropriety
of keeping the worst kind of mistress for a commander-in-chief,
and of chatting to her in an unguarded and irresponsible manner
on military affairs. This garrulity was always one of his weak-
nesses. We have seen it in evidence during the Helder campaign,
and there was at least a suspicion of it in the Flanders campaign
also. This laxity of conduct was most reprehensible in the Duke,
and although the loss of his high office was an excessive price to
pay for it, there can be no doubt that, in the existing inflamed
state of public opinion, the Cabinet were justified in contem-
plating firm steps if necessary to bring about his resignation.
His sin was an error of judgment, but persons in lofty places
cannot afford such lapses.

The personal position of the Duke is perhaps best summed up
in the words of the King to the Lord Chancellor:

'The King concurs with the Chancellor in heartily deploring
that the Duke of York should have formed any connection with
so abandoned a woman as Mrs Clarke, but his Majesty will
never permit himself to doubt for a moment the Duke of York's
patent integrity and his conscientious attention to his duty, or
to believe that in the discharge of it he has ever submitted to
undue influence.'[1]

[1] *Windsor*, 20.2.09.

Patent integrity. That is the *mot juste* throughout the Duke's public career.

It may be held that I have devoted an inordinate space to the examination of this case. But it is sadly true that to give a dog a bad name is to hang him. The Duke of York has been hanged, and the task of cutting him down is a difficult one. Even modern writers distort the story. As an example, one of the most recent books on the subject contains this passage: 'Mrs Clarke was found to be dispensing commissions in the army. Under the attacks of Colonel Wardle the Duke was compelled to resign by an adverse vote.'[1]

The repercussions of the Inquiry in the country were almost startling in their intensity. In a single night 'the immaculate patriot', as Mary Anne afterwards contemptuously called Wardle, became the hero of his country. Addresses, resolutions of thanks, speeches of adulation, engravings, songs, and even medals depicting the gallant colonel, poured upon him and flooded the land. A book was rushed out entitled *The Memoirs of Colonel Wardle*, by one Reid, the first sentence of which describes him as 'instrumental in obtaining a new era in British politics'. There was scarcely a town of any size in the country that did not vote him an address of thanks, and the *Gentleman's Magazine* at a later date recorded how 'the sapient Corporation of London voted him the Freedom of the City in a box of 100 guineas value'. Earlier it had apostrophized Wardle in these terms: 'We conceive that Colonel Wardle is deserving the thanks of the country for his manly and independent conduct in having boldly dared *single-handed* to attack the Hydra of corruption, and to assail her even in her very den.'[2]

Wardle had been promised that the affair would make him the most popular man in the country, and it had. This previously obscure member of Parliament revelled in his popularity. It looked like being as deep-founded and permanent as did the unpopularity of the Duke of York. . . .

It is on the whole a fortunate thing that we cannot foresee our own future. Wardle would hardly have had the stomach to enjoy herodom had he foreseen how soon Nemesis would over-

[1] *George IV*, by Shane Leslie, p. 128.   [2] *Gentleman's Magazine*, 1809, I, p. 273.

take him. Big results often follow from seemingly small causes. In the honeymoon heyday of his early acquaintance with Mary Anne he had, it will be remembered, lightly undertaken to furnish her new house for her – this being part of the inducement to bring her to the bar of the House. In addition to this, Wardle had advanced her £500 or £600. After the trial the Colonel conveniently forgot his promise to pay for the furniture and the upholsterer, one Francis Wright, sued him for the amount, and cited Mrs Clarke as a witness. The case was tried by Lord Ellenborough on 3 July. Wardle lost his case and was cast in damages to the tune of £1,300. But the true significance of the case was that in the course of the proceedings the facts of the conspiracy that we have outlined – the journey to the South Coast, etc. – became public for the first time. The favours of the fickle mob swung back violently in favour of the Duke. A contemporary passage in the *Gentleman's Magazine* well reflects this; it speaks of 'one of the most foul, pitiful and unmanly plots *that was ever contrived*'[1] against the Commander-in-Chief.

The 'thieves had fallen out' and the fur began to fly. The partisans of both sides rushed out with books and pamphlets, most of them recklessly libellous. Far the most libellous, remarkable, witty, and revealing was that written by Mary Anne Clarke herself. It rapidly attained fame, and even today is not entirely forgotten. She entitled it *The Rival Princes*, the princes being the Dukes of York and Kent, the latter of whom she endeavoured to drag into the conspiracy against his brother (whom she now described unctuously as a gentleman and a Prince). But the most revealing part of the book concerned herself. With shattering candour she painted her own portrait, in a passage which warrants quotation in full:

'I am of the opinion that there is not a person in England at all acquainted with the proceedings of the House of Commons . . . who is so credulous as to believe what Colonel Wardle has lately endeavoured to make the people of England credit as a divine revelation; namely that I incurred the exposure of myself, children and family together with abuse, anxiety of mind, and fatigue of person during my examination in Parliament, from *a pure patriotic zeal to serve the public*. . . . If I were to tell the same gross falsehood which has issued from *the immaculate*

[1] *Gentleman's Magazine*, 1810, II, p. 546.

Colonel Wardle, and compliment myself on having appeared against the Duke, without any motives of interest beyond the gratification of serving the public, I am sure the intelligent reader would consider me a most impudent hypocrite, and with great justice; for if I had not been well satisfied of receiving the remuneration agreed upon, not all the Jacobinial parties in Europe should have introduced my letters and person to the notice of Parliament.'[1]

The virago also fell foul of McCallum, Dodd, and even Lord Folkestone, who had taken her part so ardently. There is fortunately no need to examine the 'dirty linen' that was now washed in the public Press. The next step in Wardle's undoing was taken by himself. In an address '*To the People of the United Kingdom*', written on the morrow of the trial, Wardle had the hardihood to declare that the verdict was obtained 'by perjury alone', and he undertook to go to law on it at once. The case came on in December, and after the judge, Lord Ellenborough, had expressed the opinion that Wardle had in fact 'given a bribe which he ought not to have done', the jury decided against the Colonel without leaving the box, and worse still the Judge stigmatized as 'a conspiracy' the proceedings against the Duke. That was about the end of Gwyllin Lloyd Wardle.

The conspirators sank back into the obscurity out of which they had been so abruptly elevated. Their subsequent careers may be briefly related. McCallum died in penury next year. Glennie, rather surprisingly, became mathematical instructor at the Royal Military Academy, Woolwich. Dodd continued to be secretary to the Duke of Kent. Wardle, after failing to be elected at the next election, fled the country to avoid his creditors, and died on the Continent in 1832. Mrs Clarke, after doing nine months for libelling the Hon. William Fitzgerald, travelled on the Continent, on an annuity promised her by the Court provided she refrained from publishing her letters from the Duke of York. (In spite of this the incorrigible woman did eventually publish them in Paris.) Her daughter married a Du Maurier, and became the mother of George Du Maurier, the cartoonist, and grandmother of Sir Gerald Du Maurier. Mary Anne Clarke died at Boulogne in 1852, aged about 76.

[1] *The Rival Princes*, I, p. 74.

V

While all this turmoil between the principals was going on the Duke of York was leading a quiet life at Oatlands, making an occasional speech in the House of Lords or in the country, but keeping strictly apart from the Army. On accepting his resignation the King, who throughout maintained an invincible faith in his son, appointed old General Dundas to the 'temporary Chief Command', as he significantly called it, of the army, at the same time making it plain that he contemplated eventually restoring the Duke of York. But the worthy Dundas was nearly as much in his dotage as Amherst had been, and six months after his appointment there was a strong cry in the army for the return of its beloved Duke. The Government also was only too anxious to bring back the Duke. The war with Napoleon was far from won; at the end of 1810 our army in the Peninsula was back on the Portuguese frontier, and victory seemed as far away as ever. A strong and capable hand was as necessary at the Horse Guards as it had ever been.

The opportunity for which the Government were looking was not long in coming. Early in 1811 the old King relapsed once more into insanity – this time permanent – and the Prince of Wales on 5 February became Regent. As soon as he was comfortably settled into the saddle, with the concurrence of the Government (of which Perceval was now Prime Minister in name as well as in practice), he reappointed his brother Commander-in-Chief, Dundas having conveniently resigned. The country accepted the return of the Duke without a murmur, but Lord Milton in the House of Commons moved a vote of censure on the Government for recommending the appointment. The debate that followed was of great significance. Much had happened in the two years that had elapsed since the Duke had been hounded from office, but the same House was sitting and many Members felt uncomfortable at the recollection of their former words and votes. Some, however, remained irreconcilable. The debate consequently was almost monopolized by the old Opposition, the irreconcilables and the recanters being in roughly equal proportions. Of the latter no less than six rose in their places in succession and publicly recanted. But it is noteworthy that even the opponents of the Duke recognized the existence of a conspiracy. The following extract from *Hansard* is significant because that publication seldom records interruptions or applause. '*Lord Milton* . . . "The Duke of York had been victim of a foul conspiracy." (Here the noble Lord was interrupted by a general cry of Hear, Hear, from all parts of the House.)' The first of the open recanters was Sir Oswald Mosely, in a short speech. Mr. Gooch, another of them, asserted that 'there was not a man in the army who did not almost worship him (the Duke). . . .' He also spoke of 'as profligate a set of witnesses as had ever disgraced a tribunal'. Mr Barham, a third recanter, 'regarded the Duke of York as a grossly injured man'. Most of the other speeches were of a like complexion. Colonel Wardle sat silent in his place. Eventually he was goaded into rising – only to utter a few halting sentences concerning his law-suit. No notice was taken of his remarks: his bubble was burst.

The House divided and the motion was defeated by the over-whelming majority of 297 to 47. The mills of justice had done their work. The 'idol of the army' returned to his chair at the Horse Guards.

AT THE HORSE GUARDS AGAIN

13

When Frederick, Duke of York, sat down once more in his familiar seat at the Horse Guards the army was in much the state in which he had left it two years before. During those two years it had run on its own momentum, but a fresh impulse was required after the Dundas interregnum. There were still three years to go till the victory of Toulouse put the crown on the achievements of the British Army in the Peninsular War. The Duke wisely carried on with the same methods that had characterized his previous administration, with the result that the Army continued to grow in efficiency and self-confidence.

The Duke of Wellington on his return home in 1814 was the recipient in the House of Commons of an address of congratulation. In his reply he paid marked tribute to the work of the Commander-in-Chief, whose labours, he declared amid cheers, had alone made his victories possible. The Commons also passed a vote of thanks to York for his share in the great achievement. On this being communicated to the Duke he wrote to the Speaker: 'It is with peculiar pride I learn that the favour of the House of Commons has induced them to ascribe to any effort of mine the smallest share in securing these spendid successes.' One may well believe it, and we may note the significance of the word 'peculiar', after his past treatment by this same House of Commons.

Next year came Waterloo, and another vote of thanks from the Commons, in which they thanked him for 'his continual, effectual and unremitting attention to the duties of his office for a period of more than twenty years, during which time the Army has improved in discipline, and in science to an extent unknown before, and, under Providence, has risen to the heights of military glory'.[1]

This was the simple truth.

[1] Whitbread opposed the vote. Two days later he committed suicide.

After war comes peace, and with peace reduction of the armed forces of the Crown. In carrying out this distasteful task the Government retained the services of their old Commander-in-Chief. The work was no sinecure. The Duke had to deal with several different departments, each independent of the others, and great tact and patience and good temper were required – virtues with which York was liberally endowed. As Fortescue well puts it: 'He was liable to constant attacks upon questions of detail in Parliament and knew not to whom to entrust his defence. Indeed a less capable man than the Duke would probably have lost his hold upon the army, so eager were the politicians to encroach upon his authority. But no one could question his industry, ability or his public spirit. No one could dispute that the military forces of the country, when he first took them over, were confounded and corrupted by the jobs of politicians and by the reckless experiments of civil empirics. It was he who had reduced chaos to order, restored discipline and, with discipline, confidence, and made the British Army the most efficient in the world.'[1]

During those apparently halcyon days of the Regency the Duke of York's duties and occupations naturally veered more towards the civil side of life. He still steered clear of politics, being only occasionally drawn into its vortex, such as in the question of Catholic emancipation, and the succession to the premiership on the death of Perceval. But social and family duties claimed him increasingly. When the Emperor of Russia and the King of Prussia visited England in 1814 he had to play a prominent part both in arranging military reviews and in entertaining the foreign royalties. The visit was not repeated after Waterloo (much to the relief of the poor Queen, on whom great responsibility rested, King George being now permanently insane). But there were other duties, not all of such a pleasant nature. More and more, Frederick seemed called upon to act as mediator in family ructions, chiefly in connexion with the impossible Princess of Wales. And a modern note now enters into his activities: we find him presiding at meetings of various charitable institutions and suchlike, for which tasks he was in great demand.

The death of the Queen in 1818 threw yet another unpleasant

[1] *Fortescue*, XI, p. 44.

duty upon her second son, who was now made Guardian of the King. Many were the dutiful visits he paid to the blind, deaf and uncomprehending old monarch, till two years later a merciful Providence released King George from the sorrows of this world.

With the accession of his brother to the throne as George IV Frederick became heir presumptive, for Princess Charlotte had died a tragic death in 1817, and there was little prospect of George IV having further issue. The Duke of York was thus the first subject in the Realm, and indeed narrowly escaped becoming King a few days after his brother's accession. The new King fell ill, and for a time his life was believed to be in danger. Though George recovered, his health remained noticeably inferior to that of his brother, who was only 57, was hale and hearty, and by all the rules of life insurance should ere long succeed to the throne.

The Duke of York was now in the sunshine of his days. As year followed year the memory of the Mrs Clarke scandal grew fainter; the stout upstanding figure of the Duke became ever more familiar in the Metropolis, while his tenure of the office of Commander-in-Chief seemed ageless; a great portion of the Army could not remember the day when he had become their chief. In short, the Duke of York was now an 'institution'. His brothers were not loved by the populace – one of them was actively hated – and what affection they possessed for the Royal Family, now that old King George was dead, was centred upon his favourite son.

His social pursuits remained the same, only he had now more time to indulge in them. The chief of these were horse-racing and card-playing, two admirable ways of losing money, as he had discovered long years before. In that respect he reminds one of the Bourbons, who were not conspicuous for profiting by past mistakes. At the time of his death he owned a stud of thirty race-horses, and in spite of many failures on the turf he managed twice to win the Derby. Right up to the end he retained his love for the Sport of Kings, and his very last letter to his elder brother, written during his last illness is devoted to the subject: 'Mon Marie won again. She has now proved herself the best mare of the year. . . . It will be difficult to find a mare to beat her for the Oaks, for which she is of course the favourite.'[1]

As for cards, the less said the better. He was apparently a bad player, and his 'friends' took unmerciful advantage of this and of his love for high stakes. The vast debts he accumulated were largely due to this. Another cause was his mad project of building a great palace for himself in the grounds of St James's Palace, known since by various names, Stafford House being the most famous. The house was not finished at his death, but it had already caused a big drain on his resources and he had had to part with it.[2]

Shooting was another sport in which he delighted. As a boy, it will be remembered, he had quickly become a good shot; and throughout his life he retained a keen, quick eye and steady hand. Only three years before his death, shooting at Lord Verulam's place in Hertfordshire, he with his own gun killed ninety-eight pheasants besides other game. Watkins relates that 'he continued the sport until dark and afterwards dined with the Earl and Countess, stopped to an evening party, and between one and two o'clock set off for London, where he arrived about four, and attended the Chapel Royal at Sunday noon'.[3]

He always preferred travelling by night and the loss of sleep did not worry him. On one occasion he went for three nights in succession without going to bed at all.

Captain Gronow, who met him frequently during those years, formed a tremendous admiration for him, leaving us this graphic picture: 'Without exception one of the finest men England could boast of. He stood about six foot, was rather stout, but well proportioned, his chest broad and his frame muscular, and his face bore the stamp of authority and every feature was handsome. His brow was full and prominent, the eye greenish, beaming with benevolence, and a noble forehead completed the picture.'[4]

Lord Holland, who, being a Whig, was a political opponent, speaks of his 'alarming popularity with the military'.[5]

There are many stories of his benevolence. The following

[1] *Windsor*, 4.11.26.
[2] In order to make room for it he pulled down the house in Stableyard in which he had lived since 1807.
[3] Op. cit., p. 593. [4] *Reminiscence and Recollections, by Captain Gronow*. II, p. 114.
[5] *Holland Papers*, I, p. 37.

must suffice. One day at Oatlands he saw one of his domestics turning away a woman who was begging. He asked why she was turned away, to receive the answer: 'She is only a soldier's wife who has come here begging.' 'Only a soldier's wife!' exclaimed the Duke in wrath, 'and pray, what is your mistress but a soldier's wife? Call the poor creature back and give her some relief.' That story was not easily forgotten at Oatlands.

The United Kingdom was not destined to have a King Frederick. In the summer of 1826 the Duke's health began to fail and a long and painful illness followed. It has been described with singular fidelity and feeling by his faithful servant and devoted friend, Sir Herbert Taylor. Sir Herbert was both his private secretary, since the death of Queen Charlotte, and his executor. In the account that follows quotations are from Taylor's *The Last Illness of the Duke of York*, which was published separately and also reprinted in Huish's and Watkins's Memoirs of the Duke. In June 1826 a dropsical swelling of both legs began to appear. It had the effect of not allowing him to lie down with comfort, and a special adjustable chair was constructed for him in which for the remainder of his life he spent the nights. Visits to Brampton House and to Brighton did him no good and on 26 August the Duke went to live in the Duke of Rutland's house in Arlington Street.[1] In September the expedient of tapping was tried without giving much relief. Mortification in his feet now set in and during the next two months he suffered excruciating pain night and day. Taylor had informed the Duke of the dangerous nature of his complaint as gently as possible, and he records the following conversation that he had on 22 September.

'He told me he did his best to submit with patience and resignation; that he tried to keep up his spirits; he met his friends cheerfully, endeavoured to go correctly through what he had to do and to occupy himself at other times with reading; but when left to his own thoughts, when he went to bed and lay awake, the situation was not agreeable; the contemplation of one's end (not to be met at once but protracted possibly for months) required a struggle and tried one's resolution. But after all, he did not know that he regretted it or that he re-

[1] This house is now occupied by the Overseas League.

gretted the time that was given him which had turned his mind to serious reflections which he was certain, had been very beneficial to him.'

In October a second doctor was brought in, but the Duke begged that the fact might be kept secret, for fear that if it got about it might 'embarras the Government and influence public funds'.

From 6 November to the 20th there was a sensible improvement, and after a relapse another improvement from 8 December to the 17th. But the Duke was visibly losing strength. By the 20th his condition was regarded as critical. However, through all these weeks he still refused to give up his work. The Adjutant-General and Quartermaster-General visited him in his room daily. That this was not a mere formality was exhibited in a striking fashion. On 9 December Taylor informed him that secret orders were to be issued for embarkation of troops for Portugal. 'He was then in great pain, but he became indifferent to bodily sufferings, and immediately drew up the heads of the military arrangements (which paper in his own handwriting I now possess)[1] from which were framed detailed instructions approved by him on the following day.'

The upshot came a fortnight later, when Sir Robert Peel visited him and informed him of the safe landing of the troops in Portugal. Peel afterwards related it to the House of Commons as follows: 'Hearing of the landing of part of the troops at Lisbon he said, with a faint expression of honest triumph: "I wish any man could compare the state of the brigade of British troops disembarked at Ostend in 1794 with that of the troops now landing at Lisbon." '

On 22 December Taylor was again entrusted with the delicate duty of preparing the royal patient for death. 'After listening calmly the Duke said: "God's will be done. I am not afraid of dying. I trust I have done my duty . . . but I own it has come upon me with surprise. . . ."

'He then gave me his hand but he pressed me again to state "what was the extent of the danger and whether *immediate*". I repeated that I had been assured that it was not immediate. "Whether his case was without hope of recovery?" I gave no decided answer but said I could not extract from the physi-

[1] All trace of this paper seems to have vanished.

cians any positive opinion, but that their language was not encouraging. He said "I understand you. I may go on for a short time but may end rapidly. God's will be done. I am resigned." He then called for his official papers and transacted business with composure and his usual attention. . . . He then spoke most kindly, took me again by the hand and said "Thank you; God bless you." I had hitherto succeeded in controlling my feelings, but I could do so no longer, and I left the room.'

On Christmas Day the Duke of Wellington paid him a visit. Next day he consummated a reform for which he had laboured long, namely an arrangement for the relief of old and deserving lieutenants who were too poor to obtain promotion by purchase. There had been many difficulties in the way, but all had now been overcome, and on St Stephen's Day he signed the order giving relief. It was his last military act – and an appropriate one. On the same day he signed his will. In it he left the residue of his estate, when all debts had been paid, to his favourite sister, Sophia.[1] Alas, poor dupe! There was no residue. His assets amounted to £180,000, but his liabilities to £200,000 in round figures. Mercifully he went to his end in utter oblivion of this disastrous state of affairs.

On the 27th the Duke was visited by the King, who brought with him a special soup that was a favourite with the Duke. Sir Robert Peel also paid him a visit. Next day he was very weak, and had some fainting attacks in the morning, but recovered in the afternoon sufficiently to partake of the Sacrament at the hands of the Bishop of London. Princess Sophia and Sir Henry Taylor were also present. Afterwards he seemed better, and transacted some business. He then saw Greville, his racing trainer. Greville was much affected.

On 29 December the King again visited his brother, staying over an hour. It was to be the last time these quasi-twins were to meet in this world. On the same day and the next, he transacted business with the A.G. and Q.M.G. and he also saw his brothers Clarence and Sussex, and Princess Sophia. But a big change had come over him.

Two more days passed, and on 2 January he was shivering and subject to fainting attacks. Outside a big crowd had collected, silent and with strained expressions, waiting. . . . On

[1] The Duchess of York had died in 1820.

3 January this amazing man rallied. The doctors remarked that 'his extraordinary powers of constitution and tenacity of life defied all calculations'.

But mortification had now spread right up both legs and he was in the last stage of weakness. On the afternoon of the next day he sent for Taylor, who had not seen him for four days, and who found him dreadfully changed. Colonel Stephenson, the other executor, was also called in. 'After some interval, during which his Royal Highness breathed with great difficulty and was very faint, and during which Batchelor (his servant) bathed his temple with Cologne water, he collected his strength, and said in a steady, firm tone of voice, but so low as to be hardly audible, "I am now dying." After this he dropped his head and his lips moved for a short minute, as if in prayer.' He never spoke again. All that night and next day he lingered on, and at twenty minutes past nine at night, the 5th of January 1827, he breathed his last. His countenance was quite free from any distortion. 'Indeed it almost looked as if he had died with a smile upon it.'

So died the Soldier's Friend.

EPILOGUE

As ten o'clock approached on the morning of 8 April 1834 a stream of people could be seen wending their way down the new Lower Regent Street, across Pall Mall, and over the site of the recently dismantled Carlton House. On each side of the ground thus made vacant two imposing buildings had just been erected – the homes of the Athenaeum and the United Service Clubs, but it was not to view either of these that the crowd was collecting. Straight in front of them, at the top of the new steps leading down to the Park, a vast column reared its truncated head to the sky, its outlines scarcely visible owing to the scaffolding by which it was surrounded. Beside its foot was a huge wagon, on which lay a shapeless mass, encased in oil-cloth. It was an immense bronze statue of the late Duke of York, and the crowd had collected to witness its elevation to the top of the column. It was the nation's memorial to the late Commander-in-Chief.

Ere the Duke of York had been placed in his coffin a spontaneous demand for a worthy memorial to him had made itself heard. One Captain Tom Scott, R.A., records in his unpublished diary under date 2 January: 'His dissolution may be hourly expected. What a loss to the country and to the army he will be, especially to the latter whose friend he was.' And two days after his death the diary records that the Woolwich Mess proposed to subscribe for 'a brass statue or such other memorial as may be conceived by the army at large'. Next day a special Mess Meeting was held at which the proposal was unanimously carried. The fact that the Royal Artillery was not under the Commander-in-Chief, but under the Master-General of the Ordnance enhances the significance of this gesture.

The United Service Club was even more prompt, for on the very day after his death it was proposed, and subsequently agreed, to subscribe for a marble statue to the Duke. (This statue now stands on the grand staircase in the most prominent site in the club, and forms the frontispiece to this book.)

A month later a great public meeting, presided over by the

Duke of Wellington, resolved to erect a national memorial to the departed Chief. It was decided to leave the subscription list open for two years in order to allow all soldiers all over the world to subscribe to it. It is indeed recorded that every soldier in the army ultimately subscribed. The first proposal was that it should take the form of 'a colosal equestrian statue in front of the Horse Guards'.

The column as eventually constructed was made of Tuscan stone, with a spiral staircase of 169 steps inside. The total height of the column is 137 feet 9 inches, excluding the lightning conductor fixed on the top of the head – which the wags said was a file for the Duke's unpaid bills. Matthew Wyatt designed the column, and Richard Westmacott sculptured the statue. The latter is 13 feet 9 inches in height and weighs over seven tons. The Duke is shown in uniform, drawn sword in hand, with a cloak thrown over his shoulder. From the platform at his feet it has a striking appearance.[1]

Such was the statue that the populace had assembled on that spring morning to witness being hoisted on to its giant pedestal. The work commenced at about 11 a.m. 'Several thick ropes,' reported the *Morning Post*, 'we attached to the middle of it and at about 11 a.m. the workmen commenced raising it. In consequence of its immense weight (upwards of seven tons) the greatest care and caution were necessary to prevent any accident, and upwards of an hour was occupied in raising it little more than ten feet. It reached the top at about five o'clock in the afternoon.'

Here, then, for upwards of a century has stood the Nation's and the Army's memorial to Frederick, Duke of York, on per-

[1] The column was closed to the public for some time between 1867 and 1883. The story is related that an officer once rode his horse up the Duke of York's Steps for a wager. This action scandalised Authority, who decreed that he should be punished. Unrepentant, the misguided officer had the effrontery to declare that he would do it again. This could not be allowed; a sentry was posted at the top of the steps to prevent such an occurrence. Years passed, the officer went abroad, but still the sentry mounted duty nightly over the steps. The sentry complained one stormy night of lack of shelter, so a sentry box was erected against the column. Eventually there arose an inquisitive official at the Treasury who, during an economy drive, asked what were the duties of this sentry. Inquiries were made, but no one could say what his duties were. He was accordingly withdrawn, and the sentry box dismantled. Should anyone doubt the authenticity of this story he has only to visit the spot. In the masonry at the foot of the column he will see the nail-holes.

haps the most impressive site in the whole Metropolis. A more appropriate site could not be imagined. At its feet had stood the great house where the Duke had so often kept company with his elder brother; from its doors he had slipped away to that early-morning ride to Wimbledon Common, to return a few hours later, perfectly cool, but minus a lock of hair. To his left front lies the Horse Guards, his spiritual home for thirty-two years. His eyes are fixed in that direction. From his eyrie he looks down upon the scene of his labours with a calm and benignant gaze. There, in the centre of the building, is the window of his office, where he toiled for 'ten thousand days'. By a happy chance, over the roof of the building can be seen the new War Office – the bustling hive whence emanate orders and ordinances that once issued from the nearer and older building.

Do the workers in that hive ever chance to raise their eyes and meet that quiet gaze? Does the spirit of the 'best Commander-in-Chief the army ever had' still permeate that hive? Does that little band of officers who now carry on the work of ruling the British Army heed that gaze? And does it inspire them to emulate the unswerving and unremitting efforts for the good of the army of the 'Soldier's Friend'? If so, Frederick, Duke of York and Albany, did not live in vain.

BIOGRAPHICAL NOTE

On the death of the Duke of York a long obituary notice from the pen of Sir Walter Scott appeared in the *Annual Register*. The same year two short memoirs and a biography were published. The biography, entitled *A Biographical Memoir of His Late Royal Highness Frederick Duke of York and Albany*, by John Watkins, was addressed to the King, and might be described as a 'Court biography'. None of the above throws any light worth speaking of on his military career. Thus, up to the present day no full-dress Life of the Duke has been written, nor have his campaigns been treated with anything approaching detailed and informed criticism, except by Sir John Fortescue in his *History of the British Army*. Hence Fortescue's assessment of the military capacity of the Duke of York has been allowed to stand unchallenged.

It is a pity that no great soldier such as E. M. Lloyd, G. F. R. Henderson, or Sir Frederick Maurice has undertaken the military biography of this neglected British soldier. But that being so, we are driven back inescapably to the original sources. No attempt has ever been made to tabulate these, so it may be helpful to the military student and others if I devote some space to the subject. The list I append does not claim to be exhaustive, though I doubt if a longer list would add appreciably to our knowledge of the military career of the Duke of York.

I have listed my authorities in three groups:

    I. MSS. Sources.
    II. Contemporary Printed Sources.
    III. Later Works.

I

MSS. SOURCES

There are three main collections: those in the Public Record Office, the British Museum, and the Royal Archives at Windsor Castle.

The researcher in the Public Record Office may experience some difficulty in turning up the reference given by Fortescue and others, owing to the fact that the lists have been altered from time to time. There are two main sources, now listed as W.O.I. and W.O.VI. W.O.I. is now headed 'War Office IN Letters'. Fortescue cites it as 'Original Correspondence'. Volumes 166 to 171 cover the 1793-4 campaign, Volumes 179 to 182 the Helder campaign. They comprise mainly letters from the Duke of York and his two Adjutant-Generals to Henry Dundas, Secretary of State (and virtually War Minister).

W.O.VI. is now headed 'Secretary of State OUT Letters', cited by Fortescue as 'Secretary of State's Entry Book', and in some foreign works as 'British Army on the Continent'. (This title mystified me till I discovered on the back of the binding – and nowhere else – the above title.) Volumes 7, 8, and 11 refer to the 1793 – 4 campaign (Volumes 9 and 10 are duplicates). These volumes contain the letters from Dundas to the Duke and his Adjutant-Generals. At the end of Volumes 7 and 8, and upside down, are copies of a number of IN Letters from the front.

THE CHATHAM PAPERS. I do not, of course, claim to have examined all the 268 volumes in this massive collection. The portion that concerns us is what used to be known as the Pitt Papers, now included in the Chatham Papers. The volumes that I have found useful are:

Vol. 101. The King to Pitt.   Vol. 106. Duke of York to Pitt.
Vol. 102. Pitt to Murray.   Vol. 125. Cornwallis to Pitt.
Vol. 103. The King to Pitt.   Vol. 157. Dundas to Pitt.
              Vol. 190. Windham to Pitt.

BRITISH MUSEUM. Four volumes of *Additional Manuscripts* have proved useful:

32,133, containing letters of Malmesbury, St. Leger, Craig, etc.

37,844, relating to the recall of the Duke of York. (Most of these are printed in the Windham Papers.)

37,842, comprising letters from the Duke to Windham.

23,618, which contains some valuable plans by Colonel Hamilton Smith, notably one showing the movement of both sides in detail from 9 July to 8 November 1794.

WINDSOR ARCHIVES. These are usually described in this book by their dates, as they are filed in strictly chronological order under the names of the various Royal writers. In the case of outside writers, and in cases where the date is doubtful, I have usually quoted the number that appears on each folio.

To this incomparable collection I am deeply indebted. The Duke was an assiduous writer and a dutiful correspondent to the King, his father, from the age of 17 onwards. Moreover, during the Flanders campaign he wrote on an average two letters per week to the King, all of which have been preserved up to 2 May 1794. The later letters are unfortunately missing. The gap is to some extent filled by his letters to the Prince of Wales. Most unfortunately also he did not preserve the letters written him by the King, or if he did, they were destroyed by Sir Henry Taylor, his executor, after his death, in accordance with his instructions. These private letters from a commander in the field to his father form an almost unique collection. They throw much light on the Duke of York. We see his character gradually unfolding and developing, till, on reaching the end, we feel almost as closely acquainted with him as if we had known him in the flesh. The King's letters are chiefly to his ministers. Those of the Prince of Wales are to all and sundry. Of the IN letters, those of Pitt concerning the recall of the Duke and of Spencer Perceval regarding the Mrs Clarke affair are indispensable to the student.

II

CONTEMPORARY PRINTED SOURCES

The most detailed contemporary account of the Flanders campaign comes from a foreigner, H. E. N. Arnaudin, whose *Mémoires des Campagnes de 1793-4* is of rather mysterious origin. Nothing definite is known about the author. He seems, from internal evidence, to have been a French *émigré* at the Duke's headquarters, but it is curious that none of our extant letters or records from the front mention his name. I know of only a single copy (and that in MS.) of the work; it is in the War Office Library. It seems to have been published in France at some time, for French (but not English) writers quote from it. As far as one can judge, its facts are correct and reliable, and it contains a good deal that we do not get elsewhere. Fortescue does not appear to have had access to it. Another foreign writer, and definitely a French *émigré*, was Count L. A. H. Langeron, a man of colourful personality. He was attached to the Allied headquarters with a 'watching brief' by the Czar of Russia, in whose service he was. As such, he accompanied the Duke in the affair of Caesar's Camp, and elsewhere. He reminds one of Goslinga, the Dutch deputy who accompanied the Duke of Marlborough everywhere and 'won all his battles for him'. The particular value of Langeron's account lies in the fact that he was a neutral witness and an experienced soldier, who was free and candid in his criticisms. Unfortunately he was only a short time with the army.

Of English participants who wrote of the campaign the most important is Henry Calvert, who started as a captain in the Guards and ended as one of the Duke's most trusted staff officers, with the rank of lieutenant-colonel. His *Journal and Correspondence* consists of letters to his uncle, sister and others, and covers the whole campaign. His uncle, Sir Hew Dalrymple (afterwards to be prominent in the matter of the Convention of Cintra), was stationed at Chatham at the time, and took a close interest in the campaign, and Calvert wrote to him with surprisingly little reserve – which adds to the value of the book. Calvert was a firm believer in the Duke. Another officer on the headquarters staff, also a Guardsman, produced a book – a curious and rare work, the value of which has not been recognized. It consists of a series of letters written in verse from the front by this anonymous officer to his lady-love at home, entitled, *An Accurate and Impartial Narrative of the War*. The date of publication is not given, but it must have been strictly contemporaneous. These verses are, as Fortescue labels them, 'miserable doggerel', which perhaps accounts for their neglect, but the very fact that they are doggerel enhances their historical value, for it has enabled the author to relate his story more exactly than if he had been restricted by the claims of good poesy. Moreover, his voluminous footnotes contain many details of value, as Fortescue recognizes.

The first and almost the sole Englishman who attempted a history of the campaign was Captain L. T. Jones, but his work is a poor affair, and only deals with the year 1794 (though it contains an extremely interesting plan of the siege of Valenciennes in 1793). What would probably have been the best account in the English language was never written. Sir Henry Taylor, who would have been the author, served also on the Duke's staff, eventually acting as his private secretary. After the war he started to write his reminiscences, but they did not get far, and he afterwards destroyed all his priceless papers, together with those of the Duke, in his capacity as executor. The little that remains of his account is contained in *The Taylor Papers*. It is first hand and first class.

The Wright Letters are of more use to the history of the campaign than of the Duke, but they give a certain amount of information from an unusual angle – that of an artilleryman. (Gunners of that time were not conspicuous with the pen.)

W

Another rare work (only fifty copies were printed), but surprisingly enlightening, is Volume V of *The Harcourt Papers*, written by a woman. She was the wife of General Harcourt, and occupied a curious place in the army, sometimes acting as Quartermaster-General, and sometimes in command of the cavalry. The intrepid Mrs Harcourt insisted on going out to the front to join her husband. Here she lived with the army, entertained the Duke and all his principal officers, kept her ears cocked, missed nothing, and forgot nothing. It all went down in her astonishingly frank and illuminating letters home. Often no doubt she was reflecting the views of her husband, but some of her most shrewd observations are made when she is temporarily parted from the general. The work is badly edited, and a new edition would be a great boon to students of the campaign. It was not used by Fortescue. The most important printed collections of letters dealing with the Duke's part in the campaign are those of the Marquis Cornwallis for the latter part, Malmesbury for his relations with the Allies, and the Windham Papers for the Duke's recall. There are naturally many other letters of lesser value that I have not listed.

Of periodicals I find the *Gentleman's Magazine* most disappointing. The *Annual Register* is far more valuable; also *The Times*, the *Morning Post*, and the *St James's Chronicle*.

The French accounts, of course, deal only indirectly with the Duke, and they are not always very well informed as to the British side. Jomini's *History* can just be included under the heading 'Contemporary', but his sources do not appear to have been very profound. His comments are perhaps of more value than his facts. The standard contemporary French work is *Victoires et Conquêtes des Français de 1793 à 1815*.

The brief Helder campaign is fairly well documented. There are contemporary accounts by E. Walsh and G. Boyle, and a number of personal reminiscences by officers; of these Sir H. Bunbury's *The Great War with France* and Sir John Moore's Diary are both indispensable.

There is also a mass of contemporary literature about the Mrs Clarke case, much of it thoroughly unreliable. Of course, the main source is contained in the Parliamentary Reports; these are only slightly condensed in *A Circumstantial Report*, published at the time by the Albion Press. For the rest, Mrs Clarke's own account, *The Rival Princes*, must be consulted, even if it is more than half fable. Spencer Perceval's daily reports to the King have already been mentioned.

III

LATER WORKS

The list of worth-while English later works is dreadfully short. It is a case of Fortescue *facile princeps*. In the course of this book I have occasion from time to time to criticize statements and assessments in his *History of the British Army*, sometimes severely. But this should not be taken to imply that I have any but the profoundest admiration for that wonderful work. For a single man to accomplish it was a veritable *tour de force*. But it is not to be imagined that one man could cover such a vast field without a single blemish, and it is the duty of all who follow him, in the interest of history, to point out anything that they believe to be wrong, as regards both facts and opinions. The somewhat sketchy manner in which he cites some of his authorities, however, is most exasperating.

Phipps's monumental *Armies of the First French Republic* deals all too briefly with the Flanders campaign, and naturally from the French point of view. The same applies to his treatment of the Helder campaign. This is a great pity, for Phipps was one of our most thorough and accurate military writers, and what he has to say on the campaign is much to the point.

The only other modern English account of the Flanders campaign is by Captain Moffatt, and is in manuscript in the War Office Library. It is a painstaking factual account. This library also contains the most detailed account (MS.) of the Helder campaign by Howard. In later times three writers, Fitzgerald, Huddleston, and Fulford have included chapters on the Duke in their books. All are readable, but too slight to be of much practical value. The *Dictionary of National Biography*, strange to relate, contains many errors. French accounts of the Flanders campaign are voluminous and thorough. Chuquet blazed the trail in 1894 with his admirable *La Guerre de la Révolution*. He, unlike most French military historians, evidently took the trouble to consult our Public Record Office. His work has, however, been superseded by the French War Office publications on the war: by Dupuis for 1793 and by Coutanceau and De la Jonquiére for 1794. The best French account of the Helder is *Jourdan en Allemagne et Brune en Hollande*, by E. Gachot.

The standard accounts in German are those of Ditfurth and of Witzleben, who closely followed Ditfurth. Both are prejudiced against the British army, and have been superseded by Sybel's *History*. The latter is based largely on the Vienna archives (which for obvious reasons I have not examined). It is a judicious account, holding the balance fairly between the two sides. Ditfurth, however, is valuable for his maps, especially that on the complicated battle of Tourcoing.

BIBLIOGRAPHY

I. MANUSCRIPT SOURCES

Title	*Abbreviation*

PUBLIC RECORD OFFICE

Secretary of State IN Letters, W.O.I. — *W.O.*, I.

Secretary of State Entry Book (OUT Letters), W.O. VI. or 'British Army on the Continent' — *W.O.*, VI.

Chatham Papers. Vols. 101, 102, 103, 106, 125, 157, 190 — *Chatham Papers*

BRITISH MUSEUM

Additional manuscripts — *Add. MSS.*

ROYAL ARCHIVES, WINDSOR CASTLE

Letters to and from:

Duke of York — *Windsor*

Prince of Wales — ,,

George III — ,,

Prince Ernest — ,,

Prince Adolphus, etc. — ,,

THE HAGUE

Rijks Archiefs

General Staff Archives — *G.S. Archives*

ALKMAAR

The Town Archives

WAR OFFICE LIBRARY

The Expedition to the Helder, 1799 (Written by Howard in 1926)

II. CONTEMPORARY SOURCES

Title	*Abbreviation*

The Annual Register

Mémoires des Campagnes de 1793-4-5, by H. R. N. Arnaudin (1797) — *Arnaudin*

Sketch of the Life and Character of H.R.H. the Duke of York, Anonymous (1827)

Journal and Correspondence, by Lord Auckland (1861) — *Auckland Correspondence*

Bonne Bouche of Epicurean Rascality (in Broadsheets of 1809)

Impartial Journal, by Robert Brown (1795) — *Brown*

Campaign in Holland, by G. Boyle (1861)

Title	Abbreviation
Bulletins of the Campaigns of 1793–4	
The Great War with France, by Sir H. Bunbury (1927)	*Bunbury*
The Creevy Papers, ed. Sir H. Maxwell (1923)	
Journal and Correspondence, by Sir H. Calvert (1853)	*Calvert*
Memoirs . . . of Viscount Combermere, ed. M. W. S. Cotton (1866)	*Combermere*
Correspondence of Charles 1st Marquis of Cornwallis (1865)	*Cornwallis*
Complete Vindication of . . . the Duke of York. Anonymous (1807)	
Circumstantial Report of the Evidence . . . preferred against the Duke of York. Albion Press (1809)	*Circumstantial Report*
Letters of a Staff Officer, 1794 (Jas. Craig), ed. E. M. Lloyd in U.S. Mag. (1897)	
The Croker Papers (1884)	
Speech by J. W. Croker 14.3.1809 (1809)	
History of the Campaigns of General Pichegru, by Citoyen David (1796)	*David*
General Dyott's Diary (1908 *c.*)	
The Greville Memoirs, ed. H. Reeve (1874)	
Life and Letters of Sir G. Elliot (1859)	
General Orders and Circular Letters (1795–1827)	
Reminiscences and Recollections, by Capt. Gronow (1892)	
Works of Jas. Gillray the caricaturist, ed. T. Wright (1873)	
Life and Letters of Sir Wm. Gomme (1881)	
General Staff Archives at The Hague (1799)	*G. S. Archives*
The Harcourt Papers, ed. E. W. Harcourt (1880, etc.)	*Harcourt*
Historical Manuscripts Commission	*H. M. C.*
Fortescue Papers (Dropmore)	*Dropmore*
Charlemont Papers	*Charlemont*
Buccleugh Papers	*Buccleugh*
Histoire Politique et Militaire des Guerres de la Révolution, by Baron de Jomini (1820)	*Jomini*
British Campaign on the Continent, 1794, by L. T. Jones (1797)	*Jones*
A Laconic Epistle addressed to the Duke of York, by a military officer (1800)	
Mémoires sur les Guerres de la premiere Coalition, by L. A. H. Langeron (1895)	*Langeron*
Memorials of . . . North Holland, by Capt. Maule (1806)	
Diaries and Correspondence of Lord Malmesbury (1844)	*Malmesbury*
Diary of Sir John Moore, ed. Maurice (1904)	
An Accurate and Impartial Narrative of the War, by an Officer of the Guards (N.D.)	*Officer of the Guards*
Parliamentary Reports (1809–11)	
The Paget Papers, ed. Sir A. Paget (1896)	
Life of Spencer Perceval, by Spencer Walpole (1874)	

	Title	*Abbreviation*
PERIODICALS		

PERIODICALS
 The Times
 The Morning Post
 The St James's Chronicle

The Rival Princes, by Mrs Clarke (1809)
The Rival Dukes, by P. F. McCallum (1810)
Royal Military Calendar, by J. Phillippard (1820)
The Rival Imposters (1809)
Memoirs of Sir James Romilly (1841)
Songs of the Siege of Valenciennes, by an Old Officer
(1793)
Analysis of Reform, by B. Slacey (1810)
The Taylor Papers, ed. E. Taylor (1913   *Taylor*
Victoires et Conquêtes des Français de 1793 à 1815, by
Une Société Militaire (1818)   *Victoires*
Last Journal of Horace Walpole (1910)
Narrative of the Expedition to the Helder, by E. Walsh
(1800)
Frederick, Duke of York, J. Watkins (1827)   *Watkins*
Life of General Sir R. Wilson, ed. H. Randolph (1812)
Windham Papers, ed. Anon. (1913)   *Windham*
The Wright Letters, ed. F. A. Whinyates (1902)

III. LATER WORKS
Title   *Abbreviation*
British Military Journal (1829–30)
Lady Bessborough and her Circle, ed. Ponsonby (1940)
History of the Dutch People, by P. J. Blok (1912)
Courts and Cabinets, by the Duke of Buckingham
La Guerre de la Révolution, by A. Chuquet (1894)   *Chuquet*
Gedenkstukken der Algemeene Geschiedenis van Neder-
land, by Dr. Colenbrander (1907)   *Colenbrander*
Campagne de 1794, H. Coutanceau et C. de la Jonquière
(1907)   *Coutanceau*
La Cavalerie pendant la Révolution, Desbrieres et Sautai
(1907)   *Desbrieres*
Sir Robert Abercromby, by Lord Dunfermline (1861)   *Dunfermline*
Dictionary of National Biography
The Du Mauriers, by Daphne Du Maurier (1937)
Campagne de 1793, V. Dupuis (1906)   *Dupuis*
Die Hessen in der Feldzügen von 1793-4-5, Baron Ditfurth
(1839)   *Ditfurth*
George III, P. Fitzgerald (1881)   *Fitzgerald*
Royal Dukes and Princesses, P. Fitzgerald (1882)   *Fitzgerald*
History of the British Army, Sir J. Fortescue (1913)   *Fortescue*
Historical and Military Essays, Sir J. Fortescue (1928)
Défence Nationale, Foucart et Finot (1890)   *Foucart et Finot*
Royal Dukes, R. Fulford (1933)
Jourdan en Allemagne et Brune en Hollande, by E.   *Brune en*
Gachot (1906)   *Hollande*
Letters of King George III, ed. Dobree (1935)

Title	Abbreviation
George IV, R. Fulford (1935)	
History of the Grenadier Guards, F. W. Hamilton (1874)	
Warriors in Undress, R. J. Huddleston (1928)	
H.R.H. the Duke of York, R. Huish (1827)	*Huish*
George III, J. H. Jesse (1867)	
Life and Military Services of Viscount Lake, H. Pearse (1908)	
Duke of York's Campaigns, 1793-4, Captain Moffatt (1881) (MS.)	
Armies of the First French Republic, R. Phipps (1926)	*Phipps*
Pitt and the Great War, J. H. Rose (1911)	*Rose*
Historical Record of the 8th Hussars, J. E. Smet (1874)	
Life of Pitt, by Lord Stanhope (1870)	*Stanhope*
A Personal History of the Horse Guards, by T. H. Stocqueler (1873)	
History of the French Revolution, H. von Sybel (1867)	*Sybel*
The War Office, Past and Present, by Capt. O. Wheeler (1914)	
Prinz Frederick Josias Coburg-Saalfeld, A. von Witzleben (1859)	*Witzleben*

INDEX

A

Aa river, 176–7
Abercromby, Sir R., 40, 44, 50, 117, 119, 125, 178–82, 208, 219, 225, 238, Chap. 10, *passim*
Addington, Dr. H., 243–4
Adolphus, Prince, 76, 116
Ainslie, General, 95
Albany, The, 33, 235
Alkmaar, 263, 277–8
Amherst, Lord, 42–3, 187, 209–10, 227
Amsterdam, 262
Antwerp, 35–6, 40, 44, 160
Arnhem, 39
Arleux, 60
Arlington Street, 328
Arras, 64–5
Artillery, 49, 74, 129, 190
Artres, 51, 102
Athenæum, The, 332
Auckland, Lord, 35, 40–1, 44
Austrian Emperor, 72, 110, 122–3, 139–40, 152–9

B

Baisieux, 135
Bathurst, Countess, 32
Bavai, 89
Beaulieu, General, 84
Beaumont, 127–32, 167–8
Bentinck, Colonel, 124
Bergues, 79
Bergen, 266–72
Bergen-op-Zoom, 170, 213
Berlaimont, 88
Berlin, 19, 33

Bertry, 128
Bonnaud, General, 134, 144
Bonington, Lord, 105
Bourlon Wood, 60
Bois-le-Duc, 169, 191
Bousbec, 148
Boxtel, 177-81
Breda, 36, 109
Brownrigg, General, 240, 264, 283
Brunswick, Duke of, 19, 40, 101, 188–9
Brune, General, 259, 277–9, 281–6
Buckinghamshire, Earl of, 236, 286
Burlington, Earl of, 36
Bunbury, Captain, 268–71, 276
Buckingham House, 37, 305
Burdett, Sir F., 290, 304
Burton, F., 307
Bussche, General, 45, 139

C

Caesar's Camp, 60–2
Camphin, 135
Calvert, Harry, 75, 88, 137, 164, 184, 228, 240
Cambrai, 60–2, 130
Carter, Sam, 293–4
Carlton House, 15, 29, 332
Cassel, 14, 74
Carnot, General, 72
Cathcart, Earl of, 255-6
Chappuis, General, 130
Charles, Archduke, 117, 139–48, 163–5
Charlotte, Queen, 27, 31, 325

345

CPSIA information can be obtained
at www.ICGtesting.com
Printed in the USA
LVHW051552050721
691891LV00027B/2481